PENGUIN BOOKS

THE PENGUIN DICTIONARY OF

MODERN HUMOROUS QUOTATIONS

Fred Metcalf was born in Yorkshire and educated in Devon. He has been collecting quotations for twenty years while working as a freelance television writer in London, Sydney and Los Angeles. In the 1980s he wrote – and drew – a daily cartoon strip in the *Daily Mirror*. He lives in London.

THE PENGUIN DICTIONARY

OF

MODERN
HUMOROUS
QUOTATIONS

COMPILED BY
FRED METCALF

PENGUIN BOOKS

For my mother and father and my brothers,
Roger and Joe

Penguin Books Ltd, 27 Wrights Lane, London W8 5TZ (Publishing and Editorial)
and Harmondsworth, Middlesex, England (Distribution and Warehouse)
Viking Penguin Inc., 40 West 23rd Street, New York, New York 10010, USA
Penguin Books Australia Ltd, Ringwood, Victoria, Australia
Penguin Books Canada Ltd, 2801 John Street, Markham, Ontario, Canada L3R 1B4
Penguin Books (NZ) Ltd, 182–190 Wairau Road, Auckland 10, New Zealand

First published by Viking 1986
Published in Penguin Books 1987

Printed and bound in Great Britain by
Richard Clay Ltd, Bungay, Suffolk
Typeset in Linotronic Ehrhardt

FOREWORD

I think it was Fred Metcalf who once said, 'Humour is in the funny-bone of the beholder.' But if that observation left you unamused, please file it under 'Anon.'

I have been ever mindful, in compiling this collection of humorous quotations, that, in the wayward world of wit, what leaves one man stony-faced can leave another with his ribs and sides respectively tickled and split. It's funny, isn't it? Or not, according to taste. So it needs to be said that the quotations in this anthology are, inevitably, my choice. *I* think they're funny. (And so, presumably, do the authors.) But, as we all know, a sense of humour is something that we ourselves always have but that is sometimes sadly lacking in others.

And what is 'humour' anyway? Ever since man's first hesitant chuckle the experts have been trying to analyse what makes us laugh. A brief survey of their theories seems to point to the conclusion that humour is that quality which, when you try to define it, deserts you.

A caveat here: not all the quotations are designed to deliver a hefty comic punch. While a great number of them will, I am certain, inspire a 'mirthquake' or even a 'laff riot' (and sometimes not much else), my overall criterion was to provoke reflection as well as laughter, to give the reader something to muse on while being amused. If pressed, I would concede that more of the quotations assembled here were fished from the murky waters of scorn and cynicism than from the sparkling streams of whimsy and innocent merriment. My excuse is that my choice merely mirrors the mood of the 1980s. Who knows, a future edition might reflect the return of playful banter and good-natured joshing to the centre of the comic stage.

My original objective was to restrict my researches to the twentieth century – with one obvious exception. But it was while the boundary was being breached to admit the generous figure of Oscar Wilde that a small number of other late-nineteenth-century quotations spilled through the gap. While technically over the age limit, it was soon clear that they were as sharp and sprightly as many quotations half their age and they were therefore allowed to stay. I make no apologies for their inclusion.

My initial purpose was to produce a source book for speakers and writers. But I hope now that it will serve two other purposes. Firstly, I would like it to be a constantly rewarding haven for browsers – to whose attention I draw the comprehensive author index at the back of the book – and, secondly, I would also hope that it will serve to introduce the reader to authors previously unknown to him and whet his appetite for more of their work.

Finally, I wish to thank all those who helped me while I was devising, compiling and completing this book. I am most of all grateful for the steadfast support and understanding of Tory Rothschild. I am also deeply indebted to Kate Mortimer.

I must also record my thanks to Janet Fillingham and Sarah Tingay at my agent, Anthony Sheil Associates, to Chris Gare of Perfect Software and Jon Davies of Imperial College, London, for their technical assistance and to the staffs of Kensington Reference Library, Acton Reference Library, New Milford Public Library, New York Public Library and Los Angeles Central Public Library. I especially appreciated the assistance and patience of Donald McFarlan, my editor at Penguin Books. Also at Penguin Books I owe a debt to Liz Bland and Donna Poppy.

Thanks for their faith, friendship and forbearance are also due to Chris and Julia Allen, Patricia Allen, Jeni Barnett, Willy and Cathy Bietak, Caroline Butler, Tim and Jo Butters, Linda and Gary Chapman, Rosalind Cock, Roy and Patricia Ellsworth, David and Carina Frost, Peter and Liz Gorley, Adam and Rosy Hilton, Joyce Hodge, Jan and Eugene Hughes, Jane Kalim, Zeeb Kalim, Shelley Mallett, Wiz and Edward Mortimer, Vicky Ogden, Chris and Lavender Patten, Tricia Pombo, Sophia and Eli Schutts, Cathy Simmonds, Annie Symons, Roger Taylor and Judy Lever, Janet Unwin and John Harding, Imelda Whelehan and Andrew, Karen, Deborah, Heather and Arda Metcalf.

Fred Metcalf, London, 1985

ABSTINENCE

1 Abstinence is a good thing, but it should always be practised in moderation.
   Anon.

2 Abstainer, *n*. A weak person who yields to the temptation of denying himself a pleasure.
   Ambrose Bierce, *The Devil's Dictionary*, 1911

3 I distrust camels, and anyone else who can go a week without a drink.
   Joe E. Lewis

See also Chastity; Drink; Moderation; Prohibition; Temperance.

ABUSE

1 As to abuse – I thrive on it. Abuse, hearty abuse, is a tonic to all save men of indifferent health.
   Norman Douglas, *Some Limericks*, 1928

2 It was commonly said, though I do not vouch for the story, that Sidgwick remarked concerning Jebb, 'All the time that he can spare from the adornment of his person, he devotes to the neglect of his duties.'
   Bertrand Russell, *Some Cambridge Dons of the Nineties*, 1956

See also Hecklers; Insults; Politics – Insults.

ACCIDENTS

1 SEAGOON: He's been buried alive under a thousand tons of earth.
   MINNIE: Thank heavens he's safe.
   The Goon Show, BBC Radio, 1959

See also Disasters; Misfortune.

ACCOUNTANCY

1 An accountant is a man hired to explain that you didn't make the money you did.
   Anon.

2 . . . in your report here, it says that you are an extremely dull person. Our experts describe you as an appallingly dull fellow, unimaginative, timid, spineless, easily dominated, no sense of humour, tedious company and irrepressibly drab and awful. And whereas in most professions these would be considered drawbacks, in accountancy they are a positive boon.
   John Cleese, Graham Chapman, Terry Jones, Michael Palin and Eric Idle, *And Now for Something Completely Different*, screenplay, 1971

3 Never ask of money spent
   Where the spender thinks it went.
   Nobody was ever meant
   To remember or invent
   What he did with every cent.
   Robert Frost, 'The Hardship of Accounting'

See also Money; Professions.

ACHIEVEMENT

1 It is sobering to consider that when Mozart was my age he had already been dead for a year.
   Tom Lehrer

2 The world is divided into people who do things – and people who get the credit.
   Dwight Morrow

See also Success.

ACTING

1 Acting is all about honesty. If you can fake that, you've got it made.
   George Burns (Attrib.)

2 A. E. Matthews ambled through *This was a Man* like a charming retriever who has buried a bone and can't quite remember where.
   Noël Coward, on the Broadway production, 1926

3 My dear boy, forget about the motivation. Just say the lines and don't trip over the furniture.

Noël Coward, to an actor in his *Nude with a Violin* on Broadway, 1957 (Attrib.)

4 My very first step
Was Shakespearian 'rep'
Where an awful old 'Ham' used to train us.
I'd nothing to do
In *The Dream* and *The Shrew*
But I carried a spear
In *King John* and *King Lear*
And a hatchet in *Coriolanus*.
I ranted for years
In pavilions on piers
Till my spirits were really at zero,
Then I got a small role
Of a Tart with a soul
In a play by Sir Arthur Pinero.
Noël Coward, 'Three Theatrical Dames', song from *Night of a Hundred Stars*, London 1954

5 Your motivation is your pay packet on Friday. Now get on with it.
Noël Coward, to an actor (Attrib.)

6 I mean, the question actors most often get asked is how they can bear saying the same things over and over again night after night, but God knows the answer to *that* is, don't we all *anyway*; might as well get paid for it.
Elaine Dundy, *The Dud Avocado*, 1958

7 Acting is the most minor of gifts and not a very high-class way to earn a living. After all, Shirley Temple could do it at the age of four.
Katherine Hepburn (Attrib.)

8 The important thing in acting is to be able to laugh and cry. If I have to cry, I think of my sex life. If I have to laugh, I think of my sex life.
Glenda Jackson (Attrib.)

9 ERIC: Did you see my Bottom at Stratford-upon-Avon?
ERNIE: I'm afraid not.
ERIC: A pity – many people consider it my best part. But, above all, I consider myself a film actor.
ERNIE: Really?
ERIC: Oh, yes. For instance, did you see *Star Wars*?

ERNIE: Yes?
ERIC: So did I. Terrific, wasn't it?
Eric Morecambe and Ernie Wise, *The Morecambe and Wise Joke Book*, 1979

10 ERIC: I'll never forget the first words I spoke in the theatre.
ERNIE: What were they?
ERIC: 'This way please! Programmes! . . .'
Eric Morecambe and Ernie Wise, *The Morecambe and Wise Joke Book*, 1979

11 We used to have actresses trying to become stars; now we have stars trying to become actresses.
Sir Laurence Olivier (Attrib.)

12 Acting is standing up naked and turning around very slowly.
Rosalind Russell, *Life is a Banquet*

13 Two members of my profession who are not urgently needed by my profession, Mr Ronald Reagan and Mr George Murphy, entered politics, and they've done extremely well. Since there has been no reciprocal tendency in the other direction, it suggests to me that our job is still more difficult than their new one.
Peter Ustinov, *Any Questions*, BBC Radio, 1968

14 I love acting. It is so much more real than life.
Oscar Wilde, *The Picture of Dorian Gray*, 1891

15 He had never acted in his life and couldn't play the pin in *Pinafore*.
P. G. Wodehouse, *The Luck of the Bodkins*, 1935

See also Actors and Actresses; Film; Show Business; The Theatre; Theatre – Critics.

ACTION

1 There are two kinds of people: those who don't do what they want to do, so they write down in a diary about what they haven't done, and those who haven't time to write about it because they're out doing it.
Richard Flournoy and Lewis R. Foster, *The More the Merrier*, screenplay, 1943

2 Every normal man must be tempted at times, to spit on his hands, hoist the black flag, and begin slitting throats.
H. L. Mencken, *Prejudices*, First Series, 1919

3 CORIE: ... there isn't the least bit of adventure in you. Do you know what you are? You're a Watcher. There are Watchers in this world and there are Do-ers. And the Watchers sit around watching the Do-ers do. Well, tonight you watched and I did.
PAUL: Yeah ... Well, it was harder to watch what you did than it was for you to *do* what I was watching.
Neil Simon, *Barefoot in the Park*, 1964

See also Behaviour.

ACTORS AND ACTRESSES

1 For an actress to succeed she must have the face of Venus, the brains of Minerva, the grace of Terpsichore, the memory of Macaulay, the figure of Juno and the hide of a rhinoceros.
Ethel Barrymore (Attrib.)

2 An actor's a guy who, if you ain't talking about him, ain't listening.
Marlon Brando (Attrib.)

3 I'm now at the age where I've got to prove that I'm just as good as I never was.
Rex Harrison (Attrib.)

4 Actresses will happen in the best regulated families.
Oliver Herford

5 I never said all actors are cattle. What I said was all actors should be *treated* like cattle.
Alfred Hitchcock (Attrib.)

6 Some of the greatest love affairs I've known involved one actor, unassisted.
Wilson Mizner (Attrib.)

7 Anyone who works is a fool. I don't work – I merely inflict myself on the public.
Robert Morley (Attrib.)

8 It is a great help for a man to be in love with himself. For an actor, however, it is absolutely essential.
Robert Morley, *Playboy*, 1979

9 Scratch an actor – and you'll find an actress.
Dorothy Parker (Attrib.)

10 The physical labor actors have to do wouldn't tax an embryo.
Neil Simon, *The Sunshine Boys*, screenplay, 1975

11 Every actor in his heart believes everything bad that's printed about him.
Orson Welles (Attrib.)

See also Acting; Film; Show Business; The Theatre; Theatre – Critics.

ADOLESCENCE

1 Adolescence: a stage between infancy and adultery.
Anon.

2 Remember that as a teenager you are at the last stage in your life when you will be happy to hear that the phone is for you.
Fran Lebowitz, 'Tips for Teens', *Social Studies*, 1981

3 Should you be a teenager blessed with uncommon good looks, document this state of affairs by the taking of photographs. It is the only way anyone will ever believe you in years to come.
Fran Lebowitz, 'Tips for Teens', *Social Studies*, 1981

4 Think before you speak. Read before you think. This will give you something to think about that you didn't make up yourself – a wise move at any age, but most especially at seventeen, when you are in the greatest danger of coming to annoying conclusions.
Fran Lebowitz, 'Tips for Teens', *Social Studies*, 1981

5 You just put on your coat and hat,
And walk yourself to the laundromat.
And when you finish doing that,
Bring in the dog and put out the cat.
Yakety-yak.
Don't talk back!
Jerry Leiber and Mike Stoller, 'Yakety Yak', song for The Coasters, 1958

6 Weird clothing is *de rigueur* for teenagers, but today's generation of teens is finding it difficult to be sufficiently weird. This is

because the previous generation of teens, who went through adolescence in the sixties and seventies, used up practically all the available weirdness. After what went on in that twenty-year period, almost nothing looks strange to anyone.
P. J. O'Rourke, *Modern Manners*, 1983

7 Sex is something I really don't understand too hot. You never know *where* the hell you are. I keep making up these sex rules for myself, and then I break them right away. Last year I made a rule that I was going to stop horsing around with girls that, deep down, gave me a pain in the ass. I broke it, though, the same week I made it – the same night, as a matter of fact. I spent the whole night necking with a terrible phoney named Anne Louise Sherman. Sex is something I just don't understand. I swear to God I don't.
J. D. Salinger, *The Catcher in the Rye*, 1951

8 That's the thing about girls. Every time they do something pretty, even if they're not much to look at, or even if they're sort of stupid, you fall half in love with them, and then you never know *where* the hell you are. Girls. Jesus Christ. They can drive you crazy. They really can.
J. D. Salinger, *The Catcher in the Rye*, 1951

9 My father is a bastard,
My ma's an S.O.B.
My grandpa's always plastered,
My grandma pushes tea.
My sister wears a moustache,
My brother wears a dress.
Goodness gracious, that's why I'm a
      mess.
Stephen Sondheim, 'Gee, Officer Krupke', song from *West Side Story*, 1957

10 When I was a boy of fourteen, my father was so ignorant I could hardly stand to have the old man around. But when I got to be twenty-one, I was astonished at how much he had learned in seven years.
Mark Twain

See also Children; Teenagers; Youth.

ADULTHOOD

1 When I grow up I want to be a little boy.
Joseph Heller, *Something Happened*, 1974

2 ETH: . . . It's time he was taught you are now an adult.
RON: Exactly what I told him, Eth. I said quite firmly, I said, 'Look, Dad, you got to realize I am now a grown-up adult with all an adult's desires and capabilities.'
ETH: When did you tell him that?
RON: When he was peeling the silver paper off my Easter egg.
Frank Muir and Denis Norden, *The Glums*, London Weekend Television, 1978

See also Childhood; Parents.

ADVERSITY

1 The world is quickly bored by the recital of misfortune and willingly avoids the sight of distress.
W. Somerset Maugham, *The Moon and Sixpence*, 1919

2 By trying we can easily learn to endure adversity. Another man's, I mean.
Mark Twain, *Following the Equator*, 1897

See also Misfortune; Sympathy.

ADVERTISING

1 In the ad biz, sincerity is a commodity bought and paid for like everything else.
Newsweek, 1967

2 The codfish lays ten thousand eggs,
The homely hen lays one.
The codfish never cackles
To tell you what she's done.
And so we scorn the codfish,
While the humble hen we prize,
Which only goes to show you
That it pays to advertise.
Anon., *It Pays to Advertise*

3 When the client moans and sighs
Make his logo twice the size.
If he still should prove refractory,
Show a picture of his factory.
Only in the gravest cases
Should you show the clients' faces.
Anon.

4 Advertising agency: eighty-five per cent confusion and fifteen per cent commission.
Fred Allen

5 Everybody sat around thinking about

Panasonic, the Japanese electronics account. Finally I decided, what the hell, I'll throw a line to loosen them up . . . 'The headline is, the headline is: From Those Wonderful Folks Who Gave You Pearl Harbor.'

Complete silence . . .

Jerry Della Femina, *From Those Wonderful Folks Who Gave You Pearl Harbor*, 1970

6 The longest word in the English language is the one following the phrase: 'And now a word from our sponsor.'
Hal Eaton, *Reader's Digest*, 1949

7 Doing business without advertising is like winking at a girl in the dark: you know what you are doing, but nobody else does.
Edgar Watson Howe

8 Advertising may be described as the science of arresting the human intelligence long enough to get money from it.
Stephen Leacock

9 I think that I shall never see
A billboard lovely as a tree.
Indeed, unless the billboards fall
I'll never see a tree at all.
Ogden Nash, 'Song of the Open Road', *Happy Days*, 1933

10 Advertising is the rattling of a stick inside a swill bucket.
George Orwell

11 Advertising that uses superlatives isn't.
Harry Pesin, *Sayings to Run an Advertising Agency By*, 1966

12 Fie on clients who cannot leave copy alone and fie on copywriters who can.
Harry Pesin, *Sayings to Run an Advertising Agency By*, 1966

See also Television – Commercials.

ADVICE

1 Never eat at a place called Mom's. Never play cards with a man named Doc. And never lay down with a woman who's got more troubles than you.
Nelson Algren, *What Every Young Man Should Know*

2 I always pass on good advice. It is the only

thing to do with it. It is never any use to oneself.
Oscar Wilde, *An Ideal Husband*, 1895

3 Never put anything on paper, my boy, and never trust a man with a small black moustache.
P. G. Wodehouse, *Cocktail Time*, 1958

4 There are girls, few perhaps but to be found if one searches carefully, who when their advice is ignored and disaster ensues, do not say 'I told you so'. Mavis was not of their number.
P. G. Wodehouse, *Pearls, Girls and Monty Bodkin*, 1972

See also Opinions.

AESTHETES

1 Occasionally I have hard words to say here about aesthetes . . . Search any old lukewarm bath and you will find one of these aesthetical technicians enjoying himself. He is having a lukewarm bath, it is rather good, it is something real, something that has its roots in the soil, a tangible, valid, unique, complete, integrating, vertical experience, a diatonic spatio-temporal cognition in terms of realistic harmonic spacing, differential intervals and vector (emmanuel) analysis, of those passional orphic inferences which must be proto-morphously lodged in writing with the Manager on or before the latest closing date. Hmmmm.
Myles na Gopaleen, *The Best of Myles*, 1968

2 . . . first and foremost, of course, I'm a Cultural Attaché. But don't let that word 'culture' scare the pants off you because I can assure you I'm not one of those long-haired, limp-wristed, head-in-the-clouds, arty-crafty pooftas. No!
Sir Les Patterson (Barry Humphries), *Housewife Superstar*, one-man show, 1976

3 Dark hair fell in a sweep over his forehead. He looked like a man who would write *vers libre*, as indeed he did.
P. G. Wodehouse, *The Girl on the Boat*, 1922

4 I don't want to wrong anybody, so I won't go so far as to say that she actually wrote

poetry, but her conversation, to my mind, was of a nature calculated to excite the liveliest suspicions. Well, I mean to say, when a girl suddenly asks you out of a blue sky if you don't sometimes feel that the stars are God's daisy-chain, you begin to think a bit.
P. G. Wodehouse, *Right Ho, Jeeves*, 1934

See also Culture; Art and Artists.

AFFECTION

1 A mixture of admiration and pity is one of the surest recipes for affection.
André Maurois, *Ariel*, 1923

2 All my life affection has been showered upon me, and every forward step I have made has been taken in spite of it.
George Bernard Shaw (Attrib.)

See also Flirtation; Kissing; Love.

AGE

1 I refuse to admit that I am more than fifty-two, even if that does make my sons illegitimate.
Nancy Astor (Attrib.)

2 We talked about growing old gracefully
And Elsie who's seventy-four
Said, 'A. it's a question of being sincere,
And B., if you're supple you've nothing
   to fear.'
Then she swung upside down from a
   glass chandelier,
I couldn't have liked it more.
Noël Coward, 'I've Been to a Marvellous Party', song from *Set to Music*, 1938

3 The four stages of man are infancy, childhood, adolescence and obsolescence.
Art Linkletter, *A Child's Garden of Misinformation*, 1965

4 I was born in 1962. True. And the room next to me was 1963 . . .
Joan Rivers, *An Audience with Joan Rivers*, London Weekend Television, 1984

5 One should never trust a woman who tells one her real age. A woman who would tell one that, would tell one anything.
Oscar Wilde, *A Woman of No Importance*, 1893

6 The old believe everything: the middle-aged suspect everything: the young know everything.
Oscar Wilde, 'Phrases and Philosophies for the Use of the Young', 1894

7 Thirty-five is a very attractive age, London society is full of women of the very highest birth who have, of their own free choice, remained thirty-five for years.
Oscar Wilde, *The Importance of Being Earnest*, 1895

See also Middle Age; Old Age.

ALCOHOLISM

1 Alcoholism isn't a spectator sport. Eventually the whole family gets to play.
Joyce Rebeta-Burditt, *The Cracker Factory*, 1977

2 An alcoholic is someone you don't like who drinks as much as you do.
Dylan Thomas (Attrib.)

See also Abstinence; Drink; Temperance.

ALIMONY

1 The high cost of leaving.
Anon.

2 Alimony is like buying oats for a dead horse.
Arthur 'Bugs' Baer

3 You never realize how short a month is until you pay alimony.
John Barrymore

4 I heard from my cat's lawyer today. My cat wants $12,000 a week for Tender Vittles.
Johnny Carson, *The Tonight Show*, NBC TV, 1984

5 Alimony: bounty after the mutiny.
Max Kauffmann

6 Alimony is the curse of the writing classes.
Norman Mailer

7   She cried – and the judge wiped her tears with my checkbook.
    Tommy Manville, thirteen-times divorced American millionaire

8   If the income tax is the price we have to pay to keep the government on its feet, alimony is the price we have to pay for sweeping a woman off hers.
    Groucho Marx, *Newsday*

9   Alimony – the ransom that the happy pay to the devil.
    H. L. Mencken, *A Book of Burlesques*, 1920

10 Zsa Zsa Gabor is an expert housekeeper. Every time she gets divorced, she keeps the house.
    Henny Youngman

See also Divorce; Love – Breaking Up.

AMATEURS

1   Professionals built the *Titanic*, amateurs built the ark.
    Anon.

2   Amateur: one who plays games for the love of the thing. Unlike the professional, he receives no salary, and is contented with presents of clothes, clubs, rackets, cigarettes, cups, cheques, hotel expenses, fares, and so on.
    Beachcomber (J. B. Morton), *Beachcomber: The Works of J. B. Morton*, 1974

See also Sports.

AMBITION

1   I want to be what I was when I wanted to be what I am now.
    Graffito, London, 1980

2   The vulgar man is always the most distinguished, for the very desire to be distinguished is vulgar.
    G. K. Chesterton, *All Things Considered*, 1908

3   ETH: If Ron doesn't mix with better-class people, how's he going to get on in life? In this world it's not what you know, it's who you know, isn't it Ron?

RON: Yes, Eth. And I don't know either of them.
    Frank Muir and Denis Norden, The Glums, *Take It from Here*, BBC Radio

4   People Who Do Things exceed my endurance;
    God, for a man that solicits insurance!
    Dorothy Parker, 'Sunset Gun', 1928

5   Ambition is the last refuge of the failure.
    Oscar Wilde, 'Phrases and Philosophies for the Use of the Young', 1894

See also Achievement; Success.

AMERICA AND THE AMERICANS

1   And remember – you can't spell AMERICA without the *M* and the *R* in HUMOR.
    National Lampoon

2   Is the US ready for self-government?
    Graffito, New York, 1971

3   Americans like fat books and thin women.
    Russell Baker

4   He held, too, in his enlightened way, that Americans have a perfect right to exist. But he did often find himself wishing Mr Rhodes had not enabled them to exercise that right in Oxford.
    Max Beerbohm, *Zuleika Dobson*, 1911

5   The Yankee is a dab at electricity and crime,
    He tells you how he hustles and it takes him quite a time.
    I like his hospitality that's cordial and frank,
    I do not mind his money but I do not like his swank.
    G. K. Chesterton, 'A Song of Self-esteem', *Collected Poems*, 1933

6   The American language is in a state of flux based on the survival of the unfittest.
    Cyril Connolly, *The Sunday Times*, 1966

7   I don't know much about Americanism, but it's a damn good word with which to carry an election.
    Warren G. Harding

8 America, where overnight success is both a legend and a major industry.
John Leggett, *Ross and Tom*, 1974

9 HUSBAND (*to wife*): The egg timer is pinging. The toaster is popping. The coffeepot is perking. Is this it, Alice? Is this the great American dream?
Henry Martin, Cartoon in the *New Yorker*

10 The American people, taking one with another, constitute the most timorous, sniveling, poltroonish, ignominious mob of serfs and goosesteppers ever gathered under one flag in Christendom since the end of the Middle Ages.
H. L. Mencken, *Prejudices*, Third series, 1922

11 America's dissidents are not committed to mental hospitals and sent into exile; they thrive and prosper and buy a house in Nantucket and take flyers in the commodities market.
Ted Morgan, *On Becoming American*, 1978

12 America – a country that has leapt from barbarism to decadence without touching civilizatioń.
John O'Hara

13 The European traveller in America – at least if I may judge by myself – is struck by two peculiarities: first, the extreme similarity of outlook in all parts of the United States (except the Old South), and secondly, the passionate desire of each locality to prove that it is peculiar and different from every other. The second of these is, of course, caused by the first.
Bertrand Russell, 'Modern Homogeneity', 1930

14 Being a great power is no longer much fun.
David Schoenbaum, *New York Times*, 1973

15 Americans adore me and will go on adoring me until I say something nice about them.
George Bernard Shaw (Attrib.)

16 I like to be in America!
OK by me in America!

Everything free in America
For a small fee in America!
Stephen Sondheim, 'America', song from *West Side Story*, 1957

17 [Americans are] better at having a love affair that lasts ten minutes than any other people in the world.
Stephen Spender, interviewed in the *New York Post*, 1975

18 In the United States there is more space where nobody is than where anybody is.
That is what makes America what it is.
Gertrude Stein, *The Geographical History of America*, 1936

19 BRITISH CIVIL SERVANT: They don't stand on ceremony ... They make no distinction about a man's background, his parentage, his education. They say what they mean, and there is a vivid muscularity about the way they say it ... They are always the first to put their hands in their pockets. They press you to visit them in their own home the moment they meet you, and are irrepressibly good-humoured, ambitious and brimming with self-confidence in any company. Apart from all that I've got nothing against them.
Tom Stoppard, *Dirty Linen*, 1976

20 ... as American as English muffins and French toast.
John Russell Taylor, *The Times*, 1984

21 America is a large friendly dog in a small room. Every time it wags its tail, it knocks over a chair.
Arnold J. Toynbee

22 Losing is the great American sin.
John Tunis, quoted in the *New York Times*, 1977

23 I drive my car to the supermarket,
The way I take is superhigh,
A superlot is where I park it,
And Super Suds are what I buy.
Supersalesmen sell me tonic –
Super-Tone-O for relief.
The planes I ride are supersonic.
In trains, I like the Super Chief.
John Updike, 'Superman', *The Carpentered Hen and Other Tame Creatures*, 1958

24 All Americans lecture . . . I suppose it is something in their climate.
   Oscar Wilde, *A Woman of No Importance*, 1893

25 We have really everything in common with America nowadays, except, of course, language.
   Oscar Wilde, 'The Canterville Ghost', 1887

See also America – The South; Boston; California; Chicago; Los Angeles; New England; New York; San Francisco; Washington.

AMERICA – THE SOUTH

1 My great grandfather . . . was the first Black political candidate in the state of Mississippi. He ran for the border and made it. And the reason he ran for the border, he said, was that the people were very clannish. He didn't mind them having hang-ups, he just didn't want to be one of their hang-ups.
   Redd Foxx, *Esquire*

2 I happen to know quite a bit about the South. Spent twenty years there one night.
   Dick Gregory

3 I really am a fixin'
   To go home and start a mixin'
   Down below that Mason-Dixon line.
   I wanna go back to Alabammy,
   Back to the arms of my dear ol'
     Mammy,
   Her cookin's lousy and her hands are
     clammy,
   But what the hell, it's home.
   Yes for paradise the Southland is my
     nominee
   Just give me a hammock and a grit of
     hominy.
   Tom Lehrer, 'I Wanna Go Back to Dixie'

4 What is the difference between the South and the rest of America? It was a while before I figured out there isn't any. The South *is* America. The South is what we started out with in this bizarre, slightly troubling, basically wonderful country – fun, danger, friendliness, energy, enthusiasm and brave, crazy, tough people. After all, America is where the wildest humans on the planet came to do anything they damn pleased.
   P. J. O'Rourke, *Rolling Stone*, 1982

See also America and the Americans.

ANCESTORS

1 She's descended from a long line her mother listened to.
   Gypsy Rose Lee

2 ERIC: I come from a very old military family. One of my ancestors fell at Waterloo.
   ERNIE: Really?
   ERIC: Yes, someone pushed him off Platform Nine.
   Eric Morecambe and Ernie Wise, *The Morecambe and Wise Joke Book*, 1979

See also The Family; History; The Past; Relatives.

ANGER

1 *I* am righteously indignant; *you* are annoyed; *he* is making a fuss about nothing.
   Competition, *New Statesman*

2 He spoke with a certain what-is-it in his voice, and I could see that, if not actually disgruntled, he was far from being gruntled.
   P. G. Wodehouse, *The Code of the Woosters*, 1938

See also Abuse; Temper.

ANIMALS

1 Q: What's the difference between a buffalo and a bison?
   A: You can't wash your hands in a buffalo.
   Anon.

2 Be tender with the tadpole, and let the
     limpet thrive,
   Be merciful to mussels, don't skin your
     eels alive,
   When talking to a turtle don't mention
     calipee –

Be always kind to animals wherever you
may be.
Joseph Ashby-Sterry, 'Kindness to
Animals'

3 I shoot the Hippopotamus
With bullets made of platinum,
Because if I used leaden ones
His hide is sure to flatten 'em.
Hilaire Belloc, 'The Hippopotamus', *Bad
Child's Book of Beasts*, 1896

4 Odd things animals. All dogs look up to
you. All cats look down to you. Only a pig
looks at you as an equal.
Winston Churchill (Attrib.)

5 I do not like animals. Of any sort. I don't
even like the idea of animals. Animals are
no friends of mine. They are not welcome in my house. They occupy no space
in my heart. Animals are off my list . . . I
might more accurately state that I do not
like animals, with two exceptions. The
first being in the past tense, at which
point I like them just fine, in the form of
nice crispy spareribs and Bass Weejun
penny loafers. And the second being outside, by which I mean not merely outside,
as in outside the house, but genuinely
outside, as in outside in the woods, or
preferably outside in the South American jungle. This is, after all, only fair. I
don't go there; why should they come
here?
Fran Lebowitz, *Social Studies*, 1981

6 O Kangaroo, O Kangaroo,
Be grateful that you're in the zoo,
And not transmuted by a boomerang
To zestful tangy Kangaroo meringue.
Ogden Nash, 'The Kangaroo', *Good Inten-
tions*, 1942

7 The turtle lives 'twixt plated decks
which practically conceal its sex.
I think it clever of the turtle
In such a fix to be so fertile.
Ogden Nash, 'The Turtle', *Hard Lines*,
1931

8 Two kangaroos are talking to each other,
and one says 'Gee, I hope it doesn't rain
today, I just hate it when the children play
inside.'
Henny Youngman

See also Birds; Cats; Dogs; Fish and
Fishing; Frogs; Pets; Veterinarians.

ANTIQUES

1 Old? The only thing that kept it standing
was the woodworm holding hands.
Jerry Dennis

2 Is anybody looking for a bargain in an
Early Pennsylvania washstand in mint
condition, *circa* 1825? It's genuine pumpkin pine, with ball-and-claw feet, the
original brasses, and a smear of blood
where I tripped over it last night in the
dark. I'm holding it at $16, but not so
tightly that I wouldn't let it go to the right
party for *circa* ten cents.
S. J. Perelman, *Acres and Pains*, 1947

3 Want to have some fun? Walk into an
antique shop and say, 'What's new?'
Henny Youngman

See also History; The Past.

ANXIETY

1 Whenever he thought about Vietnam, he
felt terrible. And so at last he came to a
fateful decision. He decided not to think
about it.
Anon.

2 Caught in the grips of DESPAIR!?
Times are tough, huh, Bud? Nobody said
it was going to be a bed of roses! So now
you've made your bed, so now EAT it!
Or, you might say, you've buttered your
bread, now sleep on it! Who do you think
YOU are? GOD? What gives YOU the
right to think you should have it any
better than the NEXT guy? Forget it!
There's NO HOPE! That's right, kids!
NO HOPE! Face facts! Look at the
world situation! How long can you go on
deluding yourself that things will get
better? The only thing to do is to resign
yourself to the fatal inevitability of it all!
While waiting for death, read *Despair*.
It's your kind of comic!
Robert Crumb, *Plunge into the Depths of
Despair*, comic, 1970

3 When you don't have any money, the
problem is food. When you have money,

it's sex. When you have both, it's health. If everything is simply jake, then you're frightened of death.
J. P. Donleavy, *The Ginger Man*, 1955

4 I have a new philosophy. I'm only going to dread one day at a time.
Charles Schulz, *Peanuts*, cartoon

5 If you don't relax, I'll break my fingers. Look at this. The only man in the world with clenched hair.
Neil Simon, *The Odd Couple*, 1966

See also Crises; Fear; Hypochondria; Paranoia.

APPEARANCE

1 You look rather rash my dear your colors dont quite match your face.
Daisy Ashford, *The Young Visiters*, 1919

2 She was a vivacious girl, not pretty by any accepted standards, if anything ugly by any accepted standards, but she could speak Latin and foot a quadrille and sometimes the two simultaneously if the tempo was right.
Denis Norden, *Upon My Word*, 1974

3 . . . an individual whose appearance was so repulsive I had to have my mirrors insured.
Miss Piggy, *Miss Piggy's Guide to Life (As Told to Henry Beard)*, 1981

4 She looked, as far as her clothes went, as though she had been pulled through brambles and then pushed through a thin tube.
Gwyn Thomas, *The Alone to the Alone*, 1947

5 It is only the shallow people who do not judge by appearances.
Oscar Wilde, *The Picture of Dorian Gray*, 1891

6 She wore far too much rouge last night and not quite enough clothes. That is always a sign of despair in a woman.
Oscar Wilde, *An Ideal Husband*, 1895

7 With an evening coat and a white tie, anybody, even a stockbroker, can gain a reputation for being civilized.
Oscar Wilde, *The Picture of Dorian Gray*, 1891

8 A man who wore a tie that went twice round the neck was sure, sooner or later, to inflict some hideous insult on helpless womanhood. Add tortoiseshell-rimmed glasses, and you had what practically amounted to a fiend in human shape.
P. G. Wodehouse, *Mulliner Nights*, 1933

9 His eyes . . . were set as near together as Nature had been able to manage without actually running them into one another. His under-lip protruded and drooped. Looking at him, one felt instinctively that no judging committee of a beauty contest would hesitate a moment before him.
P. G. Wodehouse, *Psmith, Journalist*, 1915

See also Beauty; Clothes; Fashion; Looks; Style.

ARCHAEOLOGY

1 An archaeologist is the best husband a woman can have; the older she gets, the more interested he is in her.
Agatha Christie

See also Antiques; History; The Past.

ARCHITECTURE

1 In my experience, if you have to keep the lavatory door shut by extending your left leg, it's modern architecture.
Nancy Banks Smith, *Guardian*, 1969

2 I'm not sure office buildings are even architecture. They're really a mathematical calculation, just three-dimensional investments.
Gordon Bunshaft, quoted in *Fortune*, 1973

3 . . . I imagined asking her whether she liked Le Corbusier, and her replying, 'Love some – with a little Benedictine if you've got it.'
Peter De Vries, *The Tunnel of Love*, 1954

4 The village hall was one of those mid-Victorian jobs in glazed red brick which always seem to bob up in these olde-world hamlets and do so much to encourage the drift to towns.
P. G. Wodehouse, *The Mating Season*, 1949

5 The doctor can bury his mistakes, but an

architect can only advise his clients to plant vines.
Frank Lloyd Wright (Attrib.)

6 We should learn from the snail: it has devised a home that is both exquisite and functional.
Frank Lloyd Wright (Attrib.)

See also Home; Interior Decorating.

ARGUMENT

1 Keep your temper. Do not quarrel with an angry person, but give him a soft answer. It is commanded by the Holy Writ and, furthermore, it makes him madder than anything else you could say.
Anon., *Reader's Digest*, 1949

2 When people are least sure, they are often most dogmatic.
J. K. Galbraith, *The Great Crash, 1929*, 1955

3 'Shut up,' he explained.
Ring Lardner, *The Young Immigrants*, 1920

4 We might as well give up the fiction
That we can argue any view.
For what in me is pure Conviction
Is simple Prejudice in you.
Phyllis McGinley, *Times Three: 1932–1960*, 1960

5 My sad conviction is that people can only agree about what they're not really interested in.
Bertrand Russell, *New Statesman*, 1939

6 Consistency is a paste jewel that only cheap men cherish.
William Allen White, *Emporia Gazette*, 1923

7 He knew the precise psychological moment when to say nothing.
Oscar Wilde, *The Picture of Dorian Gray*, 1891

8 I can stand brute force, but brute reason is quite unreasonable. There is something unfair about its use. It is hitting below the intellect.
Oscar Wilde, *The Picture of Dorian Gray*, 1891

9 I dislike arguments of any kind. They are always vulgar, and often convincing.
Oscar Wilde, *The Importance of Being Earnest*, 1895

10 I like talking to a brick wall, it's the only thing in the world that never contradicts me.
Oscar Wilde, *Lady Windermere's Fan*, 1892

See also Fighting; Opinions.

THE ARISTOCRACY

1 I'm as drunk as the lord that I am!
John Betjeman, quoting inebriated undergraduate peer, *Evening Standard*, 1933

2 I'm not a social person but I could fall for a duke – they are a great aphrodisiac.
Tina Brown, *Tatler*, 1979

3 Democracy means government by the uneducated, while aristocracy means government by the badly educated.
G. K. Chesterton, *New York Times*, 1931

4 For the first time I was aware of that layer of blubber which encases an English peer, the sediment of permanent adulation.
Cyril Connolly, *Enemies of Promise*, 1938

5 The Stately Homes of England,
How beautiful they stand,
To prove the upper classes
Have still the upper hand;
Though the fact that they have to be rebuilt
And frequently mortgaged to the hilt
Is inclined to take the gilt
Off the gingerbread,
And certainly damps the fun
Of the eldest son.
Noël Coward, 'The Stately Homes of England', song from *Operette*, 1938

6 The Stately Homes of England
In valley, dale and glen
Produce a race of charming,
Innocuous young men.
Though our mental equipment may be slight
And we barely distinguish left from right,
We are quite prepared to fight
For our principles,

Though none of us know so far
What they really are.
Noël Coward, 'The Stately Homes of England', song from *Operette*, 1938

7 For she's never heard of Hitler, and
   she's never thought of war,
She's got twenty-seven servants, and
   she could get twenty more.
She never sees a paper, and she seldom
   reads a book,
She is worshipped by her butler,
   tolerated by her cook.
And her husband treats her nicely, and
   he's *mostly* on a horse.
While the children are entirely in the
   nursery of course.
So no wonder she is happy – she's got
   nothing else to do.
O, no wonder she is happy, for she
   hasn't got a clue,
To the future that is waiting, and the
   funny things she'll do
About . . . thirty-seven years from now.
Joyce Grenfell, 'The Countess of Cotely', song from *Stately as a Galleon*, 1978

8 Life at the Taws moved in the ordinary routine of a great English household. At 7 a gong sounded for rising, at 8 a horn blew for breakfast, at 8.30 a whistle sounded for prayers, at 1 a flag was run up at half-mast for lunch, at 4 a gun was fired for afternoon tea, at 9 a first bell sounded for dressing, at 9.15 a second bell for going on dressing, while at 9.30 a rocket was sent up to indicate that dinner was ready. At midnight dinner was over, and at 1 a.m. the tolling of a bell summoned the domestics to evening prayers.
Stephen Leacock, 'Gertrude the Governess', *Nonsense Novels*, 1911

9 A fully equipped duke costs as much to keep up as two dreadnoughts; and dukes are just as great a terror and they last longer.
David Lloyd George, speech, 1909

10 An aristocracy in a republic is like a chicken whose head has been cut off; it may run about in a lovely way, but in fact it's dead.
Nancy Mitford, *Noblesse Oblige*, 1956

11 In England, if you are a Duchess, you don't need to be well-dressed – it would be thought quite eccentric.
Nancy Mitford, *Noblesse Oblige*, 1956

12 LORD ILLINGWORTH: . . . a title is really rather a nuisance in these democratic days. As George Hartford I had everything I wanted. Now I have merely everything that other people want, which isn't nearly so pleasant.
Oscar Wilde, *A Woman of No Importance*, 1893

13 The Peerage is one book a young man about town should know thoroughly and it is the best thing in fiction the English have ever done.
Oscar Wilde, *A Woman of No Importance*, 1893

14 There is always more brass than brains in an aristocracy.
Oscar Wilde, *Vera, or The Nihilists*, 1883

15 Reluctant though one may be to admit it, the entire British aristocracy is seamed and honeycombed with immorality. If you took a pin and jabbed it down anywhere in the pages of *Debrett's Peerage* you would find it piercing the name of someone with a conscience as tender as a sunburned neck.
P. G. Wodehouse, *Mulliner Nights*, 1933

16 . . . those comfortably padded lunatic asylums which are known, euphemistically, as the stately homes of England.
Virginia Woolf, *The Common Reader*, 1925

See also The Establishment; House of Lords; Royalty; The Ruling Class; Society.

THE ARMY

1 Colonel Cathcart had courage and never hesitated to volunteer his men for any target available.
Joseph Heller, *Catch-22*, 1961

2 Einstein once said that any man who liked marching had been given his brain for nothing: just the spinal column would have done. But I wasn't Einstein. Since most of one's time in the army is wasted

anyway, I preferred to waste it by moving about in a precise manner.
Clive James, *Unreliable Memoirs*, 1980

3 It's Tommy this, an' Tommy that, an'
  'Chuck 'im out, the brute!'
But it's 'Saviour of 'is country' when the guns begin to shoot.
  Rudyard Kipling, 'Tommy', *A Choice of Kipling's Verse*, 1941

4 When I first went into the active Army, you could tell someone to move a chair across the room – now you have to tell him why.
  Major Robert Lembke, quoted in *Newsweek*, 1979

5 When the military man approaches, the world locks up its spoons and packs off its womankind.
  George Bernard Shaw, *Man and Superman*, 1903

See also The Navy; War.

ART AND ARTISTS

1 Life is very nice, but it lacks form. It's the aim of art to give it some.
  Jean Anouilh, *The Rehearsal*, 1950

2 What I'm above all primarily concerned with is the substance of life, the pith of reality. If I had to sum up my work, I suppose that's it really: I'm taking the pith out of reality.
  Alan Bennett, 'The Lonely Pursuit', *On the Margin*, BBC TV, 1966

3 A woman is fascinated not by art but by the noise made by those in the field.
  Anton Chekhov

4 The artistic temperament is a disease that afflicts amateurs.
  G. K. Chesterton, *Heretics*, 1905

5 The artist's wife will know that there is no more sombre enemy of good art than the pram in the hall.
  Cyril Connolly, *Enemies of Promise*, 1938

6 Anyone can be a cartoonist!
It's so simple even a child can do it!
'ART' is just a racket! A HOAX perpetrated on the public by so-called 'Artists' who set themselves up on a pedestal and promoted by pantywaist ivory-tower intellectuals and sob-sister 'critics' who think the world owes them a living!
  Robert Crumb, *Plunge into the Depths of Despair*, comic, 1970

7 BEVERLY: His artistic rages are awe inspiring!
SNOID: *!$!&!
BEVERLY: His untamed spirit roams the cosmos . . . he grapples with powerful unseen forces in the magic world of dark dreams!
SNOID: GRAHH!
BEVERLY: His tortured body is racked by the terrible battles raging in his soul!
SNOID: EEYAAAAHHH!
BEVERLY: I feel privileged to be a witness to this primal enactment of the creative process!
  Robert Crumb, *Snoid Comics*, 1980

8 He always did have that 'Touch of Madness' that marks the true artist and breaks the hearts of the young girls from fine homes.
  Robert Crumb, *Snoid Comics*, 1980

9 . . . at one point I found myself standing before an oil of a horse that I figured was probably a self-portrait judging from the general execution . . .
  Peter De Vries, *Let Me Count the Ways*, 1965

10 To an artist a husband named Bicket
Said, 'Turn your backside, and I'll kick it.
You have painted my wife
In the nude to the life.
Do you think for a moment that's cricket?'
  John Galsworthy

11 As my poor father used to say
In 1863,
Once people start on all this Art
Good-bye, moralitee!
And what my father used to say
Is good enough for me.
  A. P. Herbert, 'Lines for a Worthy Person'

12 The moment you cheat for the sake of beauty, you know you are an artist.
  Max Jacob, *Art Poétique*, 1922

13 Senor Dali,
   Born delirious,
   Considers it folly
   To be serious . . .
   Phyllis McGinley, *Times Three: 1932–1960*, 1960

14 The great artists of the world are never Puritans, and seldom even ordinarily respectable.
   H. L. Mencken

15 Treat a work of art like a prince: let it speak to you first.
   Arthur Schopenhauer (Attrib.)

16 What sight is sadder than the sight of a lady we admire admiring a nauseating picture.
   Logan Pearsall Smith, *All Trivia*, 1933

17 My dear Tristan, to be an artist *at all* is like living in Switzerland during a world war.
   Tom Stoppard, *Travesties*, 1975

18 The artist is a lucky dog . . . In any community of a thousand souls there will be nine hundred doing the work, ninety doing well, nine doing good, and one lucky dog painting or writing about the other nine hundred and ninety-nine.
   Tom Stoppard, *Artist Descending a Staircase*, BBC Radio, 1972

19 If Botticelli were alive today, he'd be working for *Vogue*.
   Peter Ustinov

20 If you want to know everything about me, just look at the surface of my paintings, it's all there, there's nothing more.
   Andy Warhol

21 All art is quite useless.
   Oscar Wilde, *The Picture of Dorian Gray*, 1891

22 A true artist takes no notice whatever of the public. The public to him are non-existent. He leaves that to the popular novelist.
   Oscar Wilde, 'The Soul of Man under Socialism', 1891

23 No great artist ever sees things as they really are. If he did he would cease to be an artist.
   Oscar Wilde, 'The Decay of Lying', 1889

24 She is like most artists; she has style without any sincerity.
   Oscar Wilde, 'The Nightingale and the Rose', 1888

25 I had a private income – the young artist's best friend.
   P. G. Wodehouse, *Quick Service*, 1940

26 Like all young artists nowadays, he had always held before him as the goal of his ambition the invention of some new comic animal for the motion pictures. What he burned to do, as Velazquez would have burned to do if he had lived today, was to think of another Mickey Mouse and then give up work and just sit back and watch the money roll in.
   P. G. Wodehouse, *Lord Emsworth and Others*, 1937

27 Of all the myriad individuals that went to make up the kaleidoscopic life of New York, Mrs Waddington disliked artists most. They never had any money. They were dissolute and feckless. They attended dances at Webster Hall in strange costumes and frequently played the ukelele.
   P. G. Wodehouse, *The Small Bachelor*, 1927

See also Art – Critics; Modern Art.

ART – CRITICS

1 Writing about art is like dancing about architecture.
   Anon.

ASSASSINATION

1 Assassination is the extreme form of censorship.
   George Bernard Shaw, 'The Rejected Statement', 1916

See also Murder; Revolution.

ASSERTIVENESS

1 Let people push you around. The person who says, believes, and acts on the phrase 'I ain't taking any shit from anybody' is a

very busy person indeed. This person must be ever vigilant against news vendors who shortchange him, cab drivers who take him the wrong way around, waiters who serve the other guy first, florists who are charging ten cents more per tulip than the one down the block, pharmacists who make you wait too long and cars that cut you off at the light: they are a veritable miasma of righteous indignation and never have a minute to relax and have a good time.

    Cynthia Heimel, 'Lower Manhattan Survival Tactics', *Village Voice*, 1983

2 My mother has gone to a woman's workshop on assertiveness training. Men aren't allowed. I asked my father what 'assertiveness training' is. He said, 'God knows, but whatever it is, it's bad news for me.' . . . then my mother came home and started bossing us around. She said, 'The worm has turned,' and 'Things are going to be different around here,' and things like that. Then she went into the kitchen and started making a chart dividing all the housework into three . . . she put the chart on the wall and said, 'We start tomorrow.'

    Sue Townsend, *The Secret Diary of Adrian Mole Aged 13¾*, 1982

See also Decisions; Indecision.

ASTROLOGY

1 RICHARD: What's your sign?
VICTORIA: I'm sorry – it's unlisted.
    Mel Brooks, *High Anxiety*, screenplay, 1977

2 There should be three days a week when no one is allowed to say: 'What's your sign?' Violators would have their copies of Kahlil Gibran confiscated.
    Dick Cavett, *The Dick Cavett Show*, ABC TV, 1978

3 I don't believe in astrology. The only stars I can blame for my failures are those that walk about the stage.
    Noël Coward (Attrib.)

4 The process of balancing the horoscopes of two elevens one against the other was a very delicate and difficult one. A match

between the Spurs and the Villa entailed a conflict in the heavens so vast and so complicated that it was not to be wondered at if she sometimes made a mistake about the outcome.

    Aldous Huxley, *Crome Yellow*, 1921

See also Fate; The Future; The Occult; Superstition.

ATHEISM

1 Someone asked [Bertrand] Russell at some meeting: 'Lord Russell, what will you say when you die and are brought face to face with your Maker?' He replied without hesitation: 'God,' I shall say, 'God, why did you make the evidence for your existence so insufficient?'

    A. J. Ayer, quoted in the *Standard*, 1984

2 An atheist is a man who has no invisible means of support.
    John Buchan, *Memory Hold the Door*, 1940

3 Simon darling, I'm afraid you will have to speak to the children. I caught Tristram believing in God yesterday.
    Marc, *The Trendy Ape*, cartoon, 1968

4 . . . the sort of atheist who does not so much disbelieve in God as personally dislike Him.
    George Orwell, *Down and Out in Paris and London*, 1933

5 God can stand being told by Professor Ayer and Marghanita Laski that He doesn't exist.
    J. B. Priestley, 'The BBC's Duty to Society', *Listener*, 1965

6 I was told that the Chinese said they would bury me by the Western Lake and build a shrine to my memory. I have some slight regret that this did not happen, as I might have become a god, which would have been very *chic* for an atheist.
    Bertrand Russell, *The Autobiography of Bertrand Russell*, Vol. 2, 1968

7 It's an interesting view of atheism, as a sort of *crutch* for those who can't stand the reality of God . . .
    Tom Stoppard, *Jumpers*, 1972

8 She didn't like him being an atheist, and

he wouldn't stop being an atheist, and finally he said something about Jonah and the Whale which was impossible for her to overlook. This morning she returned the ring, his letters and a china ornament with 'A Present from Blackpool' on it which he had bought her last summer while visiting relatives in the north.

P. G. Wodehouse, *The Mating Season*, 1949

See also Belief; God; Religion.

CLEMENT ATTLEE Prime Minister of Great Britain, 1945–1951 (Labour Party)

1 He seems determined to make a trumpet sound like a tin whistle . . . He brings to the fierce struggle of politics the tepid enthusiasm of a lazy summer afternoon at a cricket match.
  Aneurin Bevan, *Tribune*, 1945

2 Absolutely true – but then he [Clement Attlee] does have a lot to be modest about.
  Winston Churchill, agreeing with a colleague that Attlee was modest (possibly apocryphal)

3 . . . a sheep in sheep's clothing.
  Winston Churchill (Attrib.)

4 Charisma? He did not recognize the word except as a clue in his beloved *Times* crossword.
  James Margach, *The Abuse of Power*, 1981

5 . . . reminds me of nothing so much as a dead fish before it has had time to stiffen.
  George Orwell (Attrib.)

See also Winston Churchill; The Labour Party.

AUDIENCES

1 The best audience is intelligent, well-educated and a little drunk.
  Alben W. Barkley

2 Miss Howard let them have it, very slowly and with great feeling, accentuating the melody. She gazed thoughtfully at the ceiling, and all her audience gazed thoughtfully at other inappropriate spots, and Florence gazed at Miss Howard. Mrs Oxney found herself thinking of the late Mr Oxney, and Mrs Bertram thought about coke, and Mrs Holders thought about the enquiry she had sent to the *Sunday Gazette* about their bridge last night, and Mr Kemp with closed eyes thought about his left hip, and Mrs Bliss thought about Mind, and Miss Howard thought about the cost of the frames for her pictures, but all wore precisely the same dreamy and wistful expression.
  E. F. Benson, *Paying Guests*, 1929

3 They made me a present of Mornington Crescent,
  They threw it a brick at a time.
  Albert Chevalier, 'The Cockney Tragedian', music-hall song

4 If they liked you, they didn't applaud – they just let you live.
  Bob Hope

5 They were really tough – they used to tie their tomatoes on the end of a yo-yo, so they could hit you twice.
  Bob Hope

See also Hecklers; Speakers and Speeches.

AUNTS

1 I tell you, Jeeves, behind every poor, innocent, harmless blighter who is going down for the third time in the soup, you will find, if you look carefully enough, the aunt who shoved him into it . . . It is no use telling me there are good aunts and bad aunts. At the core, they are all alike. Sooner or later, out pops the cloven hoof.
  P. G. Wodehouse, *The Code of the Woosters*, 1938

2 It has probably occurred to all thinking men that something drastic ought to be done about aunts. If someone were to come to me and say, 'Wooster, would you be interested in joining a society whose aim will be the suppression of aunts, or at least will see to it that they are kept on a short chain and not permitted to roam hither and thither at will, scattering desolation on all sides?' I would reply

'Wilbraham,' if his name was Wilbraham, 'put me down as a foundation member.'
P. G. Wodehouse, *A Few Quick Ones*, 1959

See also Relatives; Women; Women – The Male View.

AUSTRALIA AND AUSTRALIANS

1 In the world of success and failure,
Have you noticed the genius spark
Seems brightest in folk from Australia?
We all leave an indelible mark.
You just have to go to the opera,
Or an art-show, or glance at your
  shelves
To see in a trice that Australians
Have done *terribly* well for themselves.
  Dame Edna Everage (Barry Humphries), 'Terribly Well', song, 1976

2 My son Brucie is married to a lovely lass, Joyleen. She's a Sydney girl and he's a Melbourne boy. I warned him about mixed marriages, but he takes no notice.
  Dame Edna Everage (Barry Humphries), *Russell Harty Plus*, London Weekend Television, 1973

3 You may ask me with ill-disguised envy
Why we Aussies get all the right breaks.
So here is my recipe for world-wide
  renown:
Mother's love, lots of fun, JUICY
  STEAKS!
  Dame Edna Everage (Barry Humphries), 'Terribly Well', song, 1976

4 THE GREAT AUSTRALIAN ADJECTIVE
'——'

He plunged into the —— creek,
The —— horse was —— weak,
The stockman's face was a —— study!
And though the —— horse was
  drowned
The —— rider reached the ground
Ejaculating: ——!
——!
  W. T. Goodge, *The Bulletin Reciter*, 1940

5 *Armful of chairs*: Something some people would not know whether you were up them with or not.

Bonzer: Beaut, extra grouse and fan-bloody-tastic.
Cripes: Jeez.
Dip around, A: An activity, usually contemptuous, in which a group of chefs immerse their virile members in a plate of vichyssoise.
Kookaburra's Khyber, as dry as a: A condition of the throat prior to the ingurgitation of ice cold lager.
Spit out the plum, to: To abandon an English accent.
Xenophobia: A love of Australia.
  Barry Humphries, glossary from *Bazza Pulls It Off*, 1972

6 *Australian-based*: a person of diminished aspiration who has been successfully bribed with grants and awards to resist the lure of expatriation.
  Barry Humphries, glossary from *A Nice Night's Entertainment*, 1981

7 It is Wembley in South-East Asia; a tropical Manchester.
  Barry Humphries, *Punch Down Under*, 1984

8 *Koala Triangle*: a mysterious zone in the Southern Hemisphere where persons of talent disappear without trace.
  Barry Humphries, glossary from *A Nice Night's Entertainment*, 1981

9 *Racial characteristics*: violently loud alcoholic roughnecks whose idea of fun is to throw up on your car. The national sport is breaking furniture and the average daily consumption of beer in Sydney is ten and three quarters Imperial gallons for children under the age of nine.
  P. J. O'Rourke, 'Foreigners Around the World', *National Lampoon*, 1976

10 Fair crack of the whip, who reads dictionaries, anyway? You've guessed it sport – old ladies doing the *Women's Weekly* crossword and audio typists who can't spell 'receive'. Correct me if I'm wrong but case in point:
  A red-blooded digger puts the hard word on a horny little unit down the local rubbidy . . . she looks like she'll come across so he whips her up to his brick veneer unit and they're both starkers

before the froth's gone flat on his Fosters. She's screaming for it, so what does this ratbag do? He sticks his nose (wait for it) in a copy of the *Australian Pocket Oxford Dictionary*! Viewed dispassionately thus, I ask you, readers, what strange minority need does this flaming book meet?
Sir Les Patterson (Barry Humphries), *The Sunday Times*, 1977

11 Now, I would be sticking my neck right out, asking for the chop, if I tried to kid *Sunday Times* readers that the average Australian Joe Blow talks like a limp-wristed la-dee-dah Mayfair shirtlifter. Let's face it, you can't demolish two dozen Sydney Rock oysters, a rare T-bone and six chilled tubes with a plum in your flaming mouth!
Sir Les Patterson (Barry Humphries) *The Sunday Times*, 1977

12 Australia!
Land of ravaged desert, shark-infested ocean and thirst-lashed outback.
Australia!
Land of strange, exotic creatures, freaks of evolution, ghastly victims of Mother Nature's vicious whimsy – kangaroo and platypus, potoroo and bandicoot, Richie Benaud and . . .
Peter Tinniswood, *The Brigadier Down Under*, 1983

13 THE DUCHESS OF BERWICK: Do you know, Mr Hopper, dear Agatha and I are so much interested in Australia. It must be so pretty with all the dear little kangaroos flying about.
Oscar Wilde, *Lady Windermere's Fan*, 1892

14 When I look at the map and see what an ugly country Australia is, I feel that I want to go there and see if it cannot be changed into a more beautiful form!
Oscar Wilde (Attrib.)

AUTOBIOGRAPHY

1 Autobiography is now as common as adultery – and hardly less reprehensible.
Lord Altrincham

2 Just as there is nothing between the

admirable omelette and the intolerable, so with autobiography.
Hilaire Belloc

3 Interest in autobiography should begin at home . . . my chief interest is to delight and engross myself. A modest or inhibited autobiography is written without entertainment to the writer and read with distrust by the reader.
Neville Cardus, introduction to his autobiography, 1947

4 An autobiography is an obituary in serial form with the last instalment missing.
Quentin Crisp, *The Naked Civil Servant*, 1968

5 Next to the writer of real estate advertisements, the autobiographer is the most suspect of prose artists.
Donal Henahan, *New York Times*, 1977

6 Nothing I have said is factual except the bits that sound like fiction.
Clive James, *Unreliable Memoirs*, 1980

7 Premature memoirs can only be conceited. I have no excuses against this charge, except to say that self-regard is itself a subject, and that to wait until reminiscence is justified by achievement might mean to wait for ever.
Clive James, *Unreliable Memoirs*, 1980

8 I am being frank about myself in this book. I tell of my first mistake on page 850.
Henry Kissinger, of his memoirs *The White House Years*, 1979

9 Your life story would not make a good book. Don't even try.
Fran Lebowitz, *Metropolitan Life*, 1979

10 When you put down the good things you ought to have done, and leave out the bad things you did do – that's Memoirs.
Will Rogers

11 Only when one has lost all curiosity about the future has one reached the age to write an autobiography.
Evelyn Waugh (Attrib.)

AWARDS

1 I don't deserve this, but then, I have

arthritis and I don't deserve that either.

Jack Benny, on accepting an award

2 Nobel Prize money is a lifebelt thrown to a swimmer who has already reached the shore in safety.

George Bernard Shaw (Attrib.)

See also Achievements; Show Business; Success; Winning.

B

BABIES

1 Except that right side up is best, there is not much to learn about holding a baby. There are 152 distinctly different ways – and all are right! At least all will do.
  Heywood Broun, *Collected Edition*, 1941

2 It is pretty generally held that all a woman needs to do to know all about children is to have some. This wisdom is attributed to instinct . . . I have seen mothers give beer and spaghetti and Neapolitan ice cream to children in arms, and if they got that from instinct the only conclusion possible is that instinct is not what it used to be.
  Heywood Broun, *Collected Edition*, 1941

3 The babe, with a cry brief and dismal,
  Fell into the water baptismal;
  Ere they'd gathered its plight,
  It had sunk out of sight,
  For the depth of the font was abysmal.
  Edward Gorey, 'The babe, with a cry brief and dismal', *The Listing Attic*, 1954

4 When Baby's cries grew hard to bear
  I popped him in the Frigidaire.
  I never would have done so if
  I'd known that he'd be frozen stiff.
  My wife said: 'George, I'm so unhappé!
  Our darling's now completely *frappé*!'
  Harry Graham, 'L'Enfant Glacé', *Ruthless Rhymes for Heartless Homes*, 1899

5 Training a child is more or less a matter of pot luck.
  Rod Maclean, *Reader's Digest*, 1949

6 A bit of talcum
  Is always walcum.
  Ogden Nash, 'The Baby', *Freewheeling*, 1931

7 The baby wakes up in the wee wee hours of the morning.
  Robert Robbins, *Reader's Digest*, 1949

8 GRANDMOTHER: Let me hold the baby!
  BILKO: Let you hold who? What? Who? Who? Who are you?
  MOTHER: Oh, this is my mother – the baby's grandma!
  BILKO: Oh, all right. But I don't approve of all this armhopping! . . .
  UNCLE MAX: Atishoo!
  BILKO: Who? Who? Who sneezed?
  UNCLE MAX: I sneezed. Why?
  BILKO: You'll have to go out! Out!
  UNCLE MAX: But I'm Uncle Max!
  BILKO: You should have thought of that before you sneezed! Now, out!
  Neil Simon and Terry Ryan, 'Bilko's Godson', *The Phil Silvers Show*, CBS TV, 1959

See also Birth; Children; Mothers; Pregnancy.

BACHELORS

1 A bachelor never makes the same mistake once.
  Anon.

2 I belong to Bridegrooms Anonymous. Whenever I feel like getting married, they send over a lady in a housecoat and hair curlers to burn my toast for me.
  Dick Martin, *Playboy*, 1969

3 She was another one of his near Mrs.
  Alfred McFote

4 Bachelors know more about women than married men; if they didn't, they'd be married too.
  H. L. Mencken

5 A bachelor never quite gets over the idea that he is a thing of beauty and a boy forever.
  Helen Rowland

6 Bachelors are not fashionable any more. They are a damaged lot. Too much is known about them.
  Oscar Wilde, *An Ideal Husband*, 1895

7 By persistently remaining single, a man converts himself into a permanent public temptation. Men should be more careful;

this very celibacy leads weaker vessels astray.
Oscar Wilde, *The Importance of Being Earnest,* 1895

See also Courting; Marriage.

BADGES

1 IGNORE THIS BUTTON
Badge, London, 1978

2 Politenessman says: THANK YOU FOR LOOKING AT THIS BUTTON!
Ron Barrett, *National Lampoon*

See also Graffiti.

STANLEY BALDWIN Prime Minister of Great Britain, 1923–1924, 1924–1929, 1935–1937 (Conservative Party)

1 I think Baldwin has gone mad. He simply takes one jump in the dark; looks round; and then takes another.
Lord Birkenhead, letter to Austen Chamberlain, 1923

2 Decided only to be undecided, resolved to be irresolute, adamant for drift, solid for fluidity, all-powerful to be impotent.
Winston Churchill, speech, 1936

3 He occasionally stumbled over the truth, but hastily picked himself up and hurried on as if nothing had happened.
Winston Churchill (Attrib.)

4 One could not even dignify him with the name of stuffed shirt. He was simply a hole in the air.
George Orwell, *The Lion and the Unicorn,* 1941

See also The Conservative Party.

BALLET

1 They were doing the Dying Swan at the ballet. And there was a rumor that some bookmakers had drifted into town from upstate New York and that they had fixed the ballet. There was a lot of money bet on the swan to live.
Woody Allen, nightclub act, 1960s

2 I suppose I'm the only person who re-members one of the most exciting of his

ballets – it's the fruit of an unlikely col-laboration between Nijinsky on the one hand and Sir Arthur Conan Doyle on the other. I think I'm right in saying that it was the only detective story in ballet and it was called *The Inspector de la Rose.* The choreography was by Fokine. Wasn't up to much. Just the usual Fokine rubbish.
Alan Bennett, *The South Bank Show,* London Weekend Television, 1984

See also Dance; Exercise; The Theatre.

BANKING

1 A banker is a man who lends you an umbrella when the weather is fair, and takes it away from you when it rains.
Anon.

2 . . . they all observe one rule which woe betides the banker who fails to heed it,
Which is you must never lend any money to anybody unless they don't need it.
Ogden Nash, 'Bankers are Just Like Any-body Else, except Richer', *I'm a Stranger Here Myself,* 1938

3 A lot of people will also urge you to put some money in a bank, and in fact – within reason – this is very good advice. But don't go overboard. Remember, what you are doing is giving your money to somebody else to hold on to, and I think that it is worth keeping in mind that the businessmen who run banks are so worried about holding on to things that they put little chains on all their pens.
Miss Piggy, *Miss Piggy's Guide to Life (As Told to Henry Beard),* 1981

4 There have been three great inventions since the beginning of time: fire, the wheel and central banking.
Will Rogers

See also Borrowing and Lending; Credit; Credit Cards; Money; Professions; Wealth.

BASEBALL

1 Getting a ball past his bat is like trying to sneak the sun past a rooster.
Anonymous pitcher on Hank Aaron, 1973

2 If people don't want to come out to the ball park, nobody's going to stop them.
   Yogi Berra

3 The tradition of professional baseball always has been agreeably free of chivalry. The rule is, 'Do anything you can get away with.'
   Heywood Broun

4 Say this for big league baseball – it is beyond any question the greatest conversation piece ever invented in America.
   Bruce Catton

5 I'm throwing twice as hard as I ever did. The ball's just not getting there as fast.
   'Lefty' Gomez, pitcher, New York Yankees

6 Baseball is very big with my people. It figures. It's the only time we can get to shake a bat at a white man without starting a riot.
   Dick Gregory, *From the Back of the Bus*, 1962

7 The more we lose, the more he'll fly in. And the more he flies in, the better the chance there'll be a plane crash.
   Graig Nettles, on George Steinbrenner, owner of the New York Yankees

8 The most overrated underrated player in baseball.
   Larry Ritter, on Tommy Henrich

9 The secret of managing is to keep the guys who hate you away from the guys who are undecided.
   Casey Stengel

10 The sneer has gone from Casey's lip, his teeth are clenched in hate;
   He pounds with cruel violence his bat upon the plate.
   And now the pitcher holds the ball, and now he lets it go,
   And now the air is shattered by the force of Casey's blow.
   Oh, somewhere in this favored land the sun is shining bright;
   The band is playing somewhere, and somewhere hearts are light,
   And somewhere men are laughing, and somewhere children shout;

But there is no joy in Mudville – mighty Casey has struck out.
   Ernest Lawrence Thayer, 'Casey at the Bat'

11 Baseball is almost the only orderly thing in a very unorderly world. If you get three strikes, even the best lawyer in the world can't get you off.
   Bill Veeck

See also Sport.

BATHS

1 I believe I will dip my pink-and-white body in yon Roman tub. I feel a bit gritty after the affairs of the day.
   W. C. Fields, *My Little Chickadee*, screenplay, 1940

2 Some people shave before bathing,
   And about people who bathe before shaving they are scathing,
   While those who bathe before shaving,
   Well, they imply that those who shave before bathing are misbehaving.
   Ogden Nash, 'And Three Hundred and Sixty-six in Leap Year', *Good Intentions*, 1942

3 I don't like baths. I don't enjoy them in the slightest and, if I could, I'd prefer to go around dirty.
   J. B. Priestley, *Observer*, 1979

See also Cleanliness.

THE BBC

1 The poor quivering wreck was led away to a place where he could do no harm. A home for distressed gentlefolk – or, as it is better known, the BBC Television Centre.
   He was set to work on simple tasks that his poor, befuddled mind could grasp – and now he's the producer of *Panorama*.
   Barry Took and Marty Feldman, *Round the Horne*, BBC Radio

See also Television.

THE BEATLES

1 What are the Beatles? I have never been able to understand what one beat singer

is saying. Perhaps I shall fare better with four?
  Noël Coward (Attrib.)

2 I see the Beatles have arrived from England. They were forty pounds overweight, and that was just their hair.
  Bob Hope, 1964

3 Do you remember when everyone began analysing Beatle songs? I don't think I understood what some of them were supposed to be about.
  Ringo Starr (Attrib.)

See also Music and Musicians; Rock 'n' Roll; The Sixties; Songs and Singers.

BEAUTY

1 A: How do you like bathing beauties?
  B: I don't know, I never bathed one.
  Anon.

2 *I* am beautiful; *you* have quite good features; *she* isn't bad looking, if you like that type.
  Competition, *New Statesman*

3 She wore a short skirt and a tight sweater and her figure described a set of parabolas that could cause cardiac arrest in a yak.
  Woody Allen, *Getting Even*, 1973

4 It was a blonde. A blonde to make a bishop kick a hole in a stained-glass window.
  Raymond Chandler, *Farewell, My Lovely*, 1940

5 When I go to the beauty parlor, I always use the emergency entrance. Sometimes I just go for an estimate.
  Phyllis Diller

6 After a degree of prettiness, one pretty girl is as pretty as another.
  F. Scott Fitzgerald, *Esquire*, 1936

7 'Why is it that beautiful women never seem to have any curiosity?'
  'Is it because they know they're classical? With classical things the Lord finished the job. Ordinary ugly people know they're deficient and they go on looking for the pieces.'
  Penelope Gilliatt, *A State of Change*, 1967

8 She has eyes that men adore so
  And a torso even more so.
  E. Y. Harburg, 'Lydia, the Tattooed Lady', song for Groucho Marx from *At the Circus*, 1939

9 The girl in the omnibus had one of those faces of marvellous beauty which are seen casually in the streets but never among one's friends. It was perfect in its softened classicality – a Greek face translated into English. Moreover she was fair, and her hair pale chestnut. Where do these women come from? Who marries them? Who knows them?
  Thomas Hardy, quoted in *The Early Life of Thomas Hardy, 1840–1891*, 1928

10 I'm tired of all this nonsense about beauty being only skin-deep. That's deep enough. What do you want – an adorable pancreas?
  Jean Kerr, *The Snake Has All the Lines*, 1960

See also Appearance; Cosmetics; Faces; Sexual Attraction.

BED

1 One good turn gets most of the blanket.
  Anon.

2 Lying in bed would be an altogether perfect and supreme experience if only one had a coloured pencil long enough to draw on the ceiling.
  G. K. Chesterton, 'On Lying in Bed', 1910

3 The tone now commonly taken towards the practice of lying in bed is hypocritical and unhealthy ... Instead of being regarded, as it ought to be, as a matter for personal convenience and adjustment, it has come to be regarded by many as if it were a part of essential morals to get up early in the morning. It is, upon the whole, part of practical wisdom; but there is nothing good about it or bad about its opposite.
  G. K. Chesterton, 'On Lying in Bed', 1910

4 It was such a lovely day, I thought it was a pity to get up.
  W. Somerset Maugham, *Our Betters*, 1923

See also Breakfast; Dreams; Insomnia; Sleep.

BEGGING

1 TRAMP: I haven't eaten for three days.
MAN: My dear chap – you must *force*
yourself!
   Anon.

2 TRAMP: Would you give me twenty-five
pence for a sandwich, lady?
LADY: I don't know – let me see the
sandwich.
   Gyles Brandreth, *1,000 Jokes: The Greatest
   Joke Book Ever Known*, 1980

3 Beggars should be abolished entirely! It
is annoying to give to them and it is
annoying *not* to give to them.
   Friedrich Wilhelm Nietzsche, *Thus Spake
   Zarathustra*, 1883–1892

See also Poverty; Tramps.

BEHAVIOUR

1 I never observe rules of conduct,
and therefore have given up making
them.
   George Bernard Shaw (Attrib.)

2 To be natural is such a very difficult pose
to keep up.
   Oscar Wilde, *An Ideal Husband*, 1895

See also Action.

BELGIUM

1 Belgium is the most densely populated
country in Europe . . . the land is entirely
invisible, except in the small hours of the
morning, being for the rest of the time
completely under foot . . . the sprout was
developed by Brussels agronomists, this
being the largest cabbage a housewife
could possibly carry through the teeming
streets.
   Alan Coren, *The Sanity Inspector*, 1974

2 Belgium is known affectionately to the
French as 'the gateway to Germany' and
just as affectionately to the Germans as
'the gateway to France'.
   Tony Hendra, 'EEC! It's the US of E!',
   National Lampoon, 1976

BELIEF

1 And how can I believe in God when just
last week I got my tongue caught in the
roller of an electric typewriter?
   Woody Allen, *Without Feathers*, 1976

2 In real life, Keaton believes in God. But
she also believes that the radio works
because there are tiny people inside it.
   Woody Allen, *Esquire*, 1975

3 It [the film *Love and Death*] implies that
He doesn't exist, or, if He does, He can't
really be trusted. (Since coming to this
conclusion I have twice been nearly
struck by lightning and once forced to
engage in a long conversation with a
theatrical agent.)
   Woody Allen, *Esquire*, 1975

4 Not only is there no God, but try getting a
plumber at weekends.
   Woody Allen, *Getting Even*, 1972

5 To get into hebben
Don't snap fo' a seben –
Live clean! Don't have no fault!
Oh, I takes dat gospel
Whenever it's pos'ple –
But wid a grain of salt!
   Ira Gershwin and DuBose Heyward, 'It
   Ain't Necessarily So', *Porgy and Bess*, 1935

6 Any stigma is good enough to beat a
dogma with.
   Philip Guedalla

7 I'm a man of no convictions – at least I
think I am.
   Christopher Hampton, *The Philanthropist*,
   1970

8 No matter how much I probe and prod
I cannot quite believe in God
But oh! I hope to God that he
Unswervingly believes in me!
   E. Y. Harburg, *Rhymes for the Irreverent*,
   1965

9 If there is a God, give me a sign! . . . See,
I told you that the knlupt smflrt
glpptnrr . . .
   Steve Martin, 'A Wild and Crazy Guy',
   record, 1978

10 Man is a credulous animal and must
believe something. In the absence of
good grounds for belief, he will be
satisfied with bad ones.
   Bertrand Russell, *Unpopular Essays*, 1950

11 'I've seen the light,' said the policeman, hitherto an atheist, 'and what I wanted to ask you, sir, was do I have to join the Infants' Bible Class or can I start singing in the choir right away?'
P. G. Wodehouse, *The Mating Season*, 1949

See also Atheism; The Church; Credulity; God; Heaven; Religion; Truth.

BEST-SELLERS

1 Best-sellerism is the star system of the book world. A 'best-seller' is a celebrity among books. It is a book known primarily (sometimes exclusively) for its well-knownness.
Daniel J. Boorstin, *The Image*, 1962

2 A best-seller is the gilded tomb of a mediocre talent.
Logan Pearsall Smith, *All Trivia*, 1933

See also Books; Publishing; Success; Writers; Writing.

ANEURIN (NYE) BEVAN British Labour politician, Minister of Health, 1945–1951

1 If thy Nye offend thee, pluck it out.
Clement Attlee, speech to the Labour NEC, 1955

2 He will be as great a curse to this country in peace as he was a squalid nuisance in time of war.
Winston Churchill, speech in the House of Commons, 1945

3 He enjoys prophesying the imminent end of the capitalist system and is prepared to play a part, any part, in its burial except that of a mute.
Harold Macmillan (Attrib.)

See also Winston Churchill; The Labour Party.

THE BIBLE

1 The first pair ate the first apple.
Anon.

2 And Noah he often said to his wife when he sat down to dine,

'I don't care where the water goes if it doesn't get into the wine.'
G. K. Chesterton, 'Wine and Water', *The Flying Inn*, 1914

3 CHAPTER ONE
... 26 And God saw everything He had made, and He saw that it was very good; and God said, 'It *just* goes to show Me what the private sector can accomplish. With a lot of fool regulations, this could have taken *billions of years*.'

27 And on the evening of the fifth day, *which had been* the roughest day yet, God said, 'Thank Me it's Friday.' And God made the weekend.
Tony Hendra and Sean Kelly, 'The Book of Creation', *Playboy*, 1982

4 CHAPTER ONE
In the beginning, God created dates.

2 And the date WAS Monday, July 4, 4004 BC.

3 And God said, 'Let there be Light'; and there was Light. And *when* there was Light, God *saw* the date, *that* it was an Monday, and He *got* down to work; for, verily He had an Big Job *to do*. And God made pottery shards and Silurian mollusks and Pre-Cambrian limestone strata; and flints and Jurassic mastodon tusks and Pithecanthropus erectus skulls and Cretaceous Placentalia made He; and those cave paintings at Lascaux. And that was *that* for the first Day.
Tony Hendra and Sean Kelly, 'The Book of Creation', *Playboy*, 1982

5 It is not fair to visit all
The blame on Eve, for Adam's fall;
The most Eve did was to display
Contributory negligé.
Oliver Herford, 'Eve: Apropos de Rien'

6 Say what you will about the Ten Commandments, you always come back to the pleasant fact that there are only ten of them.
H. L. Mencken (Attrib.)

7 NEWSREADER: Good even. Here beginneth the first verse of the news. It has come to pass that the seven elders of the

seven tribes have now been abiding in Sodom for seven days and seven nights. There seems little hope of an early settlement. An official spokesman said this afternoon, 'Only a miracle can save us now.'

... At the weigh-in for the big fight tomorrow, Goliath tipped the scales this even at 15 stone 3 lbs and David at 14 stone 3 lbs. David's manager said this even, 'The odd stone could make all the difference.'

... The news in brief: Lamentations 4: 18–22 and II Kings 14: 2–8.
Bill Oddie and John Cleese, *I'm Sorry I'll Read That Again*, BBC Radio

8 I read the book of Job last night – I don't think God comes well out of it.
Virginia Woolf, *The Letters of Virginia Woolf: Vol. II, 1912–1922*, 1975

See also Christianity; The Church; God; Jesus Christ; Religion.

BIGAMY

1 Bigamy is having one wife too many. Monogamy is the same thing.
Anon.

2 Q: If I married two women, would that be bigamy?
A: It would be *very* big of you!
Anon.

3 Bigamy is one way of avoiding the painful publicity of divorce and the expense of alimony.
Oliver Herford

4 There once was an old man of Lyme
Who married three wives at a time.
When asked, 'Why a third?'
He replied, 'One's absurd!
And bigamy, sir, is a crime.'
William Cosmo Monkhouse

See also Divorce; Marriage; Monogamy.

BIG BUSINESS

1 Coca-Cola Co. discovered that it had inadvertently bought Columbia Pictures Inc. Company executives had thought they were buying Columbia, the Central America country. Coca-Cola is asking the movie company for its deposit back.
Off The Wall Street Journal, 1982

2 IBM is making top corporate positions hereditary. The sweeping change is designed to take advantage of new estate tax laws and stimulate child production among the right people.
Off The Wall Street Journal, 1982

3 The meek may inherit the earth – but not its mineral rights.
J. Paul Getty

4 If the government was as afraid of disturbing the consumer as it is of disturbing business, this would be some democracy.
Kin Hubbard

5 Whenever you're sitting across from some important person, always picture him sitting there in a suit of long red underwear. That's the way I always operated in business.
Joseph P. Kennedy, quoted in *No Final Victories*, 1974

6 Nothing is illegal if a hundred businessmen decide to do it, and that's true anywhere in the world.
Andrew Young

See also Business; Capitalism; The Office.

BIRDS

1 HE: Every morning, I'd be down in the park and then I'd feed the pigeons.
SHE: What do you feed them? Popcorn?
HE: No. Every morning I'd go down to this park and I'd feed the pigeons. To my cat.
Tony Hendra and Michael O'Donoghue, National Lampoon's *Radio Dinner*, record 1972

2 Sir,
All thrushes (not only those in this neck of the Glyndebourne woods) sooner or later sing the tune of the first subject of Mozart's G minor Symphony (K. 550) – and, what's more, phrase it a sight better than most conductors. The tempo is always dead right and there is no

suggestion of an unauthorized accent on the ninth note of the phrase.

> Yours &c.,
> **Spike Hughes**, letter to *The Times*, 1962

3 How do you like that bird I sent you home for your birthday? . . . You cooked it? . . . Mama, that was a South American parrot – he spoke five languages! . . . He should have SAID something? . . .
> **George Jessel**, 'Phone Call to Mama', 1930s

4 YOUNG WOMAN IN MUSEUM: What's that bird?
W. P. KER: It's a guillemot.
YOUNG WOMAN: That's not my idea of a guillemot.
W. P. KER: It's *God's* idea of a guillemot.
> **W. P. Ker**, dialogue quoted in Geoffrey Madan's *Notebooks*, 1981

5 Many amateurs still think that when birds sing and hop around, they are being merry and affectionate. They are not, of course; they are being aggressive and demanding the price of a cup of coffee. As, however, human beings are soft at heart and in the head, I suppose we shall go on regarding this thing as a much loved garden bird, even when it beats on the window with its beak and tells you to get that goddam food out on the bird table, or else.
> **Miles Kington**, *Nature Made Ridiculously Simple*, 1983

6 A rare old bird is the pelican;
His bill holds more than his belican.
He can take in his beak
Enough food for a week;
I'm darned if I know how the helican.
> **Dixon Merritt**

7 The song of canaries
Never varies
And when they're molting
They're revolting.
> **Ogden Nash**, 'The Canary', *The Face is Familiar*, 1940

8 . . . somewhere in the woods beyond the river a nightingale had begun to sing with all the full-throated zest of a bird conscious of having had a rave notice from the poet Keats and only a couple of nights ago a star spot on the programme of the BBC.
> **P. G. Wodehouse**, *Ring for Jeeves*, 1953

See also Animals; Pets.

BIRTH

1 When I was born, I was so surprised I couldn't talk for a year and a half.
> **Gracie Allen**, *The Robert Burns Panatela Program*, CBS Radio, 1932

2 To my embarrassment, I was born in bed with a lady.
> **Wilson Mizner**

3 Congratulations. We all knew you had it in you.
> **Dorothy Parker**, telegram to friend who'd just given birth (Attrib.)

4 . . . I had a Jewish delivery: they knock you out with the first pain; they wake you up when the hairdresser shows.
> **Joan Rivers**, *An Audience with Joan Rivers*, London Weekend Television, 1984

5 My obstetrician was so dumb that when I gave birth he forgot to cut the cord. For a year that kid followed me *everywhere*. It was like having a dog on a leash.
> **Joan Rivers**, *An Audience with Joan Rivers*, London Weekend Television, 1984

6 Announcement from the proud parents of a baby daughter: 'We have skirted the issue.'
> **Earl Wilson**

7 I was caesarean born. You can't really tell, although whenever I leave a house, I go out through a window.
> **Steven Wright**, quoted in *Vanity Fair*, 1984

See also Babies; Birth Control; Fathers; Mothers; Pregnancy.

BIRTH CONTROL

1 My girlfriend just found out she's been taking aspirins instead of the pill. Well, at least she doesn't have a headache – but I do.
> *Laugh-In*, NBC TV, 1969

2 Whenever I hear people discussing birth

control, I always remember that I was the fifth.
Clarence Darrow

3 The Pill came to market and changed the sexual and real-estate habits of millions; motel chains were created to serve them.
Herbert Gold, *New York Times*, 1972

4 Sister Susie built her hopes
On the book of Marie Stopes.
But I fear from her condition
She must have read the wrong edition.
Madge Kendall

5 Contraceptives should be used on every conceivable occasion.
Spike Milligan, *The Last Goon Show of All*, BBC Radio, 1972

6 YOUNG GIRL (*to doctor*): Have I had any side effects from the pill? . . . Only promiscuity!
Don Orehek, cartoon in *Playboy*, 1969

7 Skullion had little use for contraceptives at the best of times. Unnatural, he called them, and placed them in the lower social category of things along with elastic-sided boots and made-up bow ties. Not the sort of attire for a gentleman.
Tom Sharpe, *Porterhouse Blue*, 1974

See also Birth; Pregnancy; Sex.

BIRTHDAYS

1 I think it's wonderful you could all be here for the forty-third anniversary of my thirty-ninth birthday. We decided not to light the candles this year – we were afraid Pan Am would mistake it for a runway.
Bob Hope, on his eighty-second birthday, 1985
See also Age.

BISEXUALITY

1 I can't understand why more people aren't bisexual. It would double your chances for a date on Saturday night.
Woody Allen

2 Bisexuality is not so much a cop-out as a fearful compromise.
Jill Johnston, *Lesbian Nation*, 1973

See also Homosexuality; Sex.

BOASTS

1 When you're as great as I am, it's hard to be humble.
Muhammed Ali (Attrib.)

2 If only I had a little humility, I would be perfect.
Ted Turner (Attrib.)

See also Humility; Modesty; Pride; Vanity.

THE BODY

1 Your body! After all, what is it? Just a physical covering, that's all – worth chemically thirty-two cents.
Sidney Buchman and Seton I. Miller, *Here Comes Mr Jordan*, screenplay, 1941

2 Skin is like wax paper that holds everything in without dripping.
Art Linkletter, *A Child's Garden of Misinformation*, 1965

See also Exercise; Faces; Figures; Hair; Legs; Nudity.

THE BOMB

1 Don't get smart alecksy
With the galaxy
Leave the atom alone.
E. Y. Harburg

2 Cogito ergo boom.
Susan Sontag, *Styles of Radical Will*, 1969

3 . . . the French are going the Americans one better with their Michelin bomb: it destroys only restaurants under four stars.
Robin Williams, interview in *Playboy*, 1982

See also Nuclear Power; Nuclear War; Pacifism; Peace; War.

BOOKS

1 Thank you for sending me a copy of your book. I'll waste no time in reading it.
Anon.

2 Child! do not throw this book about;
Refrain from the unholy pleasure
Of cutting all the pictures out!
Preserve it as your chiefest treasure.
   Hilaire Belloc, *Bad Child's Book of Beasts*,
   1896

3 DUFF: We've had a big best-seller . . . I
haven't got round to it yet. I suspect the
presence of allegory, which is always a
slight deterrent.
   Alan Bennett, *The Old Country*, 1978

4 MOTHER: Bobby's teacher says he ought
to have an encyclopaedia.
FATHER: Let him walk to school like I
had to.
   Gyles Brandreth, *1,000 Jokes: The Greatest
   Joke Book Ever Known*, 1980

5 I wonder what we are publishing now is
worth cutting down trees to make paper
for the stuff.
   Richard Brautigan

6 There is a good saying to the effect that
when a new book appears one should
read an old one. As an author I would not
recommend too strict an adherence to
this saying.
   Winston Churchill

7 Never lend books, for no one ever returns them; the only books I have in my
library are books that other folk have lent
me.
   Anatole France

8 ERRATUM
This slip has been inserted by mistake.
   Alisdair Gray, erratum slip inserted in
   Unlikely Stories, Mostly, 1983

9 It is the sort of book I keep meaning to
write, very slim, in large type and with
lots of illustrations. It must have taken
them at least half an hour.
   Angus McGill, *Standard*, 1983

10 They borrow books they will not buy,
They have no ethics or religions;
I wish some kind Burbankian guy
Could cross my books with homing
   pigeons.
   Carolyn Wells, 'Book-borrowers'

11 *Masterpieces* is a bouquet of pensées,

culled, garnered and even untimely
ripped from the fertile loins of the
Wellsian imagination, time-weatherered
flotsam plucked from the raging delirium
tremens of the creative process.
   Here are jewelled insights, lovingly
crafted by a veritable Fabergé amongst
wordsmiths, hand-polished erections in
the global village of contemporary sensibility, perceptions snatched from the
outer limits of human experience, great
miniatures acid-etched on the tender
film noir of the mind's membrane . . .
Masterpieces . . . The paperback!
   John Wells, *Masterpieces*, 1982

See also Best-sellers; Books – Critics;
Books – Dedications; Literature;
Novels; Publishing; Reading; Writers;
Writing.

BOOKS – CRITICS

1 He writes so well, he makes me feel like
putting my quill back in my goose.
   Fred Allen

2 That trees should have been cut down
to provide paper for this book was an
ecological affront.
   Anthony Blond, *Spectator*, 1983

3 *Sartor Resartus* is simply unreadable,
and for me that always sort of spoils a
book.
   Will Cuppy

4 One always tends to overpraise a long
book because one has got through it.
   E. M. Forster

5 From the moment I picked it [a book] up
until I laid it down, I was convulsed with
laughter. Some day I intend reading it.
   Groucho Marx (Attrib.)

6 This is not a novel to be tossed aside
lightly. It should be thrown with great
force.
   Dorothy Parker, in a book review

7 I never read a book before reviewing it –
it prejudices a man so.
   Sydney Smith

8 To see him fumbling with our rich and
delicate language is to experience all the

horror of seeing a Sèvres vase in the hands of a chimpanzee.
Evelyn Waugh, reviewing *World within World* by Steven Spender, 1951

9 George Meredith. His style is chaos illuminated by flashes of lightning. As a writer he has mastered everything except language: as a novelist he can do everything except tell a story: as an artist he is everything except articulate.
Oscar Wilde, 'The Decay of Lying', 1889

10 He leads his readers to the latrine and locks them in.
Oscar Wilde, of the novelist and playwright George Moore (Attrib.)

11 Mr Hall Caine, it is true, aims at the grandiose, but then he writes at the top of his voice. He is so loud that one cannot hear what he says.
Oscar Wilde, 'The Decay of Lying', 1889

12 Mr Henry James writes fiction as if it were a painful duty.
Oscar Wilde, 'The Decay of Lying', 1889

13 M. Zola is determined to show that, if he has not got genius, he can at least be dull.
Oscar Wilde, 'The Decay of Lying', 1889

14 One must have a heart of stone to read the death of Little Nell without laughing.
Oscar Wilde (Attrib.)

See also Books.

BOOKS – DEDICATIONS

1 To Herbert Bayard Swope without whose friendly aid and counsel every line in this book was written.
Franklin P. Adams

2 To my daughter Leonora without whose never-failing sympathy and encouragement this book would have been finished in half the time.
P. G. Wodehouse, *The Heart of a Goof*, 1926

See also Books.

BOREDOM

1 George Sanders says: 'Here are some of the things that bored me to death.'
Most Boring Tiny Enslaved Country: tiny enslaved Latvia.
Most Boring Satellite: Tiros, the weather satellite.
Most Boring Chaucerian Grammatical Form: petrified dative.
Most Boring Mathematical Concept: tangent bundles.
Most Boring New Force for Social Change: married priests.
Most Boring Telephone Pleasantry: 'Good to hear your voice.'
Most Boring Illiterate Verbalization of Approval or Awe: 'Oh, wow!'
Most Boring Sex: women.
National Lampoon, 1972

2 If you were searching for a word to describe the conversations that go on down the mine, boring would spring to your lips. Oh, God! They're very boring. If you ever want to hear things like: 'Hello, I've found a bit of coal.' 'Have you really?' 'Yes, no doubt about it, this black substance is coal all right.' 'Jolly good, the very thing we're looking for.' It's not enough to keep the mind alive, is it?
Peter Cook, 'Sitting on a Bench', monologue, 1960s

3 Ennui, felt on the proper occasions, is a sign of intelligence.
Clifton Fadiman, *Reading I've Liked*, 1958

4 Oh don't the days seem lank and long
When all goes right and nothing goes
    wrong,
And isn't your life extremely flat
With nothing whatever to grumble at!
W. S. Gilbert and Arthur Sullivan, *Princess Ida*, 1884

5 The capacity of human beings to bore one another seems to be vastly greater than that of any other animals. Some of their most esteemed inventions have no other apparent purpose, for example, the dinner party of more than two, the epic poem, and the science of metaphysics.
H. L. Mencken (Attrib.)

6 Boredom, after all, is a form of criticism.
William Phillips, *A Sense of the Present*, 1967

See also Bores.

BORES

1 Our Billy's talk is just like bottled stout,
   You draw the cork and only froth comes
   out.
   Anon., *Truth*, Brisbane, 1916

2 Doreen was okay, though. There was
   nothing wrong with her that a vasectomy
   of the vocal cords wouldn't fix.
   Lisa Alther, *Kinflicks*, 1976

3 He hasn't got much to say, but at least he
   doesn't try to say anything else.
   Robert Benchley (Attrib.)

4 He never spares himself in conversation.
   He gives himself so generously that
   hardly anybody else is permitted to give
   anything in his presence.
   Aneurin Bevan, on Winston Churchill
   (Attrib.)

5 I've just spent an hour talking to Tallulah
   for a few minutes.
   Fred Keating, on Tallulah Bankhead
   (Attrib.)

6 He is not only a bore, but he bores for
   England.
   Malcolm Muggeridge, of Sir Anthony
   Eden

7 She has the reputation of being out-
   spoken – by no one!
   Jack Paar

8 I am one of those unhappy persons who
   inspire bores to the highest flights of art.
   Edith Sitwell

9 Somebody's boring me – I think it's me.
   Dylan Thomas

10 In modern life nothing produces such an
   effect as a good platitude. It makes the
   whole world kin.
   Oscar Wilde, *An Ideal Husband*, 1895

11 MRS ALLONBY: . . . you should certainly
   know Ernest, Lady Stutfield. It is only
   fair to tell you beforehand he has got no
   conversation at all.
   LADY STUTFIELD: I adore silent men.
   MRS ALLONBY: Oh, Ernest isn't silent.
   He talks the whole time. But he has got
   no conversation.
   Oscar Wilde, *A Woman of No Importance*,
   1893

See also Boredom.

BORROWING AND LENDING

1 Don't borrow or lend, but if you must do
   one, lend.
   Josh Billings, *The Complete Works of Josh
   Billings*, 1919

2 He was an incorrigible borrower of
   money; he borrowed from all his friends;
   if he ever repaid a loan the incident failed
   to pass into history.
   Mark Twain, of Bret Harte, *Autobiography*,
   1924

See also Banking; Credit; Credit Cards;
Debt.

BOSSES

1 You can't help liking the managing
   director – if you don't, he fires you.
   Anon.

2 I don't want any yes-men around me. I
   want everybody to tell me the truth even
   if it costs them their jobs.
   Samuel Goldwyn

See also Big Business; Business; Leadership; The Office; Work.

BOSTON

1 I have just returned from Boston. It is the
   only thing to do if you find yourself up
   there.
   Fred Allen, letter to Groucho Marx, 1953

2 I come from the city of Boston,
   The home of the bean and the cod,
   Where Cabots speak only to Lowells,
   And Lowells speak only to God.
   Samuel C. Bushnell, 'Boston', 1905

3 Boston is a moral and intellectual
   nursery, always applying first principles
   to trifles.
   George Santayana

See also America and the Americans;
New England.

BOXING

1 If you ever get belted and see three
   fighters through a haze, go after the one

in the middle. That's what ruined me – I
went after the two guys on the end.
Max Baer, World Heavyweight Champion,
1934–1935

2 It is like someone jammed an electric
light bulb in your face and busted it. I
thought half my head was blowed off.
Jim Braddock, on being hit by Joe Louis,
1937

3 He floats like an anchor, stings like a
moth.
Ray Gandolf, American sports reporter on
Muhammad Ali at thirty-nine

4 I was the only fighter in Cleveland who
wore a rear-view mirror.
Bob Hope, quoted in *Bob Hope: Portrait of a
Superstar*, 1981

5 ERIC: I was a pretty handy fighter in my
youth. I could lick any man with one
hand . . .
ERNIE: Really?
ERIC: Yes. Unfortunately, I could never
find anyone with one hand who wanted a
fight.
Eric Morecambe and Ernie Wise, *The
Morecambe and Wise Joke Book*, 1979

6 ERNIE: How did the fight go?
ERIC: Well, for a minute or two I was in
with a great chance. Then it started. The
bell went – I raced out of my corner, tried
a left, then another left, then a right
hook!
ERNIE: Fantastic!
ERIC: Then my opponent came out of *his*
corner. But within a minute, I really had
him worried.
ERNIE: Why?
ERIC: He thought he'd killed me.
Eric Morecambe and Ernie Wise, *The
Morecambe and Wise Joke Book*, 1979

7 First your legs go. Then you lose your
reflexes. Then you lose your friends.
Willie Pep, World Featherweight Champion, 1942–1948, 1949–1950

8 In boxing the right cross-counter is distinctly one of those things it is more
blessed to give than to receive.
P. G. Wodehouse, *The Pothunters*, 1902

9 I'll never forget my first fight . . . all of a

sudden I found someone I knew in the
fourth row. It was me. He hit me amongst
my nose.
Henny Youngman, 1940

See also Fighting; Self-defence; Sport.

THE BRAIN

1 The brain is a wonderful organ. It starts
working the moment you get up in the
morning, and does not stop until you get
into the office.
Robert Frost

2 The left hemisphere became the one to
have if you were having only one.
Howard Gardner, *The Shattered Mind*,
1975

See also Memory.

BREAKFAST

1 My wife and I tried to breakfast together,
but we had to stop or our marriage would
have been wrecked.
Winston Churchill (Attrib.)

2 You may brag about your breakfast
  foods you eat at break of day,
Your crisp, delightful shavings and your
  stack of last year's hay,
Your toasted flakes of rye and corn that
  fairly swim in cream,
Or rave about a sawdust mash, an
  epicurean dream.
But none of these appeals to me, though
  all of them I've tried –
The breakfast that I liked the best was
  sausage mother fried.
Edgar A. Guest, 'Sausage', *Collected Verse*,
1934

3 The critical period in matrimony is
breakfast-time.
A. P. Herbert, *Uncommon Law*, 1935

4 Breakfast cereals that come in the same
colors as polyester leisure suits make
oversleeping a virtue.
Fran Lebowitz, *Metropolitan Life*, 1978

5 ERIC: I always take my wife morning tea
in my pyjamas. But is she grateful? No –
she says she'd rather have it in a cup.
Eric Morecambe and Ernie Wise, *The
Morecambe and Wise Joke Book*, 1979

6 Continental breakfasts are very sparse, usually just a pot of coffee or tea and a teensy roll that looks like a suitcase handle. My advice is to go right to lunch without pausing.
Miss Piggy, *Miss Piggy's Guide to Life* (*as told to Henry Beard*), 1981

7 In England people actually try to be brilliant at breakfast. That is so dreadful of them! Only dull people are brilliant at breakfast.
Oscar Wilde, *An Ideal Husband*, 1895

See also Bed; Eating; Eggs; Food; Morning.

BRITAIN AND THE BRITISH

1 British Xenophobia takes the form of Insularism, and the Limeys all moved to an island some time ago to 'keep themselves to themselves', which as far as the rest of the world is concerned is a good thing.
The National Lampoon Encyclopaedia of Humor, 1973

2 I have a feeling that this island is uninhabitable, and therefore people have tried to make it habitable by being reasonable with one another.
Ralf Dahrendorf, quoted in the *New York Times*, 1976

3 In peacetime the British may have many faults; but so far an inferiority complex has not been one of them.
Lord Gladwyn, *Observer*, 1967

4 The British public has always had an unerring taste for ungifted amateurs.
John Osborne, 1957

5 You should ask me whether I have any message for the British public. I have. It is this: Might must find a way. Not 'Force', remember; other nations use 'force'; we Britons alone use 'Might'.
Evelyn Waugh, *Scoop*, 1938

See also England and the English; Ireland and the Irish; Scotland and the Scots; Wales and the Welsh.

BUDGETS

1 There are several ways in which to apportion the family income, all of them unsatisfactory.
Robert Benchley

2 Some couples go over their budgets very carefully every month, others just go over them.
Sally Poplin

3 All decent people live beyond their incomes nowadays, and those who aren't respectable live beyond other people's. A few gifted individuals manage to do both.
Saki (H. H. Munro), 'The Matchmaker', 1911

4 Solvency is entirely a matter of temperament and not of income.
Logan Pearsall Smith, *Afterthoughts*, 1931

5 Anyone who lives within his means suffers from a lack of imagination.
Lionel Stander, quoted in *Playboy*, 1967

See also Accountancy; Economics; Economy; Expenses; Money; Thrift; Wealth.

BUREAUCRACY

1 Dear Mrs, Mr, Miss, or Mr and Mrs Daneeka: Words cannot express the deep personal grief I experienced when your husband, son, father or brother was killed, wounded or reported missing in action.
Joseph Heller, *Catch-22*, 1961

See also The Civil Service; Government; The Office.

BUSINESS

1 He [the businessman] is the only man who is for ever apologizing for his occupation.
H. L. Mencken (Attrib.)

See also Big Business; Bosses; Contracts; The Office; Work.

BUTTONS *see* Badges

CALIFORNIA

1 California is a great place – if you happen to be an orange.
   Fred Allen (Attrib.)

2 In California everyone goes to a therapist, is a therapist, or is a therapist going to a therapist.
   Truman Capote (Attrib.)

3 Mistresses are more common in California – in fact some of them are very common. It's easier for a man to conceal his mistress there because of the smog.
   Groucho Marx (Attrib.)

See also America and the Americans; Hollywood; Los Angeles; San Francisco.

CANADA AND THE CANADIANS

1 Canada is a country so square that even the female impersonators are women.
   Richard Benner, *Outrageous!*, screenplay, 1977

2 You have to know a man awfully well in Canada to know his surname.
   John Buchan, quoted in the *Observer*, 1950

3 Canada could have enjoyed:
   English government,
   French culture,
   and American know-how.
   Instead it ended up with:
   English know-how,
   French government,
   and American culture.
   John Robert Colombo, 'Oh Canada', 1965

4 In any world menu, Canada must be considered the vichyssoise of nations – it's cold, half-French, and difficult to stir.
   Stuart Keate (Attrib.)

5 Canada is the only country in the world that knows how to live without an identity.
   Marshall McLuhan (Attrib.)

6 *Racial characteristics*: hard to tell a Canadian from an extremely boring regular white person unless he's dressed to go outdoors. Very little is known of the Canadian country since it is rarely visited by anyone but the Queen and illiterate sport fishermen.
   P. J. O'Rourke, 'Foreigners Around the World', *National Lampoon*, 1976

CANCER

1 You know, my father died of cancer when I was a teenager. He had it before it became popular.
   Goodman Ace, quoted in the *New Yorker*, 1977

2 My final word, before I'm done,
   Is 'Cancer can be rather fun.'
   Thanks to the nurses and Nye Bevan
   The NHS is quite like heaven
   Provided one confronts the tumour
   With a sufficient sense of humour.
   I know that cancer often kills,
   But so do cars and sleeping pills;
   And it can hurt one till one sweats,
   So can bad teeth and unpaid debts.
   J. B. S. Haldane, 'Cancer's a Funny Thing', *New Statesman*, 1964

3 DRUMM: I have this . . . tummy trouble. I told a certain person – I don't know why, out of mischief, it isn't like me – I told him cancer was suspected. Quite untrue. Of course he told others, and since then my popularity has soared. I said to one man: 'I know you for a rogue and a blackguard.' Was he offended? 'You're right,' he said, 'come and have a drink.' I did.
   CHARLIE: There'll be ructions when you don't die.
   DRUMM: There will.
   Hugh Leonard, *Da*, 1973

CANDOR

1 If you can't be direct, why be?
   Lily Tomlin

CANNIBALISM

1 Cannibals are not vegetarians. They are humanitarians.
   Anon.

2 These ferocious cannibals captured a poor missionary – he gave them their first taste of religion.
   Anon.

3 A cannibal is a guy who goes into a restaurant and orders the waiter.
   Jack Benny (Attrib.)

4 I came across a tribe of cannibals who'd been converted by Roman Catholic missionaries. Now, on Friday, they only eat fishermen.
   Max Kauffmann

5 ... the better sort of Ishmaelites have been Christian for many centuries and will not publicly eat human flesh, uncooked in Lent, without special and costly dispensation from their bishop.
   Evelyn Waugh, *Scoop*, 1938

See also Expeditions; Missionaries.

CAPITALISM

1 The fundamentals of capitalist ethics require that, 'You shall earn your bread in sweat' – unless you happen to have private means.
   M. Kalecki, 'Political Aspects of Full Employment'

2 The trouble with the profit system has always been that it was highly unprofitable to most people.
   E. B. White, *One Man's Meat*, 1944

See also Big Business; Business; Conservatism; The Conservative Party; Communism; Marxism; Socialism.

CAPITAL PUNISHMENT

1 When I came back to Dublin, I was courtmartialled in my absence and sentenced to death in my absence, so I said they could shoot me in my absence.
   Brendan Behan, *The Hostage*, 1959

See also Crime; Murder; Prison.

CARS

1 Brooding upon its unexerted power,
   Deep in the gas-tank lay the gasoline
   Awaiting the inevitable hour
   When from the inward soul of the machine
   Would come the Call. Ah, hark! Man's touch awakes
   Th'ignition switch! The starting motor hums;
   A sound of meshing gears, releasing brakes!
   The call of Duty to the gas-tank comes.
   Morris Bishop, 'Gas and Hot Air', *Spilt Milk*, 1942

2 It [the Vauxhall 30-98] had great long con-rods that rose majestically and sank again lolloping with easy leisure and dipping into the sump oil.
   The old 'Thirty Ninety-eight', when you started her up, used to say, 'Guddugety-Guddugety-Gonk, Guddugety-Guddugety-Gonk' and would speak to no other motor car – unless it was one of W. O. Bentley's majestic green monsters who could civilly reply, 'Berdoobely-Berdoobely-Bonk, Berdoobely-Berdoobely-Bonk'.
   Cassandra (William Connor), *Daily Mirror*, 1961

3 The automobile changed our dress, manners, social customs, vacation habits, the shape of our cities, consumer purchasing patterns, common tastes and positions in intercourse.
   John Ketas, *The Insolent Chariots*

4 Hood ornaments. They were just lovely, and they gave a sense of respect. And they took 'em away because if you can save one human life – that's always the argument – it's worth it, if you can save one human life. Actually, I'd be willing to trade maybe a dozen human lives for a nice hood ornament. I imagine those things really did tend to stick in bicyclists.
   Michael O'Donoghue, quoted in *Playboy*, 1983

5 Dear Miss Piggy,
   My car engine turns over, but it won't start. I've checked the plugs, the points,

the condenser, the coil, the distributor, and I even sprayed carburetor cleaner in the carb, but no dice. What gives? Stuck.

Dear Stuck,
It sounds to me like your car is broken. If you need it soon, I would get it fixed.
Miss Piggy, *Miss Piggy's Guide to Life* (*As Told to Henry Beard*), 1981

6 Take most people, they're crazy about cars . . . I don't even like *old* cars. I mean they don't even interest me. I'd rather have a goddam horse. A horse is at least *human* for God's sake.
J. D. Salinger, *The Catcher in the Rye*, 1951

7 Mr Wooster being one of those easy-going young gentlemen who will drive a car but never take the trouble to study its mechanism, I felt justified in becoming technical.
'I think it is the differential gear, sir. Either that, or the exhaust.'
P. G. Wodehouse, *Carry on, Jeeves*, 1925

See also Driving; Parking; Travel.

BILLY CARTER Brother of United States President, Jimmy Carter

1 Jimmy needs Billy like Van Gogh needs stereo.
Johnny Carson, *The Tonight Show*, NBC TV, 1977

2 Billy's doing his share for the economy. He's put the beer industry back on its feet.
Jimmy Carter, quoted in *Newsweek*, 1977

See also Jimmy Carter.

JIMMY CARTER President of the United States, 1977–1981

1 Everybody seems to be disappointed in Jimmy Carter. The other day Miz Lillian was heard muttering, 'To think I voted for him.'
Joey Adams, *New York Post*, 1978

2 Jimmy's basic problem is that he's super cautious. He looks before and after he leaps.
Joey Adams, *New York Post*, 1978

3 That suave former farmer of peanuts
Changes views twice a day, driving me nuts
What he says in the morning
By night-time he's scorning
Vote Carter? You'd just have to be nuts!
Stanley K. Fisher, competition, *New York Magazine*, 1976

4 We're realists. It doesn't make much difference between Ford and Carter. Carter is your typical smiling, brilliant, back-stabbing, bull-shitting Southern nut-cutter.
Lane Kirkland, US trades union leader, 1976

5 I think Jimmy Carter as President is like Truman Capote marrying Dolly Parton. The job is just too big for him.
Rich Little (Attrib.)

6 I would not want Jimmy Carter and his men put in charge of snake control in Ireland.
Eugene McCarthy, 1976

See also The Presidency; Washington.

CATHOLICISM

1 He was of the faith chiefly in the sense that the church he currently did not attend was Catholic.
Kingsley Amis, *One Fat Englishman*, 1963

2 THE POPE: My brothers, I bring you good news and I bring you bad news. The good news is that I have just received a phone call from Christ, who has returned to earth. The bad news is that he was calling from Salt Lake City.
Monseigneur Geno Baroni, quoted in the *Wall Street Journal*

3 Confession, *n.* the acknowledgement made to a priest of a sinful act committed by a friend, neighbor or acquaintance, and to which you reacted with righteous indignation.
Ambrose Bierce, *The Devil's Dictionary*, 1911

4 . . . Catholicism is like Howard Johnson, and what they have are these franchises and they give all these people different franchises in the different countries but

they have one government, and when you buy the Howard Johnson franchise you can apply it to the geography – whatever's cool for that area – and then you, you know, pay the bread to the main office.
Lenny Bruce, *The Essential Lenny Bruce*, 1972

5 For what have they not lost, these Latins, with their Catholicism! One limerick is worth all the musty old saints in their Calendar. Saints are dead – they have died out from sheer inability to propagate their species.
Norman Douglas, *Some Limericks*, 1928

6 High Anglo-Catholics are beneath contempt –
All intellectual and moral wrecks.
They love the frills but hold themselves exempt
From self-denial in the line of sex.
James Fenton and John Fuller, 'Poem against Catholics', *New Review*, 1976

7 They call their horrid children after saints
And educate them by such dubious means
They eagerly succumb to strange complaints
Or turn psychotic in their early teens.
James Fenton and John Fuller, 'Poem against Catholics', *New Review*, 1976

8 She had once been a Catholic, but discovering that priests were infinitely more attentive when she was in process of losing or regaining faith in Mother Church, she maintained an enchantingly wavering attitude.
F. Scott Fitzgerald, *This Side of Paradise*, 1920

9 As a Roman Catholic I thank God for the heretics. Heresy is only another word for freedom of thought.
Graham Greene

10 Give me Catholicism every time. Father Cheeryble with his thurible; Father Chatterjee with his liturgy. What fun they have with all their charades and conundrums. If it weren't for the Christianity

they insist on mixing with it, I'd be converted tomorrow.
Aldous Huxley, *Time Must Have a Stop*, 1944

11 It is now quite lawful for a Catholic woman to avoid pregnancy by a resort to mathematics, though she is still forbidden to resort to physics and chemistry.
H. L. Mencken, *Minority Report*, 1956

12 A Protestant married a devout Catholic wife,
And she led him a *cat*echism and *dog*ma life.
Keith Preston, quoted in *The Lilt of the Irish*, 1978

See also Christianity; The Church; Jesus Christ; Religion; The Pope.

CATS

1 Cat, *n.* a soft, indestructible automaton provided by nature to be kicked when things go wrong in the domestic circle.
Ambrose Bierce, *The Devil's Dictionary*, 1911

2 I don't know what the cat can have eaten. Usually I know exactly what the cat has eaten. Not only have I fed it to the cat, at the cat's keen insistence, but the cat has thrown it up on the rug and someone has tracked it all the way over on to the other rug. I don't know why cats are such habitual vomiters. They don't seem to enjoy it, judging by the sounds they make while doing it. It's in their nature. A dog is going to bark. A cat is going to vomit.
Roy Blount, Jr, *Esquire*, 1984

3 You always ought to have tom cats arranged, you know – it makes 'em more companionable.
Noël Coward

4 There is something going on now in Mexico that I happen to think is cruelty to animals. What I'm talking about, of course, is cat juggling.
Steve Martin

5 The trouble with a kitten is
THAT

Eventually it becomes a
CAT.
> **Ogden Nash**, 'The Kitten', *The Face is Familiar*, 1940

6 Cats are to dogs what modern people are to the people we used to have. Cats are slimmer, cleaner, more attractive, disloyal, and lazy. It's easy to understand why the cat has eclipsed the dog as modern America's favorite pet. People like pets to possess the same qualities they do. Cats are irresponsible and recognize no authority, yet are completely dependent on others for their material needs. Cats cannot be made to do anything useful. Cats are mean for the fun of it. In fact, cats possess so many of the same qualities as some people (expensive girlfriends, for instance) that it's often hard to tell the people and the cats apart.
> **P. J. O'Rourke**, *Modern Manners*, 1983

7 We've got a cat called Ben Hur. We called it Ben till it had kittens.
> **Sally Poplin**

See also Animals; Pets.

CELEBRITIES

1 I have often thought of forming a Society for the Prevention of Cruelty to Celebrities.
   Apparently for certain individuals, men and women in the public eye are fair game to be knocked off their balance occasionally and made to look foolish. You know, a central figure at a social function isn't always as happy as he looks.
> **Noël Coward** (Attrib.)

2 To be a celebrity in America is to be forgiven everything.
> **Mary McGrory**, quoted in *New York Times*, 1976

3 A celebrity is any well-known TV or movie star who looks like he spends more than two hours working on his hair.
> **Steve Martin**, *Playboy*, 1984

See also Fame.

CENSORSHIP

1 When there is official censorship it is a sign that speech is serious. When there is none, it is pretty certain that the official spokesmen have all the loudspeakers.
> **Paul Goodman**, *Growing Up Absurd*, 1960

2 Senator Smoot (Republican, Ut.)
Is planning a ban on smut.
Oh rooti-ti-toot for Smoot of Ut.
And his reverent occiput.
Smite, Smoot, smite for Ut.,
Grit your molars and do your dut.,
Gird up your l – – ns,
Smite h – p and th – gh,
We'll all be Kansas
By and by.
> **Ogden Nash**, 'Invocation', 1931

3 If a man is pictured chopping off a woman's breast, it only gets an 'R' rating; but if, God forbid, a man is pictured kissing a woman's breast, it gets an 'X' rating. Why is violence more acceptable than tenderness?
> **Sally Struthers**, quoted in *Life*, 1984

See also Morality; Obscenity; Pornography; Prudery; Puritanism; Reformers.

NEVILLE CHAMBERLAIN
Prime Minister of Great Britain, 1937–1940 (Conservative Party)

1 Listening to a speech by Chamberlain is like paying a visit to Woolworth's. Everything in its place and nothing above sixpence.
> **Aneurin Bevan**, speech, House of Commons, 1937

2 He saw foreign policy through the wrong end of a municipal drainpipe.
> **David Lloyd George** (Attrib.)

3 . . . the mind and manner of a clothesbrush.
> **Harold Nicolson**, 1938

See also Conservatism; The Conservative Party.

CHAMPAGNE

1 Here's to champagne, the drink divine
That makes us forget our troubles.

It is made of a dollar's worth of wine
And three dollars' worth of bubbles.
Anon.

2 No government could survive without champagne. Champagne in the throat of our diplomatic people is like oil in the wheels of an engine.
Joseph Dargent, *New York Herald Tribune*, 1955

3 I hate champagne more than anything else in the world next to Seven-Up.
Elaine Dundy, *The Dud Avocado*, 1958

See also Drink; Parties; Wine.

CHARM

1 All charming people have something to conceal, usually their total dependence on the appreciation of others.
Cyril Connolly, *Enemies of Promise*, 1938

2 Charming people live up to the very edge of their charm, and behave just as outrageously as the world will let them.
Logan Pearsall Smith, *Afterthoughts*, 1931

3 A beauty is a woman you notice; a charmer is one who notices you.
Adlai Stevenson, speech at Radcliffe College, 1963

4 All charming people, I fancy, are spoiled. It is the secret of their attraction.
Oscar Wilde, 'The Portrait of Mr W. H.', 1901

CHASTITY

1 Chastity is curable, if detected early.
Graffito, Exeter, 1978

2 MRS WICKSTEED: Of course I've known for years our marriage has been a mockery. My body lying there night after night in the wasted moonlight. I know now how the Taj Mahal must feel.
Alan Bennett, *Habeas Corpus*, 1973

3 ... that melancholy sexual perversion known as continence.
Aldous Huxley, *Antic Hay*, 1923

4 As a child of eight Mr Trout had once kissed a girl of six under the mistletoe at a Christmas party, but there his sex life had come to abrupt halt.
P. G. Wodehouse, *Bachelors Anonymous*, 1973

See also Abstinence; Prudery; Puritanism; Sex; Virginity.

CHEESE

1 Poets have been mysteriously silent on the subject of cheese.
G. K. Chesterton

2 What a friend we have in cheeses!
For no food more subtly pleases,
Nor plays so grand a gastronomic part;
Cheese imported – not domestic –
For we all get indigestic
From all the pasteurizer's Kraft and
    sodden art.
William Cole, *What a Friend We Have in Cheeses!*

3 Claret, dear, not Coca-Cola,
When you're having Gorgonzola –
Be particular to serve the proper wines;
Likewise pick a Beaune, not Coke for
Pointing up a Bleu or Roquefort –
Bless the products of the bovines and
    the vines!
William Cole, *What a Friend We Have in Cheeses!*

4 Cheese. The adult form of milk.
Richard Condon, *A Talent for Loving*, 1961

5 Cheese – milk's leap forward to immortality.
Clifton Fadiman, *Any Number Can Play*, 1957

See also Eating; Food; Wine.

CHESS

1 It is impossible to win gracefully at chess. No man has yet said 'Mate!' in a voice which failed to sound to his opponent bitter, boastful and malicious.
A. A. Milne, *Not That It Matters*, 1919

CHICAGO

1 Chicago is not the most corrupt Ameri-

can city – it's the most *theatrically* corrupt.
Studs Terkel, *The Dick Cavett Show*, PBS, 1978

See also America and the Americans.

CHILDHOOD

1 ERIC: When I was eight I ran away with a circus.
ERNIE: Really?
ERIC: Yes. Then, when I was nine, they made me bring it back again.
Eric Morecambe and Ernie Wise, *The Morecambe and Wise Joke Book*, 1979

2 ERNIE: I had a pretty tough childhood myself, you know. At the age of five I was left an orphan.
ERIC: That's ridiculous! What could a five-year-old do with an orphan?
Eric Morecambe and Ernie Wise, *The Morecambe and Wise Joke Book*, 1979

3 When I was a kid, I had no watch. I used to tell the time by my violin. I used to practice in the middle of the night and the neighbors would yell, 'Fine time to practice the violin, three o'clock in the morning!'
Henny Youngman

See also Adolescence; Children; Parents; School; Teenagers; Youth.

CHILDREN

1 Insanity is hereditary. You get it from your kids.
Badge, Brussels, 1984

2 I wish I'd been a mixed infant.
Brendan Behan, *The Hostage*, 1959

3 A child develops individuality long before he develops taste. I have seen my kid straggle into the kitchen in the morning with outfits that need only one accessory: an empty gin bottle.
Erma Bombeck, *If Life is a Bowl of Cherries – What am I Doing in the Pits?*, 1978

4 I read one psychologist's theory that said, 'Never strike a child in anger.' When could I strike him? When he is kissing me on my birthday? When he is recuperating from measles? Do I slap the Bible out of his hand on a Sunday?
Erma Bombeck, *If Life is a Bowl of Cherries – What am I Doing in the Pits?*, 1978

5 It puzzles me how a child can see a dairy bar three miles away, but cannot see a 4 by 6 rug that has scrunched up under his feet and has been dragged through two rooms. Maybe you know why a child can reject a hot dog with mustard served on a soft bun at home, yet eat six of them two hours later at fifty cents each.
Erma Bombeck, *If Life is a Bowl of Cherries – What am I Doing in the Pits?*, 1978

6 I've seen kids ride bicycles, run, play ball, set up a camp, swing, fight a war, swim and race for eight hours . . . yet have to be driven to the garbage can.
Erma Bombeck, *If Life is a Bowl of Cherries – What am I Doing in the Pits?*, 1978

7 As soon as I stepped out of my mother's womb on to dry land, I realized that I had made a mistake – that I shouldn't have come, but the trouble with children is that they are not returnable.
Quentin Crisp, *The Naked Civil Servant*, 1968

8 When I was a child what I wanted to be when I grew up was an invalid.
Quentin Crisp, *The Naked Civil Servant*, 1968

9 Ah, the patter of little feet around the house. There's nothing like having a midget for a butler.
W. C. Fields (Attrib.)

10 Anybody who hates children and dogs can't be all bad.
W. C. Fields

11 I love children . . . parboiled.
W. C. Fields (Attrib.)

12 I never met a kid I liked.
W. C. Fields (Attrib.)

13 There's not a man in America who at one time or another hasn't had a secret desire to boot a child in the ass.
W. C. Fields (Attrib.)

14 Father, chancing to chastise
His indignant daughter Sue,
Said: 'I hope you realize
That this hurts me more than you.'

Susan straightway ceased to roar;
'If that's really true,' said she,
'I can stand a good deal more;
Pray go on, and don't mind me.'
Harry Graham, *Ruthless Rhymes*, 1899

15 Father heard his Children scream,
So he threw them in the stream,
Saying as he drowned the third,
'Children should be seen, *not* heard!'
Harry Graham, *Ruthless Rhymes*, 1899

16 STEPHEN: What have you got against having children?
SIMON: Well, Steve, in the first place there isn't enough room. In the second place they seem to start by mucking up their parents' lives, and then go on in the third place to muck up their own. In the fourth place it doesn't seem right to bring them into a world like this in the fifth place and in the sixth place I don't like them very much in the first place. OK.
Simon Gray, *Otherwise Engaged*, 1975

17 All God's children are not beautiful. Most of God's children are, in fact, barely presentable.
Fran Lebowitz, *Metropolitan Life*, 1978

18 Ask your child what he wants for dinner only if he's buying.
Fran Lebowitz, *Social Studies*, 1981

19 Never allow your child to call you by your first name. He hasn't known you long enough.
Fran Lebowitz, *Social Studies*, 1981

20 Notoriously insensitive to subtle shifts in mood, children will persist in discussing the color of a recently sighted cement-mixer long after one's own interest in the topic has waned.
Fran Lebowitz, *Metropolitan Life*, 1978

21 By all the published facts in the case, Children belong to the human race.

Equipped with consciousness, passions, pulse,
They even grow up and become adults.

So why's the resemblance, moral or mental,
Of children to people so coincidental?
Phyllis McGinley, 'About Children', *Times Three: 1932–1960*, 1960

22 If a child shows himself incorrigible, he should be decently and quietly beheaded at the age of twelve.
Don Marquis

23 My mother loved children – she would have given anything if I'd been one.
Groucho Marx

24 I love children. Especially when they cry – for then someone takes them away.
Nancy Mitford

25 Oh, what a tangled web do parents weave
When they think that their children are naïve.
Ogden Nash (Attrib.)

26 The quickest way for a parent to get a child's attention is to sit down and look comfortable.
Lane Olinghouse, *Wall Street Journal*

27 Do your kids a favor – don't have any.
Robert Orben, *Variety*, 1972

28 A child hasn't a grown-up person's appetite for affection. A little of it goes a long way with them; and they like a good imitation of it better than the real thing,' as every nurse knows.
George Bernard Shaw, *Getting Married*, 1911

29 In my Rogues' Gallery of repulsive small boys I suppose he would come about third.
P. G. Wodehouse, *Thank You, Jeeves*, 1934

See also Adolescence; Babies; Childhood; Orphans; Parents; School; Teenagers.

CHINESE

1 We wanted Li Wing
But we winged Willie Wong.
A sad but excusable
Slip of the tong.
Keith Preston, 'Lapsus Linguae', *Pot Shots from Pegasus*, 1929

CHRISTIANITY

1 The trouble with born-again Christians is that they are an even bigger pain the second time around.
   Herb Caen, *San Francisco Chronicle*, 1981

2 The Christian ideal has not been tried and found wanting, it has been found difficult and left untried.
   G. K. Chesterton (Attrib.)

3 Christian endeavor is notoriously hard on female pulchritude.
   H. L. Mencken, *American Mercury*, 1931

4 The act of worship, as carried on by Christians, seems to me to be debasing rather than ennobling. It involves groveling before a Being who, if He really exists, deserves to be denounced instead of respected.
   H. L. Mencken (Attrib.)

5 If I had been the Virgin Mary, I would have said 'No'.
   Stevie Smith

See also Belief; The Bible; Catholicism; Church; God; Jesus Christ; Protestantism; Religion.

CHRISTMAS

1 Christmas comes, but once a year is enough.
   Anon.

2 Our children await Christmas presents like politicians getting election returns; there's the Uncle Fred precinct and the Aunt Ruth district still to come in.
   Marcelene Cox, *Ladies' Home Journal*, 1950

3 ERNIE: Christmas always brings out the best in people, doesn't it?
   ERIC: Well, you tell my wife that.
   ERNIE: Why, is she giving you trouble?
   ERIC: I'll say. She said to me today, 'You've done absolutely nothing to help with the Christmas dinner. Absolutely nothing.'
   ERNIE: What did you say to that?
   ERIC: I said, 'What! Look at the turkey – I bought it, I've plucked it and I've stuffed it!'
   ERNIE: Good for you!

ERIC: Now, all *she's* got to do is kill it and put it in the oven.
   Eric Morecambe and Ernie Wise, *The Morecambe and Wise Joke Book*, 1979

4 It's customarily said that Christmas is done 'for the kids'. Considering how awful Christmas is and how little our society likes children, this must be true.
   P. J. O'Rourke, *Modern Manners*, 1983

5 I love the Christmas-tide and yet,
   I notice this, each year I live;
   I always like the gifts I get,
   But how I love the gifts I give!
   Carolyn Wells, 'A Thought'

6 Still xmas is a good time with all those presents and good food and i hope it will never die out or at any rate not until i am grown up and hav to pay for it all.
   Geoffrey Willans and Ronald Searle, 'How to be Topp', *The Compleet Molesworth*, 1958

7 Xmas all grown ups sa is the season for the kiddies but this do not prevent them from taking a tot or 2 from the bot and having, it may seme, a better time than us. For children in fact Xmas is often a bit of a strane wot with pretending that everything is a surprise. Above all father xmas is a strane. You canot so much as mention that there is no father xmas when some grown-sa Hush not in front of wee tim.
   Geoffrey Willans and Ronald Searle, 'How to be Topp', *The Compleet Molesworth*, 1958

8 The first rule in buying Christmas presents is to select something shiny. If the chosen object is of leather, the leather must look as if it had been well greased; if of silver, it must gleam with the light that never was on sea or land. This is because the wariest person will often mistake shininess for expensiveness.
   P. G. Wodehouse, *Louder and Funnier*, 1963

9 I love Christmas. I receive a lot of wonderful presents I can't wait to exchange.
   Henny Youngman

See also Gifts; Greetings Cards.

THE CHURCH

1 Go to church this Sunday – avoid the Christmas rush.
Graffito, London, 1979

2 At the Harvest Festival in church the area behind the pulpit was piled high with tins of IXL fruit for the old-age pensioners. We had collected the tinned fruit from door to door. Most of it came from old-age pensioners.
Clive James, *Unreliable Memoirs*, 1980

3 A church is a place in which gentlemen who have never been to heaven brag about it to people who will never get there.
H. L. Mencken (Attrib.)

4 Archbishop: a Christian ecclesiastic of a rank superior to that attained by Christ.
H. L. Mencken (Attrib.)

5 Write me a Book of Common Prayer
That is not made up of hot air
With words that are as plain as this
And, oh boy! that will take the piss
Out of those who wrote Series 3
And (I confess it) out of me.
C. H. Sisson, reacting against Series 3 Liturgy, 1979

6 'Golly! When you admonish a congregation, it stays admonished!'
P. G. Wodehouse, *Eggs, Beans and Crumpets*, 1940

7 Like so many vicars, he had a poor opinion of curates.
P. G. Wodehouse, *Meet Mr Mulliner*, 1927

8 The Bishop of Stortford was talking to the local Master of Hounds about the difficulty he had in keeping his vicars off the incense.
P. G. Wodehouse, *Mr Mulliner Speaking*, 1929

See also Catholicism; God; Jesus Christ; Protestantism; Religion.

WINSTON CHURCHILL Prime Minister of Great Britain, 1940–1945, 1951–1955 (Conservative Party)

1 I thought he was a young man of promise; but it appears he was a young man of promises.
A. J. Balfour, of Winston Churchill, 1899

2 He is a man suffering from petrified adolescence.
Aneurin Bevan

3 He mistakes verbal felicities for mental inspiration.
Aneurin Bevan (Attrib.)

4 He refers to a defeat as a disaster as though it came from God, but to a victory as though it came from himself.
Aneurin Bevan, speech in the House of Commons, 1942

5 The mediocrity of his thinking is concealed by the majesty of his language.
Aneurin Bevan (Attrib.)

6 At intervals he turned a somersault, exactly like a porpoise; and when his head reappeared at the other end of the bath, he continued precisely where he left off.
Robert Boothby, *Recollections of a Rebel*, 1975

7 Churchill was fundamentally what the English call unstable – by which they mean anybody who has that touch of genius which is inconvenient in normal times.
Harold Macmillan, 1975

8 Winston has devoted the best years of his life to preparing his impromptu speeches.
F. E. Smith (Attrib.)

See also House of Commons; Politics and Politicians.

THE CIA

1 By then, Gold had learned in Washington that the CIA was recruiting mercenaries to fight in Africa. He learned this at breakfast from his morning paper when he read:
CIA DENIES RECRUITING
MERCENARIES TO
FIGHT IN AFRICA
Joseph Heller, *Good as Gold*, 1979

See also Espionage.

CINEMA *see* Film

THE CIRCUS

1 He was engaged to a contortionist but she broke it off.
Anon.

2 He was married to an acrobat but she caught him in the act.
Anon.

3 What a life for an Acrobat!
When I watch him loop and loop
I wonder what he's thinking upside
   down on the trapeze
And if he's really happy with his head
   between his knees
And then his face gets crimson
And I know he's going to sneeze!
'Allez OOp – Allez OOp – Allez OOp!'
Noël Coward, 'The Wife of an Acrobat', *Words and Music*, 1932

See also Show Business.

THE CIVIL SERVICE

1 The Civil Service is a self-perpetuating oligarchy, and what better system is there?
Lord Armstrong, Head of the Home Civil Service, 1977

2 The besetting sin of civil servants is to mix too much with each other.
Sir William Beveridge, Director of the London School of Economics, 1924

3 Men who write minutes, who make professional assessments, who are never attacked face to face, who dwell in the Sargasso Sea of the Civil Service and who love the seaweed that conceals them.
Cassandra (William Connor), *Daily Mirror*

4 I say to myself that I must not let myself be cut off in there, and yet the moment I enter my bag is taken out of my hand, I'm pushed in, shepherded, nursed and above all cut off, alone. Whitehall envelops me.
Richard Crossman, *The Diaries of a Cabinet Minister*, 1976

5 Once it is understood that politicians are public relations officers for their publicity-shy bosses, the Civil Service Permanent Secretaries, Parliament and politics become intelligible.
David Frost and Antony Jay, *To England with Love*, 1967

6 Members rise from CMG (known sometimes in Whitehall as 'Call me God') to KCMG ('Kindly call me God') to . . . the GCMG ('God calls me God').
Anthony Sampson, *The Anatomy of Britain*, 1962

7 . . . a difficulty for every solution.
Lord Samuel, British Home Secretary, 1916 and 1931–1932

8 Britain has invented a new missile. It's called the civil servant – it doesn't work and it can't be fired.
General Sir Walter Walker, *Observer*, 1981

See also Bureaucracy; Government.

CLASS

1 As usual, I have against me the bourgeois, the officers and the diplomatists, and for me only the people who take the Metro.
Charles de Gaulle, *Observer*, 1967

2 I don't believe in class differences, but luckily my butler disagrees with me.
Marc, cartoon in *The Times*, 1976

See also The Aristocracy; Etiquette; Rich and Poor; The Ruling Class; Servants; Status.

CLEANLINESS

1 I will say this for John: he's fanatically tidy . . . Do you know, after he takes a bath he washes the soap.
Hugh Leonard, *Time Was*, 1976

2 Hygiene is the corruption of medicine by morality.
H. L. Mencken, *Prejudices*, Third Series, 1922

3 ERNIE: Why don't you wash your face – I can see what you had for breakfast this morning!
ERIC: Oh, yeah! What did I have?
ERNIE: Bacon and eggs and tomato sauce.

ERIC: Wrong! that was *yesterday* morn-
ing!
Eric Morecambe and Ernie Wise, *The
Morecambe and Wise Joke Book,* 1979

4 Have I got a mother-in-law. She's so
neat she puts paper under the cuckoo
clock.
Henny Youngman

See also Baths.

CLICHÉS

1 What does it behove us to proclaim?
Our faith.
In what does it behove us to proclaim
   our faith?
Democracy.
From what vertiginous eyrie does it
   behove us to proclaim our faith in
   democracy?
From the house-tops.
At what time should we proclaim our
   faith in democracy from the
   house-tops?
Now, more than ever.
Myles na Gopaleen, 'The Myles na Gopa-
leen Catechism of Cliché', *The Best of Myles,*
1968

CLOTHES

1 HILARY: One of the few lessons I have
learned in life is that there is invariably
something odd about women who wear
ankle socks.
Alan Bennett, *The Old Country,* 1978

2 Give me a wild tie, brother,
One with a cosmic urge!
A tie that will swear and rip and tear
When it sees my old blue serge.
Stoddard King, *The Tie that Blinds*

3 Women's clothes: never wear anything
that panics the cat.
P. J. O'Rourke, *Modern Manners,* 1983

4 Brevity is the soul of lingerie.
Dorothy Parker (Attrib.)

5 A well-tied tie is the first serious step in
life.
Oscar Wilde, *The Importance of Being
Earnest,* 1895

6 The only way to atone for being occasionally a little over-dressed is by being
always absolutely over-educated.
Oscar Wilde, 'Phrases and Philosophies for
the Use of the Young', 1894

7 Personally, if anyone had told me that a
tie like that suited me, I should have risen
and struck them on the mazzard, regard-
less of their age and sex . . .
P. G. Wodehouse, 'Jeeves in the Springtime', 1967

See also Appearance; Fashion; Footwear;
Hats; Style.

CLUBS

1 Any club that would accept me as a
member, I wouldn't want to join.
Groucho Marx (Attrib.)

See also Drink.

COINCIDENCE

1 Would You Believe It? Forty years ago,
while sunbathing in her garden, Mrs
Betty Lomax of Pugh Street, Ponders
End, lost her engagement ring. Yesterday, while digging up the very same garden, her son Wilfred ruptured himself.
Anon.

COLLABORATION

1 I never could understand how two men
can write a book together; to me that's
like three people getting together to have
a baby.
Evelyn Waugh (Attrib.)

See also Work.

COMEDY

1 Unless Cheech and Chong get run over
by a truck, the release of these albums is
likely to be the two best pieces of news in
the comedy field for a while.
National Lampoon

2 Hello:
I'm Albert Brooks and I'm speaking to
you on behalf of the Famous School For
Comedians, located on twenty-two
gorgeous acres near Arlington National
Park. How many times have you gotten
nice laughs at a party, had a friend turn to

you and say, 'You know something, (your name here), that was pretty funny. You should think about being a comedian.'

Well, your friend was right! The comedy fraternity of show business is a fast-paced, nutty, funny world. There are always openings for good comedy talent.

Albert Brooks, 'Albert Brooks' Famous School for Comedians', *Esquire*, 1972

3 Q: Is life in comedy ALWAYS fun?
A: No. But is anything ALWAYS anything?
Q: Do the Jewish people dominate the field of comedy?
A: Don't be a schmuck.
Q: What is meant when they talk about a 'one-liner'?
A: It all depends what you mean by 'they'. If 'they' are comedians, then a one-liner is a joke that is no longer than one line. If 'they' work for the Matson Steamship Co., then a one-liner probably means some kind of boat.

Albert Brooks, 'Albert Brooks' Famous School for Comedians', *Esquire*, 1972

4 Comedy, like sodomy, is an unnatural act.

Marty Feldman, *The Times*, 1969

5 An amateur thinks it's funny if you dress a man up as an old lady, put him in a wheelchair, and give the wheelchair a push that sends it spinning down a slope towards a stone wall. For a pro, it's got to be a real old lady.

Groucho Marx

6 . . . how to write a Johnny Carson monologue in five minutes or less.
FUNNY PHRASES:
'It's a biggee!'
'If I said what I'm thinking right now, this place would be a parking lot tomorrow!'
'Please, Mother, I'd rather do it myself!' (archaic)
'Would you believe (scaled down parody of the previous statement)?' (archaic)
'Where does it say that audience does monologue?'

Michael O'Donoghue, 'More to Come', *National Lampoon*, 1972

7 . . . how to write a Johnny Carson monologue in five minutes or less! Here are a few hints on delivery in case you are tempted to try the completed monologue on your friends. When Johnny loses his place, he usually 'marks time' by discussing some point of grammar with Ed ('Which is proper there, Ed, "who" or "whom"?') If a joke 'bombs', doggedly repeat the punch line. And never forget that it's impossible to overuse the word 'weird'.

That's all there is to it.

Michael O'Donoghue, 'More to Come', *National Lampoon*, 1972

8 It's whirly, it's whacky, it's slick, it's savvy; it's the madcap, daffy, fractured, ding-a-ling, ring-a-ding, loony, zany, side-splitting, rib-tickling, slap-happy, scuzzy, dreary, irksome, tedious, banal, pointless, smutty world of Phono Phunnies!

Michael O'Donoghue and Tony Hendra, National Lampoon's *Radio Dinner*, record, 1972

9 I love comedy. It's the only art form that's also a social grace. You meet a sculptor at a party, you can't say, 'He's terrific, look what he can do with the potato salad.'

Paul Reiser, Los Angeles stand-up comic, quoted in *GQ*, 1984

See also Humour; Laughter; Puns; Satire; Wit.

COMMITTEES

1 A group that takes minutes and wastes hours.
Anon.

2 A group of the unfit appointed by the unwilling to do the unnecessary.
Carl C. Byers

3 We always carry out by committee anything in which any of us alone would be too reasonable to persist.
Frank Moore Colby

4 To get something done a committee should consist of no more than three men, two of whom are absent.
Robert Copeland

5 Committee work is like a soft chair – easy to get into but hard to get out of.
  Kenneth J. Shively

See also Conferences; Decisions; Meetings.

COMMUNICATION

1 HELEN: What were you lecturing on in India?
  PATTERSON: Harold Pinter and the failure of communication.
  HELEN: How did it go?
  PATTERSON: I don't know. They didn't seem to understand a word I said.
  Malcolm Bradbury and Christopher Bigsby, *The After Dinner Game*, BBC TV, 1975

See also Letters; Telegrams; Telephones.

COMMUNISM

1 A communist is one who has nothing and wishes to share it with the world.
  Anon.

2 A communist is a socialist without a sense of humour.
  George Cutton

3 Communism might be likened to a race in which all competitors come in first with no prizes.
  Lord Inchcape, quoted in the *Observer*, 1924

4 Can you imagine lying in bed on a Sunday morning with the love of your life, a cup of tea and a bacon sandwich, and all you had to read was the *Socialist Worker*?
  Derek Jameson, Editor, *Daily Express*, 1979

5 Communism requires of its adherents that they arise early and participate in a strenuous round of calisthenics. To someone who wishes that cigarettes came already lit the thought of such exertion at an hour when decent people are just nodding off is thoroughly abhorrent.
  Fran Lebowitz, *Metropolitan Life*, 1978

6 Communists all seem to wear small caps, a look I consider better suited to tubes of toothpaste than to people.
  Fran Lebowitz, *Metropolitan Life*, 1978

7 'From each according to his ability, to each according to his needs' is not a decision I care to leave to politicians, for I do not believe that an ability to remark humorosly on the passing scene would carry much weight with one's comrades or that one could convince them of the need for a really reliable answering service.
  Fran Lebowitz, *Metropolitan Life*, 1978

8 Communism is the opiate of the intellectuals.
  Clare Booth Luce

9 The objection to a Communist always resolves itself into the fact that he is not a gentleman.
  H. L. Mencken, *Minority Report*, 1956

10 Communism is like Prohibition, it's a good idea but it won't work.
  Will Rogers, *The Autobiography of Will Rogers*, 1949

11 DOONESBURY: ... That's complete nonsense. China and Russia are deadly enemies. China invaded Vietnam. Vietnam invaded Cambodia. Russia invaded Afghanistan. The only countries communists have been invading lately are communist!
  B. D.: Of *course*, dummy! They invade each other to stay in shape!
  Garry Trudeau, *Doonesbury*, cartoon, 1983

See also Equality; Marxism; Russia and the Russians; Socialism.

COMPETITIONS

1 Bloke at work, went in for a competition and won a trip to China. That's right, to China. Fantastic. He's out there now trying to win a trip back!
  Jerry Dennis

See also Winning.

COMPLIMENTS

1 FAN: You were superb in *Romeo and Juliet*.
  ACTOR: I'll bet you say that to everyone who's superb.
  Anon.

See also Flattery; Praise.

COMPOSERS

1 Ah Mozart! He was happily married –
but his wife wasn't.
Victor Borge

See also Music and Musicians; Songs and
Singers.

COMPUTERS

1 To err is human, but to really foul things
up requires a computer.
Anon.

2 My computer dating bureau came up
with a perfect gentleman. Still, I've got
another three goes.
Sally Poplin

3 DOONESBURY: Excuse me, sir. Do you
have any user-friendly sales reps?
STORE MANAGER: You mean, consumer
compatible liveware? No, he's off today.
Garry Trudeau, *Doonesbury*, cartoon,
1983

See also Modern Life; Technology.

CONCILIATION

1 The one sure way to conciliate a tiger is
to allow oneself to be devoured.
Konrad Adenauer, first West German
Chancellor

2 An appeaser is one who feeds a crocodile
hoping it will eat him last.
Winston Churchill

See also Peace.

CONFERENCES

1 A conference is a gathering of important
people who singly can do nothing, but
together can decide that nothing can be
done.
Fred Allen

See also Committees; Meetings.

CONFORMITY

1 Consistency is the last refuge of the
unimaginative.
Oscar Wilde (Attrib.)

See also Etiquette.

CONGRESS

1 With Congress, every time they make a
joke it's a law, and every time they make a
law it's a joke.
Will Rogers

2 Reader, suppose you were an idiot.
And suppose you were a member of
Congress. But I repeat myself.
Mark Twain

See also Politics and Politicians; The
Presidency; The Senate; Washington.

CONSCIENCE

1 Conscience gets a lot of credit that
belongs to cold feet.
Anon.

2 Conscience: something that feels terrible
when everything else feels swell.
Anon., *Reader's Digest*, 1949

3 The Nonconformist Conscience makes
cowards of us all.
Max Beerbohm, 'King George the
Fourth', *Yellow Book*, 1894

4 Conscience is the inner voice that warns
us that someone may be looking.
H. L. Mencken, *Sententiae*, 1920

5 Conscience: the still small voice that
makes you feel still smaller.
James A. Sanaker, *Reader's Digest*

6 Conscience and cowardice are really the
same things. Conscience is the trade
name of the firm.
Oscar Wilde, *The Picture of Dorian Gray*,
1891

See also Duty; Guilt.

THE CONSERVATIVE PARTY

1 It is a bizarre biological fact that the
Conservative Party can be directed along
a sensible left-wing path only by a leader
with impeccable aristocratic connec-
tions.
Humphrey Berkeley, of Harold Macmillan

2 Tories are not always wrong, but they are
always wrong at the right moment.
Lady Violet Bonham-Carter

3 The Conservative Party is an organized hypocrisy.
Benjamin Disraeli, speech in the House of Commons, 1845

4 They are nothing else but a load of kippers – two-faced, with no guts.
Eric Heffer, Labour MP (Attrib.)

5 The trouble with the Conservative Party is that it has not turned the clock back a single second.
Evelyn Waugh (Attrib.)

See also Conservatism; Politics and Politicians.

CONSERVATISM

1 A conservative is someone who admires radicals a century after they're dead.
Anon.

2 When a nation's young men are conservative, its funeral bell is already rung.
Henry Ward Beecher, *Proverbs from Plymouth Pulpit*, 1887

3 POLLY: He's a socialist but he doesn't like people.
BRIAN: Nor do I, much.
POLLY: You're a Conservative. You don't have to.
Alan Bennett, *Getting On*, 1971

4 A conservative is someone who demands a square deal for the rich.
David Frost, *TVam*, 1983

5 I never dared be radical when young
For fear it would make me conservative when old.
Robert Frost, 'Precaution'

6 ... contemporary Conservatism ... is, like contemporary art, seldom much admired at the time; it only achieves acceptance and admiration in retrospect.
Sir Ian Gilmour, *Inside Right*, 1977

7 The modern conservative is engaged in one of man's oldest exercises in moral philosophy, that is the search for a superior moral justification for selfishness.
John Kenneth Galbraith

8 It is perhaps foolish to expect the Conservatives to be anything other than conservative.
Jo Grimond, Liberal politician, 1967

9 A conservative is a man who is too cowardly to fight and too fat to run.
Elbert Hubbard, *The Notebook*, 1927

10 Some fellows get credit for being conservative when they are only stupid.
Kin Hubbard

11 A conservative is a man who will not look at the new moon, out of respect for that ancient institution, the old one.
Douglas Jerrold

12 Men who are orthodox when they are young are in danger of being middle-aged all their lives.
Walter Lippmann

13 Dying and letting die, they call 'living and letting live';
They do not even make mistakes for live ones to forgive;
Wouldst thou be Nothing? Then, my son, be a conservative!
Edwin Meade Robinson, 'Conservatives'

14 A conservative is a man with two perfectly good legs who, however, has never learned to walk forward.
Franklin D. Roosevelt (Attrib.)

15 There was the Don who, whenever any reform was proposed, made exactly the same speech. He would say: 'Whenever a measure of this kind is suggested, I ask myself two questions: "Has the old system worked badly?" "Is the new system likely to work better?" I see no reason to answer either question in the affirmative, and I shall therefore vote against the proposal.'
Bertrand Russell, *Portraits from Memory*, 1956

16 A conservative is someone who believes in reform. But not now.
Mort Sahl

17 The radical invents the views. When he has worn them out, the conservative adopts them.
Mark Twain, *Notebook*, 1935

18 ... a businessman's candidate, hovering
around the status quo like a sick kitten
around a hot brick.
    William Allen White, newspaper editor,
    of Charles Evans Hughes, unsuccessful
    Republican presidential candidate, 1916

19 He thinks like a Tory, and talks like
a Radical, and that's so important
nowadays.
    Oscar Wilde, *Lady Windermere's Fan*, 1892

20 Sir,
Dr Roget included the following entry
in his Thesaurus: 'Inaction, passiveness,
abstinence from action; non-
interference; conservative policy.'
    Can there be a moral somewhere in
this?
                                    Yours, & c.
    A. J. Woodman, letter to *The Times*, 1967

See also Capitalism; The Conservative
Party; The Labour Party; The Liberal
Party; The Republican Party.

CONSUMERISM

1 Dear Ned,
Soon after I received my Acme pencil (11
cents), it rolled off the desk and on to the
floor. Upon retrieving it, I hit my head on
the desk. Can I hold Acme responsible?
                                    [Boiling Mad]

Dear Boiling,
This is what's known as an open-and-
shut case. If you don't sue them, I will.
                                    [Ned]
    R. Chast, 'Ned's Consumer Hot Line',
    cartoon, *New Yorker*, 1984

2 When Ralph Nader tells me he wants my
car to be cheap, ugly and slow, he's
imposing a way of life on me that I'm
going to resist to the bitter end.
    Timothy Leary (Attrib.)

See also Consumers; Shopping.

CONSUMERS

1 The One Who Has The Most Toys
When They Die, Wins!
    Licence-plate holder, Los Angeles, 1984

2 The customer's always right, my boys,

The customer's always right.
The son-of-a-bitch
Is probably rich
So smile with all your might.
    Noël Coward, 'The Customer's Always
    Right', *Sail Away*, 1962

3 I like to walk down Bond Street, thinking
of all the things I don't want.
    Logan Pearsall Smith, *Afterthoughts*, 1931

4 The grocer sells me addled eggs; the
        tailor sells me shoddy,
I'm only a consumer, and I am not
        anybody.
The cobbler pegs me paper soles, the
        dairyman short-weights me,
I'm only a consumer, and most
        everybody hates me.
There's turnip in my pumpkin pie and
        ashes in my pepper,
The world's my lazaretto, and I'm
        nothing but a leper;
So lay me in my lonely grave and tread
        the turf down flatter,
I'm only a consumer and it doesn't really
        matter.
    Nixon Waterman, 'Cheer for the Con-
    sumer', *The Oxford Book of American Light
    Verse*, 1979

See also Consumerism; Shopping.

CONTRACTS

1 A verbal agreement isn't worth the paper
it's written on.
    Louis B. Mayer (Attrib.)

2 Contract: an agreement that is binding
only on the weaker party.
    Frederick Sawyer

See also Big Business; Business; The
Law.

CONVERSATION

1 A gossip talks about others, a bore talks
about himself – and a brilliant conversationalist talks about you.
    Anon.

2 The trouble with telling a good story is
that it invariably reminds the other fellow
of a bad one.
    Sid Caesar

3 No man would listen to you talk if he didn't know it was his turn next.
   Edgar Watson Howe

4 The opposite of talking isn't listening. The opposite of talking is waiting.
   Fran Lebowitz, *Social Studies*, 1981

5 Buffet, ball, banquet, quilting bee,
   Wherever conversation's flowing,
   Why must I feel it falls on me
   To keep things going?
   Phyllis McGinley, *Times Three: 1932–1960*, 1960

6 We've had our clichés framed
   and hung up on the wall
   so now for conversation
   we don't have to talk at all.
   Roger McGough, 'Mute Consent', *Worse Verse*, 1969

7 Practically anything you say will seem amusing if you're on all fours.
   P. J. O'Rourke, *Modern Manners*, 1983

8 He has occasional flashes of silence that make his conversation perfectly delightful.
   The Rev. Sydney Smith, on statesman and historian Thomas Babington Macaulay (Attrib.)

9 Mr Salter's side of the conversation was limited to expressions of assent. When Lord Copper was right he said, 'Definitely, Lord Copper'; when he was wrong, 'Up to a point.'
   'Let me see, what's the name of the place I mean? Capital of Japan? Yokohama, isn't it?'
   'Up to a point, Lord Copper.'
   'And Hong Kong belongs to us, doesn't it?'
   'Definitely, Lord Copper.'
   Evelyn Waugh, *Scoop*, 1938

10 Learned conversation is either the affectation of the ignorant or the profession of the mentally unemployed.
   Oscar Wilde, 'The Critic as Artist', 1891

11 '... you wouldn't find me grousing if I were a male newt.'
   'But if you were a male newt, Madeline Bassett wouldn't look at you. Not with the eye of love, I mean.'
   'She would, if she were a female newt.'
   'But she isn't a female newt.'
   'No, but suppose she was.'
   'Well, if she was, you wouldn't be in love with her.'
   'Yes, I would, if I were a male newt.'
   A slight throbbing about the temples told me that this discussion had reached saturation point.
   P. G. Wodehouse, *Right Ho, Jeeves*, 1934

12 'What Ho!' I said, 'What Ho!' said Motty.
   'What Ho! What Ho!'
   'What Ho! What Ho! What Ho!'
   After that it seemed rather difficult to go on with the conversation.
   P. G. Wodehouse, *Carry on, Jeeves*, 1925

See also Gossip; Telephone.

COOKERY

1 Sir,
   The hymn 'Onward Christian Soldiers', sung to the right tune and in a not-too-brisk tempo, makes a very good egg timer. If you put the egg into boiling water and sing all five verses and chorus, the egg will be just right when you come to Amen.
   Letter in the *Daily Telegraph*, 1983

2 The proper way to cook a cockatoo is to put the bird and an axehead into a billy. Boil them until the axehead is soft. The cockatoo is then ready to eat.
   Anon., traditional, quoted in the *Australian*, 1954

3 Where there's smoke, there's toast.
   Anon.

4 Life is too short to stuff a mushroom.
   Shirley Conran, *Superwoman*, 1975

5 ... nobody really likes capers no matter what you do with them. Some people *pretend* to like capers, but the truth is that any dish that tastes good with capers in it, tastes even better with capers not in it.
   Nora Ephron, *Heartburn*, 1983

6 What I love about cooking is that after a hard day, there is something comforting

about the fact that if you melt butter and add flour and then hot stock, IT WILL GET THICK! It's a sure thing! It's a sure thing in a world where nothing is sure; it has a mathematical certainty in a world where those of us who long for some kind of certainty are forced to settle for crossword puzzles.
Nora Ephron, *Heartburn*, 1983

7 Couples who cook together stay together. (Maybe because they can't decide who'll get the Cuisinart.)
Erica Jong

8 Dear Miss Piggy,
Whenever I cook spaghetti, it always gets all tangled up into clumps. What am I doing wrong?
[Frustrated]

Dear Frustrated,
I am not sure, but you might try a light cream rinse, followed by a quick once-over with a blow-dryer.
Miss Piggy, *Miss Piggy's Guide to Life (As Told to Henry Beard)*, 1981

9 Do not make a stingy sandwich;
Pile the cold-cuts high;
Customers should see salami
Coming through the rye.
Alan Sherman

10 My wife does wonderful things with left-overs – she throws them out.
Herb Shriner, *Reader's Digest*, 1956

11 This week I'm going to tell you some of the many interesting things you can do with yak. There's yak à l'orange, yak pasties, yak kebab, yak fingers, yak on a spit – and yak in its jacket. But my family's favourite is a simply scrumptious desert – coupe yak. Take your yak, pluck it and bone it – take an ordinary saucepan, the type you use for broiling hippopotamus, when it's tender, cool it and smother it in raspberry ice cream, sprinkle on a little ground coconut – three tons should be enough – and serve with a hip bath of custard. Some people claim that the coconut and ice cream disguise the natural flavour of the yak meat – but when I served *my* husband

with it his immediate reaction on tasting it was –
Yak!
Barry Took and Marty Feldman, *Round the Horne*, BBC Radio, 1967

12 To make a good salad is to be a brilliant diplomatist – the problem is entirely the same in both cases. To know exactly how much oil one must put with one's vinegar.
Oscar Wilde, *Vera, or The Nihilists*, 1883

See also Breakfast; Eating; Food; Lunch; Restaurants.

CALVIN COOLIDGE President of the United States, 1923–1929

1 . . . I do wish he did not look as if he had been weaned on a pickle.
Anon., quoted by Alice Roosevelt Longworth

2 He's the greatest man who ever came out of Plymouth, Vermont.
Clarence Darrow (Attrib.)

3 Mr Coolidge's genius for inactivity is developed to a very high point. It is far from being an indolent activity. It is a grim, determined, alert inactivity which keeps Mr Coolidge occupied constantly . . . Inactivity is a political philosophy and a party program with Mr Coolidge.
Walter Lippmann, *Men of Destiny*

4 . . . simply a cheap and trashy fellow, deficient in sense and almost devoid of any notion of honor – in brief, a dreadful little cad.
H. L. Mencken, 1924

5 How can they tell?
Dorothy Parker, on being told that Coolidge was dead (Attrib.), 1933

6 He is the first president to discover that what the American people want is to be left alone.
Will Rogers, newspaper column, 1924

See also The Presidency; Washington.

COSMETICS

1 Most women are not so young as they are
painted.
   Max Beerbohm, *A Defence of Cosmetics,*
   1894

2 A girl whose cheeks are covered with
   paint
   Has an advantage with me over one
   whose ain't.
   Ogden Nash, 'Biological Reflection', *Hard
   Lines,* 1931

See also Appearance; Beauty; Faces;
Perfume.

COUNTRIES

1 . . . King Quasi of Quasiland. His country was five feet wide and eleven miles
long, and its main exports were rope and
pasta.
   Jonathan Winters, quoted by Robin
   Williams, *Playboy,* 1982

See also America and the Americans;
Foreigners.

THE COUNTRY

1 I have never understood why anybody
agreed to go on being a rustic after about
1400.
   Kingsley Amis, *The Green Man,* 1969

2 Now, nature, as I am only too well aware,
has her enthusiasts, but on the whole, I
am not to be counted among them. To
put it rather bluntly, I am not the type
who wants to go back to the land; I am the
type who wants to go back to the hotel.
   Fran Lebowitz, *Social Studies,* 1981

3 . . . to me the outdoors is what you must
pass through in order to get from your
apartment into a taxicab.
   Fran Lebowitz, *Metropolitan Life,* 1978

4 No country home is complete without a
surly figure seated in the kitchen like
Rodin's thinker, wishing she was back in
a hot little room under the Third Avenue
Elevated.
   S. J. Perelman, *Acres and Pains,* 1947

5 Lovers of the town have been content,
for the most part, to say they loved it.
They do not brag about its uplifting qualities. They have none of the infernal
smugness which makes the lover of the
country insupportable.
   Agnes Repplier, *Times and Tendencies,* 1931

6 My living in Yorkshire was so far out of
the way, that it was actually twelve miles
from a lemon.
   Sydney Smith, clergyman and wit

7 It is pure unadulterated country life.
They get up early because they have so
much to do and go to bed early because
they have so little to think about.
   Oscar Wilde, *The Picture of Dorian Gray,*
   1891

See also Farms and Farming.

COUPLES

1 Told her I had always lived alone
And I probably always would,
And all I wanted was my freedom,
And she told me that she understood.
But I let her do some of my laundry
And she slippped a few meals in between,
The next thing I remember she was all
   moved in
And I was buying her a washing machine.
   Jackson Browne, 'Ready or Not', song,
   1974

2 RICK: I mean, what AM I supposed to
call you? My 'Girl Friend'? My 'Companion'? My 'Roommate'? Nothing
sounds quite right!
   JOANIE: How about your 'Reason for
   Living'?
   RICK: No, no, I need something I can use
   around the office.
   Garry Trudeau, *Doonesbury,* cartoon

See also Courting; Engagements; Marriage; Proposals; Relationships; Sexual
Attraction.

COURAGE

1 What makes every Englishman
A fighter through and through?
It isn't roast beef or ale or home or
   mother;
It's just a little thing they sing to one
   another:

(*Refrain*)
Stiff upper lip! Stout fella!
When you're in a stew –
Sober or blotto,
This is your motto:
Keep muddling through!
> **Ira Gershwin**, 'Stiff Upper Lip', song from *A Damsel in Distress*, 1937

2   The important thing when you are going to do something brave is to have someone on hand to witness it.
> **Michael Howard**, MC, Professor of the History of War, Oxford, 1980

3   If you can keep your head when all about you are losing theirs, it's just possible you haven't grasped the situation.
> **Jean Kerr**, *Please Don't Eat the Daisies*, 1957

See also Cowardice; Fear; Heroes; War.

COURTING

1   SHE: I've heard plenty about your love-making.
HE: Oh, it's nothing.
SHE: That's what I heard.
> *Laugh-In*, NBC TV, 1969

2   A: You've been seeing my daughter Nellie for nearly a year now. What are your intentions – honorable or dishonorable?
B: You mean I've got a choice?
> **Harry Hershfield**

3   She was a lovely girl. Our courtship was fast and furious – I was fast and she was furious.
> **Max Kauffmann**

4   To differentiate between girls who put out and girls who don't. Girls who put out are tramps. Girls who don't are ladies. This is, however, a rather archaic usage of the word. Should one of you boys happen upon a girl who doesn't put out, do not jump to the conclusion that you have found a lady. What you have probably found is a lesbian.
> **Fran Lebowitz**, *Metropolitan Life*, 1978

5   Not for her potatoes
and puddings made of rice
she takes carbohydrates
like God takes advice

a surfeit of ambition
is her particular vice
Valerie fondles lovers
like a mousetrap fondles mice
> **Roger McGough**, 'Discretion', *The Mersey Sound*, 1967

6   ERIC: Who was that lady I seen you with last night?
ERNIE: You mean, '*I saw*'.
ERIC: Sorry. Who was that eyesore I seen you with last night?
> **Eric Morecambe and Ernie Wise**, *The Morecambe and Wise Joke Book*, 1979

7   The hardest task in a girl's life is to prove to a man that his intentions are serious.
> **Helen Rowland**, *Reflections of a Bachelor Girl*, 1903

8   It is assumed that the woman must wait, motionless, until she is wooed. That is how the spider waits for the fly.
> **George Bernard Shaw** (Attrib.)

9   FIREFLY (GROUCHO MARX): Oh, er, I suppose you'll think me a sentimental old fluff, but, er, would you mind giving me a lock of your hair?
MRS TEASDALE: A lock of my hair? Why, I had no idea . . .
FIREFLY: I'm letting you off easy. I was going to ask for the whole wig.
> **Arthur Sheekman and Nat Perrin**, *Duck Soup*, screenplay, 1933

10 When he dances he's all feet and when he stops he's all hands.
> **Arthur Sheekman**, *Welcome Stranger*, screenplay, 1947

11 GIRL: I saw you the other day at the corner of Hollywood and Vine winking at the girls.
RUDY VALLEE: I wasn't winking. That's a windy corner. Something got in my eye.
GIRL: She got in your car too.
> **Rudy Vallee**, *The Rudy Vallee Show*, American radio, 1930s

See also Couples; Dating; Flirtation; Rejection; Seduction; Sexual Attraction.

COWARDICE

1   Retreat, retreat,
Drop your swords and run;

Our foe is near,
Our choice is clear,
Get outa here,
Hurray for fear,
We're done.
Run away, run away,
If you run away
You live to run away another day.
  Mel Brooks, 'Retreat', song from *To Be or Not to Be*, 1984

See also Courage; Fear.

COWBOYS

1 BOY: You seem mighty thirsty. Have a long, dry ride?
COWBOY: No – I had a herring for breakfast.
BOY: What's your name stranger?
COWBOY: Folks call me . . . Strange.
BOY: Strange? What's your first name?
COWBOY: Very. But you can call me Strange.
  Parody of *Shane*, *Your Show of Shows*, NBC TV, 1950s

2 These people are simple farmers, people of the land, the common clay of the New West. You know – morons.
  Mel Brooks, *Blazing Saddles*, screenplay, 1974

3 ELLER: I'd like to say a word for the cowboy
    The road he treads is difficult and
      lonely.
    He rides for days on end
    With jist a pony fer a friend.
ADO ANNIE: I shore am feeling sorry fer the pony.
  Richard Rodgers and Oscar Hammerstein II, 'The Farmer and the Cowman', song from *Oklahoma*, 1943

See also America and the Americans.

CREATIVITY

1 When in doubt, make a fool of yourself. There is a microscopically thin line between being brilliantly creative and acting like the most gigantic idiot on earth. So what the hell, leap.
  Cynthia Heimel, 'Lower Manhattan Survival Tactics', *Village Voice*, 1983

2 Very few people possess true artistic ability. It is therefore both unseemly and unproductive to irritate the situation by making an effort. If you have a burning, restless urge to write or paint, simply eat something sweet and the feeling will pass.
  Fran Lebowitz, *Metropolitan Life*, 1978

See also Art and Artists; Ideas; Writers; Writing.

CREDIT

1 IN GOD WE TRUST. All others pay cash.
  Anon.

See also Banking; Credit Cards; Debt; Money.

CREDIT CARDS

1 FRIEND: My wife had her credit card stolen.
DAGWOOD: That's terrible!
FRIEND: It's not so terrible – the thief's been spending less than she did!
  Dean Young and Jim Raymond, *Blondie*, cartoon

See also Credit; Debt; Money.

CREDULITY

1 He had been kicked in the head when young and believed everything he read in the Sunday papers.
  George Ade, *The America of George Ade*, 1962

2 Some people will believe anything if you whisper it to them.
  Louis B. Nizer, *Thinking on Your Feet*, 1940

See also Belief; Truth.

CREMATION

1 We're all cremated equal.
  Goodman Ace, quoted in the *New Yorker*, 1977

2 SHE: Arthur.
HE: Yes, love?
SHE: I think I'd like to be cremated.
HE: OK love – get your coat on.
  Jerry Dennis

3 A: It's no good – I've got one foot in the
grate.
B: You mean 'grave'.
A: No, I mean 'grate'. I want to be
cremated.
Max Kauffmann

See also Death; Funerals.

CRICKET

1 The score piles up – somebody's
   slammed a one
And run it out: Rodmell is going gay.
Hugh with a zest that's rather overdone
Has stumped the umpire, and his loud
   hooray
Recalls the slumbering Major to the
   fray.
And now begins a kind of jamboree
Of overthrows. You think we're still at
   bay
Give me the village bat and you shall
   see.
   Beachcomber (J. B. Morton), 'Ballade of
   the Rodmell Cricket Match'

2 My wife had an uncle who could never
walk down the nave of his abbey without
wondering whether it would take spin.
   Lord Home, *The Twentieth Century Re-
   visited*, BBC TV, 1982

3 Cricket is a game which the British, not
being a spiritual people, had to invent
in order to have some concept of
eternity.
   Lord Mancroft

4 Many continentals think life is a game,
the English think cricket is a game.
   George Mikes, *How to be an Alien*, 1946

5 It's a funny kind of month, October. For
the really keen cricket fan it's when you
discover that your wife left you in May.
   Denis Norden, *She*, 1977

6 Everyone knows which comes first when
it's a question of cricket or sex – all
discerning people recognize that.
   Harold Pinter (Attrib.)

7 Personally, I have always looked upon
cricket as organized loafing.
   William Temple, Archbishop of Canter-
   bury, 1925

8 There is only one thing in criket and that
is the *strate bat*. Keep yore bat strate boy
and all will be all right in life as in criket.
So headmasters sa, but when my bat is
strate i still get bowled is that an omen
chiz. Aktually i usually prefer to hav a
slosh: i get bowled just the same but it is
more satisfactory.
   Geoffrey Willans and Ronald Searle,
   'How to be Topp', *The Compleet Molesworth*,
   1958

9 'The last time I played in a village cricket
match,' said Psmith, 'I was caught at
point by a man in braces. It would have
been madness to risk another such shock
to the system.'
   P. G. Wodehouse, *Mike*, 1909

10 The sun in heavens was beaming;
The breeze bore an odour of hay,
My flannels were spotless and gleaming,
My heart was unclouded and gay;
The ladies, all gaily apparelled,
Sat round looking on at the match,
In the tree-tops the dicky-birds
   carolled,
All was peace till I bungled that catch.
   P. G. Wodehouse, 'Missed!'

See also Sport.

CRIME

1 After an incident in Croydon involving a
prison van and a concrete mixer, police
are looking for eighteen hardened cri-
minals.
   The Two Ronnies, BBC TV

2 A kleptomaniac is a person who helps
himself because he can't help himself.
   Anon.

3 I think crime pays. The hours are good,
you travel a lot.
   Woody Allen, *Take the Money and Run*,
   screenplay, 1969

4 Al Capone, in mood benign,
Sent a massive Valentine,
Those who got his commendation
Shot up in his estimation.
   Will Bellenger, *New Statesman*, 1984

5 Thieves respect property; they merely
wish the property to become their

property that they may more perfectly respect it.

G. K. Chesterton, *The Man Who was Thursday*, 1908

6 A broad definition of crime in England is that it is any lower-class activity which is displeasing to the upper class. Crime is committed by the lower class and punished by the upper class.

David Frost and Antony Jay, *To England with Love*, 1967

7 ERNIE: Is there a price on your head?
ERIC: Yes, but I won't sell. They've offered one thousand pounds if I'm captured dead.
ERNIE: Yes?
ERIC: Two thousand pounds if I'm captured alive.
ERNIE: Yes?
ERIC: And three thousand pounds if I'm captured dead *and* alive. And all for one lousy overdue library book!
ERNIE: What's the charge?
ERIC: Tuppence a day. Oh, I see what you mean – Borrowing with Intent!

Eric Morecambe and Ernie Wise, *The Morecambe and Wise Joke Book*, 1979

8 ETH: A professional burglar! Mr Glum, you told me Ron's Uncle Charlie was a *biologist*.
MR GLUM: All I said was, he studies cell structures.

Frank Muir and Denis Norden, *The Glums*, London Weekend Television, 1978

9 I'm all for bringing back the birch. But only between consenting adults.

Gore Vidal, interviewed on *The Frost Programme*, 1966

See also Capital Punishment; Dishonesty; Kidnapping; The Law; The Mafia; Police; Prisons.

STAFFORD CRIPPS British President of the Board of Trade and Chancellor of the Exchequer, 1945–1950

1 Sir Stafford has a brilliant mind until it is made up.

Margot Asquith (Attrib.)

2 Neither of his colleagues can compare with him in that acuteness and energy of mind with which he devotes himself to so many topics injurious to the strength and welfare of the state.

Winston Churchill, speech in the House of Commons, 1946

3 There, but for the grace of God, goes God.

Winston Churchill (Attrib.), 1943

See also The Labour Party.

CRISES

1 There cannot be a crisis next week. My schedule is already full.

Henry Kissinger, *New York Times Magazine*, 1969

See also Anxiety; Despair.

CRITICISM

1 I can take any amount of criticism, so long as it is unqualified praise.

Noël Coward (Attrib.)

2 Honest criticism is hard to take, particularly from a relative, a friend, an acquaintance or a stranger.

Franklin P. Jones

3 I have never found in a long experience of politics that criticism is ever inhibited by ignorance.

Harold Macmillan

See also Abuse; Art – Critics; Critics; Critics – The Artist's View; Insults.

CRITICS

1 A good writer is not, per se, a good critic. No more than a good drunk is automatically a good bartender.

Jim Bishop

2 Either criticism is no good at all (a very defensible position) or else criticism means saying about an author the very things that would have made him jump out of his boots.

G. K. Chesterton, *Charles Dickens*, 1906

3 I could see by the way she sniffed that she was about to become critical. There had

always been a strong strain of book-reviewer blood in her.
P. G. Wodehouse, *Aunts aren't Gentlemen*, 1974

See also Art – Critics; Books – Critics; Criticism; Critics – The Artist's View; Film – Critics; Rock 'n' Roll – Critics; Theatre – Critics.

CRITICS – THE ARTIST'S VIEW

1 A critic is a bunch of biases held loosely together by a sense of taste.
Witney Balliett, *Dinosaurs in the Morning*, 1962

2 ... drooling, drivelling, doleful, depressing, dropsical drips.
Sir Thomas Beecham, 1955

3 Critics are like eunuchs in a harem: they know how it's done, they've seen it done every day, but they're unable to do it themselves.
Brendan Behan (Attrib.)

4 Critics can't even make music by rubbing their back legs together.
Mel Brooks, quoted in the *New York Times*, 1975

5 If the critics unanimously take exception to one particular scene it is advisable to move that scene to a more conspicuous place in the programme.
Noël Coward (Attrib.)

6 The day when I shall begin to worry is when the critics declare: 'This is Noël Coward's greatest play.' But I know they bloody well won't.
Noël Coward (Attrib.)

7 Taking to pieces is the trade of those who cannot construct.
Ralph Waldo Emerson (Attrib.)

8 He takes the long review of things;
He asks and gives no quarter.
And you can sail with him on wings
Or read the book. It's shorter.
David McCord, *To a Certain Most Certainly Certain Critic*

9 A drama critic is a person who surprises the playwright by informing him what he meant.
Wilson Mizner

10 Asking a working writer what he feels about critics is like asking a lamp-post what it feels about dogs.
John Osborne (Attrib.)

11 A critic is a legless man who teaches running.
Channing Polock (Attrib.)

12 A critic is a man who knows the way but can't drive the car.
Kenneth Tynan, *New York Times*, 1966

13 They search for ages for the wrong word which, to give them credit, they eventually find.
Peter Ustinov, *On Critics*, BBC Radio, 1952

14 It is exactly because a man cannot do a thing that he is the proper judge of it.
Oscar Wilde, 'The Critic as Artist', 1890

15 Has anyone ever seen a dramatic critic in the daytime? Of course not. They come out after dark, up to no good.
P. G. Wodehouse

16 ... inkstained wretches.
Alexander Woollcott

17 Rock journalism is people who can't write interviewing people who can't talk for people who can't read.
Frank Zappa (Attrib.)

See also Art – Critics; Books – Critics; Criticism; Critics; Film – Critics; Rock 'n' Roll – Critics; Theatre – Critics.

CULTS

1 What's a cult? It just means not enough people to make a minority.
Robert Altman, 1981

2 My son has taken up meditation – at least it's better than sitting doing nothing.
Max Kauffmann

3 The Amish are a surly sect.
They paint their bulging barns with hex

Designs, pronounce a dialect
Of Deutsch, inbreed, and wink at sex.
They have no use for buttons, tea,
Life insurance, cigarettes,
Churches, liquor, Sea & Ski,
Public power, or regrets.
> **John Updike**, 'The Amish', *Telegraph Poles and Other Poems*, 1969

See also Religion.

CULTURE

1 One of the basic freedoms of the Englishman is freedom from culture.
> **Lord Goodman**, Chairman of the Arts Council, 1967

2 Culture is roughly anything we do and the monkeys don't.
> **Lord Raglan** (Attrib.)

3 Mrs Ballinger is one of the ladies who pursue Culture in bands, as though it were dangerous to meet it alone.
> **Edith Wharton**, *Xingu*, 1916

See also Aesthetes; Art and Artists; The Theatre.

CYNICISM

1 Cynicism – the intellectual cripple's substitute for intelligence.
> **Russell Lynes**

2 A cynic is a man who, when he smells flowers, looks around for a coffin.
> **H. L. Mencken** (Attrib.)

3 It is a sin to believe evil of others, but it is seldom a mistake.
> **H. L. Mencken** (Attrib.)

4 A man who knows the price of everything and the value of nothing.
> **Oscar Wilde**, *Lady Windermere's Fan*, 1892

DANCE

1 Dancing is the perpendicular expression
of a horizontal desire.
Anon.

2 Down with the modern dance!
That craze we'll quickly smother.
It looks all right
If your coat's on tight
And you *really love* each other.
Down with the Shimmie Shake
That makes poor Auntie hot!
We'll see that every dance club fails,
And slap Pavlova till she wails.
What about Salomé and her seven veils?
Down with the whole damn lot!
    Noël Coward, 'Down with the Whole
    Damn Lot!', *Co-optimists*, 1928

3 Senorita Nina
From Argentina
Despised the Tango
And though she never was a girl to let a
    man go
She wouldn't sacrifice her principles for
    sex.
She looked with scorn on the gyrations
Of her relations
Who danced the Conga
And swore that if she had to stand it any
    longer
She'd lose all dignity and wring their
    silly necks!
    Noël Coward, 'Nina', *Sigh No More*,
    1945

4 Though no one ever could be keener
Than little Nina
On quite a number
Of very eligible men who did the
    Rhumba
When they proposed to her she simply
    left them flat.
She said that love should be impulsive
But not convulsive
And syncopation
Has a discouraging effect on
    procreation

And that she'd rather read a book – and
    that was that!
    Noël Coward, 'Nina', *Sigh No More*, 1945

5 May I have the pleasure of the next sadly
outdated courting ritual.
    Michael Leunig, *The Bedtime Leunig*,
    cartoon, 1981

6 Teenagers and old people may know
how to dance, but real people who go to
real parties haven't the slightest. The
only dances they even half remember
how to do are the ones they learned
twenty years ago. This is what the old
Supremes tape is for: stiff and overweight versions of the Jerk, the Mashed
Potato, the Pony, the Swim, and the
Watusi. And after six drinks everyone
will revert to the Twist.
    P. J. O'Rourke, *Modern Manners*, 1983

7 He makes you feel more danced against
than with.
    Sally Poplin

8 'Can you dance?' said the girl.
    Lancelot gave a short, amused laugh.
He was a man who never let his left hip
know what his right hip was doing.
    P. G. Wodehouse, 'Came the Dawn', *Meet
    Mr Mulliner*, 1927

See also Ballet; Exercise; The Theatre.

DATING

1 I don't believe we've met. I'm Mr Right.

If national security were at stake, would
you spend the night with a man whose
name you don't even know?

I'm glad you don't recognize me. I'd
rather have you like me for myself.

I don't dance. But I'd love to hold you
while you do.
    'Four Tested Opening Lines', advertise-
    ment, *Playboy*, 1969

2 WHAT IS A DATE?
A date, at this juncture in history, is any

prearranged meeting with a member of the opposite sex toward whom you have indecent intentions ... One does not have to sleep with, or even touch, someone who has paid for your meal. All those obligations are hereby rendered null and void, and any man who doesn't think so needs a quick jab in the kidney.
Cynthia Heimel, *Sex Tips for Girls*, 1983

3 Dates used to be made days or even weeks in advance. Now dates tend to be made the day after. That is, you get a phone call from someone who says, 'If anyone asks, I was out to dinner with you last night, okay?'
P. J. O'Rourke, *Modern Manners*, 1983

4 ... men generally pay for all expenses on a date ... Either sex, however, may bring a little gift, its value to be determined by the bizarreness of the sexual request to be made later that evening.
P. J. O'Rourke, *Modern Manners*, 1983

5 *What should a woman do if a man stands her up on a date?*
If the man is genuinely apologetic, I would let him off with a large bunch of flowers, an expensive present, and a lavish make-up dinner. On the other hand, if he treats it in an offhand manner, he is obviously the kind of person who is not going to knock himself out for you, and you should do it for him.
Miss Piggy, *Miss Piggy's Guide to Life (As Told to Henry Beard)*, 1981

See also Couples; Courting; Flirtation; Petting.

DEATH

1 Death is nature's way of telling you to slow down.
Graffito, London, 1978

2 Death is the greatest kick of all – that's why they save it till last.
Graffito, Los Angeles, 1981

3 I don't believe in an afterlife, although I am bringing a change of underwear.
Woody Allen

4 It is impossible to experience one's own death objectively and still carry a tune.
Woody Allen

5 It's not that I'm afraid to die, I just don't want to be there when it happens.
Woody Allen, *Without Feathers*, 1976

6 On the plus side, death is one of the few things that can be done as easily lying down.
Woody Allen, *Getting Even*, 1972

7 If my doctor told me I only had six minutes to live, I wouldn't brood. I'd type a little faster.
Isaac Asimov, *Life*, 1984

8 As the poets have mournfully sung,
Death takes the innocent young,
The rolling-in-money,
The screamingly-funny,
And those who are very well hung.
W. H. Auden 'The Aesthetic Point of View', *Collected Poems*, 1977

9 Dr Ramsden cannot read
The Times obituary today
He's dead.
Let monographs on silk worms
By other people be
Thrown away
Unread.
For he who best could understand and criticize them, he
Lies clay. In bed.
John Betjeman, obituary poem for Dr Walter Ramsden, 1947

10 I'd start making up this revenge list, like people I'd like to get sooner or later. And the hang-up about doing this is that you're worried about them dying, and you won't get the chance. So I started to get different ways to be offensive at the funerals ...
* Pass out baby-pictures of the deceased.
* Shake the widow's hand with an electric buzzer.
* Tell the clergyman that the deceased was a vampire and ask if you can drive a stake through his heart.
* The day after the funeral, send the widow a candygram from the deceased.
Ed Bluestone

11 Death comes along like a gas bill one can't pay – and that's all one can say about it.
  Anthony Burgess, interview, *Playboy*, 1974

12 While other people's deaths are deeply sad, one's own is surely a bit of a joke.
  James Cameron, *Observer*, 1982

13 For three days after death, hair and fingernails continue to grow but phone calls taper off.
  Johnny Carson, *The Tonight Show*, NBC TV

14 Few men by their death can have given such deep satisfaction to so many.
  Cassandra (William Connor), 'Farewell to Joseph Stalin', *Daily Mirror*, 1953

15 I am ready to meet my Maker. Whether my Maker is prepared for the ordeal of meeting me is another matter.
  Winston Churchill, on his seventy-fifth birthday, 1949

16 Mrs McFadden has gone from this life;
  She has left all its sorrows and cares;
  She caught the rheumatics in both of her legs
  While scrubbing the cellar and stairs.
  They put mustard-plasters upon her in vain;
  They bathed her in whisky and rum;
  But Thursday her spirit departed, and left
  Her body entirely numb.
  Charles Heber Clark ('Max Adeler'), 'Mrs McFadden', *Mr Slimmer's Funeral Verses for the* Morning Argus

17 We have lost our little Hanner in a very painful manner,
  And we often asked, How can her harsh sufferings be borne?
  When her death was first reported, her aunt got up and snorted
  With the grief that she supported, for it made her feel forlorn.
  She was such a little seraph that her father, who is sheriff,
  Really doesn't seem to care if he ne'er smiles in life again.
  She has gone, we hope, to heaven, at the early age of seven

(Funeral starts off at eleven), where she'll never more have pain.
  Charles Heber Clark ('Max Adeler'), 'Hanner', *Mr Slimmer's Funeral Verses for the* Morning Argus

18 It's passed on. This parrot is no more. It has ceased to be. It's expired and gone to see its maker. This is a late parrot. It's a stiff. Bereft of life. It rests in peace. If you hadn't nailed it to the perch, it would be pushing up the daisies. It's rung down the curtain and joined the choir invisible. THIS is an ex-parrot.
  John Cleese and Graham Chapman, *And Now for Something Completely Different*, 1971

19 PETE: Have you ever thought about death? Do you realize that we each must die?
  DUD: Of course we must die, but not yet. It's only half past four of a Wednesday afternoon.
  PETE: No one knows when God in His Almighty Wisdom will choose to vouch-safe His precious gift of Death.
  DUD: Granted. But chances are He won't be making a pounce at this time of day.
  Peter Cook and Dudley Moore, *The Dagenham Dialogues*, 1971

20 It's a funny old world – a man's lucky if he can get out of it alive.
  W. C. Fields, *You're Telling Me*, screenplay, 1934

21 'Hallelujah!' was the only observation
  That escaped Lieutenant-Colonel Mary Jane,
  When she tumbled off the platform in the station,
  And was cut in little pieces by the train.
  Mary Jane, the train is through yer!
  Hallelujah, Hallelujah!
  We shall gather up the fragments that remain.
  A. E. Housman, 'On the Death of a Female Officer of the Salvation Army', *Complete Poems*, 1956

22 Hardly a man is now alive
  Who recalls that in 1795
  Occurred the death of a Mr James Boswell;

A joke on his doctor, who'd thought that he was well.
Ring Lardner, 'Hardly a man is now alive'

23 Public display of mourning is no longer made by people of fashion, although some flashier kinds of widows may insist on sleeping with only black men during the first year after the death.

Normal social life, however, may not be resumed by a widow because there has been no normal social life in the United States since 1966.
P. J. O'Rourke, *Modern Manners*, 1983

24 The purpose of a funeral service is to comfort the living. It is important at a funeral to display excessive grief. This will show others how kind-hearted and loving you are and their improved opinion of you will be very comforting.

As anyone familiar with modern fiction and motion pictures knows, excessive grief cannot be expressed by means of tears or a mournful face. It is necessary to break things, hit people, and throw yourself on to the top of the coffin, at least.
P. J. O'Rourke, *Modern Manners*, 1983

25 He lies below, correct in cypress wood,
And entertains the most exclusive
   worms.
Dorothy Parker, *The Very Rich Man*

26 It costs me never a stab nor squirm
To tread by chance upon a worm.
'Aha, my little dear,' I say,
'your clan will pay me back one day.'
Dorothy Parker, 'Sunset Gun', 1928

27 GROUCHO MARX: Either this man is dead or my watch has stopped.
Robert Pirosh and George Seaton, *A Day at the Races*, screenplay, 1937

28 The late F. W. H. Myers used to tell how he asked a man at a dinner table what he thought would happen to him when he died. The man tried to ignore the question, but, on being pressed, replied: 'Oh well, I suppose I shall inherit eternal bliss, but I wish you wouldn't talk about such unpleasant subjects.'
Bertrand Russell, *Stoicism and Mental Health*, 1928

29 You haven't lived until you've died in California.
Mort Sahl

30 Boy, when you're dead, they really fix you up. I hope to hell when I *do* die somebody has sense enough to just dump me in the river or something. Anything except sticking me in a goddam cemetery. People coming and putting a bunch of flowers on your stomach on Sunday, and all that crap. Who wants flowers when you're dead? Nobody.
J. D. Salinger, *The Catcher in the Rye*, 1951

31 Eternity is a terrible thought. I mean, where's it going to end?
Tom Stoppard, *Rosencrantz and Guildenstern are Dead*, 1967

32 I did not attend his funeral; but I wrote a nice letter saying I approved of it.
Mark Twain, of a deceased politician (Attrib.)

33 The reports of my death are greatly exaggerated.
Mark Twain, cable from Europe to the Associated Press

34 Her capacity for family affection is extraordinary. When her third husband died, her hair turned quite gold from grief.
Oscar Wilde, *The Picture of Dorian Gray*, 1891

See also Cremation; Epitaphs; Funerals; Immortality; Last Words; Reincarnation; Suicide.

DEBT

1 If it isn't the sheriff it's the finance company. I've got more attachments on me than a vacuum cleaner.
John Barrymore

2 Never run into debt, not if you can find anything else to run into.
Josh Billings, *The Complete Works of Josh Billings*, 1919

See also Banking; Budgets; Extravagance; Money.

DECISIONS

1 You may be sure that when a man begins to call himself a realist he is preparing to do something that he is secretly ashamed of doing.
Sydney J. Harris

2 A decision is what a man makes when he can't get anyone to serve on a committee.
Fletcher Knebel

3 When a person tells you, 'I'll think it over and let you know' – you know.
Olin Miller

4 All our final decisions are made in a state of mind that is not going to last.
Marcel Proust

See also Assertiveness; Committees; Indecision.

CHARLES DE GAULLE
President of France 1958–1969

1 Of all the crosses I have to bear, the heaviest is the Cross of Lorraine.
Winston Churchill (Attrib.), 1943

2 When I want to know what France thinks, I ask myself.
Charles de Gaulle, quoted in *Sons of France*, 1966

3 . . . an artlessly sincere megalomaniac.
H. G. Wells (Attrib.), 1943

See also France and the French.

DEMOCRACY

1 Democracy means government by discussion but it is only effective if you can stop people talking.
Clement Attlee (Attrib.)

2 It has been said that Democracy is the worst form of government except all those other forms that have been tried from time to time.
Winston Churchill, speech in the House of Commons, November 1947

3 Democracy consists of choosing your dictators, after they've told you what you think it is you want to hear.
Alan Coren, *Daily Mail*, 1975

4 Two cheers for Democracy: one because it admits variety and two because it permits criticism. Two cheers are quite enough: there is no occasion to give three.
E. M. Forster, 'What I Believe', *Two Cheers for Democracy*, 1951

5 In an autocracy, one person has his way; in an aristocracy a few people have their way; in a democracy no one has his way.
Celia Green, *The Decline and Fall of Science*

6 One fifth of the people are against everything all the time.
Robert Kennedy, quoted in the *Observer*, 1964

7 Democracy is an interesting, even laudable, notion and there is no question but that when compared to Communism, which is too dull, or Fascism, which is too exciting, it emerges as the most palatable form of government. This is not to say that it is without its drawbacks – chief among them being its regrettable tendency to encourage people in the belief that all men are created equal. And although the vast majority need only take a quick look around the room to see that this is hardly the case, a great many remain utterly convinced.
Fran Lebowitz, *Metropolitan Life*, 1978

8 Democracy is . . . a form of religion; it is the worship of jackals by jackasses.
H. L. Mencken, *Sententiae*, 1920

9 Democracy is that system of government under which the people, having 35,717,342 native-born adult whites to choose from, including thousands who are handsome and many who are wise, pick out a Coolidge to be head of the State.
H. L. Mencken, *Prejudices*, Fifth Series, 1926

10 Democracy is the theory that the common people know what they want, and deserve to get it good and hard.
H. L. Mencken, *A Book of Burlesques*, 1916

11 Under democracy, one party always devotes its chief energies to trying to prove that the other party is unfit to rule –

and both commonly succeed, and are right.
H. L. Mencken, *Minority Report*, 1956

12 Democracy is too good to share with just anybody.
Nigel Rees, *A Year of Graffiti*, 1983

13 Democracy is a device that ensures we shall be governed no better than we deserve.
George Bernard Shaw (Attrib.)

14 Democracy substitutes election by the incompetent many for appointment by the corrupt few.
George Bernard Shaw, *Maxims For Revolutionists*, 1903

15 It is by the goodness of God that in our country we have those three unspeakably precious things: freedom of speech, freedom of conscience, and the prudence never to practice either of them.
Mark Twain

16 High hopes were once formed of democracy; but democracy means simply the bludgeoning of the people by the people for the people.
Oscar Wilde, 'The Soul of Man under Socialism', 1891

See also Equality; Government; Politics and Politicians.

THE DEMOCRATIC PARTY

1 The Democratic Party is like a man riding backward in a carriage. It never sees a thing until it has gone by.
Benjamin F. Butler

2 I never said all Democrats were saloonkeepers; what I said was all saloonkeepers were Democrats.
Horace Greeley

3 I belong to no organized party – I am a Democrat.
Will Rogers (Attrib.)

4 The Democratic Party is like a mule – without pride of ancestry or hope of posterity.
Emory Speer, Republican, Georgia (Attrib.)

See also Democrats and Republicans; Politics and Politicians; The Republican Party; Washington.

DEMOCRATS AND REPUBLICANS

1 ... while the Republicans are smart enough to make money, the Democrats are smart enough to get in office every two or three times a century and take it away from 'em.
Will Rogers, radio talk, 1934

2 Republicans raise dahlias, Dalmatians, and eyebrows. Democrats raise Airedales, kids and taxes.
Will Stanton, 'How to Tell a Democrat from a Republican', *Ladies' Home Journal*, 1962

3 Republicans sleep in twin beds – some even in separate rooms. That is why there are more Democrats.
Will Stanton, 'How to Tell a Democrat from a Republican', *Ladies' Home Journal*, 1962

4 Republicans study the financial pages of the newspaper. Democrats put them in the bottom of the bird cage.
Will Stanton, 'How to Tell a Democrat from a Republican', *Ladies' Home Journal*, 1962

See also The Democratic Party; The Republican Party.

DENMARK AND THE DANES

1 From Hamlet to Kierkegaard, the word 'Danish' has been synonymous with fun, fun, fun ... Who else would have the sense of humor to stuff prunes and toecheese into lumps of wet dough and *serve it to you for breakfast*? ... Let's hear it for those very wonderful kooky, very crazy, very whacky, very witty Danes! They're the *living end*! And vice versa.
Tony Hendra, 'EEC! It's the US of E!', *National Lampoon*, 1976

DESIRES

1 In this world there are only two tragedies.

One is not getting what one wants and the other is getting it.
Oscar Wilde, *Lady Windermere's Fan*, 1892

2 All the things I really like to do are either immoral, illegal or fattening.
Alexander Woollcott

DESPAIR

1 He's turned his life around. He used to be depressed and miserable. Now he's miserable and depressed.
David Frost, *TVam*, 1984

2 Noble deeds and hot baths are the best cures for depression.
Dodie Smith, *I Capture the Castle*, 1948

3 Bingo uttered a stricken woofle like a bull-dog that has been refused cake.
P. G. Wodehouse, *Very Good, Jeeves*, 1930

See also Crises; Suicide.

DIARIES

1 Keep a diary and one day it'll keep you.
Mae West

2 I never travel without my diary. One should always have something sensational to read in the train.
Oscar Wilde, *The Importance of Being Earnest*, 1895

DIETS

1 Diets are for those who are thick and tired of it.
Anon.

2 Eat drink and be merry, for tomorrow we diet!
Anon.

3 I've been on a constant diet for the last two decades. I've lost a total of 789 pounds. By all accounts, I should be hanging from a charm bracelet.
Erma Bombeck

4 Those magazine dieting stories always have the testimonial of a woman who wore a dress that could slipcover New Jersey in one photo and thirty days later looked like a well-dressed thermometer.
Erma Bombeck, quoted in *Time*, 1984

5 A really busy person never knows how much he weighs.
Edgar Watson Howe, *Country Town Sayings*, 1911

6 I feel about airplanes the way I feel about diets. It seems to me they are wonderful things for other people to go on.
Jean Kerr, *The Snake Has All the Lines*, 1960

7 Take, O take the cream away,
Take away the sugar, too;
Let the morning coffee stay
As a black and bitter brew.
I have gained since yesternight –
Shoot the calories on sight!
Stoddard King, *Breakfast Song in Time of Diet*

8 I went on a diet, swore off drinking and heavy eating, and in fourteen days I lost two weeks.
Joe E. Lewis

9 So I think it is very nice for ladies to be lithe and lissome,
But not so much that you cut yourself if you happen to embrace or kissome.
Ogden Nash, 'Curl Up and Diet', *I'm a Stranger Here Myself*, 1938

10 *Diet Tips*
Never eat anything at one sitting that you can't lift
Always use one of the new – and far more reliable – elastic measuring tapes to check on your waistline.
Miss Piggy, *Miss Piggy's Guide to Life (As Told to Henry Beard)*, 1981

11 My wife is on a diet. Coconuts and bananas. She hasn't lost any weight, but can she climb a tree!
Henny Youngman

See also Eating; Exercise; Figures; Foods.

DIGNITY

1 It is only people of small moral stature who have to stand on their dignity.
Arnold Bennett

2 I know of no case where a man added to his dignity by standing on it.
Winston Churchill

DIPLOMACY

1 Diplomacy, *n.* the patriotic art of lying for one's country.
Ambrose Bierce, *The Devil's Dictionary,* 1911

2 Diplomacy is the art of saying 'Nice Doggie!' till you can find a rock.
Wynn Catlin

3 Diplomacy, *n.* is the art of letting somebody else have your way.
David Frost, *TVam,* 1983

4 Diplomacy: lying in state.
Oliver Herford

5 I got a call from Haig [US Secretary of State], who offered me the job of explaining the Administration's foreign policy to the Chinese – one by one.
Henry Kissinger

6 A diplomat is a man who thinks twice before he says nothing.
Frederick Sawyer

7 A diplomat is a person who can tell you to go to hell in such a way that you actually look forward to the trip.
Caskie Stinnett, *Out of the Red,* 1960

8 . . . babies in silk hats playing with dynamite.
Alexander Woollcott (Attrib.)

See also Government; Politics and Politicians.

DISASTERS

1 'Higgledy-piggledy
Andrea Doria
Lives in the name of this
Glorious boat.
As I sit writing these
Non-navigational
Verses a – *Crash! Bang! Blurp!
Glub!* . . .
John Hollander, 'Last Words', *Jiggery-pokery: A Compendium of Double Dactyls,* 1966

See also Accidents; Misfortune.

DISC JOCKEYS

1 If you are a disc jockey, kindly remember that your job is to play records that people will enjoy dancing to and not to impress possible visiting disc jockeys with your esoteric taste. People generally enjoy dancing to songs that have words and are of reasonable length.
Fran Lebowitz, *Metropolitan Life,* 1978

2 Radio news is bearable. This is due to the fact that while the news is being broadcast the disc jockey is not allowed to talk.
Fran Lebowitz, *Metropolitan Life,* 1978

See also Music and Musicians; News; Rock 'n' Roll; Songs and Singers.

DISGUST

1 Gold was not altogether certain what, anatomically, a gorge was, but he knew that his was rising.
Joseph Heller, *Good as Gold,* 1979

See also Nausea.

DISHONESTY

1 He's the only man I ever knew who had rubber pockets so he could steal soup.
Wilson Mizner, of a Hollywood studio chief

2 It is almost always worth while to be cheated; people's little frauds have an interest which more than repays what they cost us.
Logan Pearsall Smith, *Afterthoughts,* 1931

3 Many a time in the past, when an active operator in the Street, he had done things to the Small Investor which would have caused raised eyebrows on the fo'-c's'le of a pirate sloop – and done them without a blush.
P. G. Wodehouse, *The Heart of a Goof,* 1926

See also Crime; Guilt; Lies.

DIVORCE

1 JUDGE: You want a divorce on the grounds that your husband is careless about his appearance?
WIFE: Yes, your honour – he hasn't made one for three years.
Anon.

2 For a while we pondered whether to take a vacation or get a divorce. We decided

that a trip to Bermuda is over in two weeks, but a divorce is something you always have.
Woody Allen, nightclub act, 1960s

3 Many a man owes his success to his first wife and his second wife to his success.
Jim Backus

4 The difference between divorce and legal separation is that a legal separation gives a husband time to hide his money.
Johnny Carson (Attrib.)

5 The happiest time of anyone's life is just after the first divorce.
John Kenneth Galbraith

6 . . . being divorced is like being hit by a Mack truck. If you live through it, you start looking very carefully to the right and to the left.
Jean Kerr, *Mary, Mary*, 1960

7 You don't know a woman till you've met her in court.
Norman Mailer

8 ERIC: My father was very disappointed when I was born.
ERNIE: Why? Did he want a girl?
ERIC: No, he wanted a divorce.
Eric Morecambe and Ernie Wise, *The Morecambe and Wise Joke Book*, 1979

9 When a couple decide to divorce, they should inform both sets of parents before having a party and telling all their friends. This is not only courteous but practical. Parents may be very willing to pitch in with comments, criticism and malicious gossip of their own to help the divorce along.
P. J. O'Rourke, *Modern Manners*, 1983

10 My mother and father are both speaking to solicitors. I expect they are fighting over who gets custody of me. I will be a tug-of-love child, and my picture will be in the newspapers. I hope my spots clear up before then.
Sue Townsend, *The Secret Diary of Adrian Mole Aged 13¾*, 1982

See also Alimony; Love – Breaking Up; Marriage; Rejection.

DOCTORS

1 The chief defect of Henry King
Was chewing little bits of string.
At last he swallowed some which tied
Itself in ugly Knots inside.
Physicians of the Utmost Fame
Were called at once; but when they
  came
They answered, as they took their Fees,
'There is no cure for this disease.'
Hilaire Belloc, 'Henry King', *Cautionary Tales for Children*, 1907

2 WICKSTEED: The longer I practise medicine, the more convinced I am there are only two types of cases: those that involve taking the trousers off and those that don't.
Alan Bennett, *Habeas Corpus*, 1973

3 My doctor is wonderful. Once, in 1955, when I couldn't afford an operation, he touched up the X-rays.
Joey Bishop

4 Keep away from physicians. It is all probing and guessing and pretending with them. They leave it to Nature to cure in her own time, but they take the credit. As well as very fat fees.
Anthony Burgess, *Nothing Like the Sun*, 1964

5 Doctors think a lot of patients are cured who have simply quit in disgust.
Don Herold

6 ERNIE: Doctor, I don't know what's wrong with me. Do you think I'll ever get better?
ERIC: I don't know – let me feel your purse.
ERNIE: But Doctor . . .
ERIC: Sit down and tell me all about it . . .
ERNIE: Doctor, I'm not a private patient. I'm on the National Health.
ERIC: . . . in less than two minutes.
Eric Morecambe and Ernie Wise, *The Morecambe and Wise Joke Book*, 1979

7 ERNIE: Stick your tongue out and say, 'Ah'.
ERIC: Ah.

ERNIE: Well, your tongue looks all right
– but why the postage stamp?
ERIC: So that's where I left it.
   Eric Morecambe and Ernie Wise, *The
   Morecambe and Wise Joke Book*, 1979

8 PATIENT: And I've got rheumatism on
   the back of my neck. It's a bad place to
   have rheumatism – on the back of my
   neck.
   DOCTOR: No, no – where would you
   want a better place than on the back of
   your neck?
   PATIENT: On the back of *your* neck!
      Smith and Dale, 'Dr Kronkheit and His
      Only Living Patient', American vaudeville
      act

See also Health; Hospitals; Illness;
Medicine.

DOGS

1 He knew what people thought of his
   kind: 'High Strung.' 'Spoiled Rotten.'
   'French.'
   But in the next twenty-four hours, He's
   going to change all that . . .
   He's SMALL.
   He's BLACK.
   He's MAD AS HELL.
   He's POODLE with a MOHAWK.
   'You'll never call him Fifi again!'
      Lynda Barry, 'Poodle with a Mohawk', *Big
      Ideas*, cartoon, 1983

2 You will find that the woman who is
   really kind to dogs is always one who has
   failed to inspire sympathy in men.
      Max Beerbohm, *Zuleika Dobson*, 1911

3 A dog teaches a boy fidelity, perseverance and to turn round three times
   before lying down.
      Robert Benchley

4 A dog is the only thing on earth that loves
   you more than you love yourself.
      Josh Billings, *The Complete Works of Josh
      Billings*, 1919

5 Every day, the dog and I, we go for a
   tramp in the woods. And he loves it!
   Mind you, the tramp is getting a bit fed
   up!
      Jerry Dennis

6 They had a . . . dog called Bluey. A
   known psychopath, Bluey would attack
   himself if nothing else was available. He
   used to chase himself in circles trying to
   bite his own balls off.
      Clive James, *Unreliable Memoirs*, 1980

7 ERIC: He's a lovely dog . . . Last Satur-
   day he took first prize at the cat show.
   ERNIE: How was that?
   ERIC: He took the cat.
   ERNIE: Didn't you punish him?
   ERIC: I should have done. Trouble is, I
   spoil him. It works, though. Most of the
   time I've got him eating out of my leg . . .
   Last night . . . he gave my leg quite a
   nasty bite.
   ERNIE: Did you put anything on it?
   ERIC: No, he liked it just as it was.
      Eric Morecambe and Ernie Wise, *The
      Morecambe and Wise Joke Book*, 1979

DO-IT-YOURSELF

1 The quickest way to make your own
   anti-freeze is to hide her nightie.
      Anon.

See also Home; Interior Decorating.

DREAMS

1 He dreamed he was eating shredded
   wheat and woke up to find the mattress
   half gone.
      Fred Allen

2 People who insist on telling their dreams
   are among the terrors of the breakfast
   table.
      Max Beerbohm

See also Bed; Sleep.

DRINK

1 After four martinis, my husband turns
   into a disgusting beast. And after the
   fifth, I pass out altogether.
      Anon.

2 *I* am sparkling; *you* are unusually
      talkative; *he* is drunk.
      Competition, *New Statesman*

3 It was early last December,
   As near as I remember,

I was walking down the street in tipsy
  pride;
No one was I disturbing
As I lay down by the curbing,
And a pig came up and lay down by my
  side.

As I lay there in the gutter
Thinking thoughts I shall not utter,
A lady passing by was heard to say:
'You can tell a man who boozes
By the company he chooses';
And the pig got up and slowly walked
  away.
  Anon., 'The Drunkard and the Pig', *The
  Oxford Book of American Light Verse*, 1979

4 On the chest of a barmaid in Sale
   Were tattooed the prices of ale,
   And on her behind,
   For the sake of the blind,
   Was the same information in Braille.
   Anon.

5 One reason I don't drink is that I want to
   know when I'm having a good time.
   Nancy Astor

6 Actually, it only takes one drink to get me
   loaded. Trouble is, I can't remember if
   it's the thirteenth or fourteenth.
   George Burns

7 By all means, let's breath-test pedes-
   trians involved in road accidents – if
   they're still breathing.
   The Bishop of Ely, *Observer*, 1967

8 A woman drove me to drink and I never
   even had the courtesy to thank her.
   W. C. Fields (Attrib.)

9 Either you're drunk or your braces are
   lopsided.
   W. C. Fields (Attrib.)

10 I always keep a stimulant handy in case I
   see a snake – which I also keep handy.
   W. C. Fields (Attrib.)

11 What contemptible scoundrel stole the
   cork from my lunch?
   W. C. Fields (Attrib.)

12 I don't drink. I don't like it. It makes me
   feel good.
   Oscar Levant

13 A man is never drunk if he can lay on the
   floor without holding on.
   Joe E. Lewis

14 I always wake up at the crack of ice.
   Joe E. Lewis

15 I drink to forget I drink.
   Joe E. Lewis

16 There was a young fellow named Sydney
   Who drank till he ruined his kidney.
   It shriveled and shrank
   As he sat there and drank,
   But he had a good time at it, didn't he.
   Don Marquis

17 Candy
   Is dandy
   But liquor
   Is quicker.
   Ogden Nash, 'Reflections on Ice-
   breaking', *Hard Lines*, 1931

18 One more drink and I'll be under the
   host.
   Dorothy Parker, at a cocktail party (Attrib.)

19 Water taken in moderation cannot hurt
   anybody.
   Mark Twain, *Notebook*, 1935

20 I have made an important discovery . . .
   that alcohol, taken in sufficient quantities, produces all the effects of intoxi-
   cation.
   Oscar Wilde (Attrib.)

21 He died of cirrhosis of the liver. It costs
   money to die of cirrhosis of the liver.
   P. G. Wodehouse, 'Success Story', *Nothing
   Serious*, 1950

22 I must get out of these wet clothes and
   into a dry martini.
   Alexander Woollcott (Attrib.)

23 My dad was the town drunk. A lot of
   times that's not so bad – but New York
   City?
   Henny Youngman, *Henny Youngman's
   Greatest One Liners*, 1970

See also Alcoholism; Champagne;
Hangovers; Prohibition; Restaurants;
Temperance; Thirst; Wine.

DRIVING

1 Driving in London's my pleasure
I prize it above any other,
One hand on the wheel
The fingers like steel
And the *A–Z* clenched
In the other.
   Pam Ayres, *'A–Z': Thoughts of a Late-night Knitter*, 1978

2 There are no liberals behind steering wheels.
   Russell Baker, *Poor Russell's Almanac*, 1972

3 KERMIT: Fozzie, where did you learn to drive?
   FOZZIE: I took a correspondence course.
   Jerry Juhl and Jack Burns, *The Muppet Movie*, screenplay, 1979

4 The rush-hour traffic I'd just as soon miss
When caraftercarismovinglikethis.
   Robert Lauher, *Reader's Digest*, 1964

5 . . . er, how fast were you going when Mr Adams jumped from the car? . . . Seventy-five? . . . And where was that? . . . In your driveway? . . . How far had Mr Adams gotten in the lesson? . . . Backing out?!
   Bob Newhart, 'The Driving Instructor', *The Button-down Mind of Bob Newhart*, record, 1960

6 I bought my wife a new car. She called me and said there was water in the carburetor. I said where's the car? She said in the lake.
   Henny Youngman

See also Cars; Parking.

DRUGS

1 Very little has been discovered by Weekend Update scientists to show that the smoking of marijuana is harmful in any way. White rabbits, forced to smoke eighty-seven joints a day, are encouraged not to operate heavy machinery or drive on the freeways.
   'Weekend Update', *Saturday Night Live*, NBC TV

2 Here's what another of my friends had to say, someone who used to put on earphones and get high every night, just to unwind: 'If I get high with other people, I become convinced that they think, and have always thought, that I'm pathetic. So I start saying things to prove I'm not pathetic, and then I think about the things I've just said and realize I'm much more pathetic than they even think I am.
   Marcelle Clements, 'Why the Sixties Generation Has Quit Smoking Pot', *Rolling Stone*, 1982

3 Says a former activist, 'Once marijuana was a sociopolitical and philosophical gesture. Now it just means spending hours in my room by myself looking for objects I keep misplacing.'
   Marcelle Clements, 'Why the Sixties Generation Has Quit Smoking Pot', *Rolling Stone*, 1982

4 A: It's far out, man. Like, have you ever tried it? You put your TONGUE in the HOLE, y'know, in the middle of this record. And you SPIN it, man.
   B: And what happens, man?
   A: Well, it HURTS, y'know – but the PAIN is outasight!
   Tony Hendra and Michael O'Donoghue, *National Lampoon's Radio Dinner*, record, 1972

5 If dope smoking doesn't damage your brain, how come so many teenyboppers think Cheech and Chong are funny?
   Tony Hendra and Michael O'Donoghue, *National Lampoon's Radio Dinner*, record, 1972

6 Avoid all needle drugs – the only dope worth shooting is Richard Nixon.
   Abbie Hoffman, *Steal This Book*, 1971

7 SON: Have you ever smoked opium?
   FATHER: Certainly not! Gives you constipation. Dreadful binding effect. Ever seen those pictures of the wretched poet Coleridge? Green around the gills. And a stranger to the lavatory. Avoid opium.
   John Mortimer, *A Voyage Round My Father*, screenplay, 1970

8 Drugs have taught an entire generation of American kids the metric system.
   P. J. O'Rourke, *Modern Manners*, 1983

9 Marijuana ... makes you sensitive. Courtesy has a great deal to do with being sensitive. Unfortunately marijuana makes you the kind of sensitive where you insist on everyone listening to the drum solo in Iron Butterfly's 'In-a-Gadda-Da-Vida' fifty or sixty times at 78 rpm, and that's quite rude.
R. J. O'Rourke, *Modern Manners*, 1983

10 Now they're calling taking drugs an epidemic – that's 'cos white folks are doing it.
Richard Pryor, *Richard Pryor Here and Now*, 1984

11 Pot is like a gang of Mexican bandits in your brain. They wait for thoughts to come down the road, then tie them up and trash them.
Kevin Rooney, quoted in *GQ*, 1984

12 Reality is just a crutch for people who can't cope with drugs.
Lily Tomlin

13 Cocaine is God's way of saying you're making too much money.
Robin Williams

14 ... conversation degenerates in an exponential relationship to the amount of mood-altering substances one has recently ingested. Cocaine, marijuana and ethyl alcohol fall into this category. Sex, or a lack thereof, and Hershey bars are also mood-altering substances, which may explain why it is so difficult to speak to teenagers.
Tracy Young, *Vanity Fair*, 1984

See also Drink; Smoking.

DUTY

1 When a stupid man is doing something he is ashamed of, he always declares that it is his duty.
George Bernard Shaw, *Caesar and Cleopatra*, 1898

2 ... duty is what one expects from others, it is not what one does oneself.
Oscar Wilde, *A Woman of No Importance*, 1893

3 ... my duty is a thing I never do, on principle.
Oscar Wilde, *An Ideal Husband*, 1895

See also Conscience; Ethics.

E

EARS

1 His ears make him look like a taxicab with both doors open.
Howard Hughes, on Clark Gable (Attrib.)

See also Faces; Noise; Silence.

EATING

1 *I* am an epicure; *you* are a gourmand; *he* has both feet in the trough.
Competition, *New Statesman*

2 *How to eat like a child.*
Spinach: divide into little piles. Re-arrange again into new piles. After five or six maneuvers, sit back and say you are full.
Chocolate-chip cookies: half-sit, half-lie on the bed, propped up by a pillow. Read a book. Place cookies next to you on the sheet so that crumbs get in the bed. As you eat the cookies, remove each choc-olate chip and place it on your stomach. When all the cookies are consumed, eat the chips one by one, allowing two per page.
Delia Ephron, *New York Times*, 1983

3 The best number for a dinner party is two – myself and a damn good head waiter.
Nubar Gulbenkian, quoted in the *Observer*, 1965

4 Dinner at the Huntercombes' pos-sessed 'only two dramatic features – the wine was a farce and the food a tragedy'.
Anthony Powell, *The Acceptance World*, 1955

5 Seeing is deceiving. It's eating that's believing.
James Thurber, *Further Fables for Our Time*, 1956

6 'Have you ever seen Spode eat as-paragus?'
'No.'
'Revolting. It alters one's whole conception of Man as Nature's last word.'
P. G. Wodehouse, *The Code of the Woosters*, 1938

See also Breakfast; Cookery; Dieting; Food; Fruit; Indigestion; Lunch; Picnics; Restaurants; Vegetables; Veg-etarianism.

ECOLOGY

1 Ecology became a household word. My husband became a nut on recycling. Un-til a few years ago he thought recycling was an extra setting on the washer that tore the buttons off his shirts and shred-ded his underwear. Now, he sits around making towel racks out of over-sexed coat hangers.
Erma Bombeck, *If Life is a Bowl of Cherries – What am I Doing in the Pits?*, 1978

See also Pollution.

ECONOMICS

1 If you're not confused, you're not paying attention.
Anon., *Wall Street Week*

2 There are three things not worth run-ning for – a bus, a woman or a new economic panacea; if you wait a bit another one will come along.
Derick Heathcoat-Amory, Chancellor of the Exchequer, 1958–1960

3 Price, *n.* value, plus a reasonable sum for the wear and tear of conscience in demanding it.
Ambrose Bierce, *The Devil's Dictionary*, 1911

4 Everybody is always in favour of general economy and particular expenditure.
Sir Anthony Eden

5 Blessed are the young, for they shall inherit the national debt.
Herbert Hoover

6 I learned more about economics from

one South Dakota dust storm than I did in all my years in college.
Hubert Humphrey

7 If all economists were laid end to end, they would not reach a conclusion.
George Bernard Shaw (Attrib.)

8 It is not possible for this nation to be at once politically internationalist and economically isolationist. This is just as insane as asking one Siamese twin to high dive while the other plays the piano.
Adlai Stevenson, speech in New Orleans, 1952

9 Nobody who has wealth to distribute ever omits himself.
Lev Davidorich Trotsky

10 It's a recession when your neighbor loses his job, it's a depression when you lose your own.
Harry S. Truman

11 The way to stop financial joy-riding is to arrest the chauffeur, not the automobile.
Woodrow Wilson

See also Budgets; Economy; Inflation; Money.

ECONOMY

1 Save Water, Shower with a Friend
Slogan on badge, 1970s

2 Saving is a very fine thing. Especially when your parents have done it for you.
Winston Churchill (Attrib.)

3 I would rather have my people laugh at my economies than weep for my extravagance.
King Oscar II, King of Sweden, 1872–1907

See also Budgets; Economics; Meanness; Thrift.

EDUCATION

1 My education was severely disrupted by the outbreak of World War II. It had actually taken place sixteen years previously, but I was still very upset about it.
Barry Cryer, at the Cambridge Union, quoted in *The Times*, 1984

2 Educational television should be absolutely forbidden. It can only lead to unreasonable expectations and eventual disappointment when your child discovers that the letters of the alphabet do not leap up out of books and dance around the room with royal-blue chickens.
Fran Lebowitz, *Social Studies*, 1981

3 Education! I was always led to suppose that no educated person ever spoke of notepaper, and yet I hear poor Fanny asking Sadie for notepaper. What is this education? Fanny talks about mirrors and mantelpieces, handbags and perfume, she takes sugar in her coffee, has a tassel on her umbrella, and I have no doubt that if she is ever fortunate enough to catch a husband she will call his father and mother Father and Mother. Will the wonderful education she is getting make up to the unhappy brute for all these endless pinpricks? Fancy hearing one's wife talk about notepaper – the irritation!
Nancy Mitford, *The Pursuit of Love*, 1945

4 ERIC: When it came to education, my father wanted me to have all the opportunities he never had.
ERNIE: So what did he do?
ERIC: He sent me to a girls' school.
Eric Morecambe and Ernie Wise, *The Morecambe and Wise Joke Book*, 1979

5 Education ... has produced a vast population able to read but unable to distinguish what is worth reading.
G. M. Trevelyan, *English Social History*, 1944

6 Education is an admirable thing, but it is well to remember from time to time that nothing that is worth knowing can be taught.
Oscar Wilde, 'The Critic as Artist', 1890

7 ... in England, at any rate, education produces no effect whatsoever. If it did, it would prove a serious danger to the upper classes, and would probably lead to acts of violence in Grosvenor Square.
Oscar Wilde, *The Importance of Being Earnest*, 1895

See also Examinations; School; Teachers; University.

EGGS

1 TOMMY HANDLEY: Hello, yolks – have you ever tried Itma eggs? They're all singing, all humming and all-bumen. The only eggs that are all they're cracked up to be. You'll find the maker's name stamped on the blunt end and countersigned by the rooster on the sharp end. With every dozen we give away a gas mask. Itma eggs can be whipped but they can't be beaten.
   Ted Kavanagh, *ITMA*, BBC Radio Home Service, 1939

See also Eating; Food.

EGOTISM

1 If egotism means a terrific interest in one's self, egotism is absolutely essential to efficient living.
   Arnold Bennett

2 Egotist, *n.* a person . . . more interested in himself than in me.
   Ambrose Bierce, *The Devil's Dictionary*, 1911

3 Egotism – usually just a case of mistaken nonentity.
   Barbara Stanwyck

See also Narcissism; Vanity.

DWIGHT D. EISENHOWER
President of the United States, 1953–1961

1 I doubt very much if a man whose main literary interests were in works by Mr Zane Grey, admirable as they may be, is particularly well equipped to be chief executive of this country, particularly where Indian affairs are concerned.
   Dean Acheson, US Secretary of State, 1953 (Attrib.)

2 I haven't checked these figures but eighty-seven years ago, I think it was, a number of individuals organized a governmental set-up here in this country, I believe it covered certain eastern areas, with this idea they were following up

based on a sort of national-independence arrangement and the program that every individual is just as good as every other individual . . .
   Oliver Jensen, 'The Gettysburg Address in Eisenhowerese', *New York Herald Tribune*, 1957

3 Eisenhower is the only living Unknown Soldier.
   Robert S. Kerr, Oklahoma Senator

4 If I talk over people's heads, Ike must talk under their feet.
   Adlai Stevenson, Democratic presidential candidate defeated by Eisenhower in 1952 and 1956

5 The General has dedicated himself so many times, he must feel like the cornerstone of a public building.
   Adlai Stevenson

See also The Presidency; Washington.

ELECTIONS

1 Be Thankful Only One Of Them Can Win
   Bumper sticker, Nixon/Kennedy presidential election, 1960

2 If Voting Changed Anything, They'd Make It Illegal
   Badge, London, 1983

3 Vote for the man who promises least; he'll be the least disappointing.
   Bernard M. Baruch, American businessman and presidential advisor

4 Have you ever seen a candidate talking to a rich person on television?
   Art Buchwald

5 People on whom I do not bother to dote
   Are people who do not bother to vote.
   Ogden Nash, 'Election Day is a Holiday', *Happy Days*, 1933

6 They have such refined and delicate palates
   That they can discover no one worthy of their ballots,
   And then when someone terrible gets elected

They say, There, that's just what I expected!
Ogden Nash, 'Election Day is a Holiday', *Happy Days*, 1933

See also Government; Houses of Parliament; Politics and Politicians.

ELECTRICITY

1 . . . what with having perforce to change a light bulb here and tune in a transistor radio there, I have picked up a pretty sound working knowledge of electrical matters. It is not comprehensive, God knows – I still can't fully understand why you can't boil an egg on an electric guitar . . .
Keith Waterhouse, *The Passing of the Third-floor Buck*, 1974

See also Technology.

EMBARRASSMENT

1 Man is the only animal that blushes. Or needs to.
Mark Twain, *Following the Equator*, 1897

2 There *is* a good deal to be said for blushing, if one can do it at the proper moment.
Oscar Wilde, *A Woman of No Importance*, 1893

ENEMIES

1 Love your enemy – it'll drive him nuts.
Anon.

2 He hasn't an enemy in the world – but all his friends hate him.
Eddie Cantor, *The Chase and Sanborn Hour*, NBC Radio, 1933

3 We have met the enemy, and he is us.
Walt Kelly, *Pogo* poster for Earth Day, 1971

4 Enemies to me are the *sauce piquante* to my dish of life.
Elsa Maxwell

See also Friends; War.

ENGAGEMENTS

1 She was just a passing fiancée.
Alfred McFote

See also Couples; Courting; Proposals; Weddings.

ENGLAND AND THE ENGLISH

1 The English instinctively admire any man who has no talent and is modest about it.
James Agee

2 The English may not like music but they absolutely love the noise it makes.
Sir Thomas Beecham, *A Mingled Chime*, 1944

3 So little, England. Little music. Little art. Timid. Tasteful. Nice.
Alan Bennett, *An Englishman Abroad*, BBC TV, 1983

4 His face was rosy from the cold bath, which was one of the reasons why Englishmen were stronger than anybody else, and he stronger than any other Englishman, and his whistle betokened his distinguished approval of the dealings of Providence.
E. F. Benson, *Paying Guests*, 1929

5 Think of what our nation stands for
Books from Boots and country lanes
Free speech, free passes, class distinction,
Democracy and proper drains.
John Betjeman, 'In Westminster Abbey', 1940

6 The Englishman fox-trots as he fox-hunts, with all his being, through thickets, through ditches, over hedges, through chiffons, through waiters, over saxophones, to the victorious finish: and who goes home depends on how many the ambulance will accommodate.
Nancy Boyd, (pseudonym of Edna St Vincent Millay)

7 The most dangerous thing in the world is to make a friend of an Englishman, because he'll come sleep in your closet rather than spend ten shillings on a hotel.
Truman Capote, 1966

8 When I warned them [the French Government] that Britain would fight on

alone whatever they did, their Generals told their PM and his divided Cabinet: 'In three weeks England will have her neck wrung like a chicken.' Some chicken! Some neck!
Winston Churchill, speech, Canadian Parliament, 1941

9 Mad dogs and Englishmen
Go out in the midday sun,
The Japanese don't care to.
The Chinese wouldn't dare to,
Hindoos and Argentines sleep firmly
    from twelve to one.
But Englishmen detest a siesta.
Noël Coward, 'Mad Dogs and Englishmen', *Words and Music*, 1932

10 In England, failure is all the rage.
Quentin Crisp, *The Naked Civil Servant*, 1968

11 The English think incompetence is the same thing as sincerity.
Quentin Crisp, quoted in the *New York Times*, 1977

12 Q: dwo
Q: dwo
we know of anything which can
be as dull as one englishman
A: to
e. e. cummings, *Complete Poems*, 1968

13 It is said, I believe, that to behold the Englishman at his *best* one should watch him play tip-and-run.
Ronald Firbank, *The Flower Beneath the Foot*, 1923

14 The English find ill-health not only interesting but respectable and often experience death in the effort to avoid a fuss.
Pamela Frankau, *Pen to Paper*, 1961

15 But after all, what would the English be without their sweet unreasonableness?
John Galsworthy, 'The Roof', 1929

16 Contrary to popular belief, English women do not wear tweed nightgowns.
Hermione Gingold, *Saturday Review*, 1955

17 The climate of England has been the world's most powerful colonizing impulse.
Russell Green

18 An Englishman is a man who lives on an island in the North Sea governed by Scotsmen.
Philip Guedalla, *Supers and Supermen*, 1920

19 From time immemorial, the English, saddled with a climate that produced nothing tastier than mangel-wurzels and suet, have been forced to import anything that would stay down for more than ten seconds.
Tony Hendra, 'EEC! It's the US of E!', *National Lampoon*, 1976

20 If it is good to have one foot in England, it is still better, or at least as good, to have the other out of it.
Henry James (Attrib.)

21 The Englishman's way of speaking
    absolutely classifies him,
The moment he talks he makes some
    other Englishman despise him.
Alan Jay Lerner and Frederick Loewe, 'Why Can't the English?' song from *My Fair Lady*, 1956

22 If you want to eat well in England, eat three breakfasts.
W. Somerset Maugham

23 It is good to be on your guard against an Englishman who speaks French perfectly; he is very likely to be a cardsharper or an attaché in the diplomatic service.
W. Somerset Maugham, *The Summing Up*, 1938

24 An Englishman, even if he is alone, forms an orderly queue of one.
George Mikes, *How to be an Alien*, 1946

25 Let us pause to consider the English,
Who when they pause to consider
    themselves they get all reticently
    thrilled and tinglish,
Because every Englishman is convinced
    of one thing, viz.:
That to be an Englishman is to belong
    to the most exclusive club there is.
Ogden Nash, 'England Expects', *I'm a Stranger Here Myself*, 1938

26 *Racial characteristics*: cold-blooded queers with nasty complexions and terrible teeth who once conquered half the

world but still haven't figured out central heating. They warm their beers and chill their baths and boil all their food, including bread.

P. J. O'Rourke, 'Foreigners Around the World', *National Lampoon*, 1976

27 England is the most class-ridden country under the sun. It is a land of snobbery and privilege, ruled largely by the old and silly.

George Orwell, *The Lion and the Unicorn*, 1941

28 Deploring change is the unchangeable habit of all Englishmen.

Raymond Postgate

29 The sheer inertia of Englishmen for whom the past was always sacred and inviolable and who prided themselves on their obstinacy. 'We didn't win the war,' thought Sir Godber, 'we just refused to lose it.'

Tom Sharpe, *Porterhouse Blue*, 1974

30 An Englishman thinks he is moral when he is only uncomfortable.

George Bernard Shaw, *Man and Superman*, 1903

31 Go anywhere in England where there are natural, wholesome, contented, and really nice English people; and what do you always find? That the stables are the real centre of the household . . .

George Bernard Shaw, *Heartbreak House*, 1919

32 If you eliminate smoking and gambling, you will be amazed to find that almost all an Englishman's pleasures can be, and mostly are, shared by his dog.

George Bernard Shaw (Attrib.)

33 English cuisine is generally so threadbare that for years there has been a gentlemen's agreement in the civilized world to allow the Brits pre-eminence in the matter of tea – which, after all, comes down to little more than the ability to boil water.

Wilfrid Sheed, 'Taking Pride in Prejudice', *GQ*, 1984

34 In England we have come to rely on a comfortable time-lag of fifty years or a century intervening between the perception that something ought to be done and a serious attempt to do it.

H. G. Wells, *The Work, Wealth and Happiness of Mankind*, 1931

35 . . . a typical Englishman, always dull and usually violent.

Oscar Wilde, *An Ideal Husband*, 1895

36 I don't desire to change anything in England except the weather.

Oscar Wilde, *The Picture of Dorian Gray*, 1891

37 I did a picture in England one winter and it was so cold I almost got married.

Shelley Winters

38 The English have an extraordinary ability for flying into a great calm.

Alexander Woollcott

See also Britain and the British; The English Language; London.

ENGLISH LANGUAGE

1 A spelling reformer indicted
For fudge was before the court cicted.
The judge said: 'Enough –
His candle we'll snough,
And his sepulcher shall not be whicted.

Anon., quoted in *The Devil's Dictionary* by Ambrose Bierce, 1911

2 When the American people get through with the English language, it will look as if it had been run over by a musical comedy.

Finley Peter Dunne, *Mr Dooley at His Best*, 1938

See also Grammar; Idioms; Language; Pronunciation; Speakers and Speeches; Words; Writers; Writing.

ENTRANCES AND EXITS

1 Lord Ronald said nothing; he flung himself from the room, flung himself upon his horse and rode madly off in all directions.

Stephen Leacock, 'Gertrude the Governess', *Nonsense Novels*, 1914

2 The whistle shrilled, and in a moment I was chugging out of Grand Central's

dreaming spires . . . I had chugged only a few feet when I realized that I had left without the train, so I had to run back and wait for it to start.
S. J. Perelman, *Strictly from Hunger*, 1937

3 I have nothing to declare except my genius.
Oscar Wilde, arriving at Customs in New York, 1882 (Attrib.)

4 And, closing the door with the delicate caution of one brushing flies off a sleeping Venus, he passed out of my life.
P. G. Wodehouse, *Very Good, Jeeves*, 1930

5 In this matter of shimmering into rooms the chappie is rummy to a degree.
P. G. Wodehouse, 'My Man Jeeves', 1919

6 There came from without the hoof-beats of a galloping relative, and Aunt Dahlia whizzed in.
P. G. Wodehouse, *The Code of the Woosters*, 1938

7 There was a flash of blonde hair and a whiff of Chanel No. 5 and a girl came sailing in, a girl whom I was able to classify at a single glance as a pipterino of the first water.
P. G. Wodehouse, *Jeeves and the Feudal Spirit*, 1954

EPIGRAMS

1 Epigram and truth are rarely commensurate. Truth has to be somewhat chiselled, as it were, before it will fit into an epigram.
Joseph Farrell, *Lectures of a Certain Professor*

2 An epigram is only a wisecrack that's played Carnegie Hall.
Oscar Levant

See also Proverbs; Quotations; Sayings; Wit.

EPITAPHS

1 ERNIE: What would you like them to put on your tombstone?
ERIC: Something short and simple.
ERNIE: What?
ERIC: 'Back in Five Minutes.'
Eddie Braben, *The Best of Morecambe and Wise*, 1974

2 I Would Rather Be Living in Philadelphia
W. C. Fields, suggested epitaph for himself, *Vanity Fair*, 1925

3 Excuse My Dust
Dorothy Parker, suggested epitaph for herself, *Vanity Fair*, 1925

See also Death.

EQUALITY

1 His Lordship may compel us to be equal upstairs, but there will never be equality in the servants' hall.
J. M. Barrie, *The Admirable Crichton*, 1902

2 Now that's the kind of King for me –
He wished all men as rich as he,
So to the top of every tree
Promoted everybody!
Lord Chancellors were cheap as sprats,
And Bishops in their shovel hats
Were plentiful as tabby cats –
In point of fact, too many.
Ambassadors cropped up like hay,
Prime Ministers and such as they
Grew like asparagus in May,
And Dukes were three a penny.
W. S. Gilbert and Arthur Sullivan, *The Gondoliers*, 1889

3 Inequality is as dear to the American heart as liberty itself.
W. D. Howells, *Impressions and Experiences*

4 That all men are equal is a proposition to which, in ordinary times, no sane individual has ever given his assent.
Aldous Huxley, *Proper Studies*, 1927

5 All men are born equal, but quite a few eventually get over it.
Lord Mancroft, *Observer*, 1967

6 ONE BUSINESSMAN (*to another*): Treat people as equals and the first thing you know they believe they are.
James Mulligan, cartoon in the *New Yorker*, 1982

7 All animals are equal, but some animals are more equal than others.
George Orwell, *Animal Farm*, 1946

8 Democracy demands that all of its

citizens begin the race even. Egalitarianism insists that they all *finish* even.
Roger Price, *The Great Roob Revolution*, 1970

9 Idiots are always in favour of inequality of income (their only chance of eminence), and the really great in favour of equality.
George Bernard Shaw, *The Intelligent Woman's Guide to Socialism and Capitalism*, 1928

See also Class; Communism; Democracy; Feminism; Marxism; Sexual Equality; Socialism.

ESPIONAGE

1 Variety is the life of spies.
Anon.

2 FIRST SPY: When you arrive you will meet a man in a black trench coat. He will ask you for the diamonds.
SECOND SPY: And I give him the diamonds?
FIRST SPY: No. Don't. He asks everyone for the diamonds. You will then meet a lovely redhead. Give her the diamonds.
SECOND SPY: Who is she?
FIRST SPY: That will be me.
SECOND SPY: Oh, you'll be in disguise.
FIRST SPY: No, I'm in disguise now.
Neil Simon, *Your Show of Shows*, NBC TV, 1950s

3 COLONEL HAVERSTRAP: Alright Horne – here's your equipment. These are your small arms, these are your puny hairy legs and this is your tiny bald head – you know how to use them I take it. Here's a plastic Japanese junior spy kit, comprising a small plastic dagger, the egg in bag trick, a revolving bow tie, nail through finger trick, an exploding banjo – and this . . .
HORNE: Good heavens – what is it?
COLONEL HAVERSTRAP: Ah well, the trade name is – Naughty Doggie – Fido Gets The Blame. Only use it if you're in a tight corner.
HORNE: How does it help me escape?
COLONEL HAVERSTRAP: While they're

beating the daylights out of the dog, you can slip out unnoticed.
Barry Took and Marty Feldman, *Round the Horne*, BBC Radio, 1965

See also The CIA.

THE ESTABLISHMENT

1 After a long life I have come to the conclusion that when all the Establishment is united it is always wrong.
Harold Macmillan

See also The Aristocracy; Government; Royalty; The Ruling Class; Society.

ETHICS

1 FRANKLIN: Have you ever thought, Headmaster, that your standards might perhaps be a little out of date?
HEADMASTER: Of course they're out of date. Standards always are out of date. That is what makes them standards.
Alan Bennett, *Forty Years On*, 1968

2 An ethical man is a Christian holding four aces.
Mark Twain (Attrib.)

3 Any preoccupation with ideas of what is right or wrong in conduct shows an arrested intellectual development.
Oscar Wilde, 'Phrases and Philosophies for the Use of the Young', 1894

See also Duty; Morality.

ETIQUETTE

1 Social tact is making your company feel at home, even though you wish they were.
Anon.

2 Though she lacked imagination, Brenda would go to any lengths rather than cause herself embarrassment. It was her upbringing. As a child she had been taught it was rude to say no unless she didn't mean it. If she was offered another piece of cake and she wanted it she was obliged to refuse out of politeness. And if she didn't want it she had to say yes, even if it choked her.
Beryl Bainbridge, *The Bottle Factory Outing*, 1974

3 No matter if your food is dry or it's oily,
   it's sure to look better when placed on a
   doily. Thank you!
   Ron Barrett, 'Politenessman', cartoon,
   National Lampoon, 1983

4 No matter what their religion or race,
   never sneeze in a person's face. Thank
   you!
   Ron Barrett, 'Politenessman', cartoon,
   National Lampoon, 1982

5 The man with the manners gals all adore,
   is the man who *never* spits on the floor.
   Thank you!
   Ron Barrett, 'Politenessman', *National
   Lampoon*, 1982

6 Tact consists in knowing how far to go
   too far.
   Jean Cocteau

7 No longer are her invitations sought and
      fought for eagerly,
   Her parties once so popular are now
      attended meagerly.
   A blunder unforgivable made life no
      longer livable,
   For she served the sparkling burgundy
      in glasses made for port.
   Newman Levey, 'The Glass of Fashion'

8 Dear Miss Manners,
   What am I supposed to say when I am
   introduced to a homosexual couple?
   Gentle Reader,
   'How do you do?' 'How do you do?'
   Judith Martin, *Miss Manners' Guide to
   Excruciatingly Correct Behaviour*, 1982

9 There was a brave girl of Connecticut
   Who flagged the express with her
      pecticut.
   Which her elders defined
   As presence of mind,
   But deplorable absence of ecticut.
   Ogden Nash, 'Benjamin', *The Primrose
   Path*, 1935

10 At the end of dinner it used to be that the
   men would retire to the billiard room and
   the women would go into the parlor. Men
   and women no longer separate after
   dinner, however. They now separate
   after twenty years of apparently happy
   marriage.
   P. J. O'Rourke, *Modern Manners*, 1983

11 . . . manners . . . have nothing to do with
   what you do, only how you do it. For
   example, Karl Marx was always polite in
   the British Museum. He was courteous
   to the staff, never read with his hat on,
   and didn't make lip-farts when he came
   across passages in Hegel with which he
   disagreed. Despite the fact that his political exhortations have caused the deaths
   of millions, he is today more revered
   than not. On the other hand, John W.
   Hinckley, Jr was rude only once, to a
   retired Hollywood movie actor, and
   Hinckley will be in a mental institution
   for the rest of his life.
   P. J. O'Rourke, *Modern Manners*, 1983

12 When the Chinese Ambassador's wife
      unfurls
   After three drinks of anisette,
   Don't ask if it's true about Chinese girls,
   It ain't etiquette.
   Cole Porter, 'It Ain't Etiquette', song from
   Du Barry was a Lady, 1939

13 Gentlemen do not throw wine at ladies.
   They pour it over them.
   Auberon Waugh, *Spectator*, 1983

14 Manners are especially the need of the
   plain. The pretty can get away with anything.
   Evelyn Waugh, quoted in the *Observer*,
   1962

15 'I suppose it would be a breach of hos-
   pitality if I socked my hostess's sister in
   the eye?'
      'The County would purse its lips.'
   P. G. Wodehouse, *Spring Fever*, 1948

See also Class; Conformity.

EUROPE AND THE EEC

1 The last time Britain went into Europe
   with any degree of success was on 6 June
   1944.
   Daily Express, 1980

2 Protestant fears have been aroused by
   the theory that this is a treaty *with* Rome,
   but this is not so.
   R. A. Butler, British Foreign Secretary,
   1963

3 What Caesar couldn't do, what Charle-

magne couldn't do, what Innocent III and Hitler couldn't do, it looks like the dough-faced burgher wimps of Brussels might finally be able to pull off – the unification of that portion of the earth's surface known . . . as Europe. What it took a country ten times its size less than a hundred years to accomplish, armed with only machine guns and a few trillion dollars, it has taken the squabbling, babbling tribes of Europe almost three millennia of wars, migrations, crusades, plague, pillage, partition, diets, dumas, duels, vendettas, incursions, invasions, intrusions, regicides, switching sides and genocide to accomplish.

Tony Hendra, 'EEC! It's the US of E!', *National Lampoon*, 1976

4 I do not find Northern Europe an ideal zone for human habitation. It is a fine place for industrial productivity, but its climate breeds puritans and the terrible dictates of the Protestant Work Ethic. The Romans were right to pull out when they did.

Kenneth Tynan, *The Sound of Two Hands Clapping*, 1975

5 I do not see the EEC as a great love affair. It is more like nine middle-aged couples with failing marriages meeting at a Brussels hotel for a group grope.

Kenneth Tynan, 1975

6 European Community institutions have produced European beets, butter, cheese, wine, veal and even pigs. But they have not produced Europeans.

Louise Weiss, MEP, *Observer*, 1980

7 Gloria, gloria, Europhoria!
Common faith and common goal!
Meat and milk and wine and butter
Make a smashing casserole!
Let the end of all our striving
Be the peace that love promotes,
With our hands in perfect friendship
Firmly round each other's throats!

Roger Woddis, *Spectator*, 1984

See also Foreigners; France and the French; Government; Travel; Xenophobia.

EVIL

1 Between two evils, I always pick the one I never tried before.

Mae West, *Klondike Annie*, screenplay, 1936

2 Wickedness is a myth invented by good people to account for the curious attractiveness of others.

Oscar Wilde, 'Phrases and Philosophies for the Use of the Young', 1894

See also Sin; Vice

EXAMINATIONS

1 Yes, I could have been a judge but I never had the Latin, never had the Latin for the judging, I just never had sufficient of it to get through the rigorous judging exams. They're noted for their rigour. People come staggering out saying, 'My God, what a rigorous exam.' And so I became a miner instead. A coal miner. I managed to get through the mining exams – they're not very rigorous, they only ask you one question, they say 'Who are you?' and I got seventy-five per cent on that.

Peter Cook, 'Sitting on a Bench', nightclub act, 1960s

See also Education; School; Teachers; University.

EXCESS

1 I have not been afraid of excess: excess on occasion is exhilarating. It prevents moderation from acquiring the deadening effect of a habit.

W. Somerset Maugham, *The Summing Up*, 1938

2 Drink and dance and laugh and lie,
Love, the reeling midnight through,
For tomorrow we may die!
(But, alas, we never do.)

Dorothy Parker, 'The Flaw in Paganism', *Death and Taxes*, 1931

3 I hate to advocate drugs, alcohol, violence, or insanity to anyone, but they've always worked for me.

Hunter S. Thompson

4 Moderation is a fatal thing. Nothing
succeeds like excess.
   Oscar Wilde, *A Woman of No Importance*,
   1893

See also Extravagance.

EXCUSES

1 ... several excuses are always less convincing than one.
   Aldous Huxley, *Point Counter Point*, 1928

2 ... I am prevented from coming in consequence of a subsequent engagement. I
think that would be a rather nice excuse:
it would have all the surprise of candour.
   Oscar Wilde, *The Picture of Dorian Gray*,
   1891

See also Guilt.

EXERCISE

1 I like long walks, especially when they are
taken by people who annoy me.
   Fred Allen

2 The only reason I would take up jogging
is so that I could hear heavy breathing
again.
   Erma Bombeck

3 MR UNIVERSE: Don't forget, Mr Carson,
your body is the only home you'll ever
have.
   CARSON: Yes, my home *is* pretty messy.
   But I have a woman who comes in once a
   week.
   Johnny Carson, *The Tonight Show*, NBC
   TV

4 Contrary to popular cable TV-induced
opinion, aerobics have absolutely nothing to do with squeezing our body into
hideous shiny Spandex, grinning like a
deranged orangutan, and doing cret-
inous dance steps to debauched disco
music.
   Cynthia Heimel, *Sex Tips for Girls*, 1983

5 Try This Exercise – It'll Make You Feel
Great.
   From a seated position, get up and walk
   to the bar. Mix one jigger of dry ver-
   mouth with seven jiggers of gin. Pour
   over three quarters of a cup of cracked

ice and stir well. Strain and pour into a
glass. Twist one lemon peel over the top.
Sit down and drink.
Repeat.
Build your stamina slowly and soon you'll
be able to do ten or twelve of these!
   P. J. O'Rourke, *National Lampoon*, 1979

See also Body; Diets; Sport.

EXPEDITIONS

1 The equipment for this camp had to be
carried from the railhead at Chaikhosi, a
distance of 500 miles. Five porters would
be needed for this. Two porters would be
needed to carry the food for these five,
and another would carry the food for
these two. His food would be carried by a
boy. The boy would carry his own food.
The first supporting party would be
established at 38,000 feet, also with a
fortnight's supplies which necessitated
another eight porters and a boy. In all, to
transport tents and equipment, food,
radio, scientific and photographic gear,
personal effects, and so on, 3,000 porters
and 375 boys would be required.
   W. E. Bowman, *The Ascent of Rum Doodle*,
   1956

EXPENSES

1 In Brighton she was Brenda,
She was Patsy up in Perth,
In Cambridge she was Candida
The sweetest girl on earth.
In Stafford she was Stella,
The pick of all the bunch,
But down on his expenses,
She was *Petrol, Oil and Lunch*.
   Anon.

See also Credit Cards; Money.

EXTRAVAGANCE

1 It seems he wholly lacked a sense
Of limiting the day's expense,
And money ran between his hands
Like water through the Ocean Sands.
Such conduct could not but affect
His parent's fortune, which was
   wrecked
Like many and many another one

By folly in a spendthrift son:
By that most tragical mischance,
An Only Child's Extravagance.
  Hilaire Belloc, 'Peter Goole', *More Cautionary Tales*, 1930

See also Credit; Debt; Expenses; Money.

EYES

1 A: Have your eyes ever been checked?
   B: No, Doctor, they've always been blue.
     Anon.

2 His eyes are so bad, he has to wear contact lenses to see his glasses.
     Anon.

3 Met a guy this morning with a glass eye. He didn't tell me – it just came out in the conversation.
     Jerry Dennis

4 He had but one eye and the popular prejudice runs in favour of two.
     Charles Dickens, *Nicholas Nickleby*, 1839

See also Faces; Spectacles.

FACES

1 ... a face like a wedding cake left out in the rain.
  Anon., of W. H. Auden

2 A: Her face looks like a million.
  B: Yes, all green and wrinkled.
  Anon.

3 Nature played a cruel trick upon her by giving her a waxed moustache.
  Alan Bennett, *Forty Years On*, 1968

4 I have a face that is a cross between two pounds of halibut and an explosion in an old-clothes closet. If it isn't mobile, it's dead.
  David Niven

5 ... one of those characteristic British faces that, once seen, are never remembered.
  Oscar Wilde (Attrib.)

See also Appearance; Beauty; Cosmetics; Hair; Looks.

FACTS

1 The trouble with facts is that there are so many of them.
  Samuel McChord Crothers, *The Gentle Reader*

2 Facts are ventriloquists' dummies. Sitting on a wise man's knee they may be made to utter words of wisdom; elsewhere, they say nothing, or talk nonsense, or indulge in sheer diabolism.
  Aldous Huxley, *Time Must Have a Stop*, 1944

3 Oh, don't tell me of facts – I never believe facts; you know Canning said nothing was so fallacious as facts, except figures.
  Sydney Smith

4 It is the spirit of the age to believe that any fact, no matter how suspect, is su-

perior to any imaginative exercise, no matter how true.
  Gore Vidal, *Encounter*, 1967

See also Knowledge; Truth.

FAILURE

1 There is much to be said for failure. It is more interesting than success.
  Max Beerbohm, *Mainly on the Air*, 1947

2 ... I've always been after the trappings of great luxury you see, I really, really have. But all I've got hold of are the trappings of great poverty. I've got hold of the wrong load of trappings, and a rotten load of trappings they are too, ones I could have very well done without.
  Peter Cook, 'Sitting on a Bench', nightclub act, 1960s

3 That poor man. He's completely unspoiled by failure.
  Noël Coward, of a fellow playwright (Attrib.)

4 There is the greatest practical benefit in making a few failures early in life.
  T. H. Huxley, *On Medical Education*, 1870

5 Failure has gone to his head.
  Wilson Mizner, of a still-buoyant bankrupt (Attrib.)

6 If I were not a gloriously successful person, in England they would have dismissed me as an Irishman and in America as a Socialist.
  George Bernard Shaw (Attrib.)

7 We women adore failures. They lean on us.
  Oscar Wilde, *A Woman of No Importance*, 1893

See also Success.

FAITH

1 If there was no faith there would be no

living in this world. We couldn't even eat hash with any safety.
Josh Billings, *The Complete Works of Josh Billings*, 1919

2 Faith, to my mind, is a stiffening process, a sort of mental starch, which ought to be applied as sparingly as possible.
E. M. Forster, *Two Cheers for Democracy*, 1951

3 Faith is much better than belief. Belief is when someone *else* does the thinking.
R. Buckminster Fuller

4 i once heard the survivors
of a colony of ants
that had been partially
obliterated by a cow s foot
seriously debating
the intention of the gods
towards their civilization
Don Marquis, 'certain maxims of archy', *archy and mehitabel*, 1927

5 Faith may be defined briefly as an illogical belief in the occurrence of the improbable.
H. L. Mencken, *Prejudices*, Third Series, 1922

6 I respect faith, but doubt is what gets you an education.
Wilson Mizner

7 We have not lost faith, but we have transferred it from God to the medical profession.
George Bernard Shaw (Attrib.)

8 Scepticism is the beginning of Faith.
Oscar Wilde, *The Picture of Dorian Gray*, 1891

See also Atheism; Belief; God; Heaven; Religion; Trust.

THE FALKLANDS

1 From Michael Foot's statements, one would draw the conclusion that Labour is in favour of warmongering, provided there is no war.
Labour Herald, 1982

2 Sir: Your coverage of the Falklands episode has cleared up one small point: whether you run a fairly responsible journal of the libertarian Right or a fairly entertaining magazine. You run a fairly entertaining magazine. However, there are so few of these about nowadays that I am probably justified in keeping up my subscription, though I suppose it is a bit frivolous of me.
Kingsley Amis, letter to the *Spectator*, 28 August 1982

3 Sir: Kingsley Amis's letter about your coverage of the Falklands episode has cleared up one small point: whether he is a fairly serious commentator on current events or a fairly entertaining writer of light fiction with strong political prejudices. He is a fairly entertaining writer of light fiction with strong political prejudices. However, there are so few of these about nowadays that we are probably justified in continuing to read him, though he is less entertaining and more prejudiced than he used to be.
Arthur Freeman, letter to the *Spectator*, 4 September 1982

4 The Falklands Incident was a quarrel between two bald men over a comb.
Jorge Luis Borges, 1983

5 This has been a pimple on the ass of progress festering for 200 years, and I guess someone decided to lance it.
Alexander Haig, US Secretary of State, quoted in *The Sunday Times*, 1982

6 The conflict over the Falklands is a moment dislodged from its natural home in the late nineteenth century.
Lance Morrow, *Observer*, 1982

7 Saturday 3 April
8 a.m. Britain is at war with Argentina!!! Radio Four has just announced it. I am overcome with excitement. Half of me thinks it is tragic and the other half of me thinks it is dead exciting.
10 a.m. Woke my father up to tell him Argentina has invaded the Falklands. He shot out of bed because he thought the Falklands lay off the coast of Scotland. When I pointed out that they were eight thousand miles away he got back into

bed and pulled the covers over his head.

Sue Townsend, *The Secret Diary of Adrian Mole Aged 13¾*, 1982

See also The Army; The Navy; Margaret Thatcher; War.

FAME

1 A celebrity is a person who works hard all his life to become well known, then wears dark glasses to avoid being recognized.
Fred Allen

2 It took me fifteen years to discover I had no talent for writing, but I couldn't give it up because by that time I was too famous.
Robert Benchley

3 Some are born great, some achieve greatness, and some hire public relations officers.
Daniel Boorstin, *The Image*, 1962

4 You're always a little disappointing in person because you can't be the edited essence of yourself.
Mel Brooks, interview in the *New York Post*, 1975

5 In the march up to the heights of fame there comes a spot close to the summit in which a man reads nothing but detective stories.
Heywood Broun

6 There is a lot to be said for not being known to the readers of the *Daily Mirror*.
Anthony Burgess, *Inside Mr Enderby*, 1966

7 Fame is being asked to sign your autograph on the back of a cigarette packet.
Billy Connolly

8 He's very, very well known. I'd say he's world-famous in Melbourne.
Dame Edna Everage (Barry Humphries), *Russell Harty Plus*, London Weekend Television, 1973

9 MAÎTRE D': Sorry old man. Because of the weak imagery, scanty plot and pedestrian language in your latest, we've turned your table over to Joyce Carol Oates.
William Hamilton, *William Hamilton's Anti-Social Register*, cartoon, 1974

10 Mere wealth, I am above it.
It is the reputation wide,
The playwright's pomp, the poet's pride
That eagerly I covet.
Phyllis McGinley, 'A Ballad of Anthologies', 1941

11 I'm never going to be famous. My name will never be writ large on the roster of Those Who Do Things. I don't do anything. Not one single thing. I used to bite my nails, but I don't even do that anymore.
Dorothy Parker, 'The Little Hours', *The Portable Dorothy Parker*, 1944

12 I was the toast of two continents: Greenland and Australia.
Dorothy Parker (Attrib.)

13 I'm famous. That's my job.
Jerry Rubin, *Growing (Up) at 37*, 1976

14 In the future, everyone will be famous for fifteen minutes.
Andy Warhol, 1960s

See also Celebrities; Reputation.

THE FAMILY

1 To my way of thinking, the American family started to decline when parents began to communicate with their children. When we began to 'rap', 'feed into one another', 'let things hang out' that mother didn't know about and would rather not.
Erma Bombeck, *If Life is a Bowl of Cherries – What am I Doing in the Pits?*, 1978

2 Where does the family start? It starts with a young man falling in love with a girl – no superior alternative has yet been found.
Winston Churchill (Attrib.)

3 The families of one's friends are always a disappointment.
Norman Douglas

4 A man's womenfolk, whatever their outward show of respect for his merit and authority, always regard him secretly as an ass, and with something akin to pity.
H. L. Mencken, *In Defense of Women*, 1922

5 A family is a unit composed not only of

children, but of men, women, an occasional animal, and the common cold.
Ogden Nash

6 One would be in less danger
From the wiles of the stranger
If one's own kin and kith
Were more fun to be with.
Ogden Nash, 'Family Court', *Hard Lines*, 1931

7 The Family! Home of all social evils, a charitable institution for indolent women, a prison workshop for the slaving breadwinner, and a hell for children.
August Strindberg, *The Son of a Servant*, 1886

8 Whether family life is physically harmful is still in dispute. The incidence of men who go down with a coronary upon learning that their teenage daughters are in the pudding club is indisputably higher among family men than among those who have never indulged; so is indigestion, backache, alcoholism, and going purple in the face when the bath is full of tights and knickers.
Keith Waterhouse, *The Passing of the Third-floor Buck*, 1974

See also Children; Fathers; Mothers; Parents; Relatives.

FARMS AND FARMING

1 He [Major Major's father] was a long-limbed farmer, a God-fearing, freedom-loving, law-abiding rugged individualist who held that federal aid to anyone but farmers was creeping socialism.
Joseph Heller, *Catch-22*, 1961

2 A farm is an irregular patch of nettles bounded by short-term notes, containing a fool and his wife who didn't know enough to stay in the city.
S. J. Perelman

3 A good farmer is nothing more nor less than a handy man with a sense of humus.
E. B. White, *One Man's Meat*, 1944

See also The Country.

FASHION

1 *I* have the New Look; *you* have let down

your hem; *she* has had that dress since 1934.
Competition, *New Statesman*

2 There'll be little change in men's pockets this year.
Anon., *Wall Street Journal*, 1948

3 Her hat is a creation that will never go out of style. It will look just as ridiculous year after year.
Fred Allen

4 By actual count, there are only six women in the country who looked well in a jumpsuit. Five of them were terminal and the other was sired by a Xerox machine.
Erma Bombeck, *If Life is a Bowl of Cherries – What am I Doing in the Pits?*, 1978

5 While clothes with pictures and/or writing on them are not entirely an invention of the modern age, they are an unpleasant indication of the general state of things . . . I mean, be realistic. If people don't want to listen to *you* what makes you think they want to hear from your sweater?
Fran Lebowitz, *Metropolitan Life*, 1978

6 Fashion is what one wears oneself. What is unfashionable is what other people wear.
Oscar Wilde, *An Ideal Husband*, 1895

See also Appearance; Beauty; Clothes; Looks; Style; Taste.

FASTIDIOUSNESS

1 *I* am fastidious; *you* are fussy; *he* is an old woman.
Competition, *New Statesman*

See also Cleanliness.

FATE

1 See how the Fates their gifts allot,
For A is happy – B is not.
Yet B is worthy, I dare say,
Of more prosperity than A!
W. S. Gilbert and Arthur Sullivan, *The Mikado*, 1885

2 Lots of folks confuse bad management with destiny.
Kin Hubbard

3 Unseen, in the background, Fate was
quietly slipping the lead into the boxing
glove.
P. G. Wodehouse, *Very Good, Jeeves*, 1930

FATHERS

1 Providing for one's family as a good husband and father is a watertight excuse for
making money hand over fist. Greed may
be a sin, exploitation of other people
might, on the face of it, look rather nasty,
but who can blame a man for 'doing the
best' for his children?
Eva Figes, *Nova*, 1973

2 To be a successful father there's one
absolute rule: when you have a kid, don't
look at it for the first two years.
Ernest Hemingway, quoted in *Papa
Hemingway*, 1966

3 The fundamental defect of fathers is that
they want their children to be a credit to
them.
Bertrand Russell, *New York Times*, 1963

4 Fathers should neither be seen nor
heard. That is the only proper basis for
family life.
Oscar Wilde, *An Ideal Husband*, 1895

5   'Jeeves, I wish I had a daughter. I
wonder what the procedure is?'
'Marriage is, I believe, considered the
preliminary step, sir.'
P. G. Wodehouse, *Carry on, Jeeves*, 1925

See also Children; The Family; Mothers;
Parents.

FEAR

1 He cowered before Aunt Dahlia like a
wet sock.
P. G. Wodehouse, *The Code of the Woosters*,
1938

2 The good old persp. was bedewing my
forehead by this time in a pretty lavish
manner. I don't know when I've been so
rattled.
'Do you find the room a trifle warm?'
'Oh no, no, rather not. Just right.'
P. G. Wodehouse, 'Jeeves in the Springtime', 1967

See also Anxiety; Courage; Cowardice.

FEMINISM

1 A woman who strives to be like a man
lacks ambition.
Graffito, New York, 1982

2 A woman's work is never done by men.
Graffito, London, 1980

3 Equality is a myth – women are better.
Graffito, London, 1980

4 If men could get pregnant, abortion
would be a sacrament.
Postcard produced by the Center for
Constitutional Rights

5 My father is liberated – he gave my
mother permission to vote Labour.
Graffito, London, 1980

6 Q: What happened when women stood
up for their rights?
A: They lost their seats on the bus.
The Big Book of Jokes and Riddles, 1978

7 While Manhattan's new Women's Bank
seems to be thriving, Congresswoman
Bella Abzug came out this week to quash
the rumor that the Bank's Night Deposi-
tory will be closed four to five days every
month. Mrs Abzug said that not only is
the rumor sexist, but is also a switch on
an old joke done many years ago by Jack
Carter.
'Weekend Update', *Saturday Night Live*,
NBC TV

8 These are very confusing times. For the
first time in history a woman is expected
to combine: intelligence with a sharp
hairdo, a raised consciousness with high
heels, and an open, non-sexist relationship with a tan guy who has a great
bod.
Lynda Barry, *Why are Women Crazy?*,
cartoon, *Esquire*, 1984

9 WIFE: Cooking! Cleaning! Why should
women do it?
HUSBAND: You're right – let's get an au
pair girl.
Mel Calman, *Couples*, cartoon, 1972

10 WOMAN (*in kitchen*): One man's meat is
another woman's Sunday gone.
Mel Calman, *Calman and Women*, cartoon,
1967

11 ... the major concrete achievement of the women's movement in the 1970s was the Dutch treat.
   Nora Ephron, *Heartburn*, 1983

12 We have lived through the era when happiness was a warm puppy, and the era when happiness was a dry martini, and now we have come to the era when happiness is 'knowing what your uterus looks like'.
   Nora Ephron, *Crazy Salad*, 1975

13 ... the women's movement hasn't changed *my* sex life at all. It wouldn't dare.
   Zsa Zsa Gabor, quoted in *Playboy*, 1979

14 Anyone can have the key to the executive washroom, but once a woman gets inside, what is there? A lavatory.
   Germaine Greer, quoted in *Time*, 1984

15 Is it too much to ask that women be spared the daily struggle for superhuman beauty in order to offer it to the caresses of a subhumanly ugly mate?
   Germaine Greer, *The Female Eunuch*, 1970

16 Emeralds! Aren't they divine? Jack gave them to me to shut up about Women's Lib.
   William Hamilton, *William Hamilton's Anti-Social Register*, cartoon, 1974

17 During the feminist revolution, the battle lines were again simple. It was easy to tell the enemy, he was the one with the penis. This is no longer strictly true. Some men are okay now. We're allowed to like them again. We still have to keep them in line, of course, but we no longer have to shoot them on sight.
   Cynthia Heimel, *Sex Tips for Girls*, 1983

18 Feminism is far, far from dead, but it is true that the movement has lost some of its zip. It was breezing along fine there for a while, with everyone all optimistic and fervent and charging around opening daycare centers, but things have undoubtedly slackened. Women seem scared and don't know where to look for guidance, since it seems as if all the leaders of the feminist movement have retreated into their individual lairs, emerging only at infrequent intervals to

snarl. Very upsetting, but we mustn't blame our erstwhile leaders. They're tired. They've been slogging away for years and are sick of being called strident bull-dykes. Who can blame them for being out of sorts?
   Cynthia Heimel, *Sex Tips for Girls*, 1983

19 Nobody can argue any longer about the rights of women. It's like arguing about earthquakes.
   Lillian Hellman (Attrib.)

20 *Feminist*: a woman, usually ill-favoured ... in whom the film-making instinct has displaced the maternal.
   Barry Humphries, glossary from *A Nice Night's Entertainment*, 1981

21 It is hard to fight an enemy who has outposts in your head.
   Sally Kempton, *Esquire*, 1970

22 *Ms:* the wise avoid this word entirely but (*a*) it may be used in public by harried members of the publishing world who find it necessary to abbreviate the word 'manuscript';
   (*b*) or by native residents of the south and south-western portions of United States as follows: 'I sho do ms that purty little gal.'
   Fran Lebowitz, *Metropolitan Life*, 1978

23 I'm furious about the Women's Liberationists. They keep getting up on soapboxes and proclaiming that women are brighter than men. That's true, but it should be kept very quiet or it ruins the whole racket.
   Anita Loos, *Observer*, 1973

24 No one is going to take Women's Liberation seriously until women recognize that they will not be thought of as equals in the secret privacy of men's most private mental parts until they eschew alimony.
   Norman Mailer (Attrib.)

25 Dear Miss Manners,
   As a businessman, how do I allow a businesswoman to pay for my lunch?

   Gentle Reader,
   With credit card or cash, as she prefers.
   Judith Martin, *Miss Manners' Guide to Excruciatingly Correct Behaviour*, 1983

26 Let it all hang out; let it seem bitchy, catty, dykey, frustrated, crazy, Solanesque, nutty, frigid, ridiculous, bitter, embarrassing, man-hating, libelous, pure, unfair, envious, intuitive, lowdown, stupid, petty, liberating; we are the women that men have warned us about.
   Robin Morgan, *Rat*, 1970

27 ... feminism is the result of a few ignorant and literal-minded women letting the cat out of the bag about which is the superior sex. Once women made it public that they could do things better than men, they were, of course, forced to do them. Now women have to be elected to political office, get jobs as officers of major corporations, and so on, instead of ruling the earth by batting their eyelashes the way they used to.
   P. J. O'Rourke, *Modern Manners*, 1983

28 How much fame, money, and power does a woman have to achieve on her own before you can punch her in the face?
   P. J. O'Rourke, *Modern Manners*, 1983

29 Men have always been expected to be helpful to women. The same is true now but the mode of helpfulness has changed with changing sex roles. One example will suffice. In the past a man was expected to give his seat on a bus to a woman. Today it would be much more courteous for that man to give her his job.
   P. J. O'Rourke, *Modern Manners*, 1983

30 ... there's still a place in the world for men. Women want to be a lot of things traditionally considered masculine: doctors, rock stars, body builders, presidents of the United States. But there are plenty of masculine things women have, so far, shown no desire to be: pipe smokers, first-rate spin-casters, wise old drunks, quiet. And there is one thing women can never take away from men. We die sooner.
   P. J. O'Rourke, *Modern Manners*, 1983

31 Boys don't make passes at female smartasses.
   Letty Cottin Pogrebin, *The First* Ms *Reader*, 1972

32 We're living in an age where you have to call a chick and ask her if she'll wear a dress tonight. And they say 'You're weird'.
   Tim Rose

33 ... during your innermost and private ... quest for THE TRUTH, libbywise, you might consider the following suggestion: namely, that it is naïve in the extreme for women to expect to be regarded as equals by men ... so long as they persist in a subhuman (I.E., animallike) behavior during sexual intercourse. I'm referring, as you doubtless know, to the outlandish PANTING, GASPING, MOANING, SOBBING, WRITHING, SCRATCHING, BITING, SCREAMING conniptions, and the seemingly invariable 'OH MY GOD ... OH MY GOD ... OH MY GOD' all so predictably integral to the pre-, post-, AND orgasmic stages of intercourse.
   Terry Southern, 'Letter to the Editor of *Ms*', *National Lampoon Encyclopaedia of Humor*, 1972

34 Some of us are becoming the men we wanted to marry.
   Gloria Steinham

35 Whatever women do, they must do twice as well as men to be thought half as good. Luckily, this is not difficult.
   Charlotte Whitton, former mayor of Ottawa

36 Sexual harassment at work – is it a problem for the self-employed?
   Victoria Wood, one-woman show, 1984

See also Equality; Sexual Equality; Women; Women – The Male View.

FIDELITY

1 While tearing off
   A game of golf
   I may make a play for the caddy.
   But when I do
   I don't follow through

'Cause my heart belongs to Daddy.
Cole Porter, 'My Heart Belongs to Daddy', song, 1938

See also Chastity; Infidelity; Marriage; Monogamy; Virtue.

THE FIFTIES

1 The fifties were ten years of foreplay.
Germaine Greer, *The Late Clive James*, Channel Four, 1984

FIGHTING

1 ERNIE: Did he put up a fight?
ERIC: You bet – we went at it hammer and tongs!
ERNIE: Hammer and tongs?
ERIC: Yes. I won in the end though. I had the hammer.
Eric Morecambe and Ernie Wise, *The Morecambe and Wise Joke Book*, 1979

See also Boxing; Self-defence; War.

FIGURES

1 Her husband is so bow-legged, she has to iron his underpants on a boomerang.
Anon.

2 How Dare You Presume I'd Rather Be Thin?
American Badge, 1980s

3 I had no intention of giving her my vital statistics. 'Let me put it this way,' I said. 'According to my girth, I should be a ninety-foot redwood.'
Erma Bombeck, *If Life is a Bowl of Cherries – What am I Doing in the Pits?*, 1978

4 Every so often I lose weight, and, to my utter horror and indignation, I find in the quiet of the night somebody has put it back on.
Lord Goodman, 1973

5 Is she fat? Her favorite food is seconds.
Joan Rivers, of Elizabeth Taylor, 1983

6 . . . she's so fat, she's my two best friends. She wears stretch kaftans. She's got more chins than the Chinese telephone directory.
Joan Rivers

7 Country butter and the easy life these curates lead had added a pound or two to an always impressive figure. To find the lean, finely trained Stinker of my nonage, I felt that one would have to catch him in Lent.
P. G. Wodehouse, *The Code of the Woosters*, 1938

8 The lunches of fifty-seven years had caused his chest to slip down to the mezzanine floor.
P. G. Wodehouse, *The Heart of a Goof*, 1926

9 The Right Hon. was a tubby little chap who looked as if he had been poured into his clothes and had forgotten to say 'When!'
P. G. Wodehouse, *Very Good, Jeeves*, 1930

See also The Body; Diets; Exercise; Height.

FILM

1 Imagine their delighted surprise when I read them the script of *Love and Death*, with its plot that went from war to political assassination, ending with the death of its hero caused by a cruel trick of God. Never having witnessed eight film executives go into cardiac arrest simultaneously, I was quite amused.
Woody Allen, *Esquire*, 1975

2 Making a funny film provides all the enjoyment of getting your leg caught in the blades of a threshing machine. As a matter of fact, it's not even that pleasurable; with the threshing machine the end comes much quicker.
Woody Allen, *Esquire*, 1975

3 Though they [United Artists executives] were agreed that death and atheism were indeed provocative subjects for farce, they said they would call the police if I didn't leave their office and never come back. Invoking the artistic-prerogative clause in my contract, a clause that gives me total control over what necktie I can wear while rewriting, I insisted that I go forward with the project.
Woody Allen, *Esquire*, 1975

4 An adult Western is where the hero still kisses his horse at the end, only now he worries about it.
Milton Berle, *Variety*, 1978

5 Makes *Jaws* look like a toothpaste com-
mercial.
Makes *King Kong* look like *Lassie Come Home*.
Makes *Towering Inferno* look like a
bonfire in a bungalow.
David Frost, horror film synopsis, 1978

6 It's the kissiest business in the world.
You *have* to keep kissing people.
Ava Gardner

7 It might be a fight like you see on the
screen;
A swain getting slain for the love of a
queen,
Some great Shakespearian scene
Where the Ghost and the Prince meet
And everyone ends in mincemeat.
Arthur Schwartz and Howard Dietz,
'That's Entertainment', song from *The Band Wagon*, 1953

8 Mickey Mouse, the veteran American
comic, is back in London. He is here to
launch the forthcoming series of his best
comedies, soon to be shown here by the
BBC.
Still wearing the big-buttoned
Bermuda shorts, round-topped shoes
and stitch-back gloves that made him
famous, he greeted me in the foyer at
Claridges with a sprightly grace that be-
lied his eighty-one years. A simple 'Hi
Pal!', a gentle wave of introduction to his
wife Minnie, seventy-nine, . . . and we
were sunk deep in the generous sofas,
sipping martinis and talking nostalgically
about the Good Old Days with Pluto,
Donald, Goofy and the Twins.
John Wells, *Masterpieces*, 1982

9 An actor entering through the door,
you've got nothing. But if he enters
through the window, you've got a
situation.
Billy Wilder

10 Shoot a few scenes out of focus. I want
you to win the foreign film award.
Billy Wilder, to a cameraman (Attrib.)

See also Acting; Actors and Actresses;
Film – Critics; Hollywood.

FILM – CRITICS

1 Me No Leica.
Anon., reviewing *I am a Camera*, 1955
(possibly apocryphal)

2 A mishmash: of Stalinism with New
Dealism with Hollywoodism with opportunism with shaky experimentalism with
mesmerism with onanism, all mosaicked
into a remarkable portrait of what the
makers of the film think the Soviet Union
is like – a great glad two-million-dollar
bowl of canned borscht, eminently
approvable by the Institute of Good
Housekeeping.
James Agee, reviewing *Mission to Moscow*,
1943

3 A variety show including everyone at
Paramount who was not overseas, in
hiding or out to lunch.
James Agee, reviewing *Star Spangled Rhythm*, 1942

4 I have nothing in the world against this
picture except that at least half of it
seemed to me enormously tiresome.
James Agee, reviewing *The Jolson Story*,
1946

5 I would like to recommend this film to
those who can stay interested in Ronald
Colman's amnesia for two hours and
who could with pleasure eat a bowl of
Yardley's shaving soap for breakfast.
James Agee, reviewing *Random Harvest*,
1942

6 Several tons of dynamite are set off in
this picture – none of it under the right
people.
James Agee, reviewing *Tycoon*, 1947

7 The money spent on this production
might easily have kept Mozart and
Schubert alive and busy to the age of
sixty, with enough left over to finance five
of the best movies ever made. It might
even have been invested in a good movie
musical.
James Agee, reviewing *This Time for Keeps*,
1947

8 . . . a pair of million dollar babies in a five
and ten cent flick.
Charles Champlin, reviewing *The Missouri Breaks* (starring Marlon Brando and Jack
Nicholson), *Los Angeles Times*, 1976

9 . . . so mediocre you can't get mad at it.
   Judith Crist, reviewing *Five Card Stud*,
   1968

10 This long but tiny film . . .
   Stanley Kauffmann, reviewing *Isadora*,
   1969

11 This film needs a certain something.
   Possibly burial.
   David Lardner, reviewing *Panama Hattie*,
   1942

See also Critics – The Artist's View; Film.

FISH AND FISHING

1 Oh, give me grace to catch a fish
   So big that even I
   When talking of it afterwards
   May have no need to lie.
   Anon., 'A Fisherman's Prayer'

2 ANDY: You don't know nothing about
   music. What is a scale?
   AMOS: A scale is a feather on a fish.
   ANDY: Fishes don't have feathers.
   AMOS: How about flying fishes?
   Amos 'n' Andy, 1929

3 A shark could never harm you. The
   shark is a benign creature of the sea. Of
   course, if you thrash about in the water or
   if you wear shiny bracelets, the shark will
   be attracted to you. On occasion, the
   shark has followed people out of the
   water and has gone to their blanket and
   eaten their beach ball.
       One time, the shark followed my
   brother Irving home on the Brighton
   local, and, upon being admitted to the
   apartment house, the shark entered his
   apartment – Apartment 4B – and ate his
   entire family and a brand new hat. Apart
   from that, the shark is a pussycat.
   Mel Brooks, TV interview with David
   Susskind, 1970

4 Oh, the slimy, squirmy, slithery eel!
   He swallows your hook with malignant
       zeal,
   He tangles your line and he gums your
       reel,
   The slimy, squirmy, slithery eel.
   Oh, the slimy, squirmy, slithery eel!
   He cannot be held in a grip of steel,

And when he is dead he is hard to peel,
The slimy, squirmy, slithery eel.
   Arthur Guiterman, 'Song of Hate for Eels'

5 the octopus s secret wish
   is not to be a formal fish
   he dreams that some time he may grow
   another set of legs or so
   and be a broadway music show
   Don Marquis, 'archy at the zoo', *archy and
   mehitabel*, 1927

6 All you need to be a fisherman is patience
   and a worm.
   Herb Shriner

7 The curious thing about fishing is you
   never want to go home. If you catch
   anything, you can't stop. If you don't
   catch anything, you hate to leave in case
   something might bite.
   Gladys Taber, *Ladies' Home Journal*, 1941

8 Oh, no doubt the cod is a splendid swimmer – admirable for swimming purposes
   but not for eating.
   Oscar Wilde (Attrib.)

See also Oysters; The Sea; Sport.

FLATTERY

1 Flattery must be pretty thick before anybody objects to it.
   William Feather, *The Business of Life*

2 You're the top!
   You're an Arrow collar.
   You're the top!
   You're a Coolidge dollar.
   You're the nimble tread of the feet of
       Fred Astaire.
   You're an O'Neill drama,
   You're Whistler's mama,
   You're Camembert.
   You're a rose,
   You're Inferno's Dante
   You're the nose
   On the great Durante.
   I'm just in the way, as the French would
       say 'De trop',
   But if, Baby, I'm the bottom
   You're the top.
   Cole Porter, 'You're the Top', song, 1934

3 What really flatters a man is that you think him worth flattering.
George Bernard Shaw, *John Bull's Other Island*, 1904

4 Baloney is flattery so thick it cannot be true; blarney is flattery so thin we like it.
Bishop Fulton J. Sheen

5 Flattery is like a cigarette – it's all right so long as you don't inhale.
Adlai Stevenson, speech, 1961

6 The only man who wasn't spoiled by being lionized was Daniel.
Sir H. Beerbohm Tree

See also Compliments; Praise.

FLIRTATION

1 Flirt: a woman who thinks it's every man for herself.
Anon.

2 STEVE GUTTENBERG: I'd give anything to see your thighs. I don't suppose you'd describe them for me?
KIM CATTRALL: Well, they're tan, of course. Very supple, well rounded and luxuriant to the touch.
Neal Israel, Pat Proft and Hugh Wilson, *Police Academy*, screenplay, 1984

3 George Moore unexpectedly pinched my behind. I felt rather honoured that my behind should have drawn the attention of the great master of English prose.
Ilka Chase

4 My heart is a bargain today. Will you take it?
W. C. Fields (Attrib.)

5 She plucked from my lapel the invisible strand of lint (the universal act of women to proclaim ownership).
O. Henry, 'Strictly Business', 1910

6 She's been on more laps than a napkin.
Walter Winchell

See also Couples; Courting; Love; Seduction; Sexual Attraction.

FLYING

1 Dr Rudolf Von Rudder explains how aircraft fly:
It's a simple theory. Matter is lighter than air. You see, the motors, they pull the plane forward and they cause a draft, and then it taxis faster down the field and the motors go faster and the whole plane vibrates, and then, when there's enough of a draft and a vacuum created, the plane rises off the runway into the air. From then on, it's a miracle. I don't know what keeps it up.
Mel Brooks, *Your Show of Shows*, NBC TV, 1950s

2 Beware of men on airplanes.
The minute a man reaches 30,000 feet, he immediately becomes consumed by distasteful sexual fantasies which involve doing uncomfortable things in those tiny toilets. These men should not be encouraged, their fantasies are sadly low-rent and unimaginative. Affect an aloof, cool demeanor as soon as any man tries to draw you out. Unless, of course, he's the pilot.
Cynthia Heimel, *Sex Tips for Girls*, 1983

3 Flying? I've been to almost as many places as my luggage!
Bob Hope

4 ERNIE: Hey, look at all those people down there – they look like ants.
ERIC: They *are* ants – we haven't taken off yet.
Eric Morecambe and Ernie Wise, *The Morecambe and Wise Joke Book*, 1979

5 Miss Piggy's Rules to Leave by
– *Tickets and travelling documents*: these should be kept in a handy place where you can check them several hundred times.
– *Travel arrangements*: whenever possible, avoid airlines which have anyone's first name in their titles, like Bob's International Airline or Air Fred.
– *Companions*: if you're travelling alone, beware of seatmates who by way of starting a conversation make remarks like, 'I just have to talk to someone – my teeth are spying on me' or 'Did you know that squirrels are the devil's oven mitts?'
Miss Piggy, *Miss Piggy's Guide to Life (As Told to Henry Beard)*, 1981

6 KENNETH HORNE: I relaxed in the luxury first-class compartment of the Super

Constellation Pan World Airways Swept Wing Sopwith Camel that was to take me to my rendezvous with fate. The hostess bent over me.

AIR HOSTESS: We're about to take off, sir. Would you like boiled sweets or cotton wool?

KENNETH HORNE: I won't have the boiled sweets. They just fall out of my ears. I'll just have some cotton wool.

AIR HOSTESS: Here you are, sir.

KENNETH HORNE: Thank you ... Delicious.

Barry Took and Marty Feldman, *Round the Horne*, BBC Radio, 1966

See also Flying – Fear of; Holidays; Travel.

FLYING – FEAR OF

1 ... I say to myself, 'Well, I'm strapping myself into the seat. Because if I *wasn't* strapped into this seat, there's a very good chance that I will fall *out* of this seat. If the plane came to a sudden stop. Like against a mountain.

Shelley Berman, airline routine, 1960s

2 I'll take three hours in the dentist's waiting room, with four cavities and an impacted wisdom tooth, in preference to fifteen minutes at any airport waiting for an aeroplane.

Patrick Campbell, *Daily Mail*, 1947

3 If God had intended us to fly, he would never have given us railways.

Michael Flanders (Attrib.)

4 Doc Daneeka hated to fly. He felt imprisoned in an airplane. In an airplane there was absolutely no place in the world to go except to another part of the airplane.

Joseph Heller, *Catch-22*, 1961

5 I never worry about the plane crashing. Remember – in the case of an accident, the pilot is always first on the scene.

Max Kauffmann

6 CAPTAIN: If we should have to ditch, you'll receive plenty of warning because our co-pilot becomes hysterical. And he'll start running up and down the aisles yelling 'We're going to crash!' or something like that ...

Bob Newhart, *The Grace L. Ferguson Air Line*, record

See also Fear; Flying; Travel.

FOLK MUSIC

1 A folksinger is someone who sings through his nose by ear.

Anon.

2 A folk song is a song that nobody ever wrote.

Anon.

3 For Wigan men are hearty
And Bolton men are bold,
There's something coy in a Blackpool boy
And the Bedford lads have hearts of gold,
But the chaps that live on Dartmoor
Are breezy bright and gay,
Singing Hey ha ha with a fa la la and a hey nonny no and whack folly o,
Ha ha ha ha ha ha ha ha ha ha ha ha HA HA HA HA!

Noël Coward, 'Devon', song, 1950s

4 I was involved in the Great Folk Music Scare back in the sixties. When it *almost* caught on. It was close for a time, but fortunately ...

Martin Mull, BBC TV, 1985

5 ... I've come up with a very tender and furtive madrigal, which has been passed down from father to son, until the handle dropped off. 'Tis an old Sussex courting song and tells the story of a young swain who stands beneath his loved one's bower – he's a very small swain, but then she's got a very low bower ... and he tells her of his love as follows:

Will you love me Mary-oh
When my grussets be bended low
When my orbs grow dim and my splod grows white
And my cordwangle makes an ugly sight
And my grussets be bended low-oh!
My grussets be bended low.

Barry Took and Marty Feldman, *Round the Horne*, BBC Radio, 1966

6 'Tis a hoary old folk song that I picked up from a home for hoary old folks. 'Tis a courting song or air which tells of the coming of Spring to Clapham Junction and 'tis about this young swain of they parts who every Spring feels the sap rising and gets a kind of March Madness which is common to the young men of they parts and is known as sausage fever. He wanders about the bosky haunts and verdant pasture-lands of Clapham High Street and as he hears the little hedge sparrow coughing and sees the young lambs hanging up in the butcher's shop, he feels a primeval urge. And he goes forth to seek his true love.
Barry Took and Marty Feldman, *Round the Horne*, BBC Radio, 1966

See also Music and Musicians; Songs and Singers.

FOOD

1 Tomato Ketchup.
If you do not shake the bottle
None'll come and then a lot'll.
Anon.

2 When Marilyn Monroe was married to Arthur Miller, his mother always made matzo ball soup. After the tenth time, Marilyn said, 'Gee Arthur, these matzo balls are pretty nice, but isn't there any other part of the matzo you can eat?'
Ann Barr and Paul Levy, *The Foodie Handbook*, 1984

3 INTERVIEWER: Sir, how do you survive in New York City? . . . What do you eat?
JUNGLE BOY: Pigeon.
INTERVIEWER: Don't the pigeons object?
JUNGLE BOY: Only for a minute.
Mel Brooks, *Your Show of Shows*, NBC TV, 1950

4 I have eaten octopus – or squid, I can never quite tell the difference – but never with wholehearted enjoyment on account of not caring for the taste of hot india rubber.
Noël Coward (Attrib.)

5 If there's an end
On which I'd spend

My last remaining cash,
It's sausage, friend,
It's sausage, friend,
It's sausage, friend, and mash.

. . . When Love is dead
Ambition fled,
And Pleasure, lad, and Pash,
You'll still enjoy
A sausage, boy,
A sausage, boy, and mash.
A. P. Herbert, 'Sausage and Mash'

6 Bread that must be sliced with an axe is bread that is too nourishing.
Fran Lebowitz, *Metropolitan Life*, 1978

7 Food is an important part of a balanced diet.
Fran Lebowitz, *Metropolitan Life*, 1978

8 I was standing at a bar the other day and there was a fellow there eating olives on a string. Eating olives on a string! I said, 'What are you eating them like that for?' He said, 'I may not like 'em.'
Max Miller, *The Max Miller Blue Book*, 1975

9 Parsley
Is gharsley.
Ogden Nash, 'Further Reflections on Parsley', *Good Intentions*, 1942

10 The pig, if I am not mistaken,
Supplies us sausage, ham, and bacon.
Let others say his heart is big –
I call it stupid of the pig.
Ogden Nash, 'The Pig', *Happy Days*, 1933

11 *Artichokes*. These things are just plain annoying . . . after all the trouble you go to, you get about as much actual 'food' out of eating an artichoke as you would from licking thirty or forty postage stamps. Have the shrimp cocktail instead.
Miss Piggy, *Miss Piggy's Guide to Life (As Told to Henry Beard)*, 1981

12 *Clams*. I simply cannot imagine why anyone would eat something slimy served in an ashtray.
Miss Piggy, *Miss Piggy's Guide to Life (As Told to Henry Beard)*, 1981

13 *Lobsters*. Although these are delicious, getting them out of their shells involves

giving them quite a brutal going-over. The way I look at it, they never did anything to me (although they are quite nasty-looking, and I do not like the way they stare at you from those fish tanks when you come into the restaurant – it is quite rude). On the other hand, if they serve you just the good parts already removed from the shell, that is quite a different matter, since the element of personal participation in the massacre is eliminated.

> **Miss Piggy**, *Miss Piggy's Guide to Life (As Told to Henry Beard)*, 1981

14 *Snails*. I find this a somewhat disturbing dish, but the sauce is divine. What I do is order escargots, and tell them to 'hold' the snails.

> **Miss Piggy**, *Miss Piggy's Guide to Life (As Told to Henry Beard)*, 1981

15 Madam, I have been looking for a person who disliked gravy all my life; let us swear eternal friendship.

> **Sydney Smith**, *Lady Holland's Memoir*, 1855

16 It is very poor consolation to be told that a man who has given one a bad dinner, or poor wine, is irreproachable in private life. Even the cardinal virtues cannot atone for half-cold entrées.

> **Oscar Wilde**, *The Picture of Dorian Gray*, 1891

See also Cheese; Cookery; Diets; Eating; Eggs; Fruit; Oysters; Picnics; Restaurants; Vegetables; Wine.

FOOTBALL – AMERICAN

1 Secant, cosine, tangent, sine
Logarithm, logarithm,
Hyperbolic sine
3 point 1 4 1 5 9
Slipstick, sliderule
TECH TECH TECH!

> **Anon.** cheer of the California Institute of Technology 'Beavers'

2 If the FBI went back far enough, I was always suspect: I never liked football.

> **Father Daniel Berrigan**, on his release from jail, 1972

3 Football is not a contact sport. It's a collision sport. Dancing is a good example of a contact sport.

> **Duffy Daugherty**, Michigan State University Coach, 1967

4 Pro football is like nuclear warfare. There are no winners, only survivors.

> **Frank Gifford**, quoted in *Sports Illustrated*, 1960

5 To see some of our best-educated boys spending the afternoon knocking each other down, while thousands cheer them on, hardly gives a picture of a peace-loving nation.

> **Lyndon Baines Johnson**, quoted in the *New York Times*, 1967

6 It is committee meetings, called huddles, separated by outbursts of violence.

> **George Will**, *Newsweek*, 1976

See also America and the Americans; Sport.

FOOTWEAR

1 And what about Gladiator boots. Remember them? They were the polished leather boots that hit just above the knee. You could look stylish in them or sit down. You couldn't do both.

> **Erma Bombeck**, *If Life is a Bowl of Cherries – What am I Doing in the Pits?*, 1978

2 There was a young lady of Twickenham
Whose shoes were too tight to walk
  quick in 'em.
She came back from a walk
Looking whiter than chalk
And took 'em both off and was sick in
  'em.

> **Oliver Herford**

3 Come, galoshers, be assertive,
Drop that air discreet and furtive!
Let galosh shops' stocks be lavish
With designs and hues that ravish –
Men's galoshes black and British, but
  for ladies colours skittish
(And galoshes could make rings
Round those silly plastic things
Which tie up with clumsy strings)
Let us all have this *rapprochement* with
  galoshes

And see what health and happiness it
   brings!
Paul Jennings, 'Galoshes', *Model Oddlies*

4 I am having a *rapprochement* with
   galoshes
   And some would say this heralds middle
   age;
   Yes, sneering they would say
   'Does he always wear *pince-nez*?
   Old jossers wore galoshes when ladies'
   hats were cloches,
   Ha! Woolen combinations are this
   dodderer's next stage!'
   Paul Jennings, 'Galoshes', *Model Oddlies*

See also Clothes; Legs.

GERALD FORD President of the United States, 1974–1977

1 A year ago Gerald Ford was unknown
   throughout America. Now he's unknown
   throughout the world.
   Anon., quoted in the *Guardian*, 1974

2 Richard Nixon impeached himself. He
   gave us Gerald Ford as his revenge.
   Bella Abzug

3 He looks like the guy in the science
   fiction movie who is the first to see 'The
   Creature'.
   David Frye

4 He's a very nice fellow, but that's not
   enough, gentlemen. So's my Uncle Fred.
   Hubert Humphrey (Attrib.)

5 Gerry Ford is a nice guy, but he played
   too much football with his helmet off.
   Lyndon Baines Johnson

6 Gerry Ford is so dumb that he can't fart
   and chew gum at the same time.
   Lyndon Baines Johnson (Attrib.)

7 If Ford can get away with this list of
   issues . . . and be elected on it, then I'm
   going to call the dictator of Uganda, Mr
   Amin, and tell him to start giving
   speeches on airport safety.
   Walter Mondale

8 It troubles me that he played center on
   the football team. That means he can
   only consider options for the twenty
   yards in either direction and that he has

spent a good deal of his life looking at the
world upside down through his legs.
   Martin Peretz, Editorial Director, *New
   Republic*

See also Richard Nixon; The Presidency;
The Vice-Presidency; Washington;
Watergate.

FOREIGNERS

1 Foreigners have a very roundabout and
   confused way of saying things. Here's
   how I cope. I am in a restaurant, and I
   want a piece of the delicious chocolate
   cake I see displayed on a shelf, 'Personality who bringulates les munchables,' I
   call, summoning the waiter. When he
   arrives, I give my order. 'If it does you
   please, transportez (trans-por-TAY) to
   moi's tablette one gigantical smithereeni
   de that chocolate cakefication avec as
   immense a velocité (vee-luss-ee-TAY)
   as possible.' And there you are!
   Miss Piggy, *Miss Piggy's Guide to Life (As
   Told to Henry Beard)*, 1981

See also Travel; Xenophobia.

FORGIVENESS

1 To err is human,
   To forgive takes restraint;
   To forget you forgave
   Is the mark of a saint.
   Suzanne Douglass, *Reader's Digest*, 1966

FRANCE AND THE FRENCH

1 *Pas de deux*: father of twins.
   Coup de grâce: lawnmower.
   Anon.

2 The French elections: the defeated
   Gaullists are accused of staying in
   Toulon and deserving Toulouse.
   Anon.

3 . . . xenophobia is a consequence, for the
   most part, of reading newspapers,
   although tourism is responsible to a great
   extent. Probably the worst xenophobes
   on earth are the French, a nation pro-
   tected by a cloud of garlic breath which
   still built the Maginot line to keep foreigners out. Chauvinism is a French

word which cannot even be translated, so Froggie is the emotion it describes.

The National Lampoon Encyclopaedia of Humor, 1973

4 We traveled in a big truck through the nation of France on our way to Belgium, and every time we passed through a little town, we'd see these signs – 'Boulange-rie', 'Patisserie', and 'Rue' this, and 'Rue' that, and rue the day you came here, young man. When we got to our hundred and eightieth French village, I screamed at the top of my lungs, 'The joke is over! English, PLEASE!' I couldn't believe that a whole country couldn't speak English. One third of a nation, all right, but not a whole country.

Mel Brooks, quoted by Kenneth Tynan in *Show People*, 1980

5 The simple thing is to consider the French as an erratic and brilliant people . . . who have all the gifts except that of running their country.

James Cameron, *News Chronicle*, 1954

6 Oh, how I love Humanity,
With love so pure and pringlish,
And how I hate the horrid French,
Who never will be English!

G. K. Chesterton, 'The World State', *Collected Poems*, 1933

7 France is the largest country in Europe, a great boon for drunks, who need room to fall . . .

Alan Coren, *The Sanity Inspector*, 1974

8 But there's always something fishy
    about the French!
Whether Prince or Politician
We've a sinister suspicion
That behind their *savoir-faire*
They share
A common contempt
For every mother's son of us.

Noël Coward, 'There's Always Something Fishy about the French', song from *Conversation Piece*, 1934

9 The French will only be united under the threat of danger. Nobody can simply bring together a country that has 265 kinds of cheese.

Charles de Gaulle, speech, 1951

10 It is unthinkable for a Frenchman to arrive at middle age without having syphilis and the Croix de la Légion d'honneur.

André Gide (Attrib.)

11 The French drink to get loosened up for an event, to celebrate an event, and even to recover from an event.

Geneviève Guérin, French Commission on Alcoholism, 1980

12 Bonjour.
Parlez-vous Franglais?
C'est un doddle.
Si vous êtes un fluent English-speaker, et si vous avez un 'O' Level français, Franglais est un morceau de gâteau.
Un 'O' Level de French est normale-ment inutile. Un nothing. Un wash-out. Les habitents de la France ne parlent pas 'O' Level French. Ils ne comprennent pas 'O' Level French. Un 'O' Level en français est un passeport à nowhere.

Miles Kington, *Let's Parler Franglais*, 1979

13 *Les crudités*: genitals.

Andy Kirby, competition, *New Statesman*, 1985

14 Paris is a great beauty. As such it possesses all the qualities that one finds in any other great beauty: chic, sexiness, grandeur, arrogance, and the absolute inability and refusal to listen to reason. So if you are going there you would do well to remember this: no matter how politely and distinctly you ask a Parisian a question, he will persist in answering you in French.

Fran Lebowitz, *Metropolitan Life*, 1978

15 *Fin de siècle*: tail light of a bicycle.

Russell Lucas, competition, *New Statesman*, 1985

16 When Frenchmen are talking, never lift the needle off the gramophone: it only goes back to the beginning.

Oliver Lyttleton

17 *Esprit de corps*: embalming fluid.

R. S. MacLeod, competition, *New Statesman*, 1985

18 There's something Vichy about the French.
   Ivor Novello (Attrib.), 1941

19 *Racial characteristics*: sawed-off cissies who eat snails and slugs and cheese that smells like people's feet ... Utter cowards who force their own children to drink wine, they gibber like baboons even when you try to speak to them in their own wimpy language.
   P. J. O'Rourke, 'Foreigners Around the World', *National Lampoon*, 1976

20 France is a place where the money falls apart in your hands but you can't tear the toilet paper.
   Billy Wilder

21 I have not always in my dealings with General de Gaulle found quotations from Trafalgar and Waterloo necessarily productive, and he has been very tactful about the Battle of Hastings.
   Harold Wilson, 1967

See also Charles de Gaulle; Europe and the EEC.

FRIENDS

1 Your friend is the man who knows all about you, and still likes you.
   Elbert Hubbard, *The Notebook*, 1927

2 A man of active and resilient mind out-wears his friendships just as certainly as he outwears his love affairs, his politics and his epistemology.
   H. L. Mencken, *Prejudices*, Third Series, 1922

3 A friend in need is a friend to be avoided.
   Lord Samuel

4 Whenever a friend succeeds, a little something in me dies.
   Gore Vidal, quoted in *The Sunday Times Magazine*, 1973

5 I have lost friends, some by death ... others by sheer inability to cross the street.
   Virginia Woolf, *The Waves*, 1931

See also Enemies; Love; Relationships.

FROGS

1 No animal will more repay
   A treatment kind and fair;
   At least so lonely people say
   Who keep a frog (and, by the way,
   They are extremely rare).
   Hilaire Belloc, 'The Frog', *The Bad Child's Book of Beasts*, 1896

See also Animals.

FRUIT

1 A: There's a lot of juice in this grapefruit.
   B: Yes – more than meets the eye!
   Anon.

2 Gripe: a ripe grape.
   Anon., 'Dizzy Daffinitions', *The Big Book of Jokes and Riddles*, 1978

See also Eating; Food; Vegetables.

FUNERALS

1 If you don't go to people's funerals, they won't come to yours.
   Anon.

2 In the city a funeral is just an interruption of traffic; in the country it is a form of popular entertainment.
   George Ade

3 My grandfather had a wonderful funeral. My grandfather was a very insignificant man, actually. At his funeral his hearse *followed* the other cars. It was a nice funeral, though, you would have liked it – it was a catered funeral. It was held in a big hall with accordion players. On the buffet table there was a replica of the deceased in potato salad.
   Woody Allen, *The Nightclub Years, 1964– 1968*, record, 1972

4 There is nothing like a morning funeral for sharpening the appetite for lunch.
   Arthur Marshall, *Life's Rich Pageant*, 1984

5 A damn good funeral is still one of our best and cheapest acts of theatre.
   Gwyn Thomas, *SAP*, 1974

See also Cremation; Death; Epitaphs.

THE FUTURE

1 An optimist is someone who thinks the future is uncertain.
   Anon.

2 Future, *n.* that period of time in which our affairs prosper, our friends are true and our happiness is assured.
   Ambrose Bierce, *The Devil's Dictionary*, 1911

3 . . . in 2013, the world will look like this:
   * The United States will be led by a ball-point pen, referred to as Mr Scribble.
   * The French will have the universal right to walk up to anyone they want and tell them to do anything they want them to. Their first move will be to establish cheese as the universal currency.
   * Trains will all run on time, but they will be invisible.
   * You will be able to buy briefcases in six-packs.
   * The Soviet Union, after the Purge of 2005, will be run by clowns and giant insects. Mr Scribble will *not* like them one bit.
   Kevin Curran, Peter Gaffney and Fred Graver, *National Lampoon*, 1984

See also Astrology; Fate; The Past.

G

HUGH GAITSKELL British politician, Labour Party Leader, 1955–1963

1 . . .a desiccated calculating machine.
   Aneurin Bevan (Attrib.)

GAMBLING

1 If there was no action around, he would play solitaire – and bet against himself.
   Groucho Marx, of his brother Chico (Attrib.)

2 The way his horses ran could be summed up in a word.
   Last.
   He once had a horse who finished ahead of the winner of the 1942 Kentucky Derby.
   Unfortunately, the horse started running in the 1941 Kentucky Derby.
   Groucho Marx, *Esquire*, 1972

3 . . . one of my most precious treasures . . . is an exquisite pair of loaded dice, bearing the date of my graduation from high school.
   W. C. Fields, *Let's Look at the Record*, 1939

4 The sure way of getting nothing for something.
   Wilson Mizner

5 There are two times in a man's life when he should not speculate: when he can't afford it, and when he can.
   Mark Twain

See also Debt; Horses and Horse Racing; Money; Winning.

GARDENING

1 I've had enough of gardening – I'm just about ready to throw in the trowel.
   Anon.

2 Airborne filth settling on aphis honeydew would asphyxiate all those plants which survive the sucking, biting, chewing, riddling activities of the insects, if it were not for the fact that they are generally pecked to death by sparrows, dug up, trodden on, sat on or stolen, or simply annihilated by a blast of animal urine or overwhelmed by a cloaking turd, long before that.
   Rose Blight (Germaine Greer), *The Revolting Garden*, 1979

3 Laws of Gardening:
   1. Other people's tools work only in other people's gardens.
   2. Fancy gizmos don't work.
   3. If nobody uses it, there's a reason.
   4. You get the most of what you need the least.
   Arthur Bloch, *Murphy's Law*, 1977

4 What a man needs in gardening is a cast-iron back, with a hinge in it.
   Charles Dudley Warner, *My Summer in a Garden*, 1871

5 I don't believe the half I hear,
   Nor the quarter of what I see!
   But I have one faith, sublime and true,
   That nothing can shake or slay;
   Each spring I firmly believe anew
   All the seed catalogues say!
   Carolyn Wells, *One Firm Faith*

See also Fruit; Home; Vegetables.

GAUCHENESS

1 . . . I glanced at the totally incomprehensible menu and replied, in the well-rounded, thoughtful tones of the *Michelin Guide* man doing the final check on a restaurant to which he is considering awarding three stars: 'I think I'll have the lyonnaise.' 'The lyonnaise is the potatoes, sir,' replied the waiter, contemptuously scratching his leg. 'That's what I want,' I lied, with a miserable attempt at haughtiness. 'With chips.'
   Michael Frayn, *The Day of the Dog*, 1962

See also Adolescence; Culture.

GENIUS

1 Genius is one per cent inspiration and
ninety-nine per cent perspiration.
   Thomas Alva Edison, newspaper interview, 1931

2 The public is wonderfully tolerant. It
forgives everything except genius.
   Oscar Wilde, 'The Critic as Artist', 1890

See also Intellectuals; Talent.

GENTLEMEN

1 A gentleman is one who never swears at
his wife while ladies are present.
   Anon.

2 A gentleman is one who, when he invites
a girl up to show her his etchings, shows
her his etchings.
   Anon.

3 A true gentleman is a man who knows
how to play the bagpipes – but doesn't.
   Anon.

4 I do hope I shall enjoy myself with you
. . . I am parshial to ladies if they are nice
I suppose it is my nature. I am not quite a
gentleman but you would hardly notice it.
   Daisy Ashford, *The Young Visiters*, 1919

5 A gentleman is one who never strikes a
woman without provocation.
   H. L. Mencken

6 . . . one of Nature's gentlemen, the worst
type of gentleman I know.
   Oscar Wilde, *Lady Windermere's Fan*, 1892

See also Etiquette; Men; Men – The
Female View; Society.

GERMANY AND THE GERMANS

1 . . . German – a language . . . which was
developed solely to afford the speaker the
opportunity to spit at strangers under the
guise of polite conversation.
   *The National Lampoon Encyclopaedia of
   Humor*, 1973

2 GERMAN: Will you please stop talking
about the war?
   BASIL FAWLTY: Me? You started it!
   GERMAN: We did not start it.

BASIL FAWLTY: Yes you did, you in-
vaded Poland . . .
   John Cleese and Connie Booth, *Fawlty
   Towers*, BBC TV, 1975

3 They are a fine people but quick to catch
the disease of anti-humanity. I think it's
because of their poor elimination. Germany is a headquarters for constipation.
   George Grosz

4 The Germans are like women, you can
scarcely ever fathom their depths – they
haven't any.
   Friedrich Wilhelm Nietzsche, *The Anti-
   christ*, 1888

5 *Racial characteristics*: piggish-looking
sadomasochistic automatons whose only
known forms of relaxation are swilling
watery beer from vast tubs and singing
the idiotically repetitive verses of their
porcine folk tunes . . . Their language
lacks any semblance of civilized speech.
Their usual diet consists almost wholly
of old cabbage and sections of animal
intestines filled with blood and gore.
   P. J. O'Rourke, 'Foreigners Around the
   World', *National Lampoon*, 1976

6 German is the most extravagantly ugly
language. It sounds like someone using a
sick-bag on a 747.
   William Rushton, *Holiday Inn, Ghent*, 1984

7 A verb has a hard time enough of it in this
world when it's all together. It's downright inhuman to split it up. But that's
just what those Germans do. They take
part of a verb and put it down here, like a
stake, and they take the other part of it
and put it away over yonder like another
stake, and between those two limits they
just shovel in German.
   Mark Twain, speech, New York, 1900

8 Whenever the literary German dives into
a sentence, that is the last you are going to
see of him till he emerges on the other
side of his Atlantic with his verb in his
mouth.
   Mark Twain, *A Connecticut Yankee in King
   Arthur's Court*, 1889

9 The German people are an orderly, vain,
deeply sentimental and rather insensitive

people. They seem to feel at their best when they are singing in chorus, saluting or obeying orders.
H. G. Wells, *Travels of a Republican Radical in Search of Hot Water*, 1939

See also Europe and the EEC.

GIFTS

1 You never want to give a man a present when he's feeling good. You want to do it when he's down.
Lyndon Baines Johnson (Attrib.)

2 Why is it no one ever sent me yet
One perfect limousine, do you suppose?
Ah no, it's always just my luck to get
One perfect rose.
Dorothy Parker 'One Perfect Rose', *The Portable Dorothy Parker*, 1944

3 One should never give a woman anything she can't wear in the evening.
Oscar Wilde, *An Ideal Husband*, 1895

See also Christmas; Gratitude.

WILLIAM EWART GLADSTONE Prime Minister of Great Britain, 1868–1874, 1880–1885, 1886, 1892–1894 (Liberal Party)

1 They told me how Mr Gladstone read Homer for fun, which I thought served him right.
Winston Churchill, *My Early Life*, 1930

2 He has not a single redeeming defect.
Benjamin Disraeli (Attrib.)

3 . . . honest in the most odious sense of the word.
Benjamin Disraeli (Attrib.)

4 Mr Gladstone speaks to me as if I were a public meeting.
Queen Victoria (Attrib.)

See also House of Commons; Houses of Parliament; Politics and Politicians.

GOD

1 God is alive – he just doesn't want to get involved.
Graffito, 1975

2 God is dead. But don't worry – the Virgin Mary is pregnant again.
Graffito, Los Angeles, 1981

3 God is not dead. He is alive and autographing Bibles today at Brentano's.
Graffito, New York, 1979

4 God's plan made a hopeful beginning,
But man spoiled his chances by sinning.
We trust that the story
Will end in God's glory,
But, at present, the other side's winning.
Anon., *New York Times Magazine*, 1946

5 Between projects I go into the park and bite the grass and wail, 'Why do You make me aware of the fact that I have to die one day?' God says, 'Please, I have Chinese people yelling at me, I haven't time for this.' I say all right. God is like a Jewish waiter, he has too many tables.
Mel Brooks, quoted in the *Guardian*, 1984

6 It is the final proof of God's omnipotence that he need not exist in order to save us.
Peter De Vries, *The Mackerel Plaza*, 1958

7 Good God, how much reverence can you have for a Supreme Being who finds it necessary to include such phenomena as phlegm and tooth decay in His divine system of Creation?
Joseph Heller, *Catch-22*, 1961

8 God is the immemorial refuge of the incompetent, the helpless, the miserable. They find not only sanctuary in His arms, but also a kind of superiority, soothing to their macerated egos; He will set them above their betters.
H. L. Mencken, *Minority Report*, 1956

9 It takes a long while for a naturally trustful person to reconcile himself to the idea that after all God will not help him.
H. L. Mencken, *Minority Report*, 1956

10 Is man one of God's blunders or is God one of man's blunders?
Friedrich Wilhelm Nietzsche

11 There was an Old Man with a Beard,
Who said: 'I demand to be feared.
Address Me as God,
And love Me, you sod!'

And Man did just that, which was weird.
Roger Woddis

See also Belief; The Bible; Christianity; The Church; Faith; Jesus Christ; Religion.

GOLF

1 If you want to take long walks, take long walks. If you want to hit things with a stick, hit things with a stick. But there's no excuse for combining the two and putting the results on TV. Golf is not so much a sport as an insult to lawns.
National Lampoon, 1979

2 Oh the dirty little pill
Went rolling down the hill
And rolled right into the bunker
From there to the green
I took thirteen
And then by God I sunk her!
Traditional

3 Give me my golf clubs, fresh air and a beautiful partner, and you can keep my golf clubs and the fresh air.
Jack Benny

4 The Coarse Golfer: one who has to shout 'Fore' when he putts.
Michael Green, *The Art of Coarse Golf*, 1967

5 Golf may be played on Sunday, not being a game within view of the law, but being a form of moral effort.
Stephen Leacock, 'Why I Refuse to Play Golf'

6 ERIC: My wife says if I don't give up golf; she'll leave me.
ERNIE: That's terrible.
ERIC: I know – I'm really going to miss her.
Eric Morecambe and Ernie Wise, *The Morecambe and Wise Joke Book*, 1979

7 ERIC: You know what your main trouble is?
ERNIE: What?
ERIC: You stand too close to the ball after you've hit it.
ERNIE: I still think I'm improving.
ERIC: Oh, you are. Why, only yesterday you hit the ball in one.

ERNIE: Absolutely! And anyway, this is a terrible golf course. Just look at the state of it!
ERIC: This isn't the course, you know. We left that half an hour ago.
ERNIE: Really? Is that why you keep looking at your watch?
ERIC: This isn't a watch – this is a compass!
Eric Morecambe and Ernie Wise, *The Morecambe and Wise Joke Book*, 1979

8 A: Why aren't you playing golf with the colonel any more?
B: What! Would *you* play with a man who swears and curses with every shot, who cheats in the bunkers and who enters false scores on his cards?
A: Certainly not!
B: Well neither will the colonel.
Freddie Oliver

9 Golf is a good walk spoiled.
Mark Twain

10 The uglier a man's legs are, the better he plays golf. It's almost a law.
H. G. Wells, *Bealby*, 1915

11 'After all, golf is only a game,' said Millicent.
Women say these things without thinking. It does not mean that there is any kink in their character. They simply don't realize what they are saying.
P. G. Wodehouse, *The Clicking of Cuthbert*, 1922

12 'Mortimer, you must choose between golf and me.'
'But, darling, I went round in a hundred and one yesterday. You can't expect a fellow to give up golf when he is at the top of his game.'
P. G. Wodehouse, *The Clicking of Cuthbert*, 1922

13 The least thing upsets him on the links. He misses short putts because of the uproar of the butterflies in the adjoining meadows.
P. G. Wodehouse, *The Clicking of Cuthbert*, 1922

See also Sport.

GOSSIP

1 Absolute knowledge have I none.
  But my aunt's washerwoman's sister's
      son
  Heard a policeman on his beat
  Say to a labourer on the street
  That he had a letter just last week –
  A letter that he did not seek –
  From a Chinese merchant in
      Timbuctoo,
  Who said that his brother in Cuba knew
  Of an Indian chief in a Texan town,
  Who got the dope from a circus clown,
  That a man in Klondike had it straight
  From a guy in a South American state,
  That a wild man over in Bornco
  Was told by a woman who claimed to
      know . . . etc. etc.
  Anon.

2 A recent survey of 43 scientifically selected Famous People reveals that 20.9%
  of all Famous People would rather pull
  out their own teeth than read another
  Random Note about Mick Jagger.
  'Random Notes', *Rolling Stone*

3 At last the secret is out, as it always must
      come in the end,
  The delicious story is ripe to tell to the
      intimate friend;
  Over the tea-cups and in the square the
      tongue has its desire;
  Still waters run deep, my friend, there's
      never smoke without fire.
  W. H. Auden, song from *The Ascent of F6*,
  1936

4 GIRL: Of course I wouldn't say anything
  about her unless I could say something
  good. And, oh boy, is this good . . .
  Bill King, *Collier's*, cartoon

5 If You Can't Say Something Good
  About Someone, Sit Right Here By Me.
  Alice Roosevelt Longworth, allegedly
  embroidered on a cushion in her sitting-
  room

6 Never gossip about people you don't
  know. This deprives simple artisans like
  Truman Capote of work. The best subject of gossip is someone you and your
  audience love dearly. The enjoyment of

gossip is thus doubled: to the delight of
disapprobation is added the additional
delight of pity.
  P. J. O'Rourke, *Modern Manners*, 1983

7 She always tells stories in the present
  vindictive.
  Tom Peace, *Reader's Digest*, 1957

8 The things most people want to know
  about are usually none of their business.
  George Bernard Shaw

9 I don't at all like knowing what people say
  of me behind my back. It makes one far
  too conceited.
  Oscar Wilde, *An Ideal Husband*, 1895

10 It is perfectly monstrous the way people
  go about, nowadays, saying things against
  one behind one's back that are absolutely
  and entirely true.
  Oscar Wilde, *A Woman of No Importance*,
  1893

11 There is only one thing in the world
  worse than being talked about, and that is
  not being talked about.
  Oscar Wilde, *The Picture of Dorian Gray*,
  1891

12 Gossip is when you hear something you
  like about someone you don't.
  Earl Wilson

See also Conversation; Scandals.

GOVERNMENT

1 This island is almost made of coal and
  surrounded by fish. Only an organizing
  genius could produce a shortage of coal
  and fish in Great Britain at the same
  time.
  Aneurin Bevan, speech, 1945

2 The only good government . . . is a bad
  one in a hell of a fright.
  Joyce Cary, *The Horse's Mouth*, 1944

3 The government solution to a problem is
  usually as bad as the problem.
  Milton Friedman (Attrib.)

4 CIVIL SERVANT: What I mean is that I'm
  fully seized of your aims and, of course, I
  will do my utmost to see that they're put
  into practice. To that end, I recommend

that we set up an interdepartmental committee with fairly broad terms of reference so that at the end of the day we'll be in a position to think through the various implications and arrive at a decision based on long-term considerations rather than rush prematurely into precipitate and possibly ill-conceived action which might well have unforeseen repercussions.
MINISTER: You mean, no?
    Antony Jay and Jonathan Lynn, *Yes, Minister*, BBC TV, 1981

5 It is inaccurate to say I hate everything. I am strongly in favor of common sense, common honesty and common decency. This makes me forever ineligible for any public office.
    H. L. Mencken

6 How come there's only one Monopolies Commission?
    Nigel Rees, *Graffiti 4*, 1982

7 I don't make jokes. I just watch the government and report the facts.
    Will Rogers

8 There's no trick to being a humorist when you have the whole government working for you.
    Will Rogers

9 MRS PARADOCK: There's somebody at the door wanting you to form a government.
MR PARADOCK: What does he look like?
MRS PARADOCK: He says he's working through the street directory.
    N. F. Simpson, *A Resounding Tinkle*, 1958

10 You can fool too many of the people too much of the time.
    James Thurber, *The Thurber Carnival*, 1945

11 Whenever you have an efficient government you have a dictatorship.
    Harry S. Truman, lecture at Columbia University, 1959

12 I see no need for a Royal Commission [on trades unions] which will take minutes and waste years.
    Harold Wilson, 1964

See also The Civil Service; Congress; Parliament; Politics and Politicians; The Senate; Washington.

GRAFFITI

1 – I hate graffiti.
– *I hate ALL Italian food!*
    Graffito, London, 1981

2 Alas, poor yorlik, I knew him backwards.
    Graffito, Exeter, 1984

3 If you feel strongly about graffiti, sign a partition.
    Graffito, Manchester, 1978

See also Badges.

GRAMMAR

1 The grammar has a rule absurd
Which I would call an outworn myth:
'A proposition is a word
You mustn't end a sentence with!'
    Berton Braley, *No Rule to be Afraid of*

2 I don't split 'em. When I go to work on an infinitive, I break it up in little pieces.
    Jimmy Durante (Attrib.)

3 Word has somehow got around that the split infinitive is always wrong. That is a piece with the outworn notion that it is always wrong to strike a lady.
    James Thurber

See also The English Language; Pronunciation; Writers; Writing.

GRATITUDE

1 Gratitude, like love, is never a dependable international emotion.
    Joseph Alsop, American political columnist, 1952

2 Blessed is he who expects no gratitude, for he shall not be disappointed.
    W. C. Bennett, American clergyman

See also Gifts.

GREECE AND THE GREEKS

1 *Racial characteristics*: degenerate, dirty, and impoverished descendants of a bunch of la-de-da fruit salads who invented democracy and then forgot how to

use it while walking around dressed up like girls.

P. J. O'Rourke, 'Foreigners Around the World', *National Lampoon*, 1976

See also Europe and the EEC.

GREETINGS CARDS

1 VALENTINE, I'M NOT SURE HOW I FEEL ABOUT YOU
  Christine Barber

CONGRATULATIONS AND HAPPY BIRTHDAY ON YOUR ANNIVERSARY THIS VALENTINE'S DAY, BAR MITZVAH BOY, HOPE YOU FEEL BETTER SOON
  Ed Brodsky

GOOD LUCK ON YOUR SUBWAY RIDE
  Sissy Cargill

SO YOU'VE JUST FOUND OUT YOU WERE ADOPTED!
  Jeff Monasch

THANK YOU FOR THE ONE-NIGHT STAND
  Lee Powell

BEST WISHES FOR A HAPPY AND SUCCESSFUL FIRST MARRIAGE
  Marc Rosen

DEEPEST SYMPATHY AND BELATED BIRTHDAY WISHES
  Stephen Sadowsky

IN APPRECIATION OF YOUR THANKS FOR MY RESPONSE TO YOUR BEST WISHES AFTER MY EXPRESSION OF GOOD LUCK FOLLOWING YOUR CONGRATULATIONS ON MY ANNOUNCEMENT
  Joel Schechter

SO YOU BOYCOTTED YOUR FIRST OLYMPIC GAMES!
  Ronald Weinger

'Unconventional Greeting Card Competition', *New York Magazine*, 1976

2 Don't send funny greeting cards on birthdays or at Christmas. Save them for funerals, when their cheery effect is needed.

P. J. O'Rourke, *Modern Manners*, 1983

See also Christmas.

GUILT

1 A guilty conscience is the mother of invention.
  Carolyn Wells

2 Jill had that direct, honest gaze which many nice girls have, and as a rule Bill liked it. But at the moment he could have done with something that did not pierce quite so like a red-hot gimlet to his inmost soul. A sense of guilt makes a man allergic to direct, honest gazes.

P. G. Wodehouse, *Ring for Jeeves*, 1953

See also Conscience; Crime; Sin.

HAIR

1 If you see someone with a stunning hair-cut, grab her by the wrist and demand fiercely to know the name, address and home phone number of her hairdresser. If she refuses to tell you, burst into tears.
Cynthia Heimel, *Sex Tips for Girls*, 1983

2 . . . keep away from hairdos altogether. A hairdo, by definition, always makes you look like someone else. Or think you do.
Cynthia Heimel, *Sex Tips for Girls*, 1983

3 Violet will be a good color for hair at just about the same time that brunette becomes a good color for flowers.
Fran Lebowitz, *Social Studies*, 1981

4 Why don't you get a haircut? You look like a chrysanthemum.
P. G. Wodehouse

See also Appearance; Beauty; Faces; Hats; Looks.

HALLOWEEN

1 Ducking for apples – change one letter and it's the story of my life.
Dorothy Parker, at a Halloween party (Attrib.)

HANGOVERS

1 The cocktail is a pleasant drink;
It's mild and harmless – I don't think.
When you've had one, you call for two,
And then you don't care what you do.
Last night I hoisted twenty-three
Of these arrangements into me.
My wealth increased, I swelled with pride,
I was pickled, primed, and ossified;
But R - E - M - O - R - S - E !
The water wagon is the place for me.
George Ade, 'R - E - M - O - R - S - E'

2 For a bad hangover, take the juice of two quarts of whiskey.
Eddie Condon (Attrib.)

3 I'd take a bromo, but I can't stand the noise.
Joe E. Lewis

See also Drink; Nausea.

HAPPINESS

1 Happiness is bumping into Raquel Welch . . . very slowly.
Laugh-In, NBC TV, 1969

2 VERONICA: Are you happy?
HILARY: Why does everybody keep asking me that? No. I'm not happy. But I'm not unhappy about it.
Alan Bennett, *The Old Country*, 1978

3 Happiness makes up in height for what it lacks in length.
Robert Frost, title of poem

4 Happiness is the sublime moment when you get out of your corsets at night.
Joyce Grenfell (Attrib.)

5 It's pretty hard to tell what does bring happiness; poverty and wealth have both failed.
Kin Hubbard

6 I have to tell you something. I cannot help being happy. I've struggled against it but no good. Apart from an odd five minutes here and there, I have been happy all my life. There is, I am well aware, no virtue whatever in this. It results from a combination of heredity, health, good fortune and shallow intellect.
Arthur Marshall, *Taking Liberties*, 1977

7 Gilbert White discovered the formula for complete happiness but he died before making the announcement, leaving it for me to do so. It is to be very busy with the unimportant.
A. Edward Newton, *This Book-collecting Game*

8 Happiness is a Warm Puppy.
Charles Schultz, title of Peanuts book, 1962

9 A lifetime of happiness! No man alive could bear it: it would be hell on earth.
George Bernard Shaw, *Man and Superman*, 1903

10 If only we'd stop trying to be happy we could have a pretty good time.
Edith Wharton

11 When I was young, I used to think that wealth and power would bring me happiness . . . I was right.
Gahan Wilson, *The Weird World of Gahan Wilson*, cartoon, 1975

See also Smiles; Unhappiness.

WARREN G. HARDING
President of the United States, 1921–1923

1 His speeches left the impression of an army of pompous phrases moving over the landscape in search of an idea; sometimes these meandering words would actually capture a straggling thought and bear it triumphantly a prisoner in their midst, until it died of servitude and overwork.
William G. McAdoo, unsuccessful contender for Democratic nomination for president, 1920 and 1924

2 A tin-horn politician with the manner of a rural corn doctor and the mien of a ham actor.
H. L. Mencken, *Lodge*, 1920

See also The Presidency; Washington.

HATS

1 FIRST WOMAN: Whenever I'm down in the dumps, I get myself another hat.
SECOND WOMAN: I always wondered where you found them.
Anon.

2 I began wearing hats as a young lawyer because it helped me to establish my professional identity. Before that, whenever I was at a meeting, someone would ask me to get coffee – they assumed I was a secretary.
Bella Abzug

3 A hat should be taken off when you greet a lady and left off for the rest of your life.

Nothing looks more stupid than a hat. When you put on a hat you are surrendering to the same urge that makes children wear mouse ears at Disney World or drunks wear lampshades at parties. Wearing a hat implies that you are bald if you are a man and that your hair is dirty if you are a woman. Every style of hat is identified with some form of undesirable (derby = corrupt ward heeler; fedora = Italian gangster; top hat = rich bum; pillbox = Kennedy wife, et cetera).
P. J. O'Rourke, *Modern Manners*, 1983

4 One's chapeau provides the perfect opportunity for a profound fashion statement. Your hat should not merely say, 'here is my head' but rather it should convey a sense of allure, mystery, even intrigue. Here moi's chapeau is saying, 'Oui, I have time for one quick chocolate malted in that café with the umbrellas that have tables on their handles, but then I must board the Oriental Express for a rendezvous with the Duke of Candelabra in the lovely, yet sinister, Kingdom of Rutabagia.'
Miss Piggy, *Miss Piggy's Guide to Life (As Told to Henry Beard)*, 1981

5 STICKY SITUATIONS
Someone you like is wearing an ugly hat, and she asks you to give her your honest opinion of it:
'What a lovely chapeau! But if I may make one teensy suggestion? If it blows off, don't chase it.'
Miss Piggy, *Miss Piggy's Guide to Life (As Told to Henry Beard)*, 1981

6 Hats divide generally into three classes: offensive hats, defensive hats, and shrapnel. Shrapnel hats look as if they have dropped on to the wearer's head by accident . . .
I have recently acquired a new hat of such ferocity that it has been running my whole life for me. I wake up in the morning thinking 'who shall I wear my hat at today?'
Katherine Whitehorn, 'How to Wear a Hat', *Shouts and Murmurs*, 1963

7 My dear, you're the only woman in the world who'd have known the right hat to wear on an occasion like this.
   Oscar Wilde, to Mrs Leverson, on his leaving prison, 1897 (Attrib.)

8 'Don't you like this hat?'
   'No, sir.'
   'Well, I do,' I replied rather cleverly, and went out with it tilted just that merest shade over the left eye which makes all the difference.
   P. G. Wodehouse, *Stiff Upper Lip, Jeeves*, 1963

See also Appearance; Clothes; Hair.

HAUGHTINESS

1 I am, in point of fact, a particularly haughty and exclusive person, of pre-Adamite ancestral descent. You will understand this when I tell you that I can trace my ancestry back to a protoplasmal primordial atomic globule. Consequently, my family pride is something inconceivable. I can't help it. I was born sneering.
   W. S. Gilbert and Arthur Sullivan, *The Mikado*, 1885

2 Aunt Dahlia can turn in a flash into a carbon copy of a Duchess of the old school reducing an underling to a spot of grease, and what is so remarkable is that she doesn't have to use a lorgnette; just does it all with the power of the human eye.
   P. G. Wodehouse, *Much Obliged, Jeeves*, 1971

3 Ice formed on the butler's upper slopes.
   P. G. Wodehouse, *Pigs Have Wings*, 1952

4 It was the look which caused her to be known in native bearer and halfcaste circles as 'Mgobi-Mgumbi', which may be loosely translated as She On Whom It is Unsafe To Try Any Oompus-Boompus.
   P. G. Wodehouse, *Money in the Bank*, 1946

See also Snobbery.

HEALTH

1 If you want to clear your system out, sit on a piece of cheese and swallow a mouse.
   Johnny Carson, *The Tonight Show*, NBC TV

2 Early to rise and early to bed
   Makes a male healthy, wealthy and dead.
   James Thurber

See also Diets; Exercise; Illness.

HEAVEN

1 My life I squandered waiting
   Then let my chance go by.
   One day we'll meet in Heaven.
   That Matlock in the sky.
   Alan Bennett, *Habeas Corpus*, 1973

2 What! You been keeping records on me? I wasn't so bad! How many times did I take the Lord's name in vain? One million and six? Jesus Ch . . . !
   Steve Martin, *A Wild and Crazy Guy*, record, 1978

See also Belief; God; Reincarnation; Religion.

HECKLERS

1 *Twelve Heckler Retorts*:
   * If there's ever a price on your head –
     take it!
   * Why don't you go down to the morgue and tell them you're ready!
   * Tell me, is that your lower lip or are you wearing a turtle-neck sweater?
   * You've got a fine personality, sir – but not for a human being!
   * When he was born, his father came into the room and gave him a funny look. And as you can see, he's still got it!
   * You're the sort of person Dr Spooner would have called a shining wit!
   * Will you please follow the example of your head and come to the point!
   * That reminds me of a very funny story – will you take it from there, Sir?
   * Why don't you move closer to the wall – that's plastered already!

* I'd like to help you out – tell me, which way did you come in?
* What exactly is on your mind? If you'll excuse the exaggeration?
* You've got a wonderful head on your shoulders. Tell me: whose is it?
  Anon.

See also Abuse; Audience; Insults.

HEIGHT

1 LADY RUMPERS: Rumpers was a little man too. He made no secret of his height.
  Alan Bennett, *Habeas Corpus*, 1973

2 He's so small, he's the only man I know who has turn-ups on his underpants.
  Jerry Dennis

3 He's very superstitious – he thinks it's unlucky to walk under a black cat.
  Max Kauffmann

See also The Body; Figures.

HEROES

1 We can't all be heroes because somebody has to sit on the curb and clap as they go by.
  Will Rogers

2 Formerly we used to canonize our heroes. The modern method is to vulgarize them. Cheap editions of great books may be delightful, but cheap editions of great men are absolutely detestable.
  Oscar Wilde, 'The True Function and Value of Criticism', 1890

See also Courage; War.

HISTORY

1 History is a hard core of interpretation surrounded by a pulp of disputable facts.
  Anon.

2 History is the sum total of the things that could have been avoided.
  Konrad Adenauer, Chancellor of West Germany, 1949–1963

3 History, *n.* an account, mostly false, of events mostly unimportant, which are brought about by rulers, mostly knaves, and soldiers, mostly fools.
  Ambrose Bierce, *The Devil's Dictionary*, 1911

4 History teaches us that men and nations behave wisely once they have exhausted all other alternatives.
  Abba Eban, 1970

5 History is bunk.
  Henry Ford, giving evidence in a libel action, 1919

6 History repeats itself; historians repeat each other.
  Philip Guedalla

7 History was a trash bag of random coincidences torn open in a wind. Surely, Watt with his steam engine, Faraday with his electric motor, and Edison with his incandescent light bulb did not have it as their goal to contribute to a fuel shortage some day that would place their countries at the mercy of Arab oil.
  Joseph Heller, *Good as Gold*, 1979

8 History is too serious to be left to historians.
  Iain Macleod, Leader of the House of Commons, quoted in the *Observer*, 1961

9 . . . broadly speaking, anything done against kings was to be applauded – unless, indeed, it were done by priests, like Becket, in which case one sided with the king.
  Bertrand Russell, *Portraits from Memory*, 1956

10 BLUFF KING HAL
  Henry VIII was a strong king with a very strong sense of humour and VIII wives, memorable amongst whom are Katherine the Arrogant, Anne of Cloves, Lady Jane Austin and Anne Hathaway. His beard was, however, red.
  In his youth Henry was fond of playing tennis and after his accession is believed never to have lost a set. He also invented a game called 'Bluff King Hal', which he invited ministers to play with him. The players were blindfolded and knelt down with their heads on a block of wood; they

then guessed who the King would marry next.
W. C. Sellar and R. J. Yeatman, *1066 and All That*, 1930

11 RUFUS. A RUDDY KING
This monarch was always very angry and red in the face and was therefore unpopular, so that his death was a Good Thing: it occurred in the following memorable way. Rufus was hunting one day in the New Forest, when William Tell (the memorable crackshot, inventor of Crossbow puzzles) took unerring aim at a reddish apple, which had fallen on to the King's head, and shot him through the heart. Sir Isaac Walton, who happened to be present at the time, thereupon invented the Law of Gravity. Thus was the reign of Rufus brought to a Good End.
W. C. Sellar and R. J. Yeatman, *1066 and All That*, 1930

12 Hegel was right when he said that we learn from history that men never learn anything from history.
George Bernard Shaw, *Heartbreak House*, 1919

13 'History repeats itself' and 'History never repeats itself' are about equally true.
G. M. Trevelyan

14 The one duty we have to history is to rewrite it.
Oscar Wilde, 'The Critic as Artist', 1890

See also Ancestors; Antiques; The Past.

ADOLF HITLER

1 The moustache of Hitler
Could hardly be littler
Was the thought that kept recurring
To Field Marshall Goering.
E. C. Bentley, *Complete Clerihews*, 1961

2 HITLER: I don't want war! All I want is Peace! Peace! Peace!
(*Sings*) A little piece of Poland,
A little piece of France,
A little piece of Portugal
And Austria perchance.
A little slice of Turkey
And all that that entails,

And then a piece of England, Scotland, Ireland and Wales.
Mel Brooks, *To be or Not to be*, screenplay, 1984

3 Springtime for Hitler and Germany,
Deutschland is happy and gay.
We're moving to a faster pace,
Look out, here comes the Master Race!
Springtime for Hitler and Germany,
Winter for Poland and France.
Springtime for Hitler and Germany,
Come on Germans, go into your dance!
Mel Brooks, 'Springtime for Hitler', song from *The Producers*, 1968

4 If Hitler invaded Hell I would make at least a favourable reference to the Devil in the House of Commons.
Winston Churchill, 1941, quoted in *The Grand Alliance*, 1950

5 This man is dangerous; he believes what he says.
Joseph Goebbels (Attrib.)

6 Do you think Der Führer could keep on being Der Führer
If he saw what everybody else sees every time he looks in the mührer?
Ogden Nash

See also War.

HOLIDAYS

1 Honolulu – it's got everything. Sand for the children, sun for the wife, sharks for the wife's mother.
Ken Dodd

2 ERIC: Did you know I used to be a lifeguard?
ERNIE: Really? When?
ERIC: Last summer.
ERNIE: What did you do?
ERIC: I saved women.
ERNIE: What for?
ERIC: The winter.
ERNIE: Didn't you help any men?
ERIC: Yes – I gave them the occasional woman.
Eric Morecambe and Ernie Wise, *The Morecambe and Wise Joke Book*, 1979

3 ERIC: Excuse me, are you the manager of this holiday camp?

ERNIE: I certainly am, sir – Bobkins' Holiday Camps at your service! You're one of our earliest holiday-makers this year. The camp has only been open a week.
ERIC: I know – I like to get in early while the sheets are still clean.
ERNIE: Anyway, sir, can I help you?
ERIC: Yes, it's about the roof of my chalet.
ERNIE: What about it?
ERIC: I'd like one.

> Eric Morecambe and Ernie Wise, *The Morecambe and Wise Joke Book*, 1979

4 A good holiday is one spent among people whose notions of time are vaguer than yours.

> J. B. Priestley

See also The Sea; Travel.

HOLLAND AND THE DUTCH

1 Apart from cheese and tulips, the main product of the country is advocaat, a drink made from lawyers.

> Alan Coren, *The Sanity Inspector*, 1974

2 Like the Germans, the Dutch fall into two quite distinct physical types: the small, corpulent, red-faced Edams, and the thinner, paler, larger Goudas.

> Alan Coren, *The Sanity Inspector*, 1974

3 All hail the Dutch, long-suffering neutrons in the endless movement against oppression and exploitation. Let us hear it for the Dutch, bland and obliging victims of innumerable wars which have rendered their land as flat as their treats . . . Every one of them is an uncle, not a one can muster real courage . . . All hail the Dutch, nonpeople in the people's war!

> Tony Hendra, 'EEC! It's the US of E!', *National Lampoon*, 1976

See also Europe and the EEC.

HOLLYWOOD

1 Hollywood – where people from Iowa mistake each other for movie stars.

> Fred Allen

2 You can take all the sincerity in Hollywood, place it in the navel of a fruit fly and still have room enough for three caraway seeds and a producer's heart.

> Fred Allen

3 What I like about Hollywood is that one can get along by knowing two words of English – swell and lousy.

> Vicki Baum (Attrib.)

4 Hollywood – an emotional Detroit.

> Lillian Gish

5 No one ever went broke in Hollywood underestimating the intelligence of the public.

> Elsa Maxwell

6 Just outside pious Los Angeles is Hollywood, a colony of moving picture actors. Its morals are those of Port Said.

> H. L. Mencken, *Americana*, 1925

7 . . . a delightful trip through a sewer in a glass-bottomed boat.

> Wilson Mizner

8 Hollywood is a sewer – with service from the Ritz-Carlton.

> Wilson Mizner

9 I've had several years in Hollywood and I still think the movie heroes are in the audience.

> Wilson Mizner

10 *Gandhi* was everything the voting members of the Academy would like to be: moral, tan and thin.

> Joe Morgenstern, *Los Angeles Herald-Examiner*, April 1983

11 Ten million dollars' worth of intricate and highly ingenious machinery functioning elaborately to put skin on baloney.

> George Jean Nathan

12 When Gertrude Stein returned to New York after a short sojourn in Hollywood somebody asked her . . . 'What is it like – out there?' To which, with little delay, and the minimum of careful thought the sage replied . . . 'There IS no "There" – there.'

> David Niven, *Bring on the Empty Horses*, 1975

13 Hollywood money isn't money. It's congealed snow, melts in your hand, and there you are.
   Dorothy Parker, interviewed in *Writers at Work*, 1958

14 Hollywood is where, if you don't have happiness, you send out for it.
   Rex Reed

15 Beverly Hills is very exclusive. For instance, their fire department won't make house calls.
   Mort Sahl (Attrib.)

16 They know only one word of more than one syllable here, and that is *fillum*.
   Louis Sherwin

17 A place where they shoot too many pictures and not enough actors.
   Walter Winchell

18 Everybody liked Bill Shannon, even in Hollywood, where nobody likes anybody.
   P. G. Wodehouse, *The Old Reliable*, 1951

See also Acting; Actors and Actresses; California; Film; Los Angeles.

HOME

1 They live in a beautiful little apartment overlooking the rent.
   Anon.

2 Home life as we understand it is no more natural to us than a cage is natural to a cockatoo.
   George Bernard Shaw, 'Preface', *Getting Married*, 1908

3 Home, nowadays, is a place where part of the family waits till the rest of the family brings the car back.
   Earl Wilson

See also Gardening; Interior Decorating; Real Estate.

HOMOSEXUALITY

1 – My mother made me a homosexual.
  – *If I gave her the wool, would she make me one too?*
   Graffito, London, 1978

2 My lesbianism is an act of Christian charity. All those women out there are praying for a man, and I'm giving them my share.
   Rita Mae Brown, 1978

3 If God had meant us to have homosexuals, he would have created Adam and Bruce.
   Anita Bryant, American singer and anti-Gay activist

4 Homosexuality is a sickness, just as are baby-rape or wanting to become head of General Motors.
   Eldridge Cleaver, *Soul on Ice*, 1968

5 I became one of the stately homos of England.
   Quentin Crisp, *The Naked Civil Servant*, 1968

6 I discarded a whole book because the leading character wasn't on my wavelength. She was a lesbian with doubts about her masculinity.
   Peter De Vries, quoted in the *New York Times*, 1967

7 Lesbianism has always seemed to me an extremely inventive response to the shortage of men, but otherwise not worth the trouble.
   Nora Ephron, *Heartburn*, 1983

8 TEXAN WOMAN: Are you a homo? We don't have homos in Texas – live ones, anyway.
   Susan Harris, *Soap*, ABC TV, 1978

9 It was out of the closet and into the streets for the nation's homosexuals in the seventies. This didn't do much for the streets, but on the other hand your average closet was improved immeasurably.
   Rick Meyerowitz and John Weidman, *National Lampoon*, 1980

10 It is the height of fashion to think, dress, and act like a homosexual. But, suddenly, it has become very unfashionable to be one. This may be the result of the immense fatigue everyone is feeling with the concept of equality. With blacks, Hispanics, dolphins, and so on all demanding to be treated as equals, homosexuals are just one more voice of complaint in a complaint-ridden world.

And since homosexuals are often wealthy and famous, treating them as equals is not only difficult but can actually be construed as rudeness. The whole thing is a social mess.

P. J. O'Rourke, *Modern Manners*, 1983

11 I'd rather be black than gay because when you're black you don't have to tell your mother.

Charles Pierce, American female impersonator

See also Bisexuality; Sex.

HONESTY

1 Cross my heart and hope to eat my weight in goslings.

W. C. Fields

See also Dishonesty; Morality; Trust; Truth; Virtue.

HONEYMOONS

1 Honeymoon – the morning after the knot before.

Anon.

2 Honeymooning is a very overrated occupation.

Noël Coward, *Private Lives*, 1930

See also Couples; Hotels; Sex; Weddings.

HONOURS

1 ERNIE: My name is Colonel Napoleon Davenport, DSO, MC, OBE.

ERIC: That's a funny way to spell 'Davenport'.

Eric Morecambe and Ernie Wise, *The Morecambe and Wise Joke Book*, 1979

See also Achievement; Awards.

HERBERT HOOVER President of the United States, 1929–1933

1 I was just standing out in front watching the other acts when a lady walked up to me in the lobby and said, 'Pardon me, young man, could you tell me where I could find the rest room?' and I said, 'It's just around the corner.' 'Don't give me that Hoover talk,' she said. 'I'm serious.'

Al Boasberg, *For Bob Hope*, 1930

2 In 1932, lame duck President Herbert Hoover was so desperate to remain in the White House that he dressed up as Eleanor Roosevelt. When FDR discovered the hoax in 1936, the two men decided to stay together for the sake of the children.

Johnny Carson

See also The Presidency; Washington.

HORSES AND HORSE RACING

1 It's awf'lly bad luck on Diana
Her ponies have swallowed their bits;
She fished down their throats with a spanner
And frightened them all into fits.

John Betjeman, *A Few Late Chrysanthemums*, 1954

2 If you could call the thing a horse. If it hadn't shown a flash of speed in the straight, it would have got mixed up with the next race.

P. G. Wodehouse, *Very Good, Jeeves*, 1930

3 I just played a horse yesterday so slow the jockey kept a diary of the trip.

Henny Youngman, 1940

See also Animals; Cowboys; Gambling.

HOSPITALS

1 There was a young man with a hernia
Who said to his doctor, 'Goldernia
When improving my middle
Be sure you don't fiddle
With matters that do not concernia.'

Heywood Broun

2 After two days in hospital, I took a turn for the nurse.

W. C. Fields

See also Accidents; Doctors; Health; Illness; Medicine.

HOTELS

1 Twenty-four-hour room service generally refers to the length of time that it takes for the club sandwich to arrive. This is indeed disheartening,

particularly when you've ordered scrambled eggs.

Fran Lebowitz, *Social Studies*, 1981

2 ERIC: The manager said, 'You won't find a single flea in any of my beds.' He was right – they were all married with families.

ERNIE: What sort of room did you have?

ERIC: It was quite nice actually. We had a double room with bath – pity about them being in separate buildings.

Eric Morecambe and Ernie Wise, *The Morecambe and Wise Joke Book*, 1979

3 Generally speaking, the length and grandness of a hotel's name are an exact opposite reflection of its quality. Thus the Hotel Central will prove to be a clean, pleasant place in a good part of town, and the Hotel Royal Majestic-Fantastic will be a fleabag next to a topless bowling alley.

Miss Piggy, *Miss Piggy's Guide to Life (As Told to Henry Beard)*, 1981

4 I stayed at one of the better hotels ... I was at a place called The Fractured Arms. I paid my rent in advance – they put the window back in my room ... You can imagine how big my room was – when I closed the door, the doorknob got in bed with me. It was so small, even the mice were hunchback. I had a headache, the guy next door had to take the aspirin.

Henny Youngman, 1940

See also Holidays; Restaurants; Travel.

HOUSE OF COMMONS

1 What have you done? cried Christine
You've wrecked the whole party
   machine!
To lie in the nude may be rude,
But to lie in the House is obscene!

Anon., of John Profumo who lied to the House of Commons concerning his relationship with Christine Keeler, 1963

2 I do not know what the Right Hon. Lady the Minister for Education [Miss Florence Horsbrugh] is grinning at. I was told by one of my Hon. friends this afternoon that this is a face which has sunk a thousand scholarships.

Aneurin Bevan, speech on cuts in the Education budget, House of Commons, 1953

3 If, from any speech in the House, one begins to see any results within five to ten years after it has been delivered, one will have done very well indeed.

Robert Boothby, Member of Parliament, 1936

4 I slept for two hours this afternoon in the Library of the House of Commons! A deep House of Commons sleep. There is no sleep to compare with it – rich, deep and guilty.

Henry 'Chips' Channon, 1939

5 As we had great interests there and also on general grounds, I thought that it would be a good thing to have diplomatic representation. But if you recognize anyone, it does not mean that you like him. We all, for instance, recognize the Right Hon Gentleman the Member of Ebbw Vale [Aneurin Bevan].

Winston Churchill, speech on the recognition of Communist China, House of Commons, 1952

6 BESSIE BRADDOCK: Winston, you're drunk!

CHURCHILL: Bessie, you're ugly. But tomorrow I shall be sober.

Winston Churchill, probably apocryphal

7 LADY ASTOR: If you were my husband, I'd poison your coffee.

CHURCHILL: If you were my wife, I'd drink it.

Winston Churchill, at Blenheim Palace, 1912, probably apocryphal

8 ... a Bill to make attendance at the House of Commons compulsory has been passed by three votes to two.

David Frost and Antony Jay, *To England with Love*, 1967

9 When in that House MPs divide,
If they've a brain and cerebellum, too,
They've got to leave that brain outside,
And vote just as their leaders tell 'em to.
But then the prospect of a lot

Of dull MPs in close proximity,
All thinking for themselves, is what
No man can face with equanimity.
W. S. Gilbert and Arthur Sullivan, 'Private Willis', *Iolanthe*, 1882

10 It is a truth not sufficiently appreciated that any political proposal which commends itself to both front benches of the House of Commons is at best useless and at worst against the public interest; one which also appeals to both main parties' back benches is likely to be a constitutional outrage and certain to be seriously damaging to the people's liberty, prosperity or both.
Bernard Levin, *The Times*, 1984

11 I have nothing against Hampstead. I used to live there myself when I was an intellectual. I gave that up when I became Leader of the House.
Norman St John-Stevas, *Observer*, 1980

12 Parliament is the longest running farce in the West End.
Cyril Smith, Liberal MP, 1973

13 Only people who look dull ever get into the House of Commons, and only people who are dull ever succeed there.
Oscar Wilde, *An Ideal Husband*, 1895

See also Elections; House of Lords; Parliament; Politics and Politicians.

HOUSE OF LORDS

1 The cure for admiring the House of Lords is to go and look at it.
Walter Bagehot

2 It was but a few weeks since he had taken his seat in the Lords; and this afternoon, for want of anything better to do, he strayed in.
Max Beerbohm, *Zuleika Dobson*, 1911

3 The House of Lords is the British Outer Mongolia for retired politicians.
Tony Benn, speech, 1962

4 Like many other anachronisms in British public life, the House of Lords has one supreme merit. It works.
Lord Boothby (Attrib.)

5 . . . dead, but in the Elysian fields.
Benjamin Disraeli

6 The House of Lords is a model of how to care for the elderly.
Frank Field, Labour MP, 1981

7 . . . on great matters of State it does have the vital constitutional right to say 'Yes' or 'Yes, but not for a few weeks.'
David Frost and Antony Jay, *To England with Love*, 1967

8 When Wellington thrashed Bonaparte,
As every child can tell,
The House of Peers, throughout the war,
Did nothing in particular,
And did it very well:
Yet Britain set the world ablaze
In good King George's glorious days!
W. S. Gilbert and Arthur Sullivan, 'Lord Mountararat', *Iolanthe*, 1882

9 The House of Lords is not the watchdog of the constitution: it is Mr Balfour's poodle. It fetches and carries for him. It barks for him. It bites anybody that he sets it on to!
David Lloyd George, speech, House of Commons, 1908

10 You can't say: 'The noble and gallant Lord is a silly old fool.' It just wouldn't sound right.
Lady Phillips, *Observer*, 1967

11 The House of Lords has a value . . . it is good evidence of life after death.
Lord Soper (Attrib.)

12 The House of Lords is a perfect eventide home.
Lady Stocks (Attrib.), 1970

13 LORD ILLINGWORTH: We in the House of Lords are never in touch with public opinion. That makes us a civilized body.
Oscar Wilde, *A Woman of No Importance*, 1893

See also The Aristocracy; House of Commons; Parliament; Politics and Politicians.

HOUSEWIVES

1 No one knows what her life expectancy

is, but I have a horror of leaving this world and not having anyone in the entire family know how to replace a toilet tissue spindle.
  Erma Bombeck, *If Life is a Bowl of Cherries – What am I Doing in the Pits?*, 1978

2 There was no need to do any housework at all. After the first four years the dirt doesn't get any worse.
  Quentin Crisp, *The Naked Civil Servant*, 1968

3 Cleaning your house while your kids are still growing
  Is like shoveling the walk before it stops snowing.
  Phyllis Diller, *Phyllis Diller's Housekeeping Hints*, 1966

4 I'll be there,
  Waiting until his mind is clear
  While he looks through me – right through me.
  Waiting to say, 'Good evening, dear, I'm pregnant –
  What's new with you from downtown?'
  Oh, to be loved by a man I respect,
  To bask in the glow of his perfectly understandable neglect.
  Oh to belong in the aura of his frown,
  Darling-busy frown,
  Such heaven!
  Frank Loesser, 'Happy to Keep His Dinner Warm', *How to Succeed in Business without Really Trying*, 1961

5 I hate housework! You make the beds, you do the dishes – and six months later you have to start all over again.
  Joan Rivers

See also Home; Husbands; Mothers; Women.

HUMILITY

1 It is going to be fun to watch and see how long the meek can keep the earth after they inherit it.
  Kin Hubbard, *Abe Martin's Sayings*, 1915

2 Christian humility is preached by the clergy, but practised only by the lower classes.
  Bertrand Russell, *Autobiography*, 1967

HUMOUR

1 *Caustic*: adjective applied to the wit of magistrates and judges, as in the sentence, 'The judge then asked who was this gentleman, Mussolini, who appeared to be an Italian?'
  Beachcomber (J. B. Morton), *Beachcomber: The Works of J. B. Morton*, 1974

2 Mark my words, when a society has to resort to the lavatory for its humour, the writing is on the wall.
  Alan Bennett, *Forty Years On*, 1968

3 There are best-selling humorists who do get my goat. Andy Rooney springs to mind. Wry. Who needs wry? I haven't got *time* for wry.
  Roy Blount, Jr, *Esquire*, 1984

4 There is no reason why a joke should not be appreciated more than once. Imagine how little good music there would be if, for example, a conductor refused to play Beethoven's Fifth Symphony on the ground that his audience might have heard it before.
  A. P. Herbert

5 It is better in the long run to possess an abscess or a tumor
  Than to possess a sense of humor.
  People who have senses of humor have a very good time,
  But they never accomplish anything of note, either despicable or sublime,
  Because how can anybody accomplish anything immortal
  When they realize they look pretty funny doing it and have to stop to chortle?
  Ogden Nash, 'Don't Grin, or You'll Have to Bear It', *I'm a Stranger Here Myself*, 1938

6 Wit has truth in it; wisecracking is simply calisthenics with words.
  Dorothy Parker, interviewed in *Writers at Work*, 1958

7 Humor is emotional chaos remembered in tranquility.
  James Thurber

8 Humor can be dissected, as a frog can, but the thing dies in the process and the

innards are discouraging to any but the pure scientific mind.
E. B. White

9 Nothing spoils a romance so much as a sense of humour in the woman – or the want of it in a man.
Oscar Wilde, *A Woman of No Importance,* 1893

See also Comedy; Laughter; Puns; Riddles; Satire; Tom Swifties; Wit.

HUNTING

1 We'll be talking to a gunsmith who's invented a sage-and-onion bullet that shoots the goose and stuffs it at the same time.
The Two Ronnies, BBC TV

2 If God didn't want man to hunt, he wouldn't have given us plaid shirts.
Johnny Carson, *The Tonight Show,* NBC TV

3 I only kill in self-defense. What would *you* do if a rabbit pulled a knife on you?
Johnny Carson, *The Tonight Show,* NBC TV

4 ERIC: One day we suddenly came face to face with a ferocious lion.
ERNIE: Did it give you a start?
ERIC: I didn't need one. But I'd read a book about lions, so I knew exactly what steps to take . . . long ones.
Eric Morecambe and Ernie Wise, *The Morecambe and Wise Joke Book,* 1979

5 LADY UTTERWOLD: . . . everybody can see that the people who hunt are the right people and the people who don't are the wrong ones.
George Bernard Shaw, *Heartbreak House,* 1919

6 No sportsman wants to kill the fox or the pheasant as I want to kill him when I see him doing it.
George Bernard Shaw

7 The English country gentleman galloping after a fox – the unspeakable in full pursuit of the uneatable.
Oscar Wilde, *A Woman of No Importance,* 1893

See also The Country; Sport.

HUSBANDS

1 Small band of men, armed only with wallets, besieged by a horde of wives and children.
National Lampoon, 1979

2 I've been asked to say a couple of words about my husband, Fang. How about 'short' and 'cheap'.
Phyllis Diller

3 Husbands are like fires. They go out if unattended.
Zsa Zsa Gabor

4 He tells you when you've got on too
   much lipstick,
And helps you with your girdle when
   your hips stick.
Ogden Nash, 'The Perfect Husband', *Versus,* 1949

5 A husband is what is left of the lover after the nerve has been extracted.
Helen Rowland

6 Men are horribly tedious when they are good husbands, and abominably conceited when they are not.
Oscar Wilde, *A Woman of No Importance,* 1893

See also Fathers; Housewives; Men; Men – The Female View.

HYPOCHONDRIA

1 Hypochondria is the only disease I haven't got.
Graffito, New York, 1978

2 Hypochondriac: someone who enjoys bad health.
Anon.

3 MAN (*in bed*): Even hypochondriacs get ill . . .
Mel Calman, cartoon in *Dr Calman's Dictionary of Psychoanalysis,* 1979

4 Hungry Joe collected lists of fatal diseases and arranged them in alphabetical order so that he could put his finger without delay on any one he wanted to worry about.
Joseph Heller, *Catch-22,* 1961

5 Contentment preserves one even from

catching cold. Has a woman who knew that she was well dressed ever caught a cold? – No, not even when she had scarcely a rag to her back.

Friedrich Wilhelm Nietzsche, *The Twilight of the Idols*, 1889

6 All sorts of bodily diseases are produced by half-used minds.

George Bernard Shaw

See also Health; Illness.

HYPOCRISY

1 Hypocrisy is the most difficult and nerve-racking vice that any man can pursue; it needs an unceasing vigilance and a rare detachment of spirit. It cannot, like adultery or gluttony, be practised at spare moments; it is a wholetime job.

W. Somerset Maugham, *Cakes and Ale*, 1930

See also Flattery; Lies.

IDEALISM

1 An idealist is one who, on noticing that a rose smells better than a cabbage, concludes that it will also make better soup.
  H. L. Mencken, *Sententiae*, 1920

See also Belief; Opinions.

IDEAS

1 An idea that is not dangerous is unworthy of being called an idea at all.
  Oscar Wilde, 'The Critic as Artist', 1890

See also Creativity.

IDIOMS

1 It's like the bitchenest, like neatest way to talk, I'm sure, totally. It's so awesome, I mean, fer shurr, toadly, toe-dully! To the max! Come onnnnn – bag your face, you geek, you grody totally shanky spaz, if you can't talk like a total Valley Girl, rilly, I'm shurrr. Gag me with a spoooooon! Ohhhhmigawwwd! OK: Valspeak is, I meannnnn, wow!, the funniest, most totally radical language, I guess, like in the whole mega gnarly city of Los Angeles? Fer shur-r-r!
  Bart Mills, 'A Glossary of Valspeak', *Guardian*, 1982

See also The English Language; Language.

IGNORANCE

1 What he doesn't know would make a library anybody would be proud of.
  Anon.

See also Knowledge; Stupidity.

ILLNESS

1 I've got Parkinson's disease. And he's got mine.
  Anon.

2 DOCTOR: I don't like the looks of your husband.
WIFE: I don't either, but he's good to the children.
  Joke inside Sainsbury's Christmas cracker, 1984

3 To Bary Jade
The bood is beabig brighdly, love;
The sdars are shidig too;
While I ab gazig dreabily,
Add thigkig, love, of you.
You caddot, oh! you caddot kdow,
By darlig, how I biss you –
(Oh, whadt a fearful cold I've got! –
Ck-TISH-u! Ck-ck-TISH-u!)
  Charles Follen Adams, *Yawcob Strauss and Other Poems*, 1910

4 LEE-ANN: Anyway, it must be wonderfully healthy, out here in the country. Fewer coronaries.
GAYNOR: Don't knock coronaries. They're all we women have got to guarantee us a prosperous and exciting middle age.
  Malcolm Bradbury and Christopher Bigsby, *The After Dinner Game*, BBC TV, 1975

5 I asked him if he had the results of the x-rays. He took me into his surgery . . . He gave me one of those looks of his, redolent of the cemetery, and said that I should buy day-returns from now on instead of season tickets.
  Hugh Leonard, *A Life*, 1979

6 One of the minor pleasures of life is to be slightly ill.
  Harold Nicolson, quoted in the *Observer*, 1950

7 Illness of any kind is hardly a thing to be encouraged in others. Health is the primary duty of life.
  Oscar Wilde, *Lady Windermere's Fan*, 1892

See also Doctors; Health; Hospitals; Hypochondria; Indigestion; Medicine; Nausea.

IMMORTALITY

1 If man were immortal, do you realize
what his meat bills would be?
Woody Allen

See also Death; Fame.

INDECISION

1 His indecision is final.
Anon.

2 They call him 'Jigsaw' because every
time he's faced with a problem, he goes
to pieces.
Anon.

3 Nothing is so exhausting as indecision,
and nothing is so futile.
Bertrand Russell, *The Conquest of Happiness*, 1930

See also Decisions.

INDIA

1 India is no more a political personality
than Europe. India is a geographical
term. It is no more a united nation than
the equator.
Winston Churchill, speech, 1931.

2 'Sub-' is no idle prefix in its application
to this continent.
P. J. O'Rourke, 'Foreigners Around the
World', *National Lampoon*, 1976

INDIGESTION

1 I would like to find a stew that will give
me heartburn immediately, instead of at
three o'clock in the morning.
John Barrymore

2 No country can touch us when it comes
to heartburn and upset stomachs. This
nation, under God, with liberty and justice for all, neutralizes more stomach
acid in one day than the Soviet Union
does in a year. We give more relief from
discomfort of the intestinal tract than
China and Japan combined.
   They can say what they will about us,
but we Americans know what to do with
our excess gas.
Art Buchwald, 'Acid Indigestion', *Esquire*,
1975

3 To eat is human, to digest, divine.
Mark Twain

See also Eating; Food; Illness.

INFATUATION

1 SECRETARY (*to boss*): I do think it was
terribly sweet of you to have our initials
strip-mined in the Nevada desert, but
Mr Hargrave, I already have a boyfriend.
T. Haggerty, cartoon in *National Lampoon*,
1984

2 Doris, I think I'm in love with you. I
mean, it's crazy. Really crazy! I mean
I don't even know if you've read *The
Catcher in the Rye*.
Bernard Slade, *Same Time, Next Year*, 1978

3 Infatuation is when you think that he's
as sexy as Robert Redford, as smart as
Henry Kissinger, as noble as Ralph
Nader, as funny as Woody Allen and as
athletic as Jimmy Connors. Love is when
you realize that he's as sexy as Woody
Allen, as smart as Jimmy Connors, as
funny as Ralph Nader, as athletic
as Henry Kissinger and nothing like
Robert Redford – but you'll take him
anyway.
Judith Viorst, *Redbook*, 1975

4 I'd be crazy to propose to her, but when I
see that profile of hers I feel the only
thing worth doing in the world is to grab
her and start shouting for clergymen and
bridesmaids to come running.
P. G. Wodehouse, *Plum Pie*, 1966

See also Courting; Flirtation; Love;
Romance; Sexual Attraction.

INFERIORITY

1 No one can make you feel inferior without your consent.
Eleanor Roosevelt

INFIDELITY

1 Executive Mistresses' Influence
Mounting in US Boardrooms.
 . . . Who is she? The executive mistress,
that important figure found standing behind so many top executives and kneeling
in front of still more.

A nationwide survey conducted by *Off The Wall Street Journal* shows that 86 per cent of the senior officers in 65 per cent of the Fortune 500 companies keep a mistress currently, have kept a mistress in the past or intend to find one as soon as they finish reading this article.
Off The Wall Street Journal, 1982

2 'My executive often arrives at the apartment exhausted and emotionally detached after a hard day of corporate manipulation and chicanery,' says Karen C. (not her real initial). 'He depends on me to raise his lowered interest rate and stimulate his private sector.'
Off The Wall Street Journal, 1982

3 *Off The Wall Street Journal*'s incredibly exhaustive survey of 18,845 exhausted mistresses showed that fully 75 per cent are subject to the same kind of stress, tension and high vulnerability to heart attacks, cancer and suicide suffered by the high-level executives who keep them – as well as amexophobia, the fear of abrupt credit cancellation ... Surprisingly, more than three quarters of the mistresses surveyed say they find the mistress-executive relationship to be stimulating, honest, emotionally gratifying, financially rewarding and in all ways preferable to marriage, although if the executive offered to marry them they'd grab it in a second.
Off The Wall Street Journal, 1982

4 Once, in a simpler time, mistresses were considered mere playthings, trinkets that a busy executive could enjoy at his leisure, then toss aside like a crumpled Kleenex or generic tissue. Today's mistress is a far different breed. She is better educated, better trained, more assertive and more skilled at her demanding task. Many mistresses have mastered speech, adding an entirely new facet to what was once a one-dimensional relationship.
Off The Wall Street Journal, 1982

5 WENDLE: I'm not a suspicious woman but I don't think my husband 'as been entirely faithful to me.

PELLET: Whatever makes you think that?
WENDLE: My last child doesn't resemble him in the least.
Noël Coward, 'Law and Order', *This Year of Grace*, 1928

6 I told my wife the truth. I told her I was seeing a psychiatrist. Then she told *me* the truth: that she was seeing a psychiatrist, two plumbers and a bartender.
Rodney Dangerfield

7 Stan Waltz has decided to take unto himself a wife but he hasn't decided yet whose ...
Peter De Vries, *Let Me Count the Ways*, 1965

8 You mustn't think too harshly of my secretaries. They were kind and understanding when I came to the office after a hard day at home.
Julius J. and Philip G. Epstein, *Mr Skeffington*, screenplay, 1944

9 Few things in life are more embarrassing than the necessity of having to inform an old friend that you have just got engaged to his fiancée.
W. C. Fields, *Big Money*, 1931

10 Thou shalt not commit adultery ... unless in the mood.
W. C. Fields

11 *A Code of Honor*: never approach a friend's girlfriend or wife with mischief as your goal. There are just too many women in the world to justify that sort of dishonorable behavior. Unless she's *really* attractive.
Bruce Jay Friedman, 'Sex and the Lonely Guy', *Esquire*, 1977

12 The Deacon's wife was a bit desirish
And liked her sex relations wild,
So she lay with one of the shanty Irish
And he begot the Deacon's child.
The Deacon himself was a man of money
And upright life and a bosom shirt;
Which made her infidelity funny
And gave her pleasure in doing him dirt.
And yet for all her romantic sneakin'
Out the back door and over the wall

How was she sure the child of the
  Deacon
Wasn't the Deacon's after all?
  Robert Frost, 'Pride of Ancestry'

13 The most depressing thing, you know,
the most depressing thing is that I used
to feel a certain amount of post-coital
tristesse. Well, guilt. But these days I can
scarcely be bothered to feel shifty when I
get home. Extra-marital sex is as overrated as pre-marital sex. And marital sex,
come to think of it.
  Simon Gray, *Two Sundays*, BBC TV,
  1975

14 I Could Never Have Sex With Any
Man Who Has So Little Regard For My
Husband.
  Dan Greenburg, film title

15 I said to the wife, 'Guess what I heard in
the pub? They reckon the milkman
has made love to every woman in this
road except one.' And she said, 'I'll bet
it's that stuck-up Phyllis at number
23.'
  Max Kauffmann

16 Adultery is the application of democracy
to love.
  H. L. Mencken, *Sententiae*, 1920

17 An old man of ninety got married,
The bride was so young and so bold,
In his car they both went
  honeymooning –
She married the old man for gold.
A year later he was a daddy,
At ninety he still had the knack;
He took one look at the baby –
And then gave the chauffeur the sack.
  Max Miller, 'The Hiking Song', *The Max
  Miller Blue Book*, 1975

18 Even in civilized mankind faint traces
of monogamous instinct can be
perceived.
  Bertrand Russell

19 Those who are faithful know only the
trivial side of love: it is the faithless who
know love's tragedies.
  Oscar Wilde, *The Picture of Dorian Gray*,
  1891

20 Young men want to be faithful, and are
not; old men want to be faithless, and
cannot.
  Oscar Wilde, *The Picture of Dorian Gray*,
  1891

21 SHELDRAKE: Come on, Fran – don't be
like that. You just going to sit there and
keep bawling? . . .
FRAN: How could I be so stupid? You'd
think I would have learned by now –
when you're in love with a married man,
you shouldn't wear mascara.
  Billy Wilder and I. A. L. Diamond, *The
  Apartment*, screenplay, 1960

22 I've been in love with the same woman
for forty-one years. If my wife finds out,
she'll kill me.
  Henny Youngman, *Henny Youngman's
  Greatest One Liners*, 1970

See also Bigamy; Divorce; Fidelity;
Promiscuity; Sex.

INFLATION

1 Among the things that money can't buy is
what it used to.
  Max Kauffmann

2 Time for belt tightening. You can't live
on a million a year anymore.
  Randy Newman, 1983

3 Americans are getting stronger. Twenty
years ago, it took two people to carry
ten dollars' worth of groceries. Today, a
five-year-old can do it.
  Henny Youngman

See also Economics; Money.

INHERITANCE

1 It is a gorgeous gold pocket watch. I'm
proud of it. My grandfather, on his
deathbed, sold me this watch.
  Woody Allen, *The Nightclub Years, 1965–
  1968*, record, 1972

2 'This is the last and solemn Will
Of Uncle William – known as Bill.
I do bequeath, devise and give
By Executive Mandative
The whole amount of what I've got
(It comes to a tremendous lot!)

In seizin to devote upon
My well-beloved nephew John.
(And here the witnesses will sign
Their names upon the dotted line.)'
   Hilaire Belloc, 'About John', *More Cautionary Tales*, 1930

See also Death; Money.

INJUSTICE

1 To have a grievance is to have a purpose
   in life.
   Eric Hoffer, *The Passionate State of Mind*,
   1954

See also Crime; Dishonesty; The Law.

INSANITY

1 She used to eat chops in the small hours
   and sleep in a hat. Once she arrived
   home at seven a.m. carrying a gate. Who
   am I to say there was anything wrong with
   her?
   Alan Coren, *The Sanity Inspector*, 1974

2 That's the truest sign of insanity – insane
   people are always sure they're just fine.
   It's only the sane people who are willing
   to admit they're crazy.
   Nora Ephron, *Heartburn*, 1983

3 An international team of psychiatrists
   has flown to Uganda in an attempt to
   discover exactly what makes General
   Amin tick. And, more especially, what
   makes him go cuckoo every half hour.
   David Frost, *David Frost Revue*, 1972

4 There was only one catch and that was
   Catch-22, which specified that a concern
   for one's own safety in the face of dangers
   that were real and immediate was the
   process of a rational mind. Orr was crazy
   and could be grounded. All he had to do
   was ask; and as soon as he did, he would
   no longer be crazy and would have to fly
   more missions. Orr would be crazy to fly
   more missions and sane if he didn't,
   but if he was sane he had to fly them.
   If he flew them he was crazy and
   didn't have to; but if he didn't want to
   he was sane and had to. Yossarian was
   moved very deeply by the absolute simplicity of this clause of Catch-22, and let
   out a respectful whistle.
   Joseph Heller, *Catch-22*, 1961

5 PSYCHIATRIST: The idea that all the
   people locked up in mental hospitals are
   sane while the people walking about outside are all mad is merely a literary cliché,
   put about by people who should be
   locked up. I assure you there's not much
   in it. Taken as a whole, the sane are out
   there and the sick are in here. For example, YOU are in here because you have
   delusions that sane people are put in
   mental hospitals.
   ALEXANDER: But I *am* in a mental
   hospital.
   PSYCHIATRIST: That's what I said.
   Tom Stoppard, *Every Good Boy Deserves
   Favour*, 1977

See also Illness; Paranoia; Psychiatry;
Psychoanalysis; Schizophrenia.

INSECTS

1 When the insects take over the world, we
   hope they will remember with gratitude
   how we took them along on all our
   picnics.
   Bill Vaughan

See also Pests.

INSOMNIA

1 A: How's your insomnia?
   B: Worse. I can't even sleep when it's
   time to get up.
   Anon.

2 A good cure for insomnia is to get plenty
   of sleep.
   W. C. Fields

3 When you're lying awake with a dismal
      headache, and repose is taboo'd by
      anxiety,
   I conceive you may use any language
      you choose to indulge in, without
      impropriety;
   For your brain is on fire – the
      bedclothes conspire of usual slumber
      to plunder you:

First your counterpane goes, and
   uncovers your toes, and your sheet
   slips demurely from under you;
Then the blanketing tickles – you feel
   like mixed pickles – so terribly sharp
   is the pricking,
And you're hot and you're cross, and
   you tumble and toss till there's
   nothing 'twixt you and the ticking.
Then the bedclothes all creep to the
   ground in a heap, and you pick 'em all
   up in a tangle;
Then your pillow resigns and politely
   declines to remain at its usual angle!
   W. S. Gilbert and Arthur Sullivan, 'Lord
   Chancellor', *Iolanthe*, 1882

4 CHICO MARX: Don't wake him up. He's
got insomnia. He's trying to sleep it
off.
   **George S. Kaufman and Morrie Rys-
   kind**, *A Night at the Opera*, screenplay, 1935

See also Bed; Sleep.

INSULTS

1 What he lacks in intelligence, he makes
up for in stupidity.
   Anon.

2 If I say that he's extremely stupid, I don't
mean that in any derogatory sense. I
simply mean that he's not very intelligent.
If he were more intelligent, he'd be very
clever. But he isn't and there we are.
   Alan Bennett, 'The Critics', *On the Margin*,
   BBC TV, 1966

3 I said that I didn't think Chevy Chase
could ad-lib a fart after a baked-bean
dinner. I think he took umbrage at that a
little bit.
   Johnny Carson (Attrib.)

4 A day away from Tallulah is like a month
in the country.
   Howard Dietz

5 I won't eat anything that has intelligent
life but I would gladly eat a network
executive or a politician.
   Marty Feldman

6 He has left his body to science – and
science is contesting the will.
   David Frost, *Live from London*, 1983

7 I hope you won't take this amiss, Charles,
but I don't think I've ever met a man who
reminded me less of Jeremy Irons.
   J. B. Handelsman, cartoon in the *New
   Yorker*, 1984

8 . . . like being savaged by a dead sheep.
   Denis Healey, on Geoffrey Howe's attack
   on his budget, House of Commons, 1978

9 I treasure every moment that I do not see
her.
   Oscar Levant, on Phyllis Diller (Attrib.)

10 Make yourself at home, Frank. Hit
somebody.
   Don Rickles, to Frank Sinatra (Attrib.)

11 Ricky turned on the Duke of Dunstable.
'You are without exception the worst tick
and bounder that ever got fatty degen-
eration of the heart through half a century of gorging food and swilling wine
wrenched from the lips of a starving
proletariat. You make me sick. You
poison the air. Good-bye, Uncle Alaric,'
said Ricky, drawing himself away rather
ostentatiously. 'I think we had better
terminate this interview, or I may become
brusque.'
   P. G. Wodehouse, *Uncle Fred in the Springtime*, 1939

12 The nicest thing I can say about Frances
Farmer is that she is unbearable.
   William Wyler (Attrib.)

See also Abuse; Hecklers; Politics –
Insults.

INSURANCE

1 I don't want to tell you how much insurance I carry with the Prudential, but all I
can say is: when I go, THEY go.
   Jack Benny (Attrib.)

2 Insurance, *n.* an ingenious modern game
of chance in which the player is permitted to enjoy the comfortable conviction
that he is beating the man who keeps the
table.
   Ambrose Bierce, *The Devil's Dictionary*,
   1911

3 . . . the Act of God designation on all
insurance policies; which means roughly,
that you cannot be insured for the acci-

dents that are most likely to happen to you. If your ox kicks a hole in your neighbour's Maserati, however, indemnity is instantaneous.
Alan Coren, *The Lady from Stalingrad Mansions*, 1977

4 I detest life-insurance agents. They always argue that I shall some day die, which is not so.
Stephen Leacock, *Literary Lapses*, 1910

See also Professions.

INTELLECTUALS

1 Lord Birkenhead is very clever, but sometimes his brains go to his head.
Margot Asquith

2 To the man-in-the-street, who, I'm
   sorry to say,
Is a keen observer of life,
The word 'Intellectual' suggests straight
   away
A man who's untrue to his wife.
W. H. Auden, *Collected Shorter Poems, 1927–1957*, 1966

3 To be honest, what I feel really bad about is that I don't feel worse. That is the intellectual's problem in a nutshell.
Michael Frayn, *Observer*, 1963

4 Everyone agreed that Clevinger was certain to go far in the academic world. In short, Clevinger was one of those people with lots of intelligence and no brains, and everyone knew it except those who soon found it out.
   In short, he was a dope.
Joseph Heller, *Catch-22*, 1961

5 The learned are seldom pretty fellows, and in many cases their appearance tends to discourage a love of study in the young.
H. L. Mencken

6 People who refer to themselves as intellectuals are automatically committing a social crime and, also, usually an error.
Tracy Young, *Vanity Fair*, 1984

See also Genius; Knowledge.

INTERIOR DECORATING

1 You mean you can actually spend 70,000 dollars at Woolworth's?
Bob Krasnow, after seeing Ike and Tina Turner's house

See also Do-it-yourself; Home; Style.

INTUITION

1 Intuition: that strange instinct that tells a woman she is right, whether she is or not.
Methodist Recorder

INVENTIONS

1 We owe a lot to Thomas Edison – if it wasn't for him, we'd be watching television by candlelight.
Milton Berle, *Variety*

2 You know, there's a new cloth you can wear in the rain? It gets soaking wet, but you can wear it in the rain!
Henny Youngman

See also Modern Life; Technology.

IRELAND AND THE IRISH

1 Other people have a nationality. The Irish and the Jews have a psychosis.
Brendan Behan, *Richard's Cork Leg*, 1973

2 PAT: He was an Anglo-Irishman.
MEG: In the blessed name of God, what's that?
PAT: A Protestant with a horse.
Brendan Behan, *The Hostage*, 1959

3 The English and Americans dislike only *some* Irish – the same Irish that the Irish themselves detest, Irish writers – the ones that *think*.
Brendan Behan, *Richard's Cork Leg*, 1973

4 And if ever ye ride in Ireland,
The jest may yet be said:
There is the land of broken hearts,
And the land of broken heads.
G. K. Chesterton, *Notes to a Tourist*

5 Down with the bold Sinn Fein!
We'll rout them willy-nilly.
They flaunt their crimes
In the *Belfast Times*,
Which makes *us* look so silly.

Down with the Ulster men!
They don't know which from what.
If Ireland sunk beneath the sea
How peaceful everyone would be!
You haven't said a word about the
    RUC?
Down with the whole damn lot!
    Noël Coward, 'Down with the Whole
    Damn Lot!', song from *Co-optimists*, 1920s

6 . . . the Irish behave exactly as they have
been portrayed as behaving for years.
Charming, soft-voiced, quarrelsome,
priest-ridden, feckless and happily devoid of the slightest integrity in our
stodgy English sense of the word.
    Noël Coward, *Diary*, 1960

7 I never met anyone in Ireland who
understood the Irish question, except
one Englishman who had only been there
a week.
    Major Sir Keith Fraser, MP, 1919

8 Order is an exotic in Ireland. It has been
imported from England but it will not
grow. It suits neither soil nor climate.
    J. A. Froude, *The Two Chiefs of Dunboy*,
    1889

9 Politics is the chloroform of the Irish
people, or, rather, the hashish.
    Oliver St John Gogarty, *As I Was Going
    Down Sackville Street*, 1937

10 The Irish people do not gladly suffer
common sense.
    Oliver St John Gogarty, 1935

11 Ireland is the old sow that eats her
farrow.
    James Joyce, *A Portrait of the Artist as a
    Young Man*, 1914

12 This lovely land that has always sent
Her writers and artists to banishment
And in a spirit of Irish fun
Betrayed her own leaders, one by
    one . . .
Oh Ireland my first and only love
Where Christ and Caesar are hand in
    glove!
O lovely land where the shamrock
    grows!
(Allow me, ladies, to blow my nose).
    James Joyce, 'Gas from a Burner', 1912

13 The problem with Ireland is that it's a
country full of genius, but with absolutely
no talent.
    Hugh Leonard, interview in *The Times*,
    1977

14 Every St Patrick's Day every Irishman
goes out to find another Irishman to
make a speech to.
    Shane Leslie, *American Wonderland*,
    1936

15 If, in the eyes of an Irishman, there is
anyone being more ridiculous than an
Englishman, it is an Englishman who
loves Ireland.
    André Maurois, *Ariel*, 1923

16 My one claim to originality among
Irishmen is that I never made a
speech.
    George Moore, *Ave*, 1911

17 An Irishman is a guy who:
    Believes everything he can't see, and
nothing he can.
    Has such great respect for the truth,
he only uses it in emergencies.
    Can lick any man in the house he is
sole occupant of.
    Believes salvation can be achieved by
means of a weekly envelope.
    . . . we are a very perverse, complex
people. It's what makes us lovable. We're
banking heavily that God has a sense of
humor.
    Jim Murray, *Los Angeles Times*, 1976

18 When anyone asks me about the Irish
character, I say – look at the trees.
Maimed, stark and misshapen, but fer-
ociously tenacious. The Irish have got
gab but are too touchy to be humorous.
Me too.
    Edna O'Brien

19 The English should give Ireland home
rule – and reserve the motion picture
rights.
    Will Rogers, *The Autobiography of Will
    Rogers*, 1949

20 [Gladstone] spent his declining years
trying to guess the answer to the Irish
Question; unfortunately, whenever he

was getting warm, the Irish secretly changed the Question . . .
W. C. Sellar and R. J. Yeatman, *1066 and All That*, 1930

21 The moment the very name of Ireland is mentioned, the English seem to bid adieu to common feeling, common prudence, and common sense, and to act with the barbarity of tyrants, and the fatuity of idiots.
Sydney Smith, *Peter Plymley's Letters*, 1929

22 At last I went to Ireland,
'Twas raining cats and dogs:
I found no music in the glens,
Nor purple in the bogs,
And as far as angels' laughter in the
smelly Liffy's tide –
Well, my Irish daddy said it, but the
dear old humbug lied.
George Bernard Shaw, envoi added to the song 'My Irish Daddy' by Maisie Hurl

23 The Irish are difficult for us to deal with. For one thing the English do not understand their innate love of fighting and blows. If on either side of an Irishman's road to Paradise shillelahs grew, which automatically hit him on the head, yet he would not be satisfied.
Alfred, Lord Tennyson, quoted in *Alfred, Lord Tennyson: A Memoir*, 1897

24 'Irishmen don't talk like that,' said Gussie. 'Have you read J. M. Synge's *Riders to the Sea*? If you can show me a single character in it who says "faith and begob" I'll give you a shilling. Irishmen are poets. They talk about their souls and mists and so on. They say things like, "An evening like this, it makes me wish I was back in the County Clare, watching the cows in the tall grass."'
P. G. Wodehouse, *The Mating Season*, 1949

25   'You disapprove of the Swedes?'
'Yes, sir.'
'Why?'
'Their heads are too square, sir.'

'And you disapprove of the Irish?'
'Yes, sir.'
'Why?'
'Because they are Irish, sir.'
P. G. Wodehouse, *The Small Bachelor*, 1927

See also Britain and the British.

ISRAEL

1 If we lose this war, I'll start another in my wife's name.
Moshe Dayan, during the Six-day War, 1967

See also Jews.

ITALY AND THE ITALIANS

1 The median Italian . . . is a cowardly baritone who consumes 78.3 kilometres of carbohydrates a month and drives about in a car slightly smaller than he is, looking for a divorce.
Alan Coren, *The Sanity Inspector*, 1974

2 Nobody in Rome works and if it rains in Rome *and* they happen to notice it they blame it on Milan. In Rome people spend most of their time having lunch. And they do it very well – Rome is unquestionably the lunch capital of the world.
Fran Lebowitz, *Metropolitan Life*, 1978

3 She said that all the sights in Rome were called after London cinemas.
Nancy Mitford, *Pigeon Pie*, 1940

4 Very little counts for less in Italy than the state.
Peter Nichols, *Italia, Italia*, 1973

5 By 1948 the Italians had begun to pull themselves together, demonstrating once more their astonishing ability to cope with disaster which is so perfectly balanced by their absolute inability to deal with success.
Gore Vidal, *Matters of Fact and Fiction*, 1977

See also Europe and the EEC; Venice.

JAPAN

1 Japanese food is very pretty and un-doubtedly a suitable cuisine in Japan, which is largely populated by people of below average size. Hostesses hell-bent on serving such food to occidentals would be well advised to supplement it with something more substantial and to keep in mind that almost everybody likes French fries.
   Fran Lebowitz, *Metropolitan Life*, 1978

JAZZ

1 If you have to ask what jazz is, you'll never know.
   Louis Armstrong

2 Playing 'bop' is like playing scrabble with all the vowels missing.
   Duke Ellington, *Look*, 1954

3 If you're in jazz and more than ten people like you, you're labelled 'commercial'.
   Wally Stott

See also Music and Musicians; Rock 'n' Roll; Songs and Singers.

JEALOUSY

1 The dullard's envy of brilliant men is always assuaged by the suspicion that they will come to a bad end.
   Max Beerbohm, *Zuleika Dobson*, 1911

2 Never be possessive. If a female friend lets on that she is going out with another man, be kind and understanding. If she says she would like to go out with all the Dallas Cowboys, including the coaching staff, the same rule applies. Tell her: 'Kath, you just go right ahead and do what you feel is right.' Unless you actually care for her, in which case you must see to it that she has no male contact whatsoever.
   Bruce Jay Friedman, 'Sex and the Lonely Guy', *Esquire*, 1977

3 Anybody can sympathize with the suf-ferings of a friend, but it requires a very fine nature to sympathize with a friend's success.
   Oscar Wilde, 'The Soul of Man under Socialism', 1891

4 He was a man of strong passions, and the green-eyed monster ran up his leg and bit him to the bone.
   P. G. Wodehouse, *Full Moon*, 1947

JESUS CHRIST

1 No one ever made more trouble than the 'gentle Jesus meek and mild'.
   James M. Gillis, *This Our Day*

2 Prove to me that you're no fool.
   Walk across my swimming pool.
   Tim Rice and Andrew Lloyd Webber, 'Jesus Christ Superstar', 1971

See also Belief; The Bible; Christianity; The Church; God; Heaven; Religion.

JEWS

1 How odd
   of God
   To choose
   the Jews.
   Anon.

2 Not odd
   of God.
   Goyim
   Annoy 'im.
   Leo Rosten

3 Q: Why do Jews answer a question with a question?
   A: Why shouldn't Jews answer a question with a question?
   Anon.

4 ... I landed at Orly airport and dis-covered my luggage wasn't on the same plane. My bags were finally traced to Israel where they were opened and all my trousers were altered.
   Woody Allen, *Esquire*, 1975

5 I was raised in the Jewish tradition, taught never to marry a Gentile woman, shave on Saturday and, most especially, never to shave a Gentile woman on Saturday.
Woody Allen, *Esquire*, 1975

6 We were married by a reformed rabbi in Long Island. A *very* reformed rabbi. A Nazi.
Woody Allen, *The Nightclub Years, 1964– 1968*, record, 1972

7 Mr Deasy halted, breathing hard and swallowing his breath.
– I just wanted to say, he said. Ireland, they say, has the honour of being the only country which never persecuted the jews. Do you know that? No. And do you know why?
He frowned sternly on the bright air.
– Why sir? Stephen asked, beginning to smile.
– Because she never let them in, Mr Deasy said solemnly.
James Joyce, *Ulysses*, 1922

8 If you ever forget you're a Jew, a gentile will remind you.
Bernard Malamud
See also Israel.

9 The Jewish man with parents alive is a fifteen-year-old boy and will remain a fifteen-year-old boy till they die.
Philip Roth, *Portnoy's Complaint*, 1969

See also Israel.

JINGOISM

1 He majored in English history, which was a mistake.
'*English* history!' roared the silver-maned senior Senator from his state indignantly. 'What's the matter with American history? American history is as good as any history in the world!'
Joseph Heller, *Catch-22*, 1961

See also Patriotism; Xenophobia.

JOURNALISM

1 Anyone Here Been Raped and Speaks English?
Edward Behr, book title, 1978. Inspired by an incident at an airport in the Congo, when a British TV reporter allegedly approached groups of Belgian refugees fleeing from rebel troops with this question.

2 Journalism largely consists in saying 'Lord Jones Dead' to people who never knew Lord Jones was alive.
G. K. Chesterton, *The Wisdom of Father Brown*, 1914

3 ... adjectives do most of the work, smuggling in actual information under the guise of normal journalism. Thus the use of soft-spoken (mousy), loyal (dumb), high-minded (inept), hardworking (plodding), self-made (crooked), and pragmatic (totally immoral).
John Leo, 'Journalese for the Lay Reader', *Time*, 1985

4 Cronyism is the curse of journalism. After many years I have reached the firm conclusion that it is impossible for any objective newspaperman to be a friend of a President.
Walter Lippmann

5 The art of newspaper paragraphing is to stroke a platitude until it purrs like an epigram.
Don Marquis

6 A foreign correspondent is someone who lives in foreign parts and corresponds, usually in the form of essays containing no new facts. Otherwise he's someone who flies around from hotel to hotel and thinks that the most interesting thing about any story is the fact that he has arrived to cover it.
Tom Stoppard, *Night and Day*, 1978

7 RUTH: Perhaps I'll get him a reporter doll for Christmas. Wind it up and it gets it wrong. What does it say when you press its stomach? Come on, Dick!
DICK: I name the guilty man.
Tom Stoppard, *Night and Day*, 1978

8 The public have an insatiable curiosity to know everything. Except what is worth knowing. Journalism, conscious of this, and having tradesman-like habits, supplies their demands.

Oscar Wilde, 'The Soul of Man under Socialism', 1891

9 With regard to modern journalists, they always apologize to one in private for what they have written against one in public.

Oscar Wilde, 'The Soul of Man under Socialism', 1891

10 You cannot hope
to bribe or twist,
thank God! the
British journalist.
But, seeing what
the man will do
unbribed, there's
no occasion to.

Humbert Wolfe, 'Over the Fire', *The Uncelestial City*

See also News; Newspapers.

EDWARD KENNEDY United States Senator

1 *Chappaquidick*: the name of a place brought up by candidates every time they say they are not going to bring it up.
   Mark Russell, *Presenting Mark Russell*, 1980

See also John F. Kennedy; Politics and Politicians; Washington.

JOHN F. KENNEDY President of the United States, 1961–1963

1 He taught us the courage of action in West Berlin, the wisdom of patience in South-East Asia, the action of wisdom in our space race, the patience of courage in our desegregated schools and the active patient wisdom of wise courageous action at the Guantanamo Naval Base.
   National Lampoon

2 Knock, knock.
   Who's there?
   Astronaut.
   Astronaut Who?
   Astronaut what your country can do for you – ask what you can do for your country.
   Anon.

3 ... the report is that Old Joe Kennedy told Young Jack: 'Don't worry, son. If you lose the election, I'll buy you a country.'
   Time, 1960

4 His speaking style is pseudo-Roman: 'Ask not what your country can do for you ...' Why not say, 'Don't ask ...'? 'Ask not ...' is the style of a man playing the role of being President, not of a man being President.
   Herb Gold, *New York Post*, 1962

5 Everyone's talking about how young the candidates are. And it's true. A few months ago Kennedy's mother said, 'You have a choice ... do you want to go to camp this year or run for President?'
   Bob Hope, during Kennedy/Nixon presidential campaign, 1960

6 When we got into office, the one thing that surprised me most was to find that things were just as bad as we'd been saying they were.
   John F. Kennedy, at his birthday party at the White House, 1961

See also Assassination; Edward Kennedy; Politics and Politicians; Washington.

KIDNAPPING

1 When I was kidnapped, my parents snapped into action. They rented out my room.
   Woody Allen

See also Crime; The Law.

KISSING

1 She frowned and called him Mr.
   Because in sport he kr.
   And so in spite
   That very nite
   This Mr. kr. sr.
   Anon.

2 It takes a lot of experience for a girl to kiss like a beginner.
   Ladies' Home Journal, 1948

3 A delectable gal from Augusta
   vowed that nobody ever had bussed her.
   But an expert from France
   took a bilingual chance
   and the mixture of tongues quite nonplussed her.
   Conrad Aiken, *A Seizure of Limericks*, 1965

4 ... we did one of those quick, awkward kisses where each of you gets a nose in the eye.
   Clive James, *Unreliable Memoirs*, 1980

See also Courting; Flirtation; Love; Petting; Sex.

KNOWLEDGE

1 It aint' what a man don't know that makes him a fool, but what he does know that ain't so.

   Josh Billings, *The Complete Works of Josh Billings*, 1919

2 We are here and it is now. Further than that, all human knowledge is moonshine.

   H. L. Mencken

3 I am sufficiently proud of my knowing something to be modest about my not knowing everything.

   Vladimir Nabokov, *Lolita*, 1955

See also Facts; Ignorance.

THE LABOUR PARTY

1 The Labour Party Marxists see the consequences of their own folly all around them and call it the collapse of capitalism.
Jon Akass, *Sun*, 1976

2 ... that bunch of rootless intellectuals, alien Jews and international pederasts who call themselves the Labour Party.
Alan Bennett, *Forty Years On*, 1968

3 They are not fit to manage a whelk stall.
Winston Churchill (Attrib.)

4 I do not often attack the Labour Party. They do it so well themselves.
Edward Heath, speech, 1973

5 It must never be forgotten that, whatever they say, the things that divide the [Labour] party are much greater than the things that unite it.
Frank Johnson, *The Times*, 1981

6 ... reminding us ... of the Labour Party's enduring commitment to resentment and the general, surly feeling that we are always being done by anyone in the remotest position of authority.
Frank Johnson, *The Times*, 1984

7 [Minister of Technology, Anthony Wedgwood] Benn flung himself into the Sixties technology with the enthusiasm (not to say language) of a newly enrolled Boy Scout demonstrating knot-tying to his indulgent parents.
Bernard Levin, *The Pendulum Years*, 1970

8 The 1984 Labour Party Conference last night exceeded its wildest expectations of its traditionally wild behaviour. In a pent-up frenzy of balloting ... it managed to vote against everything in sight. This has long been the position of many of the comrades where real life is concerned. But it has never been official party policy up to now, the preferred compromise being to vote in favour of conflicting things.
Michael White, *Guardian*, 1984

See also The Conservative Party; The Liberal Party; Socialism; Trades Unions.

LANGUAGE

1 BROOKS (*as 2,000-year-old man*): We spoke Rock. Basic Rock ... Two hundred years before Hebrew, there was the Rock Language. Or Rock talk.
REINER (*as interviewer*): Could you give us an example of that?
BROOKS: Yes. 'Hey, don't throw that rock at me! What are you doing with that rock? Put down that rock!'
Mel Brooks and Carl Reiner, *The 2,000-year-old Man*

2 Everybody has a right to pronounce foreign names as he chooses.
Winston Churchill (Attrib.)

3 *Watt* is the lightest of colors: 'Yew look watt as a sheet.'
Pour is having little or no means of support: 'Them folks is downriot pour.'
Ward is a unit of language: 'Pardon me. could ah have a ward with yawl?'
Owe is an overwhelming feeling of reverence: 'There's one thang I stand in owe of.'
And *Thank*: 'Ah hope yawl enjoyed raidin' this book. But just thank of what yew must sound lack to a Texan.'
Jim Everhart, *The Illustrated Texas Dictionary*

4 The word 'meaningful' when used today is nearly always meaningless.
Paul Johnson, *Observer*, 1982

5 SON: Mother, I've got something to tell you. I've just met the most wonderful girl. We love each other and we're going to get married.
MOTHER: Mama mia! What you saying? Ain't I been a gudda mudder to you, my leedle bambino? Doan I givva you lasagna, manicotti, spaghetti, ricotto, antipas-

to? Why you wanna doa dis to me? You no luvva me?

SON: Mother, you can't speak to me like this.

MOTHER: Why canna I speaka dissa way to you? Ain't I youa mudda?

SON: Mother, you can't speak to me like this because you're not Italian.

Max Kauffmann

6 Listen, someone's screaming in agony – fortunately I speak it fluently.

Spike Milligan, *The Goon Show*, BBC Radio, 1959

See also The English Language; Grammar; Idioms; Pronunciation; Punctuation.

LAST WORDS

1 Die, my dear doctor? That's the last thing I shall do.

Lord Palmerston (Attrib.), 1865

2 If this is dying, I don't think much of it.

Lytton Strachey (Attrib.), 1932

3 Either they go, or I do.

Oscar Wilde, of his new bedroom curtains (Attrib.), 1900

See also Death.

LAUGHTER

1 Laughter is the sensation of feeling good all over, and showing it principally in one spot.

Josh Billings, *The Complete Works of Josh Billings*, 1919

2 I suppose one of the reasons why I grew up feeling the need to cause laughter was perpetual fear of being its unwitting object.

Clive James, *Unreliable Memoirs*, 1980

3 One horse-laugh is worth ten thousand syllogisms. It is not only more effective; it is also vastly more intelligent.

H. L. Mencken, *Prejudices*, Fourth Series, 1924

4 He who laughs, lasts.

Mary Pettibone Poole, 'A Glass Eye at the Keyhole'

5 Aunt Dahlia guffawed more liberally than I had ever heard a woman guffaw. If there had been an aisle, she would have rolled in it ... She was giving the impression of a hyena which had just heard a good one from another hyena.

P. G. Wodehouse, *Much Obliged, Jeeves*, 1971

6 Madeline Bassett laughed the tinkling, silvery laugh which was one of the things that had got her so disliked by the better element.

P. G. Wodehouse, *The Code of the Woosters*, 1938

7 She had a penetrating sort of laugh. Rather like a train going into a tunnel.

P. G. Wodehouse, *The Inimitable Jeeves*, 1923

See also Comedy; Humour; Smiles.

THE LAW

1 COUNSEL: Have you any idea what your defence is going to be?

DEFENDANT: Well, I didn't do it, sir.

COUNSEL: Yes, well, er, I think we can afford to fill that out a little. It's not in itself a cast-iron defence.

DEFENDANT: Well I didn't do it sir! I didn't do it! And if I did it, may God strike me dead on the spot, sir!

COUNSEL: Well, we'll just give him a moment shall we ...

Alan Bennett, 'The Defending Counsel', *On the Margin*, BBC TV, 1966

2 COUNSEL: I shall of course try to discredit the character of widow Coddington. I notice she's got a Polish lodger which, in the eyes of the law, is synonymous with moral laxity. It hasn't yet been made statutory.

Alan Bennett, 'The Defending Counsel', *On the Margin*, BBC TV, 1966

3 It is illegal to make liquor privately or water publicly.

Lord Birkett (Attrib.)

4 ... all in all I'd rather have been a judge than a miner. And what is more, being a miner, as soon as you are too old and tired and sick and stupid to do the job

properly, you have to go. Well, the very opposite applies with the judges.
Peter Cook, 'Sitting on a Bench', nightclub act, 1960s

5 LAWYER (to judge): And as a precedent, your honor, I offer a Perry Mason case first televised four years ago in which . . .
Chon Day, DAC News, cartoon, 1969

6 A jury consists of twelve persons chosen to decide who has the better lawyer.
Robert Frost (Attrib.)

7 DEFENDANT: I don't recognize this court!
JUDGE: Why not?
DEFENDANT: You've had it decorated!
Eric Morecambe and Ernie Wise, The Morecambe and Wise Joke Book, 1979

8 I don't want a lawyer to tell me what I cannot do; I hire him to tell me how to do what I want to do.
J. Pierpont Morgan

9 MORGENHALL: . . . if they ever give you a brief, old fellow, attack the medical evidence. Remember, the jury's full of rheumatism and arthritis and shocking gastric troubles. They love to see a medical man put through it.
John Mortimer, The Dock Brief, 1958

10 No brilliance is needed in the law. Nothing but common sense, and relatively clean fingernails.
John Mortimer, A Voyage Round My Father, screenplay, 1972

11 . . . I don't think you can make a lawyer honest by an act of legislature. You've got to work on his conscience. And his lack of conscience is what makes him a lawyer.
Will Rogers, Sacramento, California, 1927

12 For certain people, after fifty, litigation takes the place of sex.
Gore Vidal, Evening Standard, 1981

13 JUDGE: Don't take that 'Judge not, lest ye be judged' line with me, young man.
Gahan Wilson, The Weird World of Gahan Wilson, cartoon, 1975

14 That's what comes of being a solicitor, it saps the vital juices. Johnny doesn't even embezzle his clients' money, which I

should have thought was about the only fun a solicitor can get out of life.
P. G. Wodehouse, Ice in the Bedroom, 1961

See also Crime; Injustice; Law and Order; Police.

LAW AND ORDER

1 Law and Order is like patriotism – anyone who comes on strong about patriotism has got something to hide; it never fails. They always turn out to be a crook or an asshole or a traitor or something.
Bill Mauldin

2 Distrust all in whom the impulse to punish is powerful.
Friedrich Wilhelm Nietzsche, Thus Spake Zarathustra, 1883–1892

See also Crime; The Law; Police.

LAWS

1 Murphy's Law: If anything can go wrong, it will.
O'Toole's Commentary on Murphy's Law: Murphy was an optimist.
Harper's Magazine Law: You never find an article until you replace it.
Law of Selective Gravity: An object will fall so as to do the most damage.
Jenning's Corollary: The chance of bread falling with the buttered side up is directly proportional to the cost of the carpet.
Klipstein's Corollary: The most delicate component will be the one to drop.
Arthur Bloch, Murphy's Law and Other Reasons Why Things Go Wrong, 1977

2 The Peter Principle: In a hierarchy every employee tends to rise to his level of incompetence.
Dr Lawrence J. Peter, The Peter Principle, 1969

See also Truth.

LAZINESS

1 As a boy, he swallowed a teaspoon. And he hasn't stirred since.
Anon.

2 His idea of roughing it is to turn his electric blanket down to Medium.
Anon.

3 I've found a great way to start the day – I
   go straight back to bed!
   Anon.

4 Lazy? He used to ride his bike over
   cobblestones to knock the ash off his
   ciggie.
   Les Dawson, *The Les Dawson Joke Book*,
   1979

5 The laziest man I ever met put popcorn
   in his pancakes so they would turn over
   by themselves.
   W. C. Fields (Attrib.)

6 Well, we can't stand around here doing
   nothing, people will think we're work-
   men.
   Spike Milligan, *The Goon Show*, BBC
   Radio, 1959

7 It is better to have loafed and lost than
   never to have loafed at all.
   James Thurber, *Fables for Our Time*, 1943

See also Work.

LEADERSHIP

1 In enterprise of martial kind
   When there was any fighting,
   He led his regiment from behind –
   He found it less exciting.
   But when away his regiment ran,
   His place was at the fore, O –
   That celebrated,
   Cultivated,
   Underrated
   Nobleman, The Duke of Plaza-Toro!
   W. S. Gilbert and Arthur Sullivan, 'The
   Duke of Plaza-Toro', *The Gondoliers*, 1889

2 I must follow them. I am their leader.
   Andrew Bonar Law, Conservative Prime
   Minister, 1922–1923 (Attrib.)

See also Bosses; The Presidency;
Winning.

LEGS

1 – Her legs are without equal.
   – You mean they know no parallel.
   Anon.

2 He told her her stockings were wrinkled.
   Trouble was, she wasn't wearing any.
   Anon.

3 GERALD: I have heard it said that her
   legs leave something to be desired.
   LADY D: All legs leave *something* to be
   desired, do they not. That is part of their
   function and all of their charm.
   Alan Bennett, *Forty Years On*, 1968

See also The Body; Footwear.

LETTERS

1 The great secret in life . . . not to open
   your letters for a fortnight. At the expir-
   ation of that period you will find that
   nearly all of them have answered themselves.
   Arthur Binstead, *Pitcher's Proverbs*, 1909

2 I found a letter to my sister the other day
   that I had forgotten to mail.
   It just needed a little updating to send.
   After 'the baby is . . .' I crossed out 'toilet
   trained' and wrote in 'graduating from
   high school this month'.
   Erma Bombeck, *If Life is a Bowl of Cherries
   – What am I Doing in the Pits?*, 1978

3 He's a distinguished man of letters. He
   works for the Post Office.
   Max Kauffmann

4 To the Editor of *The Times*
   Sir,
   I have just written you a long letter.
   On reading it over, I have thrown it into
   the wastepaper basket.
   Hoping this will meet with your approval.
   I am
   Sir
   Your obedient servant
   Lt. Col. A. D. Wintle, unpublished letter to
   The Times, 1946

5 What a girl! He had never in his life
   before met a woman who could write a
   letter without a postscript, and this was
   but the smallest of her unusual gifts.
   P. G. Wodehouse, *A Damsel in Distress*,
   1919

See also Communications; Greetings
Cards; Writers; Writing.

THE LIBERAL PARTY

1 Basically the Liberal Party is divided
   between wispy beards and others. Wispy

beards . . . wear T-shirts with slogans on, usually faintly dated, e.g. 'The Only Safe Fast Breeder is a Rabbit'. They tend to have ill-fitting jeans, and those heavy shoes which look like Cornish pasties. They have briefcases stuffed with documents, chiefly about community politics, nuclear power and ecology. They drink real ale.
Simon Hoggart, *On The House*, 1981

2 As usual the Liberals offer a mixture of sound and original ideas. Unfortunately, none of the sound ideas is original and none of the original ideas is sound.
Harold Macmillan, speech, 1961

3 . . . the small troupe of exhibitionists, failed vaudeville artists, juicy young Boy Scouts and degenerate old voluptuaries which is the Liberal Party.
Auberon Waugh, *Private Eye*

See also The Conservative Party; The Labour Party; Liberals; Parliament; Politics and Politicians.

LIBERALS

1 A liberal is a conservative who's been mugged by reality.
Anon.

2 The liberals can understand everything but people who don't understand them.
Anon.

3 GOOD: You know what they say; if God had been a liberal, we wouldn't have had the ten commandments. We'd have the ten suggestions.
Malcolm Bradbury and Christopher Bigsby, *The After Dinner Game*, BBC TV, 1975

4 A liberal is a man who leaves the room when a fight begins.
Heywood Broun

5 What the liberal really wants is to bring about change which will not in any way endanger his position.
Stokely Carmichael

6 A liberal is a man too broadminded to take his own side in a quarrel.
Robert Frost

7 A rich man told me recently that a liberal is a man who tells other people what to do with their money.
LeRoi Jones, *Home*, 1966

8 I can remember way back when a liberal was one who was generous with his own money.
Will Rogers

9 Liberals are variously described as limousine, double-domed, screaming, knee-jerk, professional and 'bleeding heart'.
William Safire, *The New Language of Politics*, 1968

10 . . . one who has both feet planted firmly in the air . . .
Adlai Stevenson

11 It is easy for the Liberals to say that something should be done on a bigger scale. They never have to do these things.
Patrick Gordon Walker, Labour Minister, 1967

See also The Liberal Party; Politics and Politicians.

LIBERTY

1 Liberty means responsibility. That is why most men dread it.
George Bernard Shaw, *Maxims for Revolutionists*, 1903

See also Democracy.

LIES

1 Matilda told such Dreadful Lies,
It made one Gasp and Stretch one's Eyes;
Her Aunt, who, from her Earliest Youth,
Had kept a Strict Regard for Truth,
Attempted to Believe Matilda:
The effort very nearly killed her.
Hilaire Belloc, 'Matilda', *Cautionary Tales for Children*, 1907

2 A lie can be half-way round the world before the truth has got its boots on.
James Callaghan, quoted in *The Times*, 1976

3 There is a great deal of hard lying in the

world; especially among people whose characters are above suspicion.
Benjamin Jowett (Attrib.)

4 How does a person get to be a capable liar?
That is something that I respectfully inquiar,
Because I don't believe a person will ever set the world on fire
Unless they are a capable lire.
Ogden Nash, 'Golly, How Truth Will Out!', *The Face is Familiar*, 1940

5 A little inaccuracy sometimes saves tons of explanation.
Saki (H. H. Munro), *The Square Egg*, 1924

6 A lie is an abomination unto the Lord and a very present help in trouble.
Adlai Stevenson, 1951

7 I offer my opponents a bargain: if they will stop telling falsehoods about us, I will stop telling the truth about them.
Adlai Stevenson, during the presidential campaign, 1952

8 I was brought up in a clergyman's household so I am a first-class liar.
Dame Sybil Thorndike

See also Dishonesty; Truth.

LIFE

1 Life is a hereditary disease.
Graffito, London, 1984

2 Life is a wonderful thing to talk about, or to read about in history books – but it is terrible when one has to live it.
Jean Anouilh, *Time Remembered*, 1939

3 VICAR: You know, Life – Life, is rather like opening a tin of sardines. We are all of us looking for the key. Some of us – some of us think we've found the key, don't we? We roll back the lid of the sardine tin of Life, we reveal the sardines, the riches of Life, therein and we get them out, we enjoy them. But, you know, there's always a little piece in the corner you can't get out. I wonder – I wonder, is there a little piece in the corner of your life? I know there is in mine.
Alan Bennett, *Beyond the Fringe*, 1959

4 Human life is mainly a process of filling in time until the arrival of death or Santa Claus . . .
Eric Berne, *Games People Play*, 1964

5 There are two great rules of life, the one general and the other particular. The first is that everyone can, in the end, get what he wants if he only tries. This is the general rule. The particular rule is that every individual is more or less an exception to the general rule.
Samuel Butler, *The Notebooks of Samuel Butler*, 1912

6 Life is a maze in which we take the wrong turning before we have learned to walk.
Cyril Connolly, *The Unquiet Grave*, 1944

7 Is not the whole world a vast house of assignation to which the filing system has been lost?
Quentin Crisp, *The Naked Civil Servant*, 1968

8 If you want my final opinion on the mystery of life and all that, I can give it to you in a nutshell. The universe is like a safe to which there is a combination. But the combination is locked up in the safe.
Peter De Vries, *Let Me Count the Ways*, 1965

9 It's a funny old world – a man's lucky if he gets out of it alive.
W. C. Fields, *You're Telling Me*, 1934

10 When I hear somebody sigh, 'Life is hard,' I am always tempted to ask, 'Compared to what?'
Sydney J. Harris, *Majority of One*

11 . . . life is something to do when you can't get to sleep.
Fran Lebowitz, *Metropolitan Life*, 1978

12 . . . we must first deal with the . . . question of *what is life*. Here we discover that others have preceded us and provided quite a range of answers. We consider each answer individually but we are invariably disappointed. A bowl of cherries? Too pat. A cabaret? Not in this neighborhood. Real? Hardly. Earnest? Please.
Fran Lebowitz, *Metropolitan Life*, 1978

13 The four stages of man are infancy, childhood, adolescence and obsolescence.
   Art Linkletter, *A Child's Garden of Misinformation*, 1965

14 The basic fact about human existence is not that it is a tragedy, but that it is a bore. It is not so much a war as an endless standing in line.
   H. L. Mencken, *Prejudices*, Sixth Series, 1927

15 Life's a tough proposition, and the first hundred years are the hardest.
   Wilson Mizner

16 Life is not for everyone.
   Michael O'Donoghue, quoted in *Playboy*, 1983

17 My whole life is a movie. It's just that there are no dissolves. I have to live every agonizing moment of it. My life needs editing.
   Mort Sahl

18 Life is too short for men to take it seriously.
   George Bernard Shaw, *Back to Methuselah*, 1921

19 Life is a gamble at terrible odds – if it was a bet, you wouldn't take it.
   Tom Stoppard, *Rosencrantz and Guildenstern are Dead*, 1967

20 Oh, isn't life a terrible thing, thank God?
   Dylan Thomas, *Under Milk Wood*, 1954

21 Life is like an overlong drama through which we sit being nagged by the vague memories of having read the reviews.
   John Updike, *The Coup*, 1979

22 Life is much too important a thing ever to talk seriously about it.
   Oscar Wilde, *Vera, or The Nihilists*, 1883

See also Death.

LIMERICKS

1 The limerick packs laughs anatomical
Into space that is quite economical.
But the good ones I've seen
So seldom are clean
And the clean ones so seldom are
   comical.
   Anon.

2 The limerick's an art-form complex
Whose contents run chiefly to sex.
It's famous for virgins
And masculine urgin's
And vulgar erotic effects.
   Anon., quoted in W. S. Baring-Gould's *The Lure of the Limerick*, 1968

3 There was an old man of St Bees
who was stung on the arm by a wasp.
When asked, 'Does it hurt?'
He said, 'No, it doesn't,
I'm so glad it wasn't a hornet.'
   Anon.

4 Well, it's partly the shape of the thing
That gives the old limerick wing;
These accordian pleats
Full of airy conceits
Take it up like a kite on a string.
   Anon., quoted in W. S. Baring-Gould's *The Lure of the Limerick*

5 The limerick's, admitted, a verse form:
a terse form: a curse form; a hearse
   form.
It may not be lyric,
and at best it's Satyric,
and a whale of a tail in perverse form.
   Conrad Aiken, *A Seizure of Limericks*, 1965

6 Most women loathe limericks, for the same reason that calves hate cookbooks.
   Gershon Legman

7 The limerick, peculiar to English,
Is a verse form that's hard to extinguish.
Once Congress in session
Decreed its suppression
But people got around it by writing the
   last line without any rhyme or meter.
   Professor T. J. Spencer

See also Poets and Poetry.

ABRAHAM LINCOLN President of the United States, 1860–1865

1 Abe – have you got a pencil and paper there? Would you take this down? 'You can fool all of the people some of the time and some of the people all of the time. But you can't fool all of the people all the

time.' . . . Well, you keep doing it differently, Abe. The last quote I got was 'You can fool all the people all the time . . .'

Bob Newhart, 'Abe Lincoln versus Madison Avenue', *The Button-down Mind of Bob Newhart*, record, 1960

See also The Presidency.

LITERATURE

1 Literature exists so that where one man has lived finely, ten thousand may afterwards live finely.
Arnold Bennett

2 He [Clevinger] knew everything about literature except how to enjoy it.
Joseph Heller, *Catch-22*, 1961

3 At tea in cocktail weather,
The lady authors gather.
Their hats are made of feather.
They talk of Willa Cather.
They talk of Proust and Cather,
And how we drift, and wither.
Where wends the lady author,
Martinis do not wither.
Phyllis McGinley, 'Publisher's Party', *Times Three: 1932–1960*, 1960

4 A man with his belly full of the classics is an enemy of the human race.
Henry Miller, *Tropic of Cancer*, 1930

5 If F. Scott and Zelda are Class
Cellini made things out of brass,
And Dacron is fur,
Air-Wick smells like myrrh,
And plastic's as good as stained glass!
Michael O'Donoghue, *The National Lampoon Encyclopaedia of Humor*, 1973

6 A classic is something that everybody wants to have read and nobody wants to read.
Mark Twain, *The Disappearance of Literature*, 1900

7 I hate vulgar realism in literature. The man who would call a spade a spade should be compelled to use one. It is the only thing he is fit for.
Oscar Wilde, *The Picture of Dorian Gray*, 1891

See also Books; Novels; Poets and Poetry; Quotations; Reading; William Shakespeare; Writers; Writing.

DAVID LLOYD GEORGE Prime Minister of Great Britain, 1916–1922 (Liberal Party)

1 He couldn't see a belt without hitting below it.
Margot Asquith (Attrib.)

2 He did not seem to care which way he travelled, providing he was in the driver's seat.
Lord Beaverbrook, *The Decline and Fall of Lloyd George*, 1963

3 The Happy Warrior of Squandermania.
Winston Churchill, debate in House of Commons on 1929 Budget

See also Liberals; The Liberal Party; Politics and Politicians.

LONDON

1 London is a splendid place to live for those who can get out of it.
Lord Balfour of Burleigh, quoted in the *Observer*, 1944

2 I don't know what London's coming to – the higher the buildings the lower the morals.
Noël Coward, 'Law and Order', *This Year of Grace*, 1928

3 London is a university with ten million graduates qualified to live and let live.
Oliver St John Gogarty, *As I Was Going Down Sackville Street*, 1937

4 When it's three o'clock in New York, it's still 1938 in London.
Bette Midler, quoted in *The Times*, 1978

5 London is too full of fogs – and serious people. Whether the fogs produce the serious people or whether the serious people produce the fogs, I don't know, but the whole thing rather gets on my nerves.
Oscar Wilde, *Lady Windermere's Fan*, 1892

See also Britain and the British; England and the English.

LONELINESS

1 I Feel So Miserable Without You, It's
Almost Like Having You Here.
Stephen Bishop, song title

2 There are no books like a dame
And nothin' looks like a dame.
There are no drinks like a dame
And nothin' thinks like a dame,
Nothin' acts like a dame
Or attracts like a dame.
There ain't a thing that's wrong with any
man here
That can't be cured by putting him near
A girly, womanly, female, feminine
dame!
Oscar Hammerstein II, 'There is Nothin'
Like a Dame', song from *South Pacific*, 1949

3 If there's anything worse than a woman
living alone, it's a woman saying she likes
it.
Stanley Shapiro and Maurice Richlin,
Pillow Talk, screenplay, 1959

4 When so many are lonely as seem to be
lonely, it would be inexcusably selfish to
be lonely alone.
Tennessee Williams, *Camino Real*, 1953

LOOKS

1 As a beauty I'm not a great star,
There are others more handsome by far,
But my face I don't mind it,
Because I'm behind it –
'Tis the folks in the front that I jar.
Anthony Euwer, 'The Face', *The Oxford
Book of American Light Verse*, 1979

2 Phyllis Diller's had so many face lifts,
there's nothing left in her shoes.
Bob Hope

3 Men seldom make passes
At girls who wear glasses.
Dorothy Parker, 'News Item', *The Portable
Dorothy Parker*, 1944

4 Circumstances alter faces.
Carolyn Wells

5 As long as a woman can look ten years
younger than her own daughter, she is
perfectly satisfied.
Oscar Wilde, *The Picture of Dorian Gray*,
1891

6 Good looks are a snare that every sen-
sible man would like to be caught in.
Oscar Wilde, *The Importance of Being
Earnest*, 1895

See also Appearance; Beauty; Clothes;
Faces; Fashion; Style.

LOS ANGELES

1 I don't want to live in a city where the
only cultural advantage is that you can
make a right turn on a red light.
Woody Allen and Marshall Brickman,
Annie Hall, screenplay, 1977

2 They don't throw their garbage away.
They make it into television shows.
Woody Allen and Marshall Brickman,
Annie Hall, screenplay, 1977

3 'I went to Los Angeles once,' goes a
favorite line, 'but I couldn't find it.'
Herb Caen, *Vanity Fair*, 1984

4 A big hard-boiled city with no more
personality than a paper cup.
Raymond Chandler, *The Little Sister*, 1949

5 ... is a large citylike area surrounding
the Beverly Hills Hotel ... In 1956
the population of Los Angeles was
2,243,901. By 1970 it had risen to
2,811,801, 1,650,917 of whom are currently up for a series.
Fran Lebowitz, *Social Studies*, 1981

6 The chief products of Los Angeles are
novelizations, salad, game-show hosts,
points, muscle tone, mini-series and re-
writes. They export all of these items
with the twin exceptions of muscle tone
and points, neither of which seem to
travel well.
Fran Lebowitz, *Social Studies*, 1981

7 Is it true what they say about Los
Angeles, that Los Angeles is erratic,
That in the sweet national symphony
of common sense Los Angeles is the
static?
Yes it is true, Los Angeles is not only
erratic, not only erotic, Los Angeles is
crotchety, centrifugal, vertiginous,
esoteric and exotic.
Ogden Nash, 'Don't Shoot Los Angeles',
Good Intentions, 1942

8 I have a theory about L.A. architecture. I think all the houses had a costume party and they all came as other countries.
Michael O'Donoghue, quoted in *Playboy*, 1983

9 Seventy-two suburbs in search of a city.
Dorothy Parker (Attrib.)

10 The violet hush of twilight was descending over Los Angeles as my hostess, Violet Hush, and I left its suburbs headed towards Hollywood. In the distance a glow of huge piles of burning motion-picture scripts lit up the sky. The crisp tang of frying writers and directors whetted my appetite. How good it was to be alive, I thought, inhaling deep lungfuls of carbon monoxide.
S. J. Perelman, *Strictly from Hunger*, 1937

11 The difference between Los Angeles and yogurt is that yogurt has real culture.
Tom Taussik, *Legless in Gaza*, 1982

See also America and the Americans; California; Hollywood.

LOVE

1 People in love, it is well known, suffer extreme conceptual delusions; the most common of these being that other people find your condition as thrilling and eye-watering as you do yourselves.
Julian Barnes, *Observer*, 1984

2 If it is your time love will track you down like a cruise missile. If you say 'No! I don't want it right now.' That's when you'll get it for sure. Love will make a way out of no way. Love is an exploding cigar which we willingly smoke.
Lynda Barry, *Big Ideas*, cartoon, 1983

3 Love . . . the delightful interval between meeting a beautiful girl and discovering that she looks like a haddock.
John Barrymore (Attrib.)

4 Love is like the measles – all the worse when it comes late in life.
Douglas Jerrold

5 He gave her a look you could have poured on a waffle.
Ring Lardner

6 Pride – that's a luxury a woman in love can't afford.
Clare Boothe Luce

7 Love is only the dirty trick played on us to achieve continuation of the species.
W. Somerset Maugham, *A Writer's Notebook*, 1949

8 Love is based on a view of women that is impossible to those who have had any experience with them.
H. L. Mencken, *Prejudices*, Fourth Series, 1924

9 Love is like war: easy to begin but very hard to stop.
H. L. Mencken

10 Love is the delusion that one woman differs from another.
H. L. Mencken, *A Mencken Chrestomathy*, 1949

11 To fall in love you have to be in the state of mind for it to take, like a disease.
Nancy Mitford

12 ETH: Oh, Ron . . .
RON: Yes, Eth?
ETH: You did *mean* those three little words you whispered to me in the cinema, didn't you?
RON: 'Course I did, Eth . . . I *had* seen it.
Frank Muir and Denis Norden, 'The Glums', *Take It from Here*, BBC Radio

13 More than a catbird hates a cat,
Or a criminal hates a clue,
Or the Axis hates the United States,
That's how much I love you.
Ogden Nash, 'To My Valentine', *Good Intentions*, 1942

14 Every love's the love before
In a duller dress.
Dorothy Parker, 'Summary', *Death and Taxes*, 1931

15 Love is like quicksilver in the hand. Leave the fingers open and it stays. Clutch it, and it darts away.
Dorothy Parker (Attrib.)

16 Oh, life is a glorious cycle of song,
A medley of extemporanea;
And love is a thing that can never go wrong;

And I am Marie of Roumania.
Dorothy Parker, 'Comment', *Enough Rope*, 1926

17 Scratch a lover and find a foe.
Dorothy Parker

18 Love is not the dying moan of a distant violin – it is the triumphant twang of a bedspring.
S. J. Perelman (Attrib.)

19 Electric eels, I might add, do it,
Though it shocks 'em, I know,
Why ask if shad do it?
Waiter, bring me shad roe.
In shallow shoals, English soles do it,
Gold-fish in the privacy of bowls, do it,
Let's do it, let's fall in love.
Cole Porter, 'Let's Do It', song, 1930

20 Old sloths who hang down from twigs
   do it,
Though the effort is great,
Sweet guinea-pigs do it,
Buy a couple and wait.
The world admits bears in pits do it,
Even pekineses in the Ritz, do it,
Let's do it, let's fall in love.
Cole Porter, 'Let's Do It', song, 1930

21 I can see from your utter misery, from your eagerness to misunderstand each other, and from your thoroughly bad temper, that this is the real thing.
Peter Ustinov, *Romanoff and Juliet*, 1957

22 I can understand companionship. I can understand bought sex in the afternoon. I cannot understand the love affair.
Gore Vidal, *The Sunday Times*, 1973

23 Love is much nicer to be in than an automobile accident, a tight girdle, a higher tax bracket or a holding pattern over Philadelphia.
Judith Viorst, *Redbook*, 1975

24 Love is the same as like except you feel sexier. And more romantic. And also more annoyed when he talks with his mouth full. And you also resent it more when he interrupts you. And you also respect him less when he shows any weakness. And furthermore, when you ask him to pick you up at the airport and

he tells you he can't do it because he's busy, it's only when you love him that you hate him.
Judith Viorst, *Redbook*, 1975

25 Love conquers all things except poverty and toothache.
Mae West

26 . . . a really *grand passion* is comparatively rare nowadays. It is the privilege of people who have nothing to do. That is the one use of the idle classes in a country.
Oscar Wilde, *A Woman of No Importance*, 1893

27 It's curious how, when you're in love, you yearn to go about doing acts of kindness to everybody. I am bursting with a sort of yeasty benevolence these days, like one of those chaps in Dickens. I very nearly bought you a tie in London, Bertie.
P. G. Wodehouse, *The Mating Season*, 1949

28 'Love,' she said, 'seems to pump me full of vitamins. It makes me feel as if the sun were shining and my hat was right and my shoes were right and my frock was right and my stockings were right, and somebody had just left me ten thousand a year.'
P. G. Wodehouse, *Spring Fever*, 1948

See also Affection; Flirtation; Infatuation; Love – Breaking Up; Romance; Seduction; Sex; Sexual Attraction.

LOVE – BREAKING UP

1 *What to do with your time*
DO: *Drink black coffee and smoke numerous cigs. You NEED to eat and this will do. *Find out who 'she' is and introduce yourself. Scrutinize her appearance and comfort yourself with thoughts of her large pores or taste in clothes. *Drink mass quantities of alcohol and watch TV all you can. *Abandon personal hygiene and cleaning your house. *Kick his car.
DON'T: *Take up a new hobby. When the most hellish period has passed you will be unable to do this activity ever again in your life. *Try to meet a new

lovemate through church organizations or night classes in ballroom dancing. *Try to feel happy or good for thirty days. *Go anywhere or do anything. *Go near high bridges, open windows, trucks that are moving fast or couples holding hands.

Lynda Barry, *Big Ideas*, cartoon, 1983

2 She always believed in the old adage – leave them while you're looking good.

Anita Loos, *Gentlemen Prefer Blondes*, 1925

3 There is one thing I would break up over, and that is if she caught me with another woman. I won't stand for that.

Steve Martin

4 *Is there a 'cure' for a broken heart?*
Only time can heal your broken heart, just as only time can heal his broken arms and legs.

Miss Piggy, *Miss Piggy's Guide to Life (As Told to Henry Beard)*, 1981

5 My boyfriend and I broke up. He wanted to get married, and I didn't want him to.

Rita Rudner, quoted in *Ms*, 1984

6 There is always something ridiculous about the emotions of people whom one has ceased to love.

Oscar Wilde, *The Picture of Dorian Gray*, 1891

7 I was in rare fettle and the heart had touched a new high. I don't know anything that braces one up like finding you haven't got to get married after all.

P. G. Wodehouse, *Jeeves in the Offing*, 1960

See also Alimony; Divorce; Infidelity; Love.

LUNCH

1 Never drink black coffee at lunch; it will keep you awake in the afternoon.

Jilly Cooper, *How to Survive from Nine to Five*, 1970

See also Eating; Food; Restaurants.

LUXEMBOURG

1 On a clear day, from the terrace . . . you can't see Luxembourg at all. This is because a tree is in the way.

Alan Coren, *The Sanity Inspector*, 1974

See also Europe and the EEC.

DOUGLAS MACARTHUR
American Army General

1 MacArthur is the type of man who thinks that when he gets to heaven, God will step down from the great white throne and bow him into His vacated seat.
   Harold Ickes, *Diary*, 1933

2 I fired him because he wouldn't respect the authority of the President. That's the answer to that. I didn't fire him because he was a dumb son of a bitch, although he was, but that's not against the law for generals. If it was, half to three quarters of them would be in jail.
   Harry S. Truman, on his sacking of General MacArthur as Commander-in-Chief of the US forces in Korea, 1951, quoted in *Plain Speaking: An Oral Biography of Harry S. Truman* by Merle Miller

See also The Army; War.

JAMES RAMSAY MACDONALD
Prime Minister of Great Britain, 1924, 1929–1931, 1931–1935 (Labour Party)

1 I have waited fifty years to see the Boneless Wonder sitting on the Treasury bench.
   Winston Churchill, speech, House of Commons, 1933

2 We know that he has, more than any other man, the gift of compressing the largest amount of words into the smallest amount of thought.
   Winston Churchill, speech, House of Commons, 1933

3 He had sufficient conscience to bother him, but not sufficient to keep him straight.
   David Lloyd George (Attrib.)

See also The Labour Party; Politics and Politicians.

THE MAFIA

1 Death is one of the worst things that can happen to a Cosa Nostra member, and many prefer simply to pay a fine.
   Woody Allen, 'A Look at Organized Crime', *New Yorker*

See also Crime.

MANKIND

1 Man is a beautiful machine that works very badly. He is like a watch of which the most that can be said is that its cosmetic effect is good.
   H. L. Mencken, *Minority Report*, 1956

MARRIAGE

1 Marriage is not a word but a sentence.
   Anon.

2 Marriage is the price men pay for sex, sex is the price women pay for marriage.
   Anon.

3 For the first year of marriage I had a basically bad attitude. I tended to place my wife underneath a pedestal.
   Woody Allen, nightclub act, 1960s

4 You must come to our house next time. Absolute peace. Neither of us ever says a word to each other. That's the secret of a successful union.
   Alan Ayckbourn, *Absent Friends*, 1975

5 The other night I said to my wife Ruth, 'Do you feel that the sex and excitement has gone out of our marriage?' Ruth said, 'I'll discuss it with you during the next commercial.'
   Milton Berle, *Variety*

6 HORNCASTLE: The whole point of marriage is to stop you getting anywhere near real life. You think it's a great struggle with the mystery of being. It's more like ... being smothered in warm cocoa. There's sex, but it's not what you think. Marvellous, for the first fortnight. Then every Wednesday. If there isn't a good late-night concert on the Third.

Meanwhile you become a biological functionary. An agent of the great female womb, spawning away, dumping its goods in your lap for succour. Daddy, daddy, we're here and we're expensive.
Malcolm Bradbury, *Love on a Gunboat*, BBC TV, 1977

7 Dr Heinrich von Heartburn's advice on keeping one's marriage alive: Make it interesting . . . I showed a friend of mine once how to keep his marriage exciting . . . One day he'd come home from work, his wife would open the door, he's a French soldier . . . The next day he's a policeman, he comes in, he starts to run around with the handcuffs and the badges, and the next day he don't come through the door, he jumps through the window, he's a clown. He somersaults all over the living room and throws his wife all around the place. [*Pause*] She left him. He was a maniac.
Mel Brooks, *Your Show of Shows*, NBC TV

8 Wedlock: the deep, deep peace of the double bed after the hurly-burly of the *chaise longue*.
Mrs Patrick Campbell

9 A man's friends like him but leave him as he is: his wife loves him and is always trying to turn him into somebody else.
G. K. Chesterton, *Orthodoxy*, 1908

10 I think of my wife, and I think of Lot, And I think of the lucky break he got.
William Cole, 'Marriage Couplet', *The Oxford Book of American Light Verse*, 1979

11 We sleep in separate rooms, we have dinner apart, we take separate vacations — we're doing everything we can to keep our marriage together.
Rodney Dangerfield

12 It is true that I never should have married, but I didn't want to live without a man. Brought up to respect the conventions, love had to end in marriage. I'm afraid it did.
Bette Davis, *The Lonely Life*, 1962

13 Never go to bed mad. Stay up and fight.
Phyllis Diller, *Phyllis Diller's Housekeeping Hints*, 1966

14 Every woman should marry — and no man.
Benjamin Disraeli, *Lothair*, 1870

15 The reason husbands and wives do not understand each other is because they belong to different sexes.
Dorothy Dix

16 *A Lexicon for Fighting Marital Fights, Arranged According to Subject*
Amnesia: 'Who do you think you ARE?'
Apology: 'PARdon me for LIVing!'
Family Tree: 'She's YOUR mother, not mine.'
Hearing impairments: 'Could you speak up a little? They can't hear you in Europe.'
Language barrier: 'What's the matter, don't you understand English?'
Mining: 'I hadn't realized we'd descended to that level.'
Wildlife: 'That's right, use physical violence. That's all an animal like you knows anyway.'
Dan Greenburg and Suzanne O'Malley, *How to Avoid Love and Marriage*, 1983

17 *Fighting: Style and Syntax*
Anything you say in a marital fight will have more bounce if you utilize a melodramatic style and an archaic syntax. A statement like 'I'm sorry I ever met you' is effective enough, but how much more piquant is the same communication expressed as: '*I rue the day* I met you' . . . Asking whether your mate has time for a discussion is tapioca pudding compared with asking whether your mate *would deign to favor you* with his or her attention.
Dan Greenburg and Suzanne O'Malley, *How to Avoid Love and Marriage*, 1983

18 *Wallpaper Design for the Marital Bedroom*
EXCUSE ME COULD YOU PLEASE SAY THAT AGAIN I DON'T BELIEVE I HEARD YOU CORRECTLY LISTEN JUST WHO THE HELL DO YOU THINK YOU ARE FOR GOD'S SAKE WHAT AM I SUPPOSED TO BE YOUR SERVANT DON'T YOU DARE TALK TO ME IN THAT TONE OF VOICE I GUESS WE JUST AREN'T MEANT TO BE TOGETHER THAT'S ALL I'VE HAD IT UP TO HERE WITH YOU

THAT'S RIGHT YOU HEARD ME THAT'S NOT MEANT TO BE A THREAT WE'RE JUST IN DIFFERENT TIMES IN OUR LIFE O.K. GO AHEAD THEN LEAVE I'LL HELP YOU PACK YOUR BAGS I GUESS WE DON'T NEED TO BE TOGETHER OH THAT'S CUTE REAL CUTE I DON'T HAVE TO STAND
Dan Greenburg and Suzanne O'Malley, *How to Survive Love and Marriage,* 1983

19 Marriage is a great institution – no family should be without it.
Bob Hope

20 Zsa Zsa Gabor got married as a one-off and it was so successful she turned it into a series.
Bob Hope

21 I never knew what real happiness was until I got married. And by then it was too late.
Max Kauffmann

22 The trouble was, I went into marriage with both eyes closed – her father closed one and her brother closed the other.
Max Kauffmann

23 Marrying a man is like buying something you've been admiring for a long time in a shop window. You may love it when you get it home, but it doesn't always go with everything else in the house.
Jean Kerr, *The Snake Has All the Lines,* 1960

24 We do not squabble, fight or have rows. We collect grudges. We're in an arms race, storing up warheads for the domestic Armageddon.
Hugh Leonard, *Time Was,* 1976

25 WIFE: Mr Watt next door blows his wife a kiss every morning as he leaves the house. I wish you'd do that.
HUSBAND: But I hardly know the woman!
Alfred McFote

26 When a man brings his wife flowers for no reason – there's a reason.
Molly McGee

27 The fundamental trouble with marriage is that it shakes a man's confidence in himself, and so greatly diminishes his general competence and effectiveness. His habit of mind becomes that of a commander who has lost a decisive and calamitous battle. He never quite trusts himself thereafter.
H. L. Mencken, *Prejudices,* Second Series, 1920

28 . . . just as I am unsure of the difference between flora and fauna and flotsam and jetsam.
I am quite sure that marriage is the alliance of two people one of whom never remembers birthdays and the other never forgetsam.
Ogden Nash, 'I Do, I Will, I Have', *Versus,* 1949

29 To keep your marriage brimming
With love in the marriage cup,
Whenever you're wrong, admit it;
Whenever you're right, shut up.
Ogden Nash, 'A Word to Husbands', *Everyone but Thee and Me,* 1962

30 Marriage is popular because it combines the maximum of temptation with the maximum of opportunity.
George Bernard Shaw, *Maxims for Revolutionists,* 1903

31 Marriage is a great institution, but I'm not ready for an institution yet.
Mae West (Attrib.)

32 How marriage ruins a man. It's as demoralizing as cigarettes, and far more expensive.
Oscar Wilde, *Lady Windermere's Fan,* 1892

33 I am not in favour of long engagements. They give people the opportunity of finding out each other's character before marriage, which I think is never advisable.
Oscar Wilde, *The Importance of Being Earnest,* 1895

34 It's most dangerous nowadays for a husband to pay any attention to his wife in public. It always makes people think that he beats her when they're alone.
Oscar Wilde, *Lady Windermere's Fan,* 1892

35 Men marry because they are tired;

women because they are curious. Both are disappointed.
> Oscar Wilde, *A Woman of No Importance*, 1893

36 The amount of women in London who flirt with their own husbands is perfectly scandalous. It looks so bad. It is simply washing one's clean linen in public.
> Oscar Wilde, *The Importance of Being Earnest*, 1895

37 The one charm of marriage is that it makes a life of deception absolutely necessary for both parties.
> Oscar Wilde, *The Picture of Dorian Gray*, 1891

38 There's nothing in the world like the devotion of a married woman. It's a thing no married man knows anything about.
> Oscar Wilde, *Lady Windermere's Fan*, 1892

39 In Hollywood all marriages are happy. It's trying to live together afterwards that causes all the problems.
> Shelley Winters (Attrib.)

40 Do you know what it means to come home at night to a woman who'll give you a little love, a little affection, a little tenderness? It means you're in the wrong house, that's what it means.
> Henny Youngman, *Henny Youngman's Greatest One Liners*, 1970

41 Some people ask the secret of our long marriage. We take time to go to a restaurant two times a week. A little candlelight, dinner, soft music and dancing. She goes Tuesdays, I go Fridays.
> Henny Youngman

42 Take my wife . . . please!
> Henny Youngman

43 The first part of our marriage was very happy. But then, on the way back from the ceremony . . .
> Henny Youngman

See also Bigamy; Divorce; The Family; Weddings.

MARTYRDOM

1 Martyrdom is the only way in which a

man can become famous without ability.
> George Bernard Shaw, *Essays in Fabian Socialism*, 1908

2 . . . a thing is not necessarily true because a man dies for it.
> Oscar Wilde, 'The Portrait of Mr W. H.', 1889

See also Faith; Religion.

MARXISM

1 I could go for Marxism as long as it meant overthrowing a junta, but I don't want to *live* under it.
> Roy Blount, Jr, *Playboy*, 1983

2 M is for Marx
And clashing of classes
And movement of masses
And massing of asses.
> Cyril Connolly

See also Communism; Russia and the Russians; Socialism.

MATHEMATICS

1 'Tis a favorite project of mine
A new value of pi to assign.
I would fix it at 3
For it's simpler, you see,
Than 3 point 14159.
> Professor Harvey L. Carter

See also Computers; Metrication.

MAXIMS

1 Nothing is so useless as a general maxim.
> Thomas Macaulay

2 To do each day two things one dislikes is a precept I have followed scrupulously: every day I have got up and I have gone to bed.
> W. Somerset Maugham

See also Epigrams; Politics – Axioms; Proverbs; Sayings.

MEANNESS

1 When it comes to paying, he's the first to put his hand in his pocket. And leave it there.
> Anon.

2 ROBBER: Don't make a move, this is a stick-up!
BENNY: What?
ROBBER: You heard me.
BENNY: Mister . . . Mister, put down that gun.
ROBBER: Shut up . . . now, come on . . . your money or your life . . . [*Long pause*] . . . Look bud, I said, 'Your money or your life.'
BENNY: I'm thinking it over!
Jack Benny, *The Jack Benny Show*, NBC Radio, 1948

3 LENNIE: Oh, come on, Fletch. You are mean.
FLETCHER: No, I'm not. Thrifty, perhaps. Frugal.
LENNIE: He unwraps Bounty bars under water so I can't hear he's got one.
Dick Clement and Ian La Frenais, 'Poetic Justice', *Porridge*, BBC TV

4 They asked Jack Benny if he would do something for the Actor's Orphanage – so he shot both his parents and moved in.
Bob Hope

5 My Uncle Tom has a peculiarity I've noticed in other very oofy men. Nick him for the paltriest sum, and he lets out a squawk you can hear at Land's End. He has the stuff in gobs, but he hates giving it up.
P. G. Wodehouse, *Right Ho, Jeeves*, 1934

See also Budgets; Economy; Thrift.

MEDICINE

1 A minor operation: one performed on somebody else.
Anon.

2 And in our new series, *Medical Hints by Well-known Actresses*, tonight, your very own Googie Withers – and what to do if it does.
The Two Ronnies, BBC TV

3 Medicine: The Nation's Number One Killer.
National Lampoon, 1975

4 TB or not TB, that is the congestion.
Woody Allen, *Everything You Always Wanted to Know about Sex*, screenplay, 1972

5 DOCTOR: A pint is a perfectly normal quantity to take!
BLOOD DONOR: You don't seriously expect me to believe that! I mean, I came here in all good faith to help my country. I don't mind giving a reasonable amount, but a pint – that's very nearly an armful!
Ray Galton and Alan Simpson, for Tony Hancock in *The Blood Donor*, BBC TV, 1961

6 ERIC: I went to see the specialist about my slipped disc.
ERNIE: What happened?
ERIC: He said he'd have me back on my feet in a fortnight.
ERNIE: And did he?
ERIC: Yes – I had to sell the car to pay him.
Eric Morecambe and Ernie Wise, *The Morecambe and Wise Joke Book*, 1979

7 Let no one suppose that the words doctor and patient can disguise from the parties the fact that they are employer and employee.
George Bernard Shaw, *The Doctor's Dilemma*, 1913

8 DR KRUGMAN: So we open the kid up, and what do you think we find? Three buttons, a thumb tack, and twenty-seven cents in change . . . The parents couldn't afford to pay for the operation, so I kept the twenty-seven cents.
Billy Wilder and I. A. L. Diamond, *The Fortune Cookie*, screenplay, 1966

See also Doctors; Health; Hospitals; Illness.

MEDIOCRITY

1 Some men are born mediocre, some men achieve mediocrity, and some men have mediocrity thrust upon them. With Major Major it had been all three.
Joseph Heller, *Catch-22*, 1961

THE MEDITERRANEAN

1 VERONICA: The Mediterranean? Not any more, dear. It's the Elsan of Europe.
Alan Bennett, *The Old Country*, 1978

See also Holidays; Travel.

MEETINGS

1 I met Curzon in Downing Street from whom I got the sort of greeting a corpse would give to an undertaker.
Stanley Baldwin

2 Meetings ... are rather like cocktail parties. You don't want to go, but you're cross not to be asked.
Jilly Cooper, *How to Survive from Nine to Five*, 1970

3 Meetings are indispensable when you don't want to do anything.
J. K. Galbraith, *Ambassador's Journal*, 1969

4 *The Law of Triviality*. Briefly stated, it means that the time spent on any item of the agenda will be in inverse proportion to the sum involved.
C. Northcote Parkinson, 'High Finance', *Parkinson's Law*, 1957

See also Committees; Conferences; Parties.

MEMORY

1 Our memories are card indexes consulted, and then put back in disorder by authorities whom we do not control.
Cyril Connolly, *The Unquiet Grave*, 1945

2 I have a memory like an elephant. In fact, elephants often consult me.
Noël Coward (Attrib.)

3 A retentive memory may be a good thing, but the ability to forget is the true token of greatness.
Elbert Hubbard, *The Notebook*, 1927

4 HARRY SECOMBE: Good morning – my name is Neddy Seagoon.
SPIKE MILLIGAN: What a memory you have!
Spike Milligan, *The Goon Show*, BBC Radio, 1955

5 ERIC: My wife's got a terrible memory.
ERNIE: Really?
ERIC: Yes, she never forgets a thing.
Eric Morecambe and Ernie Wise, *The Morecambe and Wise Joke Book*, 1979

6 No woman should have a memory.

Memory in a woman is the beginning of dowdiness.
Oscar Wilde, *A Woman of No Importance*, 1893

See also The Brain.

MEN

1 *Meet the Snoid*
Now here's a dude with absolute self-confidence! Never had a self-doubt in his entire life! And no qualms of conscience have ever stood in his way! The result: this ugly little creep has more cute girls chasing after him than a 747 jetplane can haul! There's no law to prevent the landscape from being littered with the women this nasty little fellow has used up and thrown away!
Robert Crumb, *Snoid Comics*, 1980

2 American men are all mixed up today ... There was a time when this was a nation of Ernest Hemingways. REAL MEN. The kind of men who could defoliate an entire forest to make a breakfast fire – and then wipe out an endangered species while hunting for lunch. But not anymore. We've become a nation of wimps. Pansies. Alan Alda types who cook and clean and 'relate' to their wives. Phil Donahue clones who are 'sensitive' and 'vulnerable' and 'understanding' of their children. And where's it gotten us? I'll tell you where. The Japanese make better cars. The Israelis, better soldiers ... And the rest of the world is using our embassies for target practice.
Bruce Feirstein, 'Real Men Don't Eat Quiche', *Playboy*, 1982

3 Is there a way to accept the concept of the female orgasm and still command the respect of your foreign-auto mechanic?
Bruce Feirstein, 'Real Men Don't Eat Quiche', *Playboy*, 1982

4 Men have a much better time of it than women; for one thing they marry later; for another thing they die earlier.
H. L. Mencken

See also Fathers; Gentlemen; Husbands; Men – The Female View; Men and Women; Parents.

MEN – THE FEMALE VIEW

1 Women have their faults
Men have only two:
Everything they say,
Everything they do.
    Anon.

2 Every man who is high up loves to think he has done it all himself; and the wife smiles, and lets it go at that. It's our only joke. Every woman knows that.
    J. M. Barrie, *What Every Woman Knows,* 1908

3 It's no news to anyone that nice guys finish last. Almost every female I know has had the uncomfortable experience of going out with a 'nice man'. Spelled 'N-E-R-D'. How many times has your girlfriend said, 'He's SO sweet and so cute so why don't I like him?' Let's face it, when an attractive but ALOOF ('cool') man comes along, there are some of us who offer to shine his shoes with our underpants. If he has a mean streak, somehow this is 'attractive'. There are thousands of scientific concepts as to why this is so, and yes, yes, it's very sick – but none of this helps.
    Lynda Barry, *Big Ideas,* cartoon, 1983

4 I refuse to consign the whole male sex to the nursery. I insist on believing that some men are my equals.
    Brigid Brophy

5 I'd never seen men hold each other. I thought the only thing they were allowed to do was shake hands or fight.
    Rita Mae Brown

6 The male is a domestic animal which, if treated with firmness and kindness, can be trained to do most things.
    Jilly Cooper, *Cosmopolitan,* 1972

7 PELLET: Men are all alike.
    WENDLE: Only some more than others.
    Noël Coward, 'Law and Order', *This Year of Grace,* 1928

8 . . . beware of men who cry. It's true that men who cry are sensitive to and in touch with feelings, but the only feelings they tend to be sensitive to and in touch with are their own.
    Nora Ephron, *Heartburn,* 1983

9 Macho does not prove mucho.
    Zsa Zsa Gabor

10 The only place men want depth in a woman is in her *décolletage.*
    Zsa Zsa Gabor (Attrib.)

11 Probably the only place where a man can feel really secure is in a maximum security prison, except for the imminent threat of release.
    Germaine Greer, *The Female Eunuch,* 1970

12 None of you [men] ask for anything – except everything, but just for so long as you need it.
    Doris Lessing, *The Golden Notebook,* 1962

13 I require only three things of a man. He must be handsome, ruthless and stupid.
    Dorothy Parker, quoted in *You Might As Well Live,* 1971

14 Some men break your heart in two,
Some men fawn and flatter,
Some men never look at you;
And that cleans up the matter.
    Dorothy Parker, 'Experience', *Enough Rope,* 1926

15 Women find men who have a sense of humor EXTREMELY SEXY! You don't have to look like Robert Redford. All you have to do is tickle her funny bone, and she'll follow you anywhere! If you can make her laugh, you've got it made!
    MAN: One to call her Dad and the other to open the Diet Pepsi!
    WOMAN: Oh stop! You're KILLING me! Take off all your clothes quick!
    Mimi Pond, *Mimi Pond's Secrets of the Powder Room,* cartoon, 1983

16 I like two kinds of men: domestic and foreign.
    Mae West

17 It's not the men in my life that count; it's the life in my men.
    Mae West

18 When women go wrong, men go right after them.
    Mae West

19 No nice men are good at getting taxis.
    Katharine Whitehorn, *Observer*, 1977

See also Men; Women – The Male View.

MEN AND WOMEN

1 Give a woman an inch and she thinks
   she's a ruler.
   Stars and Stripes

2 I married beneath me. All women do.
   Nancy Astor

3 The first time Adam had a chance, he
   laid the blame on women.
   Nancy Astor

4 . . . all women dress like their mothers,
   that is their tragedy. No man ever does.
   That is his.
   Alan Bennett, *Forty Years On*, 1968

5 The sad lesson of life is that you treat a
   girl like that with respect, and the next
   guy comes along and he's banging the
   hell out of her.
   Art Buchwald, *Herald Tribune*, 1975

6 In the sex-war, thoughtlessness is the
   weapon of the male, vindictiveness of the
   female.
   Cyril Connolly, *The Unquiet Grave*, 1945

7 Most women set out to try to change a
   man, and when they have changed him
   they do not like him.
   Marlene Dietrich (Attrib.)

8 Men and women do not have the faintest
   idea of what to do with one another. Each
   sex looks at the other with suspicion. The
   slightest gesture (scratching an ear), the
   most casual remark ('How are your
   tomatoes?') are seen as hostile acts. Now
   that women are equal, they feel awful
   about it and wonder if they should have
   pushed so hard. Men would like to reach
   out and help but are afraid they will be
   smashed in the head.
   Bruce Jay Friedman, 'Sex and the Lonely
   Guy', *Esquire*, 1977

9 'They eat him, same as a hen-spider
   eats a cock-spider. That's what women
   do – if a man lets 'em.'
   'Indeed,' commented Flora.
   'Ay – but I said "if" a man lets 'em.

Now I – I don't let no woman eat me – I
eats them instead.'
   Flora thought an appreciative silence
was the best policy to pursue at this
point . . .
   'That shocks you, eh?' said Seth, mis-
interpreting her silence . . .
   'I'm afraid I wasn't listening to all of it,'
she replied, 'but I am sure it was very
interesting. You must tell me all about
your work sometime. What do you do
now, on the evenings when you aren't –
er – eating people.'
   Stella Gibbons, *Cold Comfort Farm*, 1932

10 . . . we can call each other girls, chicks,
    broads, birds and dames with equanim-
    ity. Many of us prefer to do so since the
    word 'woman', being two syllables, is
    long, unwieldy, and earnest.
       But a man must watch his ass. Never
    may a man be permitted to call any
    female a 'chick'. He may call you a broad
    or a dame only if he is a close friend and
    fond of John Garfield movies. The term
    'bird', generally used by fatuous English-
    men, is always frowned upon.
       Cynthia Heimel, *Sex Tips for Girls*, 1983

11 Women complain about sex more often
    than men. Their gripes fall into two
    major categories: (1) Not enough. (2)
    Too much.
       Ann Landers, *Ann Landers Says Truth is
    Stranger . . .* 1968

12 A man's womenfolk, whatever their out-
    ward show of respect for his merit and
    authority, always regard him secretly as
    an ass, and with something akin to pity.
       H. L. Mencken, *In Defense of Women*, 1922

13 On one issue at least, men and women
    agree: they both distrust women.
       H. L. Mencken (Attrib.)

14 Society is now influenced, shaped, and
    even to a large extent controlled by
    women. This is a far cry from the world
    of our childhood, when society was con-
    trolled by . . . Well, as the author recalls,
    society was controlled by Mom. Christ-
    mas dinner for all the relatives, square
    dancing, the PTA, split-level ranch
    houses with two and a half baths – surely

no man thought these up. Feminism seems to be a case of women having won a leg-wrestling match with their own other leg. There is only one thing for men to do in response to this confusing situation, which is the same thing men have always done, which is anything women want.
P. J. O'Rourke, *Modern Manners*, 1983

15 Boys don't make passes at female smart-asses.
Letty Cottin Pogrebin, *The First Ms Reader*, 1972

16 God created man, and finding him not sufficiently alone, gave him a companion to make him feel his solitude more.
Paul Valéry, *Tel Quel*, 1943

17 A man can be happy with any woman as long as he does not love her.
Oscar Wilde, *The Picture of Dorian Gray*, 1891

18 Between men and women there is no friendship possible. There is passion, enmity, worship, love, but no friendship.
Oscar Wilde, *Lady Windermere's Fan*, 1892

19 Women are never disarmed by compliments. Men always are. That is the difference between the sexes.
Oscar Wilde, *An Ideal Husband*, 1895

20 Men play the game; women know the score.
Roger Woddis, *Spectator*

See also Couples; Men; Men – The Female View; Relationships; Women; Women – The Male View.

METRICATION

1 On 1 July 1977 all US humor will be converted to the metric system, bringing American humor into conformity with the humor of the rest of the world. On that date, the decimal metric system of risibles, mimics, mockers, grims, and merdes will replace such US Customary humor units as jokes, jibes, jests, railleries, satires, burlesques, and clowning around as the proper measure of comic activity.
P. J. O'Rourke, *National Lampoon*, 1977

2 I adore
a Viennese waltz in 3/4
but my love would not survive
a change to 0.75
Fritz Spiegl, 'Decimal Waltz', *Worse Verse*, 1969

See also Mathematics.

MIDDLE AGE

1 Middle age is when we can do just as much as ever – but would rather not.
Anon.

2 Years ago we discovered the exact point, the dead centre of middle age. It occurs when you are too young to take up golf and too old to rush up to the net.
Franklin P. Adams, *Nods and Becks*, 1944

3 I have everything now I had twenty years ago – except now it's all lower.
Gypsy Rose Lee, quoted in *Newsweek*, 1968

4 Middle age is when, whenever you go on holiday, you pack a sweater.
Denis Norden, *My Word*, BBC Radio, 1976

5 But it's hard to be hip over thirty
When everyone else is nineteen,
When the last dance we learned was the Lindy,
And the last we heard, girls who looked like Barbra Streisand
Were trying to do something about it.
Judith Viorst, *It's Hard to be Hip Over Thirty . . .*, 1968

See also Age; Old Age.

MISFORTUNE

1 Calamities are of two kinds: misfortune to ourselves and good fortune to others.
Ambrose Bierce, *The Devil's Dictionary*, 1911

See also Accidents; Disasters.

MISSIONARIES

1 A missionary is a person who teaches cannibals to say grace before they eat him.
Anon.

2 Poor Uncle Harry
  Having become a missionary
  Found the natives' morals rather crude.
  He and Aunt Mary
  Swiftly imposed an arbitrary
  Ban upon them shopping in the nude.
  They all considered this silly and
      decided to rebel,
  They burnt his boots and several suits
      which made a horrible smell,
  The subtle implication was that Uncle
      could go to hell . . .
    Noël Coward, 'Uncle Harry', song from
    Pacific 1860, 1946

3 Missionaries, my dear! Don't you realize
  that missionaries are the divinely provided food for destitute and under-
  fed cannibals? Whenever they are on
  the brink of starvation, Heaven in its
  infinite mercy sends them a nice plump
  missionary.
    Oscar Wilde (Attrib.)

See also Cannibalism; Christianity; The
Church; Religion.

MISTAKES

1 All wrong-doing is done in the sincere
  belief that it is the best thing to do.
    Arnold Bennett

2 If only one could have two lives: the first
  in which to make one's mistakes, which
  seem as if they have to be made; and the
  second in which to profit by them.
    D. H. Lawrence, *The Collected Letters of
    D. H. Lawrence*, 1962

3 Nowadays most people die of a sort of
  creeping common sense, and discover
  when it is too late that the only things one
  never regrets are one's mistakes.
    Oscar Wilde, *The Picture of Dorian Gray*,
    1891

4 Whenever a man does a thoroughly
  stupid thing, it is always from the noblest
  of motives.
    Oscar Wilde, *The Picture of Dorian Gray*,
    1891

MODERATION

1 Moderation is a virtue only in those who
  are thought to have an alternative.
    Henry Kissinger, *Observer*, 1982

See also Abstinence; Temperance.

MODERN ART

1 GALLERY OWNER: Now this, Mr
  Kingsley, is Paul Klee. In Klee you see
  everything one looks for in modern
  art: rapid capital growth, sound long-
  term prospects, and excellent relative
  liquidity.
    William Hamilton, *William Hamilton's
    Anti-Social Register*, cartoon, 1974

2 Skill without imagination is craftsman-
  ship and gives us many useful objects
  such as wickerwork picnic baskets. Imagination without skill gives us modern
  art.
    Tom Stoppard, *Artist Descending a Stair-
    case*, BBC Radio, 1972

3 Another unsettling element in modern
  art is that common symptom of immatur-
  ity, the dread of doing what has been
  done before.
    Edith Wharton, *The Writing of Fiction*, 1925

4 . . . collecting contemporary art, the
  leading edge, the latest thing, warm and
  wet from the Loft, appeals specifically
  to those who feel most uneasy about
  their own commercial wealth . . . See?
  I'm not like THEM – those Jaycees,
  those United Fund chairmen, those
  Young Presidents, those mindless
  New York A.C. GOYISHEH hog-
  jowled, stripe-tied goddamn-good-to-
  see-you-you-old-bastard-you oyster-bar
  trenchermen . . . Avant-garde art, more
  than any other, takes the Mammon and
  the Moloch out of money, puts Levi's,
  turtlenecks, muttonchops, and other
  mantles and laurels of bohemian grace
  upon it.
    Tom Wolfe, *The Painted Word*, 1975

5 It was the thaw! It was spring again! The
  press embraced Pop Art with priapic
  delight. That goddamned Abstract Ex-
  pressionism had been so solemn, so

grim ... 'Shards of interpenetrated sensibility make their way, tentatively, through a not always compromisable field of cobalt blue –' How could you write about the freaking stuff? Pop Art you could have fun with.

Tom Wolfe, *The Painted Word*, 1975

See also Art and Artists; Modern Life.

MODERN LIFE

1 VERONICA: I saw somebody peeing in Jermyn Street the other day. I thought, Is this the end of civilization as we know it. Or is it simply somebody peeing in Jermyn Street?

Alan Bennett, *The Old Country*, 1978

2 And where's the roof of golden thatch?
The chimney-stack of stone?
The crown-glass panes that used to match
Each sunset with their own?
Oh now the walls are red and smart
The roof has emerald tiles.
The neon sign's a work of art
And visible for miles.

John Betjeman, 'The Village Inn', *A Few Late Chrysanthemums*, 1954

3 It's hard for me to get used to these changing times. I can remember when the air was clean and sex was dirty.

George Burns

4 I have tried at various times in my life to grasp the rudiments of such inventions as the telephone, the camera, wireless telegraphy and even the ordinary motor-car, but without success. Television, of course, and radar and atomic energy are so far beyond my comprehension that my brain shudders at the thought of them and scurries for cover like a primitive tribesman confronted for the first time with a Dunhill cigarette lighter.

Noël Coward (Attrib.)

5 The marvels of modern technology include the development of a soda can which, when discarded, will last forever – and a $7,000 car, which, when properly cared for, will rust out in two or three years.

Paul Harwitz, *Wall Street Journal*

6 The past few years have seen a steady increase in the number of people playing music in the streets. The past few years have also seen a steady increase in the number of malignant diseases. Are these two facts related?

Fran Lebowitz, *Metropolitan Life*, 1978

7 There is one fault that I must find with
the twentieth century,
And I'll put it in a couple of words: Too
adventury.
What I'd like would be some nice dull
monotony
If anyone's gotony.

Ogden Nash, 'Put Back those Whiskers, I Know You', *Good Intentions*, 1942

8 Ev'rythin's up to date in Kansas City.
They've gone about as fur as they c'n
go!
They went and built a skyscraper seven
stories high –
About as high as a buildin' orta grow.
Ev'rythin's like a dream in Kansas City.
It's better than a magic-lantern show.
Y' c'n turn the radiator on whenever you
want some heat,
With ev'ry kind o' comfort ev'ry house is
all complete,
You c'n walk to privies in the rain an'
never wet yer feet –
They've gone about as fur as they c'n
go!
Yes, sir!
They've gone about as fur as they c'n
go!

Richard Rodgers and Oscar Hammerstein II, 'Kansas City', song from *Oklahoma*, 1943

9 No man ... who has wrestled with a self-adjusting card table can ever quite be the man he once was.

James Thurber, 'Sex ex Machina', *Let Your Mind Alone*, 1937

See also Inventions; Modern Art; Progress; Space; Technology; Video Games.

MODESTY

1 Modesty is the art of encouraging people to find out for themselves how wonderful you are.

Anon.

2 Modesty is a vastly overrated virtue.
  J. K. Galbraith (Attrib.)

3 Modesty: the gentle art of enhancing
  your charm by pretending not to be aware
  of it.
  Oliver Herford

4 A modest man is usually admired – if
  people ever hear of him.
  Edgar Watson Howe, *Ventures in Common
  Sense*, 1919

See also Humility; Morality; Virginity.

MONEY

1 Money isn't everything: usually it isn't
  even enough.
  Anon.

2 Money is better than poverty, if only for
  financial reasons.
  Woody Allen, *Without Feathers*, 1972

3 Can money make your hands get rough,
  As washing dishes does?
  Can money make you smell the way
  That cooking fishes does?
  It may buy you gems and fancy clothes
  And juicy steaks to carve,
  But it cannot build your character
  Or teach you how to starve!
  . . . Money *isn't* everything
  As long as you have dough!
  Oscar Hammerstein II, 'Money isn't
  Everything', song from *Allegro*, 1947

4 All right, so I like spending money! But
  name one other extravagance!
  Max Kauffmann

5 Money is like a sixth sense without which
  you cannot make a complete use of the
  other five.
  W. Somerset Maugham

6 Money can't buy friends but you can get
  a better class of enemy.
  Spike Milligan, *Puckoon*, 1963

7 The great rule is not to talk about money
  with people who have much more or
  much less than you.
  Katharine Whitehorn

8 I don't want money. It is only people who
  pay their bills who want that, and I never
  pay mine.
  Oscar Wilde, *The Picture of Dorian Gray*,
  1891

See also Banking; Budgets; Credit;
Credit Cards; Debt; Economics; Economy; Rich and Poor; Taxation; Wealth.

MONOGAMY

1 Monogamy leaves a lot to be desired.
  Graffito, London, 1982

See also Bigamy; Fidelity; Marriage.

MORALITY

1 We know of no spectacle so ridiculous as
  the British public in one of its periodical
  fits of morality.
  Thomas Macaulay

2 Morality consists in suspecting other
  people of not being legally married.
  George Bernard Shaw, *The Doctor's
  Dilemma*, 1906

3 PICKERING: Have you no morals, man?
  DOOLITTLE: Can't afford them, Gov-
  ernor.
  George Bernard Shaw, *Pygmalion*, 1912

4 Moral indignation is jealousy with a halo.
  H. G. Wells

5 A man who moralizes is usually a hypo-
  crite, and a woman who moralizes is
  invariably plain.
  Oscar Wilde, *Lady Windermere's Fan*, 1892

6 Morality is simply the attitude we adopt
  to people whom we personally dislike.
  Oscar Wilde, *An Ideal Husband*, 1895

See also Conscience; Puritanism; Reformers; Rogues; Standards; Virtue.

MORNING

1 The average, healthy, well-adjusted
  adult gets up at seven thirty in the morning feeling just plain terrible.
  Jean Kerr, *Please Don't Eat the Daisies*, 1957

2 Don't forget I was up early this morning.
  I was up at the crack of 6, took a brisk
  walk to the window, was back in bed by
  6.05. I stood under that cold shower for

ten minutes. Tomorrow I'm going to turn the water on.
Henny Youngman, 1940

See also Breakfast.

MOTHERS

1 Never marry a man who hates his mother because he'll end up hating you.
Jill Bennett (Attrib.)

2 The parting injunctions
Of mothers and wives
Are one of those functions
That poison their lives.
Clarence Day, *Scenes from Mesozoic*

3 Nobody can misunderstand a boy like his own mother.
Norman Douglas (Attrib.)

4 Few misfortunes can befall a boy which bring worse consequences than to have a really affectionate mother.
W. Somerset Maugham, *A Writer's Notebook*, 1949

5 No woman can shake off her mother. There should be no mothers, only women.
George Bernard Shaw, *Too True to be Good*, 1934

6 MOTHER: Do you love me, Albert?
ALBERT: Yes.
MOTHER: Yes – what?
ALBERT: Yes, please.
Tom Stoppard, *Albert's Bridge*, BBC Radio, 1967

7 On her face was the look of a mother whose daughter had seen the light and will shortly be marrying a deserving young clergyman with a bachelor uncle high up in the shipping business.
P. G. Wodehouse, *Blandings Castle and Elsewhere*, 1935

See also Children; Fathers; Housewives; Women.

MOTHERS-IN-LAW

1 My mother-in-law broke up my marriage. My wife came home from work one day and found me in bed with her.
Lenny Bruce

2 The mother-in-law thinks I'm effeminate: not that I mind that because, beside her, I am!
Les Dawson, *The Les Dawson Joke Book*, 1979

3 I haven't spoken to my mother-in-law for eighteen months – I don't like to interrupt her.
Ken Dodd

4 Behind every successful man stands a surprised mother-in-law.
Hubert Humphrey, speech, 1964

5 ERIC: But I will say this for her: there was one time in my life when I think I would have cut my throat if it wasn't for my mother-in-law.
ERNIE: How d'you mean?
ERIC: She was using my razor.
Eric Morecambe and Ernie Wise, *The Morecambe and Wise Joke Book*, 1979

See also Husbands; Marriage; Women.

MURDER

1 From Number Nine, Penwiper Mews,
There is really abominable news:
They've discovered a head
In the box for the bread
But nobody seems to know whose.
Edward Gorey

2 ERIC: It was the corpse. He had a gun in his hand and a knife in his back. Who d'you think poisoned him?
ERNIE: Who?
ERIC: Nobody. He'd been strangled.
Eric Morecambe and Ernie Wise, *The Morecambe and Wise Joke Book*, 1979

3 If the desire to kill and the opportunity to kill came always together, who would escape hanging?
Mark Twain

4 Murder is always a mistake ... One should never do anything that one cannot talk about after dinner.
Oscar Wilde, *The Picture of Dorian Gray*, 1891

5 It's the old problem, of course – the one that makes life so tough for murderers – what to do with the body.
P. G. Wodehouse, *The Code of the Woosters*, 1938

See also Assassination; Capital Punishment; Crime; The Law; Police.

MUSIC AND MUSICIANS

1 There was an Old Person of Tring
Who, when somebody asked her to sing,
Replied, 'Aren't it odd?
I can never tell "God
Save the Weasel" from "Pop Goes the King."'
Anon., *New York Times Magazine*, 1946

2 The music teacher came twice a week to bridge the awful gap between Dorothy and Chopin.
George Ade

3 It is quite untrue that the English people don't appreciate music. They may not understand it but they absolutely love the noise it makes.
Sir Thomas Beecham

4 Madam, you have between your legs an instrument capable of giving pleasure to thousands – and all you can do is scratch it.
Sir Thomas Beecham, to lady cellist (Attrib.)

5 We cannot expect you to be with us all the time, but perhaps you could be good enough to keep in touch now and again.
Sir Thomas Beecham, to musician at rehearsal (Attrib.)

6 Extraordinary how potent cheap music is.
Noël Coward, *Private Lives*, 1930

7 I hate music, especially when it's played.
Jimmy Durante

8 Away with the music of Broadway,
Be off with your Irving Berlin,
Oh, I give no quarter
To Kern or Cole Porter,
And Gershwin keeps pounding on tin.
How can I be civil
While hearing this drivil,

It's strictly for night-clubbing souses.
Oh, give me the free 'n' easy
Waltz that is Viennesy
And,
Go tell the band
If they want a hand,
The waltz must be Strauss's.
George and Ira Gershwin, 'By Strauss', song from *The Show is On*, 1936

9 I only know two tunes. One of them is 'Yankee Doodle' and the other isn't.
Ulysses S. Grant

10 Classical music is the kind we keep thinking will turn into a tune.
Kin Hubbard, *Abe Martin's Sayings*, 1915

11 This world is a difficult world, indeed,
And people are hard to suit,
And the man who plays on the violin,
Is a bore to the man with the flute.
Walter Learned, *Consolation*

12 There was a time when music knew its place. No longer. Possibly this is not music's fault. It may be that music fell in with a bad crowd and lost its sense of common decency . . . The first thing that music must understand is that there are two kinds of music – good music and bad music. Good music is music that I want to hear. Bad music is music that I don't want to hear.
Fran Lebowitz, *Metropolitan Life*, 1978

13 The kids today are quite right about the music their parents listened to: most of it was trash. The parents are quite right about what their young listen to: most of it is trash too.
Gene Lees, 'Rock', *High Fidelity*, 1967

14 Music-hall songs provide the dull with wit, just as proverbs provide them with wisdom.
W. Somerset Maugham, *A Writer's Notebook*, 1949

15 Without music, life would be a mistake.
Friedrich Wilhelm Nietzsche, *The Twilight of the Idols*, 1889

16 When you are about thirty-five years old, something terrible always happens to music.
Steve Race, BBC Radio, 1982

17 Music is essentially useless, as life is.
   George Santayana, *Little Essays*, 1920

18 Artists who say they practise eight hours
   a day are liars or asses.
   Andres Segovia, 1980

19 . . . music is the brandy of the damned.
   George Bernard Shaw, *Man and Superman*, 1903

20 I wish the Government would put a tax
   on pianos for the incompetent.
   Edith Sitwell, *Edith Sitwell: Selected Letters
   1916–1964*, 1970

21 I like Wagner's music better than anybody's. It is so loud that one can talk the
   whole time without people hearing what
   one says.
   Oscar Wilde, *The Picture of Dorian Gray*,
   1891

22 Musical people are so absurdly unreasonable. They always want one to be
   perfectly dumb at the very moment when
   one is longing to be absolutely deaf.
   Oscar Wilde, *An Ideal Husband*, 1895

23 Music makes one feel so romantic – at
   least it always got on one's nerves – which
   is the same thing nowadays.
   Oscar Wilde, *A Woman of No Importance*,
   1893

24 It was loud in spots and less loud in other
   spots, and it had that quality which I have
   noticed in all violin solos of seeming to
   last much longer than it actually did.
   P. G. Wodehouse, *The Mating Season*, 1949

See also Composers; Folk Music; Jazz;
Opera; Rock 'n' Roll; Songs and Singers;
Violins.

NAMES

1 Said Jerome K. Jerome to Ford Madox
  Ford,
  'There's something, old boy, that I've
      always abhorred:
  When people address me and call me
      "Jerome",
  Are they being standoffish, or too much
      at home?'
  Said Ford, 'I agree;
  It's the same thing with me.'
  William Cole, 'Mutual Problem', *The
  Oxford Book of American Light Verse*, 1979

2 Marie-Joseph? It's a *lovely* name! It just
  sounds silly, that's all.
  **Dame Edna Everage (Barry Hum-
  phries)**, *Housewife Superstar*, one-man
  show, 1976

3 Now why did you name your baby 'John'?
  Every Tom, Dick and Harry is named
  'John'.
  Sam Goldwyn (Attrib.)

4 'Yossarian? Is that his name? Yossarian? What the hell kind of a name is
  Yossarian?'
  Lieutenant Scheisskopf had the facts
  at his finger tips. 'It's Yossarian's name,
  sir,' he explained.
  Joseph Heller, *Catch-22*, 1961

5 No good can come of association with
  anything labelled Gwladys or Ysobel or
  Ethyl or Mabelle or Kathryn. But particularly Gwladys.
  P. G. Wodehouse, *Very Good, Jeeves*, 1930

NARCISSISM

1 'He fell in love with himself at first sight
  and it is a passion to which he has always
  remained faithful. Self-love seems so
  often unrequited.'
  Anthony Powell, *The Acceptance World*,
  1955

2 A narcissist is someone better looking
  than you are.
  Gore Vidal

See also Egotism; Vanity.

NAUSEA

1 *Chuck, Enough to make you*: (see under
  Chunder, Technicolor Yawn, Hurl, Play
  the Whale, Park the Tiger, Cry Ruth).
  Chunder: to enjoy oneself in reverse.
  Technicolour Yawn: Liquid Laugh.
  Barry Humphries, glossary from *Bazza
  Pulls It Off*, 1972

2 I've had liquid laughs in bars
  And I've hurled from moving cars
  And I've chuckled when and where it
      suited me
  But, if I could choose a spot
  To regurgitate me lot
  Then I'd chunder in the old Pacific sea.
  Barry Humphries, 'The Old Pacific Sea',
  1964

3 Don't worry – the white wine came up
  with the fish.
  Herman J. Mankiewicz, after being sick at
  a Hollywood party (Attrib.)

4 Every authority on etiquette discusses
  how to put things into your stomach, but
  very few discuss how to get them back out
  in a hurry. Actually, there is no way to
  make vomiting courteous. You have to do
  the next best thing, which is to vomit in
  such a way that the story you tell about it
  later will be amusing.
  P. J. O'Rourke, *Modern Manners*, 1983

See also Drink; Hangovers; Illness.

THE NAVY

1 The Navy's a very gentlemanly business.
  You fire at the horizon to sink a ship and
  then you pull people out of the water and
  say, 'Frightfully sorry, old chap.'
  William Golding, *The Sunday Times*, 1984

2 The trouble with modern navies is that
  they have to operate in water, which is
  ridiculous stuff to get around in and

offers no decent cover at all, except for Davy Jones's locker.

Tony Hendra, 'EEC! It's the US of E!', *National Lampoon*, 1976

See also The Army; The Sea; Ships; War.

NEEDS

1 That I am totally devoid of sympathy for, or interest in, the world of groups is directly attributable to the fact that *my* two greatest needs and desires – smoking cigarettes and plotting revenge – are basically solitary pursuits.

Fran Lebowitz, *Metropolitan Life*, 1978

NEGOTIATIONS

1 When a man tells me he's going to put all his cards on the table, I always look up his sleeve.

Lord Hore-Belisha, Secretary of State for War, 1937–1940

NEUTRALITY

1 Q: Which is the most neutral country in the world?

A: Czechoslovakia – it doesn't even interfere in its own internal affairs.

Anon.

2 We know what happens to people who stay in the middle of the road. They get run over.

Aneurin Bevan

3 The middle of the road is all of the usable surface. The extremes, right and left, are in the gutters.

Dwight D. Eisenhower

4 An independent is a guy who wants to take the politics out of politics.

Adlai Stevenson

NEW ENGLAND

1 The most serious charge which can be brought against New England is not Puritanism but February.

Joseph Wood Krutch, *The Twelve Seasons*, 1949

2 There is a sumptuous variety about the New England weather . . . In the spring I

have counted one hundred and thirty-six different kinds of weather inside of four and twenty hours.

Mark Twain, speech, 1876

See also America and the Americans; Boston.

NEWS

1 It's not the world that's got so much worse but the news coverage that's got so much better.

G. K. Chesterton (Attrib.)

2 *News*: anything that makes a woman say, 'For heaven's sake!'

Edgar Watson Howe

3 No News Is Preferable.

Fran Lebowitz, *Metropolitan Life*, 1978

See also Journalism; Newspapers.

NEWSPAPERS

1 Instead of being arrested, as we stated, for kicking his wife down a flight of stairs and hurling a lighted kerosene lamp after her, the Rev. James P. Wellman died unmarried four years ago.

Anon., from an American newspaper, quoted by Sir Edward Burne-Jones in a letter to Lady Horner

2 I keep reading between the lies.

Goodman Ace

3 He had been kicked in the head by a mule when young, and believed everything he read in the Sunday papers.

George Ade

4 I read the newspaper avidly. It is my one form of continuous fiction.

Aneurin Bevan (Attrib.)

5 I love the weight of American Sunday newspapers. Pulling them up off the floor is good for the figure.

Noël Coward (Attrib.)

6 I'm the Clergyman who's never been to London,
I'm the Clergyman who's never been to Town,
An enterprising journalist approached me

And every word I said he jotted down,
I had to face a battery of cameras
And hold an extra service in the snow
And all because I've *never* been to
  London
And haven't got the *least* desire to go!
  Noël Coward, 'The Hall of Fame', *Words and Music*, 1932

7 When I say 'start' let's have five seconds of silence. (*Pause*) That's pretty good. That gives something for the news media to quote with absolute accuracy.
  Bobby Knight, Indiana basketball coach, 1982

8 Everything you read in the newspapers is absolutely true except for the rare story of which you happen to have first-hand knowledge.
  Erwin Knoll

9 People everywhere confuse
What they read in newspapers with
  news.
  A. J. Liebling, *New Yorker*, 1956

10 You should always believe all you read in the newspapers, as this makes them more interesting.
  Rose Macaulay, *A Casual Commentary*, 1925

11 All successful newspapers are ceaselessly querulous and bellicose. They never defend anyone or anything if they can help it; if the job is forced upon them, they tackle it by denouncing someone or something else.
  H. L. Mencken, *Prejudices*, First Series, 1919

12 Any man with ambition, integrity – and $10,000,000 dollars – can start a daily newspaper.
  Henry Morgan, 1950

13 Early in life I had noticed that no event is ever correctly reported in a newspaper.
  George Orwell, *Collected Essays, Journalism and Letters*, 1968

14 I hope we never live to see the day when a thing is as bad as some of our newspapers make it.
  Will Rogers, 1934

15 [A device] unable ... to discriminate between a bicycle accident and the collapse of civilization.
  George Bernard Shaw

16 An editor is one who separates the wheat from the chaff and prints the chaff.
  Adlai Stevenson

17 MILNE: Junk journalism is the evidence of a society that has got at least one thing right, that there should be nobody with the power to dictate where responsible journalism begins.
  Tom Stoppard, *Night and Day*, 1978

18 RUTH: I'm with you on the free press. It's the newspapers I can't stand.
  Tom Stoppard, *Night and Day*, 1978

19 'With regard to Policy, I expect you already have your own views. I never hamper my correspondents in any way. What the British public wants first, last and all the time is News. Remember that the Patriots are in the right and are going to win. *The Beast* stands by them four square. But they must win quickly. The British public has no interest in a war that drags on indecisively. A few sharp victories, some conspicuous acts of personal bravery on the Patriot side and a colourful entry into the capital. That is *The Beast* Policy for the war.'
  Evelyn Waugh, *Scoop*, 1938

20 In the old days men had the rack, now they have the Press.
  Oscar Wilde, 'The Soul of Man under Socialism', 1891

21 It is useless to dangle rich bribes before our eyes. *Cosy Moments* cannot be muzzled. You doubtless mean well, according to your – if I may say so – somewhat murky lights, but we are not for sale, except at ten cents weekly. From the hills of Maine to the Everglades of Florida, from Sandy Hook to San Francisco, from Portland, Oregon, to Melonsquashville, Tennessee, one sentence is in every man's mouth. And what is that sentence? I give you three guesses. You give it

up? It is this: '*Cosy Moments* cannot be muzzled!'
P. G. Wodehouse, *Psmith, Journalist*, 1915

See also Journalism; News.

NEW YORK

1 I love short trips to New York; to me it is the finest three-day town on earth.
James Cameron, *Witness*, 1966

2 It seemed almost intolerably shining, secure and well dressed, as though it was continually going to gay parties while London had to stay at home and do the housework.
Noël Coward, 1943

3 We'll have Manhattan,
The Bronx and Staten
Island too.
We'll try to cross
Fifth Avenue.
As black as onyx
We'll find the Bronnix
Park Express.
Our Flatbush flat, I guess,
Will be a great success,
More or less.
Lorenz Hart, 'Manhattan', song, 1925

4 This is New York, a combat zone, and everyone has to have an angle or they're not allowed over the bridges or through the tunnels. Let them have their angles, it's what they live for. You've got better things to worry about, like making sure the people that actually matter don't try any funny stuff.
Cynthia Heimel, 'Lower Manhattan Survival Tactics', *Village Voice*, 1983

5 Well, little old Noisyville-on-the-Subway is good enough for me.
O. Henry, *Strictly Business*, 1910

6 A city where everyone mutinies but no one deserts.
Harry Hershfield

7 A car is useless in New York, essential everywhere else. The same with good manners.
Mignon McLaughlin, *The Second Neurotic's Notebook*, 1966

8 New York, the nation's thyroid gland.
Christopher Morley, *Shore Leave*

9 In New York beautiful girls can become more beautiful by going to Elizabeth Arden,
And getting stuff put on their faces and waiting for it to harden,
And poor girls with nothing to their names but a letter or two can get rich and joyous
From a brief trip to their loyous.
So I can say with impunity
That New York is a city of opportunity.
Ogden Nash, 'A Brief Guide to New York', *Many Long Years Ago*, 1945

10 The Bronx?
No, thonx!
Ogden Nash, 'Geographical Reflection', *New Yorker*, 1931

11 Vulgar of manner, overfed,
Overdressed and underbred;
Heartless, Godless, hell's delight,
Rude by day and lewd by night . . .
Crazed with avarice, lust and rum,
New York, thy name's Delirium.
Byron Rufus Newton, *Owed to New York*, 1906

12 . . . I've been a New Yorker for ten years, and the only people who are nice to us turn out to be Moonies.
P. J. O'Rourke, *Rolling Stone*, 1982

13 There's no room for amateurs, even in crossing the streets.
George Segal, quoted in *Newsweek*, 1972

14 It's not Mecca, it just smells like it.
Neil Simon, *California Suite*, screenplay, 1978

15 WILLIAMS: Next thing I knew, I was in New York.
INTERVIEWER: Was that a heavy adjustment for you to make?
WILLIAMS: I was the walking epitome of fur*shirr* meets yo'ass. On my first day in New York, I went to school dressed like a typical California kid: I wore tie-up yoga pants and a Hawaiian shirt, and I kept stepping in dog shit with my thongs.
Robin Williams, interview in *Playboy*, 1982

16 The Sheridan Apartment House stands in the heart of New York's Bohemian and artistic quarter. If you threw a brick from any of its windows, you would be certain to brain some rising interior decorator, some Vorticist sculptor or a writer of revolutionary *vers libre*.
   P. G. Wodehouse, *The Small Bachelor*, 1927

See also America and the Americans.

NEW ZEALAND

1 Terrible Tragedy in the South Seas. Three million people trapped alive!
   Tom Scott, *Listener*, 1979

RICHARD NIXON President of the United States, 1969–1974

1 A new book has been released entitled *Friends of Richard Nixon*. It is only one page longer than the work, *Famous Antarctic Television Personalities of the Eighteenth Century*. President Ford said, 'I've spent most of this week reading it, finding it challenging in its scope.'
   'Weekend Update', *Saturday Night Live*, NBC TV

2 In Washington, so the story goes, Republican top strategists huddled, and all were glum indeed – except one. 'I'm sure we'll win, there's no doubt about it,' he enthused. Everyone wanted to know the reason for his confidence. Answer: 'I have a deep and abiding faith in the fundamental bigotry of the American people.'
   Time, 1960, (the Republican Presidential candidate was Nixon)

3 There's a theory that provides an answer to the question of President Nixon's attitude to gambling. There was once a small boy in California who had a pony he was very fond of. One day a gambler came to town and, engaging the boy in a game of cards, won the pony. The boy swore never to gamble again . . .
   The reader will have guessed by now that I am telling Richard Nixon's story. He was that gambler.
   Anon.

4 He told us he was going to take crime out of the streets. He did. He took it into the damn White House.
   Rev. Ralph D. Abernathy

5 . . . a Main Street Machiavelli.
   Patrick Anderson

6 Look, Nixon's no dope. If the people really *wanted* moral leadership, he'd give them moral leadership.
   Charles Barsotti, cartoon in the *New Yorker*

7 Nixon is a purposeless man, but I have great faith in his cowardice.
   Jimmy Breslin

8 . . . a naïve, inept, maladjusted Throttlebottom.
   Emanuel Celler

9 Nixon just isn't half the man Hitler was.
   Richard Dudman, *St Louis Post Dispatch*

10 Do you realize the responsibility I carry? I'm the only person standing between Richard Nixon and the White House.
   John F. Kennedy

11 The only problem with drawing Nixon is restraint. Your tendency is to let your feelings come out. He's such a loathsome son of a bitch, and he looks so loathsome.
   Bill Mauldin, political cartoonist

12 Ever since Nixon, nobody has asked me why I am teaching a course like Policy Choice as Value Conflict.
   Professor Bruce Payne, Duke University, North Carolina

13 Richard Nixon means never having to say you're sorry.
   Wilfrid Sheed, *GQ*, 1984

14 Let's face it, there's something perversely endearing about a man so totally his own worst enemy that even achieving the presidency was merely something he had to do in order to be able to lose it.
   Paul Slansky

15 He is the kind of politician who would cut down a redwood tree and then mount the stump to make a speech for conservation.
   Adlai Stevenson, 1956

16 . . . McCarthyism in a white collar.
   Adlai Stevenson

17 ... a little man in a big hurry.
   Robert A. Taft

18 ... the integrity of a hyena and the style of a poison toad.
   Hunter S. Thompson

19 When the cold light of history looks back on Richard Nixon's five years of unrestrained power in the White House, it will show that he had the same effect on conservative/Republican politics as Charles Manson and the Hell's Angels had on hippies and flower people.
   Hunter S. Thompson

20 Richard Nixon is a no-good lying bastard. He can lie out of both sides of his mouth at the same time, and even if he caught himself telling the truth, he'd lie just to keep his hand in.
   Harry S. Truman

21 ... it is quite extraordinary! He will even tell a lie when it is not convenient to. That is the sign of a great artist ...
   Gore Vidal, interviewed on *Russell Harty Plus*, London Weekend Television, 1972

See also Gerald Ford; The Presidency; The Vietnam War; Washington; Watergate.

NOISE

1 Don't get annoyed if your neighbour plays his hi-fi at two o'clock in the morning. Call him at four and tell him how much you enjoyed it.
   Anon.

2 Noise, *n.* a stench in the ear. The chief product and authenticating sign of civilization.
   Ambrose Bierce, *The Devil's Dictionary*, 1911

See also Ears; Silence.

NONSENSE

1 I never saw a Purple Cow,
   I never hope to see one;
   But I can tell you anyhow,
   I'd rather see than be one.
   Gelett Burgess, 'The Purple Cow', *The Burgess Nonsense Book*, 1901

2 Ah, yes! I wrote the 'Purple Cow' –
   I'm Sorry, now, I Wrote it!
   But I can Tell you, Anyhow,
   I'll Kill you if you Quote it!
   Gelett Burgess, 'Cinq Ans Après', *The Burgess Nonsense Book*, 1901

See also Humour.

THE NOSE

1 JIMMY DURANTE: Hey, where are my glasses?
   FRIEND: They're on your nose!
   JIMMY DURANTE: Be more specific!
   Jimmy Durante

See also Faces; Perfumes; Smells; Sneezing.

NOVELS

1 Every novel should have a beginning, a muddle and an end.
   Peter De Vries

2 WAGNER: One of the things that makes novels less plausible than history, I find, is the way they shrink from coincidence.
   Tom Stoppard, *Night and Day*, 1978

3 I quite admit that modern novels have many good points. All I insist on is that, as a class, they are quite unreadable.
   Oscar Wilde, 'The Decay of Lying', 1889

4 Every author really wants to have letters printed in the papers. Unable to make the grade, he drops down a rung of the ladder and writes novels.
   P. G. Wodehouse

5 It has been well said that an author who expects results from a first novel is in a position similar to that of a man who drops a rose petal down the Grand Canyon of Arizona and listens for the echo.
   P. G. Wodehouse, *Cocktail Time*, 1958

6 'I write about stalwart men, strong but oh so gentle, and girls with wide grey eyes and hair the colour of ripe wheat, who are always having misunderstandings and going to Africa. The men, that is. The girls stay at home and marry the wrong bimbos. But there's a happy ending. The

bimbos break their necks in the hunting field and the men come back in the last chapter and they and the girls get together in the twilight, and all around is the scent of English flowers and birds singing their evensong in the shrubbery. Makes me shudder to think of it.'

P. G. Wodehouse, *Ice in the Bedroom*, 1961

7 Nothing induces me to read a novel except when I have to make money by writing about it. I detest them.

Virginia Woolf

See also Books; Literature; Writers; Writing.

NUCLEAR POWER

1 What's all this fuss about plutonium? How can something named after a Disney character be dangerous?

They say that if there is a leak in a nuclear power plant the radiation can kill you. Nix! Radiation cannot kill you because it contains absolutely no cholesterol. They say atomic radiation can hurt your reproductive organs. My answer is, so can a hockey stick. But we don't stop building *them*.

I told my wife that there was a chance that radiation might hurt my reproductive organs but she said in her opinion it's a small price to pay.

Johnny Carson, *The Tonight Show*, NBC TV

See also Electricity; Nuclear War.

NUCLEAR WAR

1 No first-class war can now be fought
Till all that can be sold is bought.
So do get going helter-skelter
And sell each citizen a shelter
Wherein, while being bombed and strafed, he
Can reek and retch and rot in perfect safety.

Kenneth Burke, 'Civil Defense', *Collected Poems 1915–1967*

2 Don'tcha worry, honey chile,
Don'tcha cry no more,

It's jest a li'l ole atom bomb
In a li'l ole lim'ted war.
It's jest a bitsy warhead, chile,
On a li'l ole tactical shell,
And all it'll do is blow us-all
To a li'l ole lim'ted hell.

Marya Mannes, 'On Limited Warfare', *Subverse*

3 I had that bomb dispatched to Moscow the moment we got imminent warning red. Ah, those Ruskies didn't think we had the means of delivering the bomb ... they overlooked the fact that we have the finest postal system in the world.

Spike Milligan and John Antrobus, *The Bed-sitting Room*, 1963

4 On this the first anniversary of the Nuclear Misunderstanding which led to World War III, I'd like to point out that under a Labour Administration, this was the shortest World War on record, two minutes twenty-eight seconds precisely, including the signing of the Peace Treaty ...

Spike Milligan and John Antrobus, *The Bed-sitting Room*, 1963

See also The Bomb; Nuclear Power; Pacifism; War.

NUDITY

1 Don't miss our show! Six beautiful dancing girls! Five beautiful costumes!

Poster outside nightclub, London

2 If God had wanted us to walk around naked, we would have been born that way.

Anon.

3 The trouble with nude dancing is that not everything stops when the music does.

Robert Helpmann, dancer and choreographer

4 I'm not *against* half-naked girls – not as often as I'd like to be ...

Benny Hill, *The Benny Hill Show*, Thames TV, 1984

5 Full-frontal nudity . . . has now become accepted by every branch of the theatrical profession with the possible exception of lady accordion-players.
   Denis Norden, *You Can't Have Your Kayak and Heat It*, 1973

6 I didn't pay three pounds fifty just to see half a dozen acorns and a chipolata.
   Noël Coward, after watching the male nude scenes in David Storey's *The Changing Room*, 1972

See also The Body; Censorship; Pornography; Prudery; Sex.

O

OBSCENITY

1 Obscenity is whatever gives a judge an erection.
   Anon.

2 It's a heavy breather wanting to reverse the charges . . .
   Marc, cartoon in *The Times*, 1977

3 Obscenity is what happens to shock some elderly and ignorant magistrate.
   Bertrand Russell, *Look*, 1954

4 Obscenity can be found in every book except the telephone directory.
   George Bernard Shaw

5 Under certain circumstances, profanity provides a relief denied even to prayer.
   Mark Twain

See also Censorship; Pornography; Puritanism; Sex; Swearing; Vulgarity.

OBSTINACY

1 Like all weak men, he laid an exaggerated stress on not changing one's mind.
   W. Somerset Maugham, *Of Human Bondage*, 1915

2 *I* am firm; *you* are obstinate; *he* is a pig-headed fool.
   Bertrand Russell, *Brains Trust*, BBC Radio

3 He has one of those terribly weak natures that are not susceptible to influence.
   Oscar Wilde, *An Ideal Husband*, 1895

THE OCCULT

1 Some things have got to be believed to be seen.
   Ralph Hodgson

2 Two spoons of sherry
   Three oz. of yeast,
   Half a pound of unicorn,
   And God bless the feast.
   Shake them in the colander
   Bang them to a chop,

Simmer slightly, snip up nicely,
Jump, skip, hop.
Knit one, knot one, purl two together,
Pip one and pop one and pluck the
   secret feather.
   T. H. White, 'The Witch's Work Song', *The Sword in the Stone*, 1938

See also Astrology; Superstition.

THE OFFICE

1 A memorandum is written not to inform the reader but to protect the writer.
   Dean Acheson

2 BOSS (*to Departmental Head*): How many people work in your office?
   DEPT. HEAD: About half of them, sir.
   Gyles Brandreth, *1,000 Jokes: The Greatest Joke Book Ever Known*, 1980

3 PERSONNEL MANAGER: I like your qualifications Gribson – you have the makings of a first-class underling.
   Hector Breeze, cartoon in *Private Eye*

4 A secretary is not a thing
   Wound by key, pulled by string.
   Her pad is to write in,
   And not spend the night in,
   If that's what you plan to enjoy.
   No!
   Frank Loesser, 'A Secretary is Not a Toy', song from *How to Succeed in Business without Really Trying*, 1961

5 Your face is a company face.
   It smiles at executives then goes back in place.
   The company furniture?
   Oh, it suits me fine.
   The company letterhead?
   A valentine.
   Anything you're against?
   Unemployment.
   Frank Loesser, 'The Company Way', song from *How to Succeed in Business without Really Trying*, 1961

6 . . . an office is not a tea-bar, matrimonial

bureau, betting shop, reading room, fashion house or smoking lounge, but a place where paperwork necessary to good management is originated and eventually filed.

Keith Waterhouse, *The Passing of the Third-floor Buck*, 1974

7 I yield to no one in my admiration for the office as a social centre, but it's no place actually to get any work done.

Katharine Whitehorn, *Sunday Best*

See also Big Business; Business; Work.

OLD AGE

1 DOCTOR: You're going to live to be eighty.
PATIENT: I AM eighty!
DOCTOR: What did I tell you?
Anon.

2 We think he's dead, but we're afraid to ask.
Anonymous Committee Member, of 79-year-old Chairman of House Committee, Washington, 1984

3 I used to dread getting older because I thought I would not be able to do all the things I wanted to do, but now that I am older I find that I don't want to do them.
Nancy Astor, on her eightieth birthday, 1959

4 I will never be an old man. To me, old age is always fifteen years older than I am.
Bernard Baruch

5 WICKSTEED: No. Not too old at fifty-three.
A worn defeated fool like me.
Still the tickling lust devours
Long stretches of my waking hours.
Busty girls in flowered scanties
Hitching down St Michael panties.
Easing off their wet-look boots,
To step into their birthday suits.
Alan Bennett, *Habeas Corpus*, 1973

6 You only have to survive in England and all is forgiven you . . . if you can eat a boiled egg at ninety in England they think you deserve a Nobel Prize.
Alan Bennett, *The South Bank Show*, London Weekend Television, 1984

7 I have my eighty-seventh birthday coming up and people ask what I'd most appreciate getting. I'll tell you: a paternity suit.
George Burns

8 I'm at that age now where just putting my cigar in its holder is a thrill.
George Burns

9 We talked about growing old gracefully
And Elsie who's seventy-four
Said, 'A, it's a question of being sincere,
And B, if you're supple you've nothing
to fear.'
Then she swung upside down from a
glass chandelier,
I couldn't have liked it more.
Noël Coward, 'I've Been to a Marvellous Party', *Set to Music*, 1938

10 We're a dear old couple and we *hate* one another
And we've hated one another for a long, long time.
Since the day that we were wed, up to the present,
Our lives, we must confess,
Have been progressively more unpleasant.
We're just sweet old darlings who despise one another
With a thoroughness approaching the sublime,
But through all our years
We've been affectionately known
As the Bronxville Darby and Joan.
Noël Coward, 'Bronxville Darby and Joan', *Sail Away*, 1962

11 Old age is life's parody.
Simone de Beauvoir, *The Coming of Age*, 1972

12 Very, very, very few
People die at ninety-two.
I suppose that I shall be
Safer still at ninety-three.
Willard R. Espy, 'Actuarial Reflection'

13 Being an old maid is like death by

drowning, a really delightful sensation after you cease to struggle.
Edna Ferber

14 I've joined the Olde Thyme Dance
    Club, the trouble is that there
Are too many ladies over, and no
    gentlemen to spare.
It seems a shame, it's not the same,
But still it has to be,
Some ladies have to dance together,
One of them is me.
    Joyce Grenfell, 'Stately as a Galleon',
    Stately as a Galleon, 1978

15 Stately as a galleon, I sail across the floor,
Doing the Military Two-step, as in the
    days of yore.
I dance with Mrs Tiverton; she's light
    on her feet, in spite
Of turning the scale at fourteen stone,
    and being of medium height.
so gay the band
So giddy the sight,
Full evening dress is a must,
But the zest goes out of a beautiful waltz
When you dance it bust to bust.
    Joyce Grenfell, 'Stately as a Galleon',
    Stately as a Galleon, 1978

16 I don't feel eighty. In fact I don't feel
anything till noon. Then it's time for my
nap.
    Bob Hope

17 You know you're getting old when the
candles cost more than the cake.
    Bob Hope

18 Seventy is wormwood
Seventy is gall
But it's better to be seventy
Than not alive at all.
    Phyllis McGinley

19 A man's only as old as the woman he
feels.
    Groucho Marx

20 Anyone can get old. All you have to do is
live long enough.
    Groucho Marx

21 One of the many pleasures of old age is
giving things up.
    Malcolm Muggeridge

22 Senescence begins
And middle age ends
The day your descendants
Outnumber your friends.
    Ogden Nash, 'Crossing the Border', *You
    Can't Get There from Here*, 1957

23 Growing old is like being increasingly
penalized for a crime you haven't committed.
    Anthony Powell, *Temporary Kings*, 1973

24 The denunciation of the young is a
necessary part of the hygiene of older
people, and greatly assists the circulation
of the blood.
    Logan Pearsall Smith, *Afterthoughts*, 1931

25 The greatest problem about old age is
the fear that it may go on too long.
    A. J. P. Taylor, *Observer*, 1981

26 MRS ALLONBY: I delight in men over
seventy, they always offer one the
devotion of a lifetime.
    Oscar Wilde, *A Woman of No Importance*,
    1893

See also Age; Middle Age.

OPERA

1 The opera is like a husband with a foreign title: expensive to support, hard to
understand, and therefore a supreme
social challenge.
    Cleveland Amory, NBC TV, 1961

2 I do not mind what language an opera is
sung in so long as it is a language I don't
understand.
    Sir Edward Appleton, *Observer*, 1955

3 No good opera plot can be sensible, for
people do not sing when they are feeling
sensible.
    W. H. Auden, quoted in *Time*, 1961

4 People are wrong when they say that
opera is not what it used to be. It *is* what it
used to be. That is what is wrong with it.
    Noël Coward

5 Opera in English is, in the main, just
about as sensible as baseball in Italian.
    H. L. Mencken

6 The genuine music-lover may accept the

carnal husk of opera to get at the kernel of actual music within, but that is no sign that he approves the carnal husk or enjoys gnawing through it.

H. L. Mencken, *Prejudices*, Second Series, 1920

7 There was a time when I heard eleven operas in a fortnight . . . which left me bankrupt and half-idiotic for a month.

J. B. Priestley, 'All about Ourselves', 1923

8 *Parsifal* is the kind of opera that starts at six o'clock. After it has been going three hours, you look at your watch and it says 6.20.

David Randolph

9 Tenors are noble, pure and heroic and get the soprano, if she has not tragically expired before the final curtain. But baritones are born villains in opera.

Leonard Warren, *New York World-Telegram and Sun*, 1957

10 Now momma an' poppa they gotta ragazzo
So much-a he eat-a they call a-heem Fatso
He cry-a so loud-a they theenk eet-a propera
Some day he grow up-a an' seeng at L'opera
Tenoré per'aps or a-basso profondo
For heem-a they spare-a no sforzo or fondo
An cart a-heem off to La Scala Milano;
But Fatso he seeng like da clapped-out soprano,
La vocé don't flow, eet a-got no vibrato
Da notes a-come out-a all corsa an' flat-o.

J. J. Webster, 'La Forza del Destino', *Everyman's Book of Nonsense*, 1981

11 An unalterable and unquestioned law of the musical world required that the German text of French operas sung by Swedish artists should be translated into Italian for the clearer understanding of English speaking audiences.

Edith Wharton, *The Age of Innocence*, 1920

See also Music and Musicians; Songs and Singers; The Theatre.

OPINION POLLS

1 If, when faced with a Gallup Quiz,
I tell the pollster
To mind his own biz,
Do you suppose
I'm one of the 'Don't Nose'?

Freddie Oliver, *Worse Verse*, 1969

2 Glad you brought that up, Jim. The latest research on polls has turned up some interesting variables. It turns out, for example, that people will tell you any old thing that pops into their heads.

Charles Saxon, cartoon in the *New Yorker*, 1984

See also Opinions.

OPINIONS

1 Too bad all the people who know how to run the country are busy driving taxi cabs and cutting hair.

George Burns

2 Steer clear of overviews. Those of us who have the situation in Lebanon in perspective and know exactly how to plot a gay rights campaign are usually morons. We snap at our children when they have innocent homework questions. We don't notice when our lover has a deadline. We forget to call our best friend back when she's just had root canal.

Homework, root canal and deadlines are the important things in life, and only when we have these major dramas taken care of can we presume to look at the larger questions.

Cynthia Heimel, 'Lower Manhattan Survival Tactics', *Village Voice*, 1983

3 If nobody ever said anything unless he knew what he was talking about, a ghastly hush would descend upon the earth.

Sir Alan Herbert

4 The degree of one's emotion varies inversely with one's knowledge of the facts – the less you know, the hotter you get.

Bertrand Russell

5 The fact that an opinion has been widely held is no evidence whatever that it is not utterly absurd.
   Bertrand Russell, *Marriage and Morals*, 1929

6 . . . an unbiased opinion is always absolutely valueless.
   Oscar Wilde, 'The Critic as Artist', 1890

7 ERNEST: Simply this: that in the best days of art there were no art-critics.
   GILBERT: I seem to have heard that observation before, Ernest. It has all the vitality of error and all the tediousness of an old friend.
   Oscar Wilde, 'The Critic as Artist', 1890

See also Advice; Argument; Opinion Polls.

OPPORTUNISM

1 Dear Prime Minister,
   Thank you for your letter. I am delighted to have the opportunism to serve in your Cabinet.
   Anon.

2 I would rather be an opportunist and float than go to the bottom with my principles round my neck.
   Stanley Baldwin

See also Selfishness.

OPORTUNITY

1 Opportunity, *n.* a favorable occasion for grasping a disappointment.
   Ambrose Bierce, *The Devil's Dictionary*, 1911

2 I despise making the most of one's time: half the pleasures of life consist of the opportunities one has neglected.
   Oliver Wendell Holmes, Jr

OPTIMISM

1 An optimist is a man who starts a crossword puzzle with a fountain pen.
   Anon.

2 Optimism is the content of small men in high places.
   F. Scott Fitzgerald, *The Crack-up*, 1945

3 an optimist is a guy
   that has never had
   much experience
   Don Marquis, 'certain maxims of archy', *archy and mehitabel*, 1927

See also Optimism and Pessimism; Pessimism.

OPTIMISM AND PESSIMISM

1 The optimist proclaims that we live in the best of all possible worlds; and the pessimist fears this is true.
   James Branch Cabell, *The Silver Stallion*, 1926

2 O, merry is the optimist,
   With the troops of courage leaguing
   But a dour trend
   In any friend
   Is somehow less fatiguing.
   Phyllis McGinley, 'Song against Sweetness and Light', *A Pocketful of Wry*, 1940

3 'Twixt the optimist and the pessimist
   The difference is droll:
   The optimist sees the doughnut
   But the pessimist sees the hole.
   McLandburgh Wilson, 'Optimist and Pessimist'

See also Optimism; Pessimism.

ORGIES

1 You get a better class of person at orgies, because people have to keep in trim more. There is an awful lot of going round holding in your stomach, you know. Everybody is very polite to each other. The conversation isn't very good but you can't have everything.
   Gore Vidal, interviewed on *Russell Harty Plus*, London Weekend Television, 1972

See also Promiscuity; Sex.

ORPHANS

1 At six I was left an orphan. What on earth is a six-year-old supposed to do with an orphan?
   Anon.

2 Gertrude De-Mongmorenci McFiggin had known neither father nor mother.

They had both died years before she was born.

> **Stephen Leacock**, 'Gertrude the Governess', *Nonsense Novels*, 1911

See also Children; Parents.

OYSTERS

1 An oyster is a fish built like a nut.
> **Anon.**

2 Than an oyster
There's nothing moister.
> **Anon.**

3 According to experts, the oyster
In its shell – or crustacean cloister –
May frequently be
Either he or a she
Or both, if it should be its choice ter.
> **Berton Braley**

4 The oyster's a confusing suitor;
It's masc., and fem., and even neuter.
But whether husband, pal or wife
It leads a painless sort of life.
I'd like to be an oyster, say,
In August, June, July or May.
> **Ogden Nash**, 'The Oyster', *Free Wheeling*, 1931

See also Eating; Fish and Fishing; Food; The Sea.

PACIFISM

1 Join the Army, see the world, meet interesting people – and kill them.
Pacifist badge, 1978

2 Sometime they'll give a war and nobody will come.
Carl Sandburg, *The People, Yes*, 1936

See also Peace; Protest; War.

PARANOIA

1 Just Because You're Paranoid Doesn't Mean They Aren't Out To Get You.
Anon., slogan on badge, 1970s

2 PSYCHIATRIST (*to patient*): You're suffering from paranoia. Anyone'll tell you.
Hector Breeze, cartoon in *Private Eye*

3 I told my psychiatrist that everyone hates me. He said I was being ridiculous – everyone hasn't met me yet.
Rodney Dangerfield

See also Anxiety; Fear; Insanity.

PARENTS

1 I will never understand children. I never pretended to. I meet mothers all the time who make resolutions to themselves. 'I'm going to develop patience with my children and go out of my way to show them I am interested in them and what they do. I am going to understand my children.' These women wind up making rag rugs, using blunt scissors.
Erma Bombeck, *If Life is a Bowl of Cherries – What am I Doing in the Pits?*, 1978

2 Once a child knows that a square millimetre is .00155 square inches, will he ever have respect for a mother who once measured the bathroom for carpeting and found out that she had enough left over to slipcover New Jersey?
Erma Bombeck, *If Life is a Bowl of Cherries – What am I Doing in the Pits?*, 1978

3 FATHER (*to son*): Don't forget – I fought at El Alamein so you could be free *to worry* about the collapse of the ecosystem!
Hector Breeze, cartoon in *Private Eye*

4 Parenthood: that state of being better chaperoned than you were before marriage.
Marcelene Cox, *Ladies' Home Journal*, 1944

5 The first half of our lives is ruined by our parents, and the second half by our children.
Clarence Darrow

6 Parents – people who use the rhythm method of birth control.
May Flink

7 The real menace in dealing with a five-year-old is that in no time at all you begin to sound like a five-year-old.
Jean Kerr, *Please Don't Eat the Daisies*, 1957

8 They fuck you up, your mum and dad.
They may not mean to, but they do.
They fill you with the faults they had
And add some extra, just for you.
Philip Larkin, 'This be the Verse', *High Windows*, 1974

9 *Parental expressions every child should know*:
Some day you'll thank me.
(Statement made by parent who has successfully asserted authority, in order to soften the victory.)
I don't want to hear any more about it.
(Assertion of parental authority after parent has lost argument with child.)
Judith Martin, *Miss Manners' Guide to Rearing Perfect Children*, 1984

10 He is too experienced a parent ever to make positive promises.
Christopher Morley, *Thunder on the Left*, 1936

11 Children aren't happy with nothing to ignore

And that's what parents were created for.
Ogden Nash, 'The Parent', *Happy Days*, 1933

12 ... parents ... are sometimes a bit of a disappointment to their children. They don't fulfil the promise of their early years.
Anthony Powell, *A Buyer's Market*, 1952

13 If parents would only realize how they bore their children.
George Bernard Shaw, *Misalliance*, 1910

14 Parentage is a very important profession; but no test of fitness for it is ever imposed in the interest of the children.
George Bernard Shaw, *Everybody's Political What's What?*, 1944

15 I have found the best way to give advice to your children is to find out what they want and then advise them to do it.
Harry S. Truman, television interview, 1955

16 All women become like their mothers. That is their tragedy. No man does. That is his.
Oscar Wilde, *The Importance of Being Earnest*, 1895

17 Few parents nowadays pay any regard to what their children say to them. The old-fashioned respect for the young is fast dying.
Oscar Wilde, *The Importance of Being Earnest*, 1895

18 The longer I live the more keenly I feel that whatever was good enough for our fathers is not good enough for us.
Oscar Wilde, *The Picture of Dorian Gray*, 1891

19 To lose one parent ... may be regarded as a misfortune; to lose both looks like carelessness.
Oscar Wilde, *The Importance of Being Earnest*, 1895

See also Children; The Family; Fathers; Mothers.

PARKING

1 I just solved the parking problem. I bought a parked car.
Henny Youngman

See also Cars; Driving.

PARLIAMENT

1 Westminster is the power house transmitting socially sanctioned aggression. It inevitably becomes the Mecca for all those who wish, even as they did in their nurseries, but now without fear of disapproval, to scream with anger, spit at their enemies, bitingly attack opponents, boldly hit out at wrongs, real and imagined. Like moths around a flame, the aggressive flutter around Westminster. Outside Dartmoor and the armed forces, there are no more aggressive men than those sitting in our Parliament.
Leo Abse, Private Member, 1973

2 I had better recall before someone else does, that I said on one occasion that all was fair in love, war and parliamentary procedure.
Michael Foot

3 An angry Parliamentary debate has the same effect upon national events as a slammed door has upon domestic arguments. It is emphatic; it is deeply, though momentarily, satisfying; and it settles nothing at all.
David Frost and Antony Jay, *To England with Love*, 1967

4 ... like playing squash with a dish of scrambled eggs.
Harold Nicolson, on debating with Nancy Astor in the House of Commons, 1943

5 There are three golden rules for Parliamentary speakers: 'Stand up. Speak up. Shut up.'
J. W. Lowther, Speaker of the House of Commons, 1919

6 The essentially feminine role of Parliament in the constitutional process does indeed put one in mind of the traditional wife in a male (or government) dominated national household. What the

master says goes. Parliament may advise, complain, criticize, protest, delay, nag, scream its head off but it does what it's told in the end.

Norman Shrapnel, quoted in *Westminster Man* by Austin Mitchell, 1982

See also Government; House of Commons; House of Lords; Politics and Politicians.

PARTIES

1 It is not done to let anybody be too happy. The moment two people seem to be enjoying one another's company, a good hostess introduces a third element or removes the first.
Virginia Graham

2 The cocktail party is easily the worst invention since castor oil.
Elsa Maxwell

3 ERIC: It was a Gay Nineties Party. It was terrible.
ERNIE: Why was that?
ERIC: All the men were gay and all the women were ninety.
Eric Morecambe and Ernie Wise, *The Morecambe and Wise Joke Book*, 1979

4 A cocktail party is what you call it when you invite everyone you know to come over to your house at six p.m., put cigarettes out on your rug, and leave at eight to go somewhere more interesting for dinner without inviting you. Cocktail parties are very much on their way out among rug-owning, hungry, snubbed people.
P. J. O'Rourke, *Modern Manners*, 1983

5 A small boy, who was a stickler for the literal truth, once said to me that it was wrong to say 'Good-bye' when you had not enjoyed yourself at a party. I enquired what should be substituted for it. He suggested 'Bad-bye'. I have never tried this.
Arthur Ponsonby, *Casual Observations*

6 I delight in the idea of a party but find no pleasure in the reality. The result is that I can neither keep away from parties nor enjoy them.
J. B. Priestley, *All about Ourselves and Other Essays*, 1956

7 The cocktail party – a device for paying off obligations to people you don't want to invite to dinner.
Charles Merrill Smith, *Instant Status*, 1972

8 Nothing is more irritating than not being invited to a party you wouldn't be seen dead at.
Bill Vaughan, *Reader's Digest*, 1959

9 Lord Copper quite often gave banquets; it would be an understatement to say that no one enjoyed them more than the host, for no one else enjoyed them at all, while Lord Copper positively exulted in every minute.
Evelyn Waugh, *Scoop*, 1938

10 There must be some good in the cocktail party to account for its immense vogue among otherwise sane people.
Evelyn Waugh, 'Wine in Peace and War'

See also Champagne; Dance; Drink; Society; Wine.

THE PAST

1 Nothing is more responsible for the good old days than a bad memory.
Franklin P. Adams

2 Mind you, six bob *was* six bob in them days. You could buy three penny worth of chips and still have change from sixpence.
Alan Bennett, 'The Lonely Pursuit', *On the Margin*, BBC TV, 1966

3 ED: The instant past is as past as slightly pregnant is pregnant!
Michael Frayn, *Clouds*, 1976

See also Ancestors; Antiques; Archaeology; History.

PATRIOTISM

1 An author's first duty is to let down his country.
Brendan Behan, *Guardian*, 1960

2 'My country, right or wrong' is a thing no patriot would think of saying except in a desperate case. It is like saying, 'My mother, drunk or sober'.
   G. K. Chesterton, *The Defendant*

3 The English, the English, the English
   are best
   I wouldn't give tuppence for all of the
   rest.
   Michael Flanders and Donald Swann, 'Song of Patriotic Prejudice', song from *At the Drop of Another Hat*, 1964

4 The less a statesman amounts to, the more he loves the flag.
   Kin Hubbard

5 Whenever you hear a man speak of his love for his country, it is a sign that he expects to be paid for it.
   H. L. Mencken

6 Patriotism is often an arbitrary veneration of real estate above principles.
   George Jean Nathan

7 At a sporting event, both men and women should stand during the national anthem . . . Black people should remain seated for a couple of bars and then stand up very slowly to show that, even though they got a raw deal and never asked to come here in the first place, they're still patriotic deep down inside. Aging hippies, members of the Socialist Workers' Party, Vietnam combat veterans, and other nut cases should be sure to stand up because that's what Robert De Niro would do if he were playing them in a movie. He would stand up for the national anthem to show that although he's crazy, it's an American kind of craziness. This makes everyone feel better.
   P. J. O'Rourke, *Modern Manners*, 1983

8 Patriotism is the willingness to kill and be killed for trivial reasons.
   Bertrand Russell

9 Patriotism is the virtue of the vicious.
   Oscar Wilde (Attrib.)

See also Jingoism; Xenophobia.

PEACE

1 It's co-existence
   Or no existence.
   Bertrand Russell

2 Gone are those pleasant nineteenth-century days when a country could remain neutral and at peace just by saying it wanted to.
   William Shirer

See also Conciliation; Fighting; Pacifism; War.

PERFUME

1 Perfume is a subject dear to my heart. I have so many favourites: Arome de Grenouille, Okéfénôkée, Eau Contraire, Fume de Ma Tante, Blast du Past, Kèrmes, Je Suis Swell, and Attention S'il Vous Plaît, to name but a few.
   Miss Piggy, *Miss Piggy's Guide to Life (As Told to Henry Beard)*, 1981

See also Cosmetics; Smells.

PERSONALITY

1 The Texan turned out to be good-natured, generous and likeable. In three days no one could stand him.
   Joseph Heller, *Catch-22*, 1961

PESSIMISM

1 Life is divided into the horrible and the miserable.
   Woody Allen and Marshall Brickman, *Annie Hall*, screenplay, 1977

2 There are bad times just around the
      corner,
   There are dark clouds hurtling through
      the sky
   And it's no good whining
   About a silver lining
   For we know from experience that they
      won't roll by,
   With a scowl and a frown
   We'll keep our peckers down
   And prepare for depression and doom
      and dread,
   We're going to unpack our troubles
      from our old kit bag

And wait until we drop down dead.
  Noël Coward, 'There are Bad Times Just Around the Corner', song from *Globe Revue*, 1952

3 A pessimist is a man who has been compelled to live with an optimist.
  Elbert Hubbard, *The Notebook*, 1927

4 Things are going to get a lot worse before they get worse.
  Lily Tomlin

See also Optimism; Optimism and Pessimism.

PESTS

1 What makes
common house flies
trying
is
that they keep
multiflieing.
  Niels Mogens Bodecker, 'House Flies', *Hurry, Hurry Mary Dear*

See also Insects.

PETS

1 . . . when I was young, I wanted a dog and we had no money . . . I couldn't get a dog because it was too much and they finally opened up in my neighborhood in Flatbush, a damaged pet shop. They sold damaged pets at discount, you know, you could get a bent pussy cat if you wanted; a straight camel, you know. I got a dog that stuttered. Like, cats would give him a hard time and he would go b-b-b-b-bow wow!
  Woody Allen, recorded live at Mr Kelly's, Chicago, 1964

2 You will find that the woman who is really kind to dogs is always one who has failed to inspire sympathy in men.
  Max Beerbohm, *Zuleika Dobson*, 1911

3 But don't you see darling? Giving him an unaffected name like 'Spot' would really be the most affected thing of all.
  William Hamilton, *William Hamilton's Anti-Social Register*, cartoon, 1974

4 If you [a pet] have been named after a human being of artistic note, run away from home. It is unthinkable that even an animal should be obliged to share quarters with anyone who calls a cat Ford Madox Ford.
  Fran Lebowitz, *Social Studies*, 1981

5 No animal should ever jump up on the dining-room furniture unless absolutely certain that he can hold his own in the conversation.
  Fran Lebowitz, *Social Studies*, 1981

6 The black dog was the only intelligent member of the family. He died a few years later. He was poisoned, and no one will convince me it wasn't suicide.
  Hugh Leonard, *Da*, 1973

7 ERNIE: What's that you've got there?
ERIC: A lobster.
ERNIE: A lobster? Are you taking it home for tea?
ERIC: No, it's had its tea – now I'm taking it to the pictures.
  Eric Morecambe and Ernie Wise, *The Morecambe and Wise Joke Book*, 1979

8 And now a word for dog lovers. Kinky.
  Bill Oddie and Graeme Garden, *I'm Sorry I'll Read That Again*, BBC Radio

See also Cats; Dogs; Veterinarians.

PETTING

1 . . . [he] twisted my nipples as though tuning a radio.
  Lisa Alther, *Kinflicks*, 1976

2 The requirements of romantic love are difficult to satisfy in the trunk of a Dodge Dart.
  Lisa Alther, *Kinflicks*, 1976

3 Whoever called it necking was a poor judge of anatomy.
  Groucho Marx

4 Half the time, if you really want to know the truth, when I'm horsing around with a girl I have a helluva lot of trouble just finding what I'm looking for, for God's sake, if you know what I mean. Take this girl that I just missed having sexual intercourse with, that I told you about. It took me about an hour just to get her goddam

brassière off. By the time I did get it off, she was about ready to spit in my eye.
  J. D. Salinger, *The Catcher in the Rye*, 1951

See also Courting; Kissing; Sex.

PHILANTHROPY

1 Giving away a fortune is taking Christianity too far.
  Charlotte Bingham

2 No people do so much harm as those who go about doing good.
  Mandell Creighton

3 A large part of altruism, even when it is perfectly honest, is grounded upon the fact that it is uncomfortable to have unhappy people about one.
  H. L. Mencken, *Prejudices*, Fourth Series, 1924

4 A show of altruism is respected in the world chiefly for selfish motives ... Everyone figures himself profiting by it tomorrow.
  H. L. Mencken

5 High-toned humanitarians constantly overestimate the sufferings of those they sympathize with.
  H. L. Mencken, *Minority Report*, 1956

6 In the United States doing good has come to be, like patriotism, a favorite device of persons with something to sell.
  H. L. Mencken

7 A good deed never goes unpunished.
  Gore Vidal

8 Philanthropy seems to have become simply the refuge of people who wish to annoy their fellow creatures.
  Oscar Wilde, *An Ideal Husband*, 1895

9 'I have got to take a few pints of soup to the deserving poor,' said Myrtle. 'I'd better set about it. Amazing the way these bimbos absorb soup. Like sponges.'
  P. G. Wodehouse, *Eggs, Beans and Crumpets*, 1940

See also Wealth.

PHILOSOPHY

1 What if everything is an illusion and nothing exists? In that case, I definitely overpaid for my carpet.
  Woody Allen, *Without Feathers*, 1976

2 I vastly prefer Sartre's plays to his philosophy. Existentialism works much better in the theatre than in theory.
  A. J. Ayer, quoted in Kenneth Tynan's *Show People*, 1980

3 Philosophy is common sense in a dress suit.
  Oliver S. Braston, *Philosophy*

4 ... philosophy professors are weird guys. You can really freak them out easy. 'Hey, prof, you know how to give yourself déjà vu? Ask yourself this question: Hey, prof, you know how to give yourself déjà vu?'
  Bob Dubac, quoted in *GQ*, 1984

5 Sir,
  My husband, T. S. Eliot, loved to recount how late one evening he stopped a taxi. As he got in, the driver said: 'You're T. S. Eliot.' When asked how he knew, he replied: 'Ah, I've got an eye for a celebrity. Only the other evening I picked up Bertrand Russell, and I said to him: "Well, Lord Russell, what's it all about," and, do you know, he couldn't tell me.'
  Valerie Eliot, letter to *The Times*, 1970

6 There once was a man who said: 'God
  Must think it exceedingly odd
  If he finds that this tree
  Continues to be
  When there's no one about in the
    Quad.'
  Monsignor Ronald Knox

7 Dear Sir, Your astonishment's odd;
  I am always about in the Quad;
  And that's why the tree
  Will continue to be
  Since observed by Yours Faithfully,
    God.
  Anonymous reply to Monsignor Ronald Knox (*see above*)

8 Most philosophical treatises show the

human cerebrum loaded far beyond its Plimsoll Mark.
H. L. Mencken, *Prejudices*, Fourth Series, 1924

9 There is no record in human history of a happy philosopher.
H. L. Mencken, *Prejudices*, Fourth Series, 1924

10 People become who they are. Even Beethoven became Beethoven.
Randy Newman

11 ... as I grew up I became increasingly interested in philosophy, of which they [his family] profoundly disapproved. Every time the subject came up they repeated with unfailing regularity, 'What is mind? No matter. What is matter? Never mind.' After some fifty or sixty repetitions, this remark ceased to amuse me.
Bertrand Russell, *Portraits from Memory*, 1956

12 I think that bad philosophers may have a certain influence, good philosophers, never.
Bertrand Russell

13 The point of philosophy is to start with something so simple as to seem not worth stating, and to end with something so paradoxical that no one will believe it.
Bertrand Russell, *Logic and Knowledge*, 1956

14 Philosophers are as jealous as women; each wants a monopoly of praise.
George Santayana, *Dialogues in Limbo*, 1925

15 A Chinaman of the T'ang Dynasty – and, by which definition, a philosopher – dreamed he was a butterfly, and from that moment he was never quite sure that he was not a butterfly dreaming it was a Chinese philosopher.
Tom Stoppard, *Rosencrantz and Guildenstern are Dead*, 1966

16 ... if rationality were the criterion for things being allowed to exist, the world would be one gigantic field of soya bears!
Tom Stoppard, *Jumpers*, 1972

17 I'll have to get myself articled to a philosopher ... Start at the bottom. Of course, a philosopher's clerk wouldn't get the really interesting work straight off. I know that. It'd be a matter of filing the generalizations, tidying up the paradoxes, laying out the premises before the boss gets in – that kind of thing; but after I've learned the ropes I might get a half-share in a dialectic, perhaps, and work up towards a treatise ...
Tom Stoppard, *Albert's Bridge*, BBC Radio, 1967

18 ... since an arrow shot towards a target first had to cover half the distance, and then half the remainder, and then half the remainder after that, and so on *ad infinitum*, the result was ... that though the arrow is always approaching its target, it never quite gets there, and San Sebastian died of fright.
Tom Stoppard, *Jumpers*, 1972

19 Philosophy teaches us to bear with equanimity the misfortunes of others.
Oscar Wilde (Attrib.)

See also Knowledge.

PHOTOGRAPHY

1 A: Do you know it's costing me more than two thousand pounds to have my house painted?
B: Wouldn't it be cheaper just to have it photographed?
Anon.

2 My photographs do me an injustice. They look just like me.
Phyllis Diller

3 Some hate broccoli, some hate bacon
I hate having my picture taken.
How can your family claim to love you
And then demand a picture of you?
Ogden Nash, 'Waiting for the Birdie', *I'm a Stranger Here Myself*, 1938

4 *Aperture*. A little hole in the camera through which a wife, child, dog, cat pawing a ball of wool, wedding, swan, Norman church, father up to his neck in sand, interesting old alley, sailor sticking his head out of a porthole, or Midlands

couple who were the life and soul of the party that last night in Ibiza, may be observed by the photographer.

Keith Waterhouse, 'A–Z of Photography', *The Passing of the Third-floor Buck*, 1974

PICNICS

1 Upon this theme
I'll briefly touch:
Too far
To go
To eat
Too much.
  A. A. Lattimer, 'Picnic', *Liberty*

See also Eating; Food.

PLAGIARISM

1 If you steal from one author, it's plagiarism; if you steal from many, it's research.
  Wilson Mizner

2 The only 'ism she believes in is plagiarism.
  Dorothy Parker, of a woman writer (Attrib.)

3 Immature artists imitate. Mature artists steal.
  Lionel Trilling

See also Cheating; Literature.

POETS AND POETRY

1 Anon., Idem, Ibid. and Trad.
Wrote much that is morally bad:
Some ballads, some chanties,
All poems on panties –
And limericks, too, one must add.
  Anon.

2 Little Mary from Boston, Mass.
Stepped into water up to her ankles.
It doesn't rhyme now,
But wait till the tide comes in.
  Graffito, New Haven, 1976

3 Elegy, *n*. A composition in verse, in which, without employing any of the methods of humor, the writer aims to produce in the reader's mind the dampest kind of dejection. The most famous English example begins somewhat like this:
The cur foretells the knell of parting day;
The loafing herd winds slowly o'er the lea
The wise man homeward plods; I only stay
To fiddle-faddle in a minor key.
  Ambrose Bierce, *The Devil's Dictionary*, 1911

4 I know that poetry is indispensable, but to what I couldn't say.
  Jean Cocteau, quoted in the *Observer*, 1955

5 He tells you, in the sombrest notes,
If poets want to get their oats,
The first step is to slit their throats.
The way to divide
The sheep of poetry from the goats
Is suicide.
  James Fenton, 'Letter to John Fuller', *Children in Exile*, 1984

6 A true sonnet goes eight lines and then takes a turn for the better or worse and goes six or eight lines more.
  Robert Frost

7 Writing free verse is like playing tennis with the net down.
  Robert Frost, speech at Milton Academy, Mass., 1935

8 . . . I found a simple plan
Which makes the lamest lyric scan!
When I've a syllable de trop,
I cut it off, without apol.:
This verbal sacrifice, I know,
May irritate the schol.:
But all must praise my dev'lish cunn.
Who realize that Time is Mon.
  Harry Graham, 'Poetical Economy', *Deportmental Ditties*, 1909

9 There is no money in poetry; but then there is no poetry in money, either.
  Robert Graves

10 It's hard to say why writing verse
Should terminate in drink or worse.
  A. P. Herbert, *Punch*

11 Show me a poet and I'll show you a shit.
  A. J. Liebling

12 Publishing a volume of verse is like dropping a rose petal down the Grand Canyon and waiting for the echo.
Don Marquis

13 The crown of literature is poetry. It is its end and aim. It is the sublimest activity of the human mind. It is the achievement of beauty and delicacy. The writer of prose can only step aside when the poet passes.
W. Somerset Maugham, *Saturday Review*, 1957

14 *Vers libre*: a device for making poetry easier to read and harder to write.
H. L. Mencken, *A Book of Burlesques*, 1916

15 Having considered the matter in – of course – all its aspects, I have decided that there is no excuse for poetry. Poetry gives no adequate return in money, is expensive to print by reason of the waste of space occasioned by its form, and nearly always promulgates illusory concepts of life. But a better case for the banning of all poetry is the simple fact that most of it is bad. Nobody is going to manufacture a thousand tons of jam in the expectation that five tons may be eatable. Furthermore, poetry has the effect on the negligible handful who read it of stimulating them to write poetry themselves. One poem, if widely disseminated, will breed perhaps a thousand inferior copies.
Myles na Gopaleen, *The Best of Myles*, 1968

16 I'd rather be a great bad poet than a bad good poet.
Ogden Nash

17 Poets aren't very useful.
Because they aren't consumeful or very produceful.
Ogden Nash

18 A poem is a form of refrigeration that stops language going bad.
Peter Porter

19 The writing of more than seventy-five poems in any fiscal year should be punishable by a fine of $500.
Ed Sanders, 'Codex White Blizzard', *Montemora*, 1980

20 All poets' wives have rotten lives
Their husbands look at them like knives.
Delmore Schwartz (Attrib.)

21 Poetry is like fish: if it's fresh, it's good; if it's stale, it's bad; and if you're not certain, try it on the cat.
Osbert Sitwell

22 A publisher of today would as soon see a burglar in his office as a poet.
Henry de Vere Stacpoole

23 Poetry is trouble dunked in tears.
Gwyn Thomas

24 . . . a form of poetry which cannot possibly hurt anybody, even if translated into French.
Oscar Wilde, review in *Pall Mall Gazette*

25 All bad poetry springs from genuine feeling. To be natural is to be obvious, and to be obvious is to be inartistic.
Oscar Wilde, 'The Critic as Artist', 1890

26 We have been able to have fine poetry in England because the public do not read it, and consequently do not influence it. The public like to insult poets because they are individual, but once they have insulted them, they leave them alone.
Oscar Wilde, 'The Soul of Man under Socialism', 1891

27 Peotry is sissy stuff that rhymes. Weedy people say la and fie and swoon when they see a bunch of daffodils. Aktually there is only one piece of peotry in the english language.

The Brook
i come from haunts of coot and hern
i make a sudden sally
and-er-hem-er-hem-the fern
to bicker down a valley.
Geoffrey Willans and Ronald Searle, 'Down With Skool!', *The Compleet Molesworth*, 1958

28 I may as well tell you that if you are going about the place thinking things pretty, you will never make a modern poet. Be poignant, man, be poignant!
P. G. Wodehouse, *The Small Bachelor*, 1927

29 She could never forget that the man she loved was a man with a past. He had been a poet. Deep down in her soul there was always the corroding fear lest at any moment a particularly fine sunset or the sight of a rose in bud might undo all the work she had done, sending Rodney hot-foot once more to his Thesaurus and rhyming dictionary. It was for this reason that she always hurried him indoors when the sun began to go down and refused to have rose trees in her garden.
   P. G. Wodehouse, *Nothing Serious*, 1950

See also Limericks; Literature; Writers; Writing.

POLAND AND THE POLES

1 There are few virtues that the Poles do not possess – and there are few mistakes they have ever avoided.
   Winston Churchill, speech, House of Commons, 1945

POLICE

1 I have never seen a situation so dismal that a policeman couldn't make it worse.
   Brendan Behan (Attrib.)

2 When a felon's not engaged in his employment
   Or maturing his felonius little plans
   His capacity for innocent enjoyment
   Is just as great as any honest man's
   Our feelings we with difficulty smother
   When constabulary duty's to be done
   Ah, take one consideration with another
   A policeman's lot is not a happy one.
   W. S. Gilbert and Arthur Sullivan, 'A Policeman's Lot is Not a Happy One', song from *The Pirates of Penzance*, 1880

3 Are you going to come quietly or do I have to use ear-plugs?
   Spike Milligan, *The Goon Show*, BBC Radio

See also Crime; The Law; Law and Order; Prison.

POLITICS – AXIOMS

1 It is a good thing to follow the First Law of Holes; if you are in one, stop digging.
   Denis Healey, 1983

2 If it walks like a duck, and quacks like a duck, then it just may be a duck.
   Walter Reuther, trades union leader, on how to tell a communist

3 He who slings mud, usually loses ground.
   Adlai Stevenson (Attrib.), 1954

4 If you can't stand the heat, get out of the kitchen.
   Harry S. Truman

See also Politics and Politicians.

POLITICS – INSULTS

1 It is fitting that we should have buried the Unknown Prime Minister by the side of the Unknown Soldier.
   Lord Asquith, of Bonar Law, British Prime Minister, 1922

2 When they circumcised Herbert Samuel, they threw away the wrong bit.
   David Lloyd George, on his fellow Liberal, 1930s

3 Sir Alec Douglas-Home, when he was a British Foreign Secretary, said he received the following telegram from an irate citizen: 'To hell with you. Offensive letter follows.'
   William Safire, *The New Language of Politics*, 1968

4 . . . when political ammunition runs low, inevitably the rusty artillery of abuse is always wheeled into action.
   Adlai Stevenson, speech, 1952

See also Abuse; Insults; Politics and Politicians.

POLITICS AND POLITICIANS

1 Politics makes estranged bedfellows.
   Goodman Ace

2 The first requirement of a statesman is that he be dull. This is not always easy to achieve.
   Dean Acheson, American statesman, 1970

3 A: Have you ever taken a serious political stand on anything?
   B: Yes, for twenty-four hours I refused to eat grapes.
   Woody Allen, *Sleeper*, screenplay, 1973.

4 Politics – the gentle art of getting votes from the poor and campaign funds from the rich, by promising to protect each from the other.
Oscar Ameringer

5 There are three groups that no British Prime Minister should provoke: the Vatican, the Treasury and the miners.
Stanley Baldwin (Attrib.)

6 The politician is an acrobat. He keeps his balance by saying the opposite of what he does.
Maurice Barrès, *Mes cahiers*, 1896–1923

7 Here richly, with ridiculous display,
The Politician's corpse was laid away.
While all of his acquaintances sneered
      and slanged,
I wept: for I had longed to see him
      hanged.
Hilaire Belloc

8 When the audience is a mixed group, the speaker finds a quick kinship in geography. He will always have a soft spot for Devil's Gulch, Arizona, because his mother was born eighteen miles from there. Or for East Overshoe, Illinois, because his Uncle Henry ran a poolroom there in 1912. At worst, he can always call a town his 'second home' on the ground that he once stayed overnight at the local hotel and had his laundry done.
Robert Bendiner, 'How to Listen to Campaign Oratory if You Have to', *Look*, 1960

9 Politics is the art of looking for trouble, finding it whether it exists or not, diagnosing it incorrectly, and applying the wrong remedy.
Sir Ernest Benn, quoted in the *Observer*, 1930

10 I always wanted to get into politics but I was never light enough to get in the team.
Art Buchwald

11 If you take yourself seriously in politics, you've had it.
Lord Carrington, British Foreign Secretary, 1979–1982

12 Every politician is emphatically a promising politician.
G. K. Chesterton, *The Red Moon of Meru*

13 Political ability is the ability to foretell what is going to happen tomorrow, next week, next month and next year. And to have the ability afterward to explain why it didn't happen.
Winston Churchill

14 Politics are almost as exciting as war and quite as dangerous. In war you can only be killed once, but in politics many times.
Winston Churchill

15 Since a politician never believes what he says, he is surprised when others believe him.
Charles de Gaulle, quoted in *Newsweek*, 1962

16 Politics is not the art of the possible. It consists in choosing between the disastrous and the unpalatable.
J. K. Galbraith, *Ambassador's Journal*, responding to R. A. Butler's 'Politics is the Art of the Possible', 1969

17 Probably the most distinctive characteristic of the successful politician is selective cowardice.
Richard Harris, 'Annals of Legislation', *New Yorker*, 1968

18 A politician will do anything to keep his job – even become a patriot.
William Randolph Hearst, editorial, 1933

19 'What a lovely, lovely moon
And it's in the constituency too.'
Alan Jackson, 'The Young Politician'

20 The *press conference* is a politician's way of being informative without saying anything. Should he accidentally say something, he has at his side a *press officer* who immediately explains it away by 'clarifying' it.
Emery Kelen, *Platypus at Large*, 1960

21 Mothers all want their sons to grow up to be President but they don't want them to become politicians in the process.
John F. Kennedy (Attrib.)

22 Politicians are the same all over. They promise to build a bridge even when there's no river.
Nikita Krushchev, remark at Glen Cove, New York, 1960

23 Being in politics is like being a football coach. You have to be smart enough to understand the game and stupid enough to think it's important.
    Eugene McCarthy

24 I have never found, in a long experience of politics, that criticism is ever inhibited by ignorance.
    Harold Macmillan, after his son Maurice had written to *The Times* criticizing the Conservative Government, 1963

25 When you're abroad, you're a statesman; when you're at home, you're just a politician.
    Harold Macmillan

26 A politician is an animal that can sit on a fence and keep both ears to the ground.
    H. L. Mencken

27 If experience teaches us anything at all, it teaches us this: that a good politician, under democracy, is quite as unthinkable as an honest burglar.
    H. L. Mencken, *Prejudices*, Fourth Series, 1924

28 I have spent much of my life fighting the Germans and fighting the politicians. It is much easier to fight the Germans.
    Field Marshall Lord Montgomery, *Observer*, 1967

29 Politics is the diversion of trivial men who, when they succeed at it, become important in the eyes of more trivial men.
    George Jean Nathan

30 Political language – and with variations this is true of all political parties, from Conservatives to Anarchists – is designed to make lies sound truthful and murder respectable, and to give an appearance of solidity to pure wind.
    George Orwell, 'Politics and the English Language', *Shooting an Elephant*, 1950

31 It is now known that men enter local politics solely as a result of being unhappily married.
    G. Northcote Parkinson, *Parkinson's Law*, 1957

32 Politicians who complain about the media are like ships' captains who complain about the sea.
    Enoch Powell (Attrib.)

33 All politics are based on the indifference of the majority.
    James Reston

34 There is no more independence in politics than there is in jail.
    Will Rogers

35 A conservative is a man with two perfectly good legs who, however, has never learned to walk forwards ... A reactionary is a somnambulist walking backwards ... A radical is a man with both feet firmly planted – in the air.
    Franklin D. Roosevelt, 'Fireside Chat', 1939

36 The most successful politician is he who says what everybody is thinking most often and in the loudest voice.
    Theodore Roosevelt

37 Our great democracies still tend to think that a stupid man is more likely to be honest than a clever man, and our politicians take advantage of this prejudice by pretending to be even more stupid than nature made them.
    Bertrand Russell, *New Hopes for a Changing World*, 1951

38 A government which robs Peter to pay Paul can always depend on the support of Paul.
    George Bernard Shaw, *Everybody's Political What's What?*, 1944

39 He knows nothing and he thinks he knows everything. That points *clearly* to a political career.
    George Bernard Shaw, *Major Barbara*, 1905

40 An independent is the guy who wants to take the politics out of politics.
    Adlai Stevenson, quoted in *The Stevenson Wit*, 1966

41 Greater love hath no man than this, that he lay down his friends for his political life.
    Jeremy Thorpe, on Harold Macmillan's drastic Cabinet reshuffle, 1962

42 Ninety-eight per cent of the adults in this country are decent, hard-working, honest Americans. It's the other lousy two per cent that get all the publicity. But then – we elected them.
Lily Tomlin

43 A statesman is a politician who's been dead ten or fifteen years.
Harry S. Truman, quoted in *New York World-Telegram*, 1958

44 Politicians are always deeply shocked to see anything in the newspapers which is not about themselves or their piffling preoccupations, but very few people, in fact, are remotely interested in either.
Auberon Waugh, *Spectator*, 1984

45 When we have finally stirred ourselves to hang them all, I hope our next step will be to outlaw political parties outside Parliament on the grounds that, like amusement arcades, they attract all the least desirable members of society.
Auberon Waugh, *Spectator*, 1984

See also Winston Churchill; Congress; Conservatism; The Conservative Party; Elections; Government; House of Commons; House of Lords; Parliament; Politics – Axioms; Politics – Insults; Power; The Presidency; The Vice-Presidency.

POLLUTION

1 I simply can't believe nice communities release effluents.
William Hamilton, *William Hamilton's Anti-Social Register*, cartoon, 1974

2 Little Bo-Peep
Has lost her sheep
And thinks they may be roaming;
They haven't fled;
They've all dropped dead
From nerve gas in Wyoming.
Frank Jacobs, 'Little Bo-Peep', *Mad Magazine*, 1972

See also Ecology.

THE POPE

1 It often happens that I wake at night and begin to think about a serious problem and decide I must tell the Pope about it. Then I wake up completely and remember that I *am* the Pope.
Pope John XXIII

See also Catholicism; God; Religion.

POPULARITY

1 Being popular is important. Otherwise, people might not like you.
Mimi Pond, *The Valley Girl's Guide To Life*, 1982

2 Every effect that one produces gives one an enemy. To be popular one must be a mediocrity.
Oscar Wilde, *The Picture of Dorian Gray*, 1891

See also Celebrities; Fame.

PORNOGRAPHY

1 Pornography is in the groin of the beholder.
Anon.

2 The Citizens' Committee to Clean Up New York's Porn-Infested Areas continued its series of rallies today, as a huge, throbbing, pulsating crowd sprang erect from nowhere and forced its way into the steaming nether region surrounding the glistening, sweaty intersection of Eighth Avenue and Forty-Second Street. Thrusting, driving, pushing its way into the usually receptive neighborhood, the excited throng, now grown to five times its original size, rammed itself again and again and again into the quivering, perspiring, musty dankness, fluctuating between eager anticipation and trembling revulsion. Now, suddenly, the tumescent crowd and the irresistible area were one heaving, alternately melting and thawing turgid entity, ascending to heights heretofore unexperienced. Then, with a gigantic, soul-searching, heart-stopping series of eruptions, it was

over. Afterwards, the crowd had a cigarette and went home.

'Weekend Update', *Saturday Night Live*, NBC TV

3 A WORD ABOUT PORNOGRAPHY
You'll need it. Lots of it. The dirty, filthy, degrading kind. But keep it *well hidden*! Don't discount secret wall panels, trick drawers, holes in the yard, etc., especially if you have teenage boys or a Baptist wife with a housecleaning obsession. Also keep in mind that you could die at any moment, and nothing puts a crimp in a funeral worse than having the bereaved family wonder what kind of sick, perverted beast you were under that kind and genteel exterior.

John Hughes, 'Very Married Sex', *National Lampoon*, 1979

4 At last, an unprintable book that is readable.

Ezra Pound, of Henry Miller's *Tropic of Cancer*, 1934

5 Fill in the blank with the best word or phrase:
*He awoke with a start when two —— slipped naked into his bed.
A: Federal judges B: Militant feminists C: Burglars D: Teenaged girls
Seeing her 42-inch ——, I grew excited.
A: Husband B: Bowling trophy C: Bust D: Heels

Alphonse Simonaitis, 'Porno Writer's Aptitude Test', *Playboy*

6 Perhaps it would help . . . to compose a letter . . . to *The Times*:
Dear Sir,
I hope I am not a prude, but I feel compelled to lodge a protest against the ever-increasing flood of obscenity in dreams. Many of my friends have been as shocked and sickened as myself by the filth that is poured out nightly as soon as our eyes are closed. It is certainly not my idea of 'home entertainment'.
Night after night, the most disgraceful scenes of perversion and bestiality are perpetrated behind my eyelids . . . It is

imperative that official action should be taken . . .

Kenneth Tynan, *The Sound of Two Hands Clapping*, 1975

7 Western man, especially the Western critic, still finds it very hard to go into print and say: 'I recommend you to go and see this because it gave me an erection.'

Kenneth Tynan, *Playboy*, 1977

8 The worst that can be said about pornography is that it leads not to 'anti-social' acts but to the reading of more pornography.

Gore Vidal, *Reflections upon a Sinking Ship*, 1969

See also Censorship; Nudity; Puritanism; Sex; Sexual Perversions.

POTENTIAL

1 Whom the Gods wish to destroy they first call promising.

Cyril Connolly, *Enemies of Promise*, 1938

POVERTY

1 The trouble with being poor is that it takes up all your time.

Willem de Kooning

2 I used to think I was poor. Then they told me I wasn't poor, I was needy. Then they told me it was self-defeating to think of myself as needy. I was deprived. Then they told me that underprivileged was overused. I was disadvantaged. I still don't have a dime. But I have a great vocabulary.

Jules Feiffer, cartoon in the *Village Voice*, 1965

3 When I was a kid, my family was so poor I had to wear my brother's hand-me-downs – at the same time he was wearing them.

Redd Foxx, *Esquire*, 1972

4 He couldn't even afford to buy his little boy a yo-yo for Christmas. He just managed to get him a yo.

Max Kauffmann

5 The furnace tolls the nell of falling
   steam,
   The coal supply is virtually done,
   And at this price, indeed it does not
   seem
   As though we could afford another ton.
   Now fades the glossy, cherished
   anthracite;
   The radiators lose their temperature:
   How ill avail, on such a frosty night,
   The 'short and simple flannels of the
   poor'.
   Christopher Morley, 'Elegy Written in a
   Country Coal-bin', 1921

6 MENDOZA: I am a brigand: I live by
   robbing the rich.
   TANNER: I am a gentleman: I live by
   robbing the poor.
   George Bernard Shaw, *Man and Superman*, 1903

7 What is the matter with the poor is
   Poverty: what is the matter with the rich
   is Uselessness.
   George Bernard Shaw, *Maxims for Revolutionists*, 1903

8 Who made your millions for you? Me and
   my like. What's kep' us poor? Keepin'
   you rich.
   George Bernard Shaw, *Major Barbara*,
   1907

9 Poverty is no disgrace to a man, but it is
   confoundedly inconvenient.
   Sydney Smith, *His Wit and Wisdom*, 1900

10 We who are liberal and progressive know
   that the poor are our equals in every
   sense except that of being equal to us.
   Lionel Trilling, *The Liberal Imagination*,
   1950

11 ... a poor man who is ungrateful, un-
   thrifty, discontented, and rebellious, is
   probably a real personality, and has much
   in him. He is at any rate a healthy protest.
   As for the virtuous poor, one can pity
   them, of course, but one cannot possibly
   admire them. They have made private
   terms with the enemy, and sold their
   birthright for very bad pottage.
   Oscar Wilde, 'The Soul of Man under
   Socialism', 1891

12 I should fancy that the real tragedy of the
   poor is that they can afford nothing but
   self-denial.
   Oscar Wilde, *The Picture of Dorian Gray*,
   1891

13 There is only one class in the community
   that thinks more about money than the
   rich, and that is the poor. The poor can
   think of nothing else.
   Oscar Wilde, 'The Soul of Man under
   Socialism', 1891

See also Begging; Debt; Rich and Poor;
Wealth.

POWER

1 A friend in power is a friend lost.
   Henry Adams, *The Education of Henry
   Adams*, 1906

2 It is certainly more agreeable to have
   power to give than to receive.
   Winston Churchill

3 Power is the ultimate aphrodisiac.
   Henry Kissinger, quoted in the *Guardian*,
   1976

4 Power corrupts, but lack of power
   corrupts absolutely.
   Adlai Stevenson, 1963

See also Government; Politics and Politicians; The Ruling Class.

PRAISE

1 Some people pay a compliment as if they
   expected a receipt.
   Kin Hubbard

2 I can live for two months on a good
   compliment.
   Mark Twain

3 LADY WINDERMERE: ... I don't like
   compliments, and I don't see why a man
   should think he is pleasing a woman
   enormously when he says to her a
   whole heap of things that he doesn't
   mean.
   Oscar Wilde, *Lady Windermere's Fan*, 1892

See also Compliments; Flattery.

PRAYER

1 Forgive, O Lord, my little jokes on Thee
And I'll forgive Thy great big one on me.
Robert Frost, 'Cluster of Faith', *In the Clearing*, 1962

2 Prayer gives a man the opportunity of getting to know a gentleman he hardly ever meets. I do not mean his maker, but himself.
William Inge, Dean of St Paul's Cathedral, 1911–1934

3 Prayer must never be answered: if it is, it ceases to be prayer and becomes correspondence.
Oscar Wilde (Attrib.)

4 . . . when the Gods wish to punish us they answer our prayers.
Oscar Wilde, *An Ideal Husband*, 1895

See also The Church; God; Heaven; Religion.

PREGNANCY

1 A woman who took the pill with a glass of pond water has been diagnosed three months stagnant.
The Two Ronnies, BBC TV

2 GIRL: Mother, I'm afraid I'm pregnant.
MOTHER: Are you sure it's yours?
Anon.

3 Someone's gonna have to explain it to me,
I'm not sure what it means,
My baby's feeling funny in the mornings,
She's having trouble getting into her jeans.
Her waistline seems to be expanding
Although she never feels like eating a thing,
I guess we'll reach some understanding
When we see what the future will bring.
Jackson Browne, 'Ready or Not', song, 1974

See also Babies; Birth; Birth Control; Mothers; Sex.

THE PRESIDENCY

1 If Presidents don't do it to their wives, they do it to the country.
Mel Brooks

2 When I was a boy I was told that anybody could become President; I'm beginning to believe it.
Clarence Darrow

3 Higgledy-piggledy,
Benjamin Harrison,
Twenty-third President,
Was, and, as such,
Served between Clevelands, and
Save for this trivial
Idiosyncracy,
Didn't do much.
John Hollander, 'Historical Reflections', *Jiggery-pokery: A Compendium of Double Dactyls*, 1966

4 You're asking the leader of the Western world a chickenshit question like that?
Lyndon Baines Johnson, to reporter (Attrib.)

5 When we got into office, the thing that surprised me most was to find that things were just as bad as we'd been saying they were.
John F. Kennedy, speech in Washington, 1961

6 In America any boy may become President and I suppose it's just one of the risks he takes.
Adlai Stevenson, speech in Indianapolis, 1952

7 The best reason I can think of for not running for President of the United States is that you have to shave twice a day.
Adlai Stevenson

8 All the President is, is a glorified public relations man who spends his time flattering, kissing, and kicking people to get them to do what they are supposed to do anyway.
Harry S. Truman, letter to his sister, 1947

9 Any man who has had the job I've had and didn't have a sense of humor wouldn't still be here.
Harry S. Truman (Attrib.), 1955

10 Any American who is prepared to run for President should automatically, by definition, be disqualified from ever doing so.
   Gore Vidal (Attrib.)

11 The presidential system just won't work any more. Anyone who gets in under it ought not to be allowed to serve.
   Gore Vidal, 1980

See also The Vice-Presidency; Washington.

PRIDE

1 Godolphin Horne was Nobly Born;
   He held the Human Race in Scorn,
   And lived with all his Sisters where
   His father lived, in Berkeley Square.
   And oh! the Lad was Deathly Proud!
   He never shook your Hand or Bowed,
   But merely smirked and nodded thus:
   How perfectly ridiculous!
   Alas! That such Affected Tricks
   Should flourish in a Child of Six!
   Hilaire Belloc, 'Godolphin Horne', *Cautionary Tales for Children*, 1907

See also Boasts; Egotism; Vanity.

PRINCIPLES

1 I don't like principles ... I prefer prejudices.
   Oscar Wilde, *An Ideal Husband*, 1895

2 The Rev. 'Stinker' Pinker was dripping with high principles ...
   P. G. Wodehouse, *The Code of the Woosters*, 1938

See also Morality; Standards.

PRISON

1 It was my belief that they bought the books for the prison by weight. I once got a *Chums* annual for 1917 and a Selfridge's furniture catalogue for my non-fiction or education book.
   Brendan Behan, *Borstal Boy*, 1958

2 OFFICER: And the next time you try to escape, you'll be shot at dawn.

ERIC: I'm not worried – I don't get up till nine o'clock.
   Eddie Braben, *The Best of Morecambe and Wise*, 1974

3 GOVERNOR: I have always found Christmas to be a very difficult time.
   WARDER: Yes, sir. So open to abuse. Contraband, bartering, smuggling. There isn't a Christmas cake comes inside that isn't laced with marijuana.
   GOVERNOR: What are we doing about that?
   WARDER: I've taken precautions, sir. I've put Mr Barrowclough on to sampling all the food parcels.
   GOVERNOR: Has he anything to report?
   WARDER: He's still too stoned to tell me, sir.
   Dick Clement and Ian La Frenais, *Porridge*, BBC TV, 1976

4 LENNIE: ... human weakness takes many forms. Desire, greed, lust – we're all here for different reasons aren't we?
   FLETCHER: With respect, Godber, we're all here for the same reason – we got caught.
   Dick Clement and Ian La Frenais, 'Poetic Justice', *Porridge*, BBC TV

5 PRISONER: ... I'm going out soon, like.
   GOVERNOR: Good, good. Well, don't fall back into your old ways.
   PRISONER: No chance of that, sir. Not since t'wife passed away.
   GOVERNOR: Oh, I'm sorry. When was this?
   PRISONER: A few weeks before I came inside.
   GOVERNOR: Poor woman, what happened?
   PRISONER: I murdered her.
   GOVERNOR: (*taken aback*) Well, see that it doesn't happen again.
   Dick Clement and Ian La Frenais, *Porridge*, BBC TV, 1976

6 Prison is a Socialist's Paradise, where equality prevails, everything is supplied and competition is eliminated.
   Elbert Hubbard

7 That is the whole beauty of prisons – the benefit is not to the prisoner, of being

reformed or rehabilitated, but to the public. Prisons give those outside a resting period from town bullies and horrible characters, and for this we should be very grateful.
  Roy Kerridge, *The Lone Conformist,* 1984

8 ERIC: I'll never forget my mother's words to me when I first went to jail.
ERNIE: What did she say?
ERIC: Hello, son.
  Eric Morecambe and Ernie Wise, *The Morecambe and Wise Joke Book,* 1979

9 Anyone who has been to an English public school will always feel comparatively at home in prison. It is the people brought up in the gay intimacy of the slums who find prison so soul-destroying.
  Evelyn Waugh, *Decline and Fall,* 1928

See also Crime; The Law; Law and Order.

PROBLEMS

1 There's no problem so big or complicated that it can't be run away from.
  Graffito, London, 1979

2 In my experience, the worst thing you can do to an important problem is discuss it. You know – I really do think this whole business of non-communication is one of the more poignant fallacies of our zestfully over-explanatory age. Most of us understand as much as we need to without having to be told.
  Simon Gray, *Otherwise Engaged,* 1975

3 She probably laboured under the common delusion that you made things better by talking about them.
  Rose Macaulay, *Crewe Train,* 1926

4 When a man laughs at his troubles he loses a great many friends. They never forgive the loss of their prerogative.
  H. L. Mencken

See also Questions.

PROCRASTINATION

1 If a thing's worth doing, it's worth doing late.
  Frederick Oliver

See also Punctuality.

PROFESSIONS

1 All professions are conspiracies against the laity.
  George Bernard Shaw, *The Doctor's Dilemma,* 1906

See also Accountancy; Banking; Insurance; Work.

PROGRESS

1 Carnation Milk is the best in the land;
Here I sit with a can in my hand –
No tits to pull, no hay to pitch,
You just punch a hole in the son of a
  bitch.
  Anon., 'The Virtues of Carnation Milk', quoted in *Confessions of an Advertising Man,* David Ogilvy, 1963

2 My father worked for the same firm for twelve years. They fired him. They replaced him with a tiny gadget this big. It does everything that my father does, only it does it much better. The depressing thing is my mother ran out and bought one.
  Woody Allen, *The Nightclub Years, 1964– 1968,* record, 1972

3 GEORGE: Books are on their way out, nowadays, didn't you know that. Words are on their last legs. Words, print and also thought. That's also for the high jump. The sentence, that dignified entity with subject and predicate, is shortly to be made illegal. Wherever two or three words are gathered together, you see, there is a grave danger that thought might be present. All assemblies of words will be forbidden, in favour of patterns of light, videotape, every man his own telecine.
  Alan Bennett, *Getting On,* 1971

4 All progress is based upon a universal

innate desire of every organism to live beyond its income.
Samuel Butler, *Note Books*, 1912

5 The reason that men oppose progress is not that they hate progress but that they love inertia.
Ellert Hubbard, *The Notebook*, 1927

6 Progress might have been all right once but it has gone on far too long.
Ogden Nash

See also The Future; Inventions; Modern Life.

PROHIBITION

1 Once, during Prohibition, I was forced to live for days on nothing but food and water.
W. C. Fields

2 I am certain that the good Lord never intended grapes to be made into jelly.
Fiorello La Guardia

3 prohibition makes you
want to cry
into your beer and
denies you the beer
to cry into
Don Marquis, 'certain maxims of archy', *archy and mehitabel*, 1927

4 The South is dry and will vote dry. That is, everybody sober enough to stagger to the polls will.
Will Rogers, 'Oklahoma City', 1926

See also Abstinence; Drink; Temperance.

PROMISCUITY

1 She's the original good time that was had by all.
Bette Davis, of another actress (Attrib.)

2 'Has it ever occurred to you that in your promiscuous pursuit of women you are merely trying to assuage your subconscious fears of sexual impotence?'
'Yes, sir, it has.'
'Then why do you do it?'
'To assuage my fears of sexual impotence.'
Joseph Heller, *Catch-22*, 1961

3 Lady Capricorn, he understood, was still keeping open bed.
Aldous Huxley, *Antic Hay*, 1923

4 What is a promiscuous person? It's usually someone who is getting more sex than you are.
Victor Lownes, *Playboy*, 1985

5 You were born with your legs apart. They'll send you to your grave in a Y-shaped coffin.
Joe Orton, *What the Butler Saw*, 1969

6 The girl speaks eighteen languages and can't say no in any of them.
Dorothy Parker, of a famous actress (Attrib.)

7 I used to be Snow White, but I drifted.
Mae West (Attrib.)

See also Infidelity; Orgies; Prostitution; Sex.

PROMISES

1 Half the promises people say were never kept, were never made.
Edgar Watson Howe

PRONUNCIATION

1 Q: What word is always pronounced wrong?
A: 'Wrong'.
The Big Book of Jokes and Riddles, 1978

2 Aitches don't make artists – there ain't no 'H' in 'Art'.
Albert Chevalier, 'The Cockney Trajedian', music-hall song

3 You can't be happy with a woman who pronounces both *d*'s in Wednesday.
Peter De Vries, *Sauce for the Goose*, 1981

4 Dear Miss Manners,
When is a *vase* a *vahz*?

Gentle Reader,
When it is filled with *dah-zies*.
Judith Martin, *Miss Manners' Guide to Excruciatingly Correct Behaviour*, 1982

See also The English Language; Language; Words.

PROPOSALS

1 BOY: Don't you understand? I want to marry you. I want you to be the mother of my children.
GIRL: But how many do you have?
Anon.

2 HE: I'd like to marry your daughter.
FATHER: Have you seen my wife yet?
HE: Yes, I have. But I prefer your daughter.
Anon.

3 FATHER: The man who marries my daughter will get a prize.
CLAUD: Can I see the prize first?
Gyles Brandreth, *1,000 Jokes: The Greatest Joke Book Ever Known*, 1980

4 Before I was married I was courting my wife ten years. Before I was married. Then I went round to see her father. And I looked straight at him. He said, 'Hello.' I said, 'Hello.' He said, 'What do you want?' I said, 'I've been courting your daughter for ten years.' He said, 'So what?' I said, 'I want to marry her.' He said, 'I thought you wanted a pension.' He said, 'If you marry my daughter, I'll give you three acres and a cow.'
You're quite right – you're quite right. I'm still waiting for the three acres.
Max Miller, *The Max Miller Blue Book*, 1975

5 ERIC: Would you like to hear how I asked her father for his daughter's hand in marriage? I said, 'Sir, the bright sunshine of your daughter's smile has dispelled the dark clouds of my depression!' He said, 'Are you proposing or is this the weather forecast?' . . . I said, 'I would like your daughter for my wife.' He said, 'But I've never even seen your wife. Bring her round and we'll talk about it.'
ERNIE: You got through to him eventually?
ERIC: Yes – he said, 'So you want to marry my daughter? Don't you think you'd better see my wife first?' I said, 'I have, sir, and I still want to marry your daughter.'
Eric Morecambe and Ernie Wise, *The Morecambe and Wise Joke Book*, 1979

6 Once a week is quite enough to propose to anyone, and it should always be done in a manner that attracts some attention.
Oscar Wilde, *An Ideal Husband*, 1895

7 He had been building one of those piles of thought, as ramshackle and fantastic as a Chinese pagoda, half from words let fall by gentlemen in gaiters, half from the litter in his own mind, about duck shooting and legal history, about the Roman occupation of Lincoln and the relations of country gentlemen with their wives, when, from all this disconnected rambling, there suddenly formed itself in his mind the idea that he would ask Mary to marry him.
Virginia Woolf, *Night and Day*, 1919

See also Couples; Courting; Engagements; Weddings.

PROSTITUTION

1 The big difference between sex for money and sex for free is that sex for money usually costs less.
Brendan Francis, quoted in *Playboy*, 1985

2 Prostitution gives her an opportunity to meet people. It provides fresh air and wholesome exercise, and it keeps her out of trouble.
Joseph Heller, *Catch-22*, 1961

See also Promiscuity; Sex; Vice.

PROTEST

1 Gay Whales Against the Bomb!
Slogan on badge, London, 1982

2 Non-violence is a flop. The only bigger flop is violence.
Joan Baez, *Observer*, 1967

3 In the whole range of human occupations is it possible to imagine a poorer thing to be than an iconoclast? It is the lowest of all the unskilled trades.
G. K. Chesterton, *Daily News*, 1905

4 Light your faith and you can light the world – set fire to the church of your choice.
Tony Hendra and Michael O'Donoghue, National Lampoon's *Radio Dinner*, 1972

5 FOLK SINGER: Next I want to sing a song
about the House Rules Committee and
how the legislative functions of Congress
are tyrannized over by its procedural
calendar, dominated in turn by an all-
powerful chairman hamstringing the
processes of democracy.
  Edward Koren, cartoon in the *New Yorker*

6 It is not difficult to be unconventional in
the eyes of the world when your uncon-
ventionality is but the convention of your
set.
  W. Somerset Maugham, *The Moon and
  Sixpence*, 1919

7 MILNE: I never got used to the way the
house Trots fell into the jargon back in
Grimsby – I mean, on any other subject,
like the death of the novel, or the sex life
of the editor's secretary, they spoke
ordinary English, but as soon as they
started trying to get me to join the strike it
was as if their brains had been taken out
and replaced by one of those little golf-
ball things you get in electric typewriters
... 'Betrayal' ... 'Confrontation' ...
'Management' ... My God, you'd need
a more supple language than that to
describe an argument between two
amoebas.
  Tom Stoppard, *Night and Day*, 1978

8 Agitators are a set of interfering med-
dling people, who come down to some
perfectly contented class of the community and sow the seeds of discontent
among them. That is the reason why
agitators are so absolutely necessary.
  Oscar Wilde, 'The Soul of Man under
  Socialism', 1891

See also Revolution; Terrorism.

PROTESTANTISM

1 The chief contribution of Protestantism
to human thought is its massive proof
that God is a bore.
  H. L. Mencken, *Minority Report*, 1956

See also Catholicism; Christianity; The
Church; God; Jesus Christ; Prayer;
Religion.

PROVERBS

1 Sick yaks leave light tracks.
  P. Clifton, 'Meaningless Proverbs', *New
  Statesman*, 1967

2 One does not moisten a stamp with the
Niagara Falls.
  P. W. R. Foot, 'Meaningless Proverbs', *New
  Statesman*, 1969

3 No leg's too short to reach the ground.
  Lyndon Irving, 'Meaningless Proverbs',
  New Statesman, 1967

4 She that knows why knows wherefore.
  Jim Snell, 'Meaningless Proverbs', *New
  Statesman*, 1983

5 He digs deepest who deepest digs.
  Roger Woddis, 'Meaningless Proverbs',
  New Statesman, 1969

See also Epigrams; Maxims; Politics –
Axioms; Sayings.

PRUDERY

1 MOTHER: Any road, you seem to know a
lot about it.
SON: Lesbianism? Yes, well I come
across it in literature.
MOTHER: Well, I hope it *is* in literature
and not in Halifax.
  Alan Bennett, *Me! I'm Afraid of Virginia
  Woolf*, London Weekend Television, 1978

2 I'm an intensely shy and vulnerable
woman. My husband has never seen me
naked. Nor has he expressed the least
desire to do so.
  Dame Edna Everage (Barry Humphries), *Housewife Superstar*, one-man
  show, 1976

See also Censorship; Chastity; Morality;
Nudity; Pornography; Puritanism.

PSYCHIATRY

1 Psychiatry – the care of the id by the odd.
  Anon.

2 There was a young man from Toledo
Who traveled around incognito,
The reason he did
Was to bolster his id
While appeasing his savage libido.
  Anon.

3 You go to a psychiatrist when you're slightly cracked and keep going until you're completely broke.
Anon.

4 A psychiatrist is the next man you start talking to after you start talking to yourself.
Fred Allen

5 PSYCHIATRIST (*to patient*): You're lucky Mrs Pindleby – most shoplifters aren't rich enough to be kleptomaniacs.
Hector Breeze, cartoon in *Private Eye*

6 Anybody who goes to see a psychiatrist ought to have his head examined.
Samuel Goldwyn (Attrib.)

7 A neurotic is a person who builds a castle in the air. A psychotic is the person who lives in it. A psychiatrist is the one who collects the rent.
Jerome Lawrence

8 My psychiatrist and I have decided that when we both think I'm ready, I'm going to get in my car and drive off the Verrazano Bridge.
Neil Simon, *The Last of the Red Hot Lovers*, 1969

9 One should only see a psychiatrist out of boredom.
Muriel Spark

10 A psychiatrist is a man who goes to the Folies Bergère and looks at the audience.
Dr Mervyn Stockwood, Anglican bishop, quoted in the *Observer*, 1961

11 Sir Roderick Glossop . . . is always called a nerve specialist, because it sounds better, but everybody knows that he's really a sort of janitor to the looney-bin.
P. G. Wodehouse, *The Inimitable Jeeves*, 1923

See also Anxiety; Insanity; Paranoia; Psychoanalysis; Psychology; Schizophrenia.

PSYCHOANALYSIS

1 *Psychoanalysist*: A Jewish boy who can't stand the sight of blood.
Anon.

2 I was in group analysis when I was younger 'cause I couldn't afford private. I was captain of the Latent Paranoid Softball Team. We played all the neurotics on a Sunday morning. The Nail-Biters against the Bed-Wetters.
Woody Allen, *The Nightclub Years, 1964–1968*, record, 1972

3 ANNIE: Oh, you see an analyst?
ALVY: Y-y-yeah, just for fifteen years?
ANNIE: Fifteen years?
ALVY: Yeah, uh, I'm going to give him one more year and then I'm going to Lourdes.
Woody Allen and Marshall Brickman, *Annie Hall*, screenplay, 1977

4 My analyst doesn't understand me . . .
Mel Calman, *Dr Calman's Dictionary of Psychoanalysis*, cartoon, 1979

5 Psychoanalysis is confession without absolution.
G. K. Chesterton

6 *The Benefits of Therapy*
If you happen to have experience with Freudian analysis, group psychotherapy, est or some other form of training, your communications to your mate during marital squabbles will be considerably enhanced. For example, if you happen to be in therapy, here are some phrases you might use:
1. 'My psychiatrist says you're inhibiting me.'
2. 'My shrink says I'm not supposed to let you talk to me like that.'
3. 'Nobody in my group has these kinds of problems with *their* husbands.'
Dan Greenburg and Suzanne O'Malley, *How to Avoid Love and Marriage*, 1983

7 You will . . . be able to utilize the special words and phrases you have learned in therapy. Your mate will find these particularly grating. For example:
1. 'Will you stop ACTING OUT and start RELATING?'

2. 'You know what this is about?
TRANSFERENCE.'
3. 'What's the psychological PAYOFF
in all this for you?'
4. 'Boy, do you have a lot of REPRES-
SED RAGE.'
5. 'You're a classic example of ANAL-
RETENTIVE behavior.'
Dan Greenburg and Suzanne O'Malley,
How to Avoid Love and Marriage, 1983

8 'You seem to be reacting to your boyfriend as if he were your father,' your
shrink may say stonily (unless she is a
strict Freudian, in which case she'll shut
up and wait until you think of it yourself,
a process that usually takes ten years.
This is why strict Freudians have such
lovely summer houses).
Cynthia Heimel, *Sex Tips for Girls*, 1983

9 There were 117 psychoanalysts on the
Pan Am flight to Vienna and I'd been
treated by at least six of them. And
married a seventh.
Erica Jong, *Fear of Flying*, 1973

10 Psychoanalysis is the disease it purports
to cure.
Karl Kraus

See also Psychiatry; Psychology.

PSYCHOLOGY

1 The difference between a conjuror and a
psychologist is that one pulls rabbits out
of a hat while the other pulls habits out of
a rat.
Anon.

2 Did you hear what the white rat said to
the other white rat? ... I've got that
psychologist so well trained that every
time I ring the bell he brings me something to eat.
David Mercer, *A Suitable Case for Treatment*, BBC TV, 1962

3 The object of all psychology is to give us a
totally different idea of the things we
know best.
Paul Valéry, *Tel Quel*, 1943

See also The Brain; Psychiatry;
Psychoanalysis.

THE PUBLIC

1 The public have an insatiable curiosity to
know everything, except what is worth
knowing.
Oscar Wilde, 'The Soul of Man under
Socialism', 1891

PUBLISHING

1 As repressed sadists are said to become
policemen or butchers, so those with an
irrational fear of life become publishers.
Cyril Connolly, *Enemies of Promise*, 1938

2 Never buy an editor or publisher a lunch
or a drink until he has bought an article,
story or book from you. This rule is
absolute and may be broken only at your
peril.
John Creasey

3 It is with publishers as with wives: one
always wants somebody else's.
Norman Douglas

4 Great editors do not discover nor produce great authors; great authors create
and produce great publishers.
John Farrar, *What Happens in Book
Publishing*, 1957

5 I don't believe in publishers who wish to
butter their bannocks on both sides while
they'll hardly allow an author to smell
treacle. I consider they are too grabby
altogether and like Methodists they love
to keep the Sabbath and everything else
they can lay their hands on.
Amanda Ros

6 I object to publishers: the one service
they have done me is to teach me to do
without them. They combine commercial rascality with artistic touchiness and
pettiness, without being either good
business men or fine judges of literature.
All that is necessary in the production of
a book is an author and a bookseller,
without any intermediate parasite.
George Bernard Shaw, letter, 1895

See also Best-sellers; Books; Literature;
Novels; Poets and Poetry; Writers;
Writing.

PUNCTUALITY

1 Punctuality is something that, if you have it, there's often no one around to share it with you.
Anon.

2 Punctuality: the art of guessing correctly how late the other party is going to be.
P. C. F., *Saturday Evening Post*

3 The only way of catching a train I ever discovered is to miss the train before.
G. K. Chesterton (Attrib.)

4 I have noticed that the people who are late are often so much jollier than the people who have to wait for them.
E. V. Lucas, *Reading, Writing and Remembering*, 1932

5 I've been on a calendar, but never on time.
Marilyn Monroe, *Look*, 1962

6 Being early is an unpardonable sin. If you are early, you'll witness the last-minute confusion and panic that always attend making anything seem effortlessly gracious. Looking in on this scene is almost as rude as asking someone where he got his face-lift.
P. J. O'Rourke, *Modern Manners*, 1983

7 The trouble with being punctual is that there's nobody there to appreciate it.
Harold Rome

8 Punctuality is the virtue of the bored.
Evelyn Waugh, *Diaries*, 1976

9 He was always late on principle, his principle being that punctuality is the thief of time.
Oscar Wilde, *The Picture of Dorian Gray*, 1891

See also Procrastination.

PUNS

1 A pun is a short quip followed by a long groan.
Anon.

2 The inveterate punster follows a conversation as a shark follows a ship.
Stephen Leacock (Attrib.)

3 A pun is the lowest form of humor – when you don't think of it first.
Oscar Levant

See also Comedy; Humour; Laughter; Wit.

PURITANISM

1 A puritan's a person who pours righteous indignation into the wrong things.
G. K. Chesterton (Attrib.)

2 We have long passed the Victorian era, when asterisks were followed after a certain interval by a baby.
W. Somerset Maugham, *The Constant Wife*, 1926

3 Puritanism: the haunting fear that someone, somewhere, may be happy.
H. L. Mencken, *Sententiae*, 1920

4 Everyone knows about those archaic 'blue laws' – but here are some we *guarantee* you've never heard of.
In Connecticut, it is a felony to exhibit a vasectomy scar while jaywalking with a nun.
In New York it is illegal to wear a blue suit with brown shoes while seducing a haberdasher's daughter.
In Maine it is against the law for an unmarried woman to have a checking account at a sperm bank.
Larry Tritton, *Playboy*

5 The prig is a very interesting psychological study, and though of all poses a moral pose is the most offensive, still to have a pose at all is something.
Oscar Wilde, 'The Critic as Artist', 1890

See also Censorship; Morality; Prudery.

QUESTIONS

1 No question is so difficult to answer as that to which the answer is obvious.
   George Bernard Shaw

2 The 'silly question' is the first intimation of some totally new development.
   Alfred North Whitehead

See also Problems; Questions and Answers.

QUESTIONS AND ANSWERS

1 Of what question is the following the answer: 'Coal Mine'?
   The question: What should you say when asked to identify your lump of coal?
   Anon.

2 Of what question is the following the answer: '9W'?
   The question: Tell me, is that Richard Wagner with a 'V'?
   Anon.

3 Of what question is the following the answer: 'Washington Irving'?
   The question: Who was the first President of the United States, Max?
   Anon.

See also Questions.

QUOTATIONS

1 Hush little bright line,
   Don't you cry,
   You'll be a cliché
   By and by.
   Fred Allen

2 Quotation: something that somebody said that seemed to make sense at the time.
   Egon J. Beaudoin

3 The surest way to make a monkey out of a man is to quote him.
   Robert Benchley

4 *Quoting*: the act of repeating erroneously the words of another.
   Ambrose Bierce, *The Devil's Dictionary*, 1911

5 Next to being witty yourself, the best thing is to quote another's wit.
   Christian N. Bovee

6 I might repeat to myself, slowly and soothingly, a list of quotations beautiful from minds profound; if I can remember any of the damn things.
   Dorothy Parker, 'The Little Hours', *The Portable Dorothy Parker*, 1944

7 If, with the literate, I am
   Impelled to try an epigram,
   I never seek to take the credit;
   We all assume that Oscar said it.
   Dorothy Parker, 'Oscar Wilde', *Sunset Gun*, 1928

8 I often quote myself. It adds spice to my conversation.
   George Bernard Shaw

9 To be occasionally quoted is the only fame I care for.
   Alexander Smith, *Dreamthorp*, 1863

10 In the dying world I come from, quotation is a national vice.
   Evelyn Waugh

11 I don't know if you happen to be familiar with a poem called 'The Charge of the Light Brigade' by the bird Tennyson whom Jeeves had mentioned when speaking of the fellow whose strength was as the strength of ten . . . the thing goes, as you probably know,
   Tum tiddle umpty-pum
   Tum tiddle umpty-pum
   Tum tiddle umpty-pum
   and this brought you to the snapperoo or pay-off which was 'someone had blundered'.
   P. G. Wodehouse, *Jeeves and the Feudal Spirit*, 1954

See also Literature.

RACE

1 Racial prejudice is a pigment of the imagination.
Graffito, Greenwich, 1980

2 BLACK MAN: As a matter of racial pride we want to be called 'Blacks'.
Which has replaced the term 'Afro-American' –
Which replaced 'Negroes' –
Which replaced 'Colored People' –
Which replaced 'Darkies' –
Which replaced 'Blacks'.
Jules Feiffer, cartoon in the *Village Voice*, 1967

3 The Ku Klux Klan. They wear white sheets and their hats have a point – which is more than can be said for their beliefs.
David Frost and Michael Shea, *A Mid-Atlantic Companion*, 1986

4 I'll say this about one of us living in an all-white suburb. Crabgrass isn't our biggest problem.
Dick Gregory

5 I waited five days at a white lunch counter but when they finally served me, they didn't have what I wanted anyway.
Dick Gregory, 1960

6 I was so excited when I came North and sat in the front of the bus, that I missed my stop.
Dick Gregory, 1957

7 Wouldn't it be a hell of a thing if all this was burnt cork and you people were being tolerant for nothing?
Dick Gregory

8 Whereas black people can call each other 'nigger' with impunity, a white person may not presume to do so unless he doesn't mind dying.
Cynthia Heimel, *Sex Tips for Girls*, 1983

9 I want to be the white man's brother, not his brother-in-law.
Martin Luther King (Attrib.)

10 Absolute equality, that's the thing; and throughout the ages we have always defended to the death the sacred right of every Black man, no matter how lowly, to be equal to every other Black man.
Hugh Leonard, *Time Was*, 1976

11 He's really awfully fond of colored people. Well, he says himself, he wouldn't have white servants.
Dorothy Parker, 'Arrangement in Black and White', *The Portable Dorothy Parker*, 1944

12 Beware of Greeks bearing gifts, colored men looking for loans and whites who understand the Negro.
Adam Clayton Powell, Black congressman

13 You ever notice how *nice* white people get when there's a bunch of niggers around? Why, they talk to everybody – 'Hi! How ya doin'? I don't know ya, but here's my wife. Hello!'
Richard Pryor, comedy routine quoted in *Playboy*, 1979

RAILWAYS

1 STATION ANNOUNCER: The train now arriving on Platforms 6, 7, 8 and 9 . . . is coming in sideways.
Anon.

2 My heart is warm with the friends I make,
And better friends I'll not be knowing;
Yet there isn't a train I wouldn't take
No matter where it's going.
Edna St Vincent Millay, 'Travel', *Collected Poems*, 1956

3 STATION ANNOUNCER: . . . the train now standing on Platform 3 will, we hope, in due course be moved back on to the lines . . . will the passengers who have taken the 4.15 train from Platform 8 to Ponders End, please bring it back again at once . . .
Richard Murdoch and Kenneth Horne, *Much Binding in the Marsh*, BBC Radio, 1947

4 Oh, some like trips in luxury ships,
  And some in gasoline wagons,
  And others swear by the upper air
  And the wings of flying dragons.
  Let each make haste to indulge his taste,
  Be it beer, champagne or cider;
  My private joy, both man and boy,
  Is being a railroad rider.
    Ogden Nash, 'Riding on a Railroad Train',
    I'm a Stranger Here Myself, 1938

5 Your train leaves at eleven forty-five and
    it is now but eleven thirty-nine and a
    half,
  And there is only one man ahead of you
    at the ticket window so you have
    plenty of time, haven't you, well I
    hope you enjoy a hearty laugh,
  Because he is Dr Fell, and he is
    engaged in an intricate maneuver
  He wants to go to Sioux City with
    stopovers at Plymouth Rock, Stone
    Mountain, Yellowstone Park, Lake
    Louise and Vancouver . . .
    Ogden Nash, 'Dr Fell and Points West',
    Good Intentions, 1942

See also Travel.

READING

1 There are times when I think that the
  reading I have done in the past has had
  no effect except to cloud my mind and
  make me indecisive.
    Robertson Davies

2 When I want to read a book, I write
  one.
    Benjamin Disraeli

3 . . . magazines all too frequently lead to
  books and should be regarded by the
  prudent as the heavy petting of literature.
    Fran Lebowitz, *Metropolitan Life*, 1978

4 Oh! DO you remember Paper Books
  When paper books were thrilling,
  When something to read
  Was seldom Gide
  Or Proust or Peacock
  Or Margaret Mead
  And seldom Lionel Trilling?
    Phyllis McGinley, *Times Three: 1932–
    1960*, 1960

5 The chief knowledge that a man gets
  from reading books is the knowledge that
  very few of them are worth reading.
    H. L. Mencken (Attrib.)

6 Don't read science fiction books. It'll
  look bad if you die in bed with one on the
  nightstand. Always read stuff that will
  make you look good if you die in the
  middle of it.
    P. J. O'Rourke, *National Lampoon*, 1979

7 When you come to the end of a crime
  novel, something at least in this huge,
  chaotic world has been settled.
    J. B. Priestley, quoted in the *Manchester
    Guardian Weekly*

8 There are two motives for reading a
  book; one, that you enjoy it; the other,
  that you can boast about it.
    Bertrand Russell

9 People say that life is the thing, but I
  prefer reading.
    Logan Pearsall Smith, *Trivia*, 1917

See also Books; Literature; Newspapers;
Novels; Poets and Poetry; William
Shakespeare; Writers; Writing.

RONALD REAGAN President of
the United States, 1981–

1 National Security Advisor [William P.]
  Clark arrived in Lebanon thought he was
  in Israel.
    He wasn't disturbed by the logis-
  tical error. 'I'm not sure who's the President of which,' he remarked. Clark
  said he planned to use his ignorance as a
  way to mediate tense relations between
  the two countries by 'avoiding name
  calling'.
    Off The Wall Street Journal, 1982

2 [Secretary of State, Alexander] Haig
  found a Nicaraguan insurgent under his
  desk. Haig said this proves 'beyond an
  irrefutable iota of a doubt' there are
  communist influences in El Salvador and
  the State Department. Haig said the
  Nicaraguan 'was so small I almost missed
  him', and that he couldn't produce the
  Nicaraguan rebel for reporters because,
  'just as I was bringing him on over here,

he slipped through my fingers and disappeared under my rug'.
Off The Wall Street Journal, 1982

3 He has not the remotest idea of what he is about to say, and having said it he has not the remotest recollection of what it was. One can pray only that the Russians are alive to this fact, since if they are not, then none of us will be alive to anything else.
Alan Coren, *Punch*, 1984

4 Ronald Reagan doesn't dye his hair – he's just prematurely orange.
Gerald Ford (Attrib.)

5 I believe that Ronald Reagan can make this country what it once was – an arctic region covered with ice.
Steve Martin (Attrib.)

6 Reaganomics, that makes sense to me. It means if you don't have enough money, it's because poor people are hoarding it.
Kevin Rooney, quoted in *GQ*, 1984

7 . . . a triumph of the embalmer's art.
Gore Vidal

8 There's a lot to be said for being *nouveau riche* and the Reagans mean to say it all.
Gore Vidal, 1981

9 I still think Nancy does most of his talking; you'll notice that she *never* drinks water when Ronnie speaks.
Robin Williams, interview in *Playboy*, 1982

See also The Presidency; Washington.

REAL ESTATE

1 GROUCHO MARX: This is the heart of the residential district. Every lot is a stone's throw from the station. As soon as they throw enough stones, we're going to build a station.
George S. Kaufman and Morrie Ryskind, *The Cocoanuts*, screenplay, 1929

See also Home.

RECORDS

1 The World Record holder for blowing a bugle whilst riding a bike uphill dragging four hundredweight of pig iron and holding his breath is buried at . . .
Spike Milligan

2 Clufton Bay Bridge is the fourth biggest single-span double-track shore-to-shore railway bridge in the world bar none.
Tom Stoppard, *Albert's Bridge*, BBC Radio, 1967

See also Achievement; Winning.

REFORMERS

1 The urge to save humanity is almost always only a false-face for the urge to rule it.
H. L. Mencken, *Minority Report*, 1956

See also Censorship; Morality.

REGRETS

1 The only thing I regret about my life is the length of it. If I had to live my life again, I'd make all the same mistakes – only sooner.
Tallulah Bankhead

2 The follies which a man regrets most in his life are those which he didn't commit when he had the opportunity.
Helen Rowland

3 OLD-AGE PENSIONER (*to his wife*): My only regret is I did it my way.
James Stevenson, cartoon in the *New Yorker*, 1974

REINCARNATION

1 If I believed in reincarnation, I'd come back as a sponge.
Woody Allen, *Seventeen*, 1972

See also Belief; Death; Heaven.

REJECTION

1 HE: In the barrel you're a pickle
In the gold mine you're a nickel,
You're the tack inside my shoe.
Yeah! I can do without you!
SHE: In the bosom you're a dagger

You're a mangy carpetbagger.
In the theater you're the boo!
I can do without you!
Sammy Fain and Paul Francis Webster,
'I Can Do Without You', song from *Calamity Jane*, 1953

2 ERIC: See that terrific blonde over there?
ERNIE: Yes?
ERIC: She's been annoying me all evening!
ERNIE: I bet she hasn't even *looked* at you!
ERIC: Right – that's what's annoying me!
Eric Morecambe and Ernie Wise, *The Morecambe and Wise Joke Book*, 1979

3 ... his efforts at conversation were returned unopened.
Sally Poplin

See also Courting; Divorce.

RELATIONSHIPS

1 Relations between the sexes are so complicated that the only way you can tell if two members of the set are 'going together' is if they are married. Then, almost certainly, they are not.
Cleveland Amory, *Who Killed Society?*, 1960

2 *Relationship*: The civilized conversationalist uses this word in public only to describe a seafaring vessel carrying members of his family.
Fran Lebowitz, *Metropolitan Life*, 1978

See also Couples; Friends; Marriage; Romance.

RELATIVES

1 You see this watch? This is an absolutely fantastic, very fine, elegant gold watch which speaks of breeding and was sold to me by my grandfather on his deathbed.
Woody Allen

2 We must all be very kind to Auntie Jessie,
For she's never been a Mother or a Wife,
You mustn't throw your toys at her
Or make a vulgar noise at her,
She hasn't led a very happy life.

You must never lock her playfully in the bathroom
Or play tunes on her enamelled Spanish comb.
Though unpleasant to behold
She's a heart of purest gold
And Charity you know begins at home.
Noël Coward, 'We Must All be Very Kind to Auntie Jessie', song, 1920s

3 Extraordinary thing about the lower classes in England – they are always losing their relations. They are extremely fortunate in that respect.
Oscar Wilde, *An Ideal Husband*, 1895

4 I can't help detesting my relations. I suppose it comes from the fact that none of us can stand other people having the same faults as ourselves.
Oscar Wilde, *The Picture of Dorian Gray*, 1891

5 Relations are simply a tedious pack of people, who haven't got the remotest knowledge of how to live, nor the smallest instinct about when to die.
Oscar Wilde, *The Importance of Being Earnest*, 1895

6 A strange, almost unearthly light comes into the eyes of wronged uncles when they see a chance of getting a bit of their own back from erring nephews.
P. G. Wodehouse, *Uncle Dynamite*, 1948

7 Aunts as a class are like Napoleon. They expect their orders to be carried out without a hitch and don't listen to excuses.
P. G. Wodehouse, *Much Obliged, Jeeves*, 1971

8 Many a fellow who looks like the dominant male and has himself photographed smoking a pipe curls up like carbon paper when confronted by an aunt.
P. G. Wodehouse, *The Mating Season*, 1949

See also Aunts; The Family.

RELATIVITY

1 It is impossible to travel faster than light, and certainly not desirable, as one's hat keeps blowing off.
Woody Allen, *Side Effects*, 1980

2 It is said that there are, besides Dr Einstein himself, only two men who can claim to have grasped the Theory in full. I cannot claim to be either of these ... The attempt to conceive Infinity had always been quite arduous enough for me. But to imagine the absence of it; to feel that perhaps we and all the stars beyond our ken are somehow cosily (though awfully) closed in by curtain curves beyond which is nothing; and to convince myself, by the way, that this exterior is not (in virtue of *being* nothing) something, and therefore ... but I lose the thread.
   Max Beerbohm, 'A Note on the Einstein Theory', *Mainly on the Air*, 1947

3 Albert Einstein got prepared,
Took a *c* and had it 2,
Multiplied by *m* – that's right! –
e, by gum! – the speed of light.
   Will Bellenger, *New Statesman*, 1984

4 There was a young lady named Bright
Whose speed was far faster than light;
She went out one day
In a relative way,
And returned the previous night.
   Professor A. H. Reginald Buller, *Punch*

5 I simply ignored an axiom.
   Albert Einstein, on relativity (Attrib.)

6 When a man sits with a pretty girl for an hour, it seems like a minute. But let him sit on a hot stove for a minute – and it's longer than any hour. That's relativity.
   Albert Einstein

See also Science and Scientists.

RELIGION

1 HILARY: I imagine when it comes to the next prayer book they won't write He, meaning Him with a capital *h*. God will be written in the lower case to banish any lurking sense of inferiority his worshippers might feel.
   Alan Bennett, *The Old Country*, 1978

2 SCHOOLMASTER: Now you're sure you've got the Catechism all buttoned up, Foster?

FOSTER: I'm still a bit hazy about the Trinity, sir.
SCHOOLMASTER: Three in one, one in three, perfectly straightforward. Any doubts about that see your maths master.
   Alan Bennett, *Forty Years On*, 1968

3 Every day people are straying away from the church and going back to God.
   Lenny Bruce, *The Essential Lenny Bruce*, 1972

4 There is something wrong with a man if he does not want to break the Ten Commandments.
   G. K. Chesterton, quoted in the *Observer*, 1925

5 He represented what any minister will tell you is the bane of parish work: somebody who has got religion. It's as embarrassing to a cleric of sensibility as 'poetry lovers' are to a poet.
   Peter De Vries, *The Mackerel Plaza*, 1958

6 I do benefits for all religions – I'd hate to blow the hereafter on a technicality.
   Bob Hope

7 Perhaps the most lasting pleasure in life is the pleasure of *not* going to church.
   William Inge, Dean of St Paul's Cathedral, 1911–1934 (Attrib.)

8 We must respect the other fellow's religion, but only in the sense and to the extent that we respect his theory that his wife is beautiful and his children smart.
   H. L. Mencken, *Minority Report*, 1956

9 After coming in contact with a religious man, I always feel that I must wash my hands.
   Friedrich Wilhelm Nietzsche, *The Anti-christ*, 1888

10 Religions die when they are proved to be true. Science is the record of dead religions.
   Oscar Wilde, 'Phrases and Philosophies for the Use of the Young', 1894

11 To all things clergic
I am allergic.
   Alexander Woollcott (Attrib.)

See also The Bible; Catholicism; The

Church; God; Jesus Christ; Missionaries; Prayer; Protestantism.

THE REPUBLICAN PARTY

1 The Republican Convention opened with a prayer. If the Lord can see his way to bless the Republican Party the way it's been carrying on, then the rest of us ought to get it without even asking.
   Will Rogers, 1928

2 The Republicans have a habit of having three bad years and one good one, and the good one always happens to be election year.
   Will Rogers (Attrib.)

3 The Republicans have their splits after the election and the Democrats have theirs just before the election.
   Will Rogers (Attrib.)

4 A conservative Republican is one who doesn't believe anything new should ever be tried for the first time. A liberal Republican is one who *does* believe something should be tried for the first time – but not now.
   Mort Sahl

5 I like Republicans, have grown up with them, worked with them and would trust them with anything in the world, except public office.
   Adlai Stevenson

See also Congress; Conservatism; The Senate; Washington.

REPUTATION

1 One can survive everything nowadays, except death, and live down anything except a good reputation.
   Oscar Wilde, *A Woman of No Importance*, 1893

See also Celebrities; Fame.

RESIGNATIONS

1 Galbraith's law states that anyone who says he won't resign four times, will.
   John Kenneth Galbraith, 1973

See also Unemployment; Work.

RESPECTABILITY

1 He must be quite respectable. One has never heard his name before in the whole course of one's life, which speaks volumes for a man, nowadays.
   Oscar Wilde, *A Woman of No Importance*, 1893

RESTAURANTS

1 GEORGE: I ate on the Motorway. At the Grill n'Griddle. I had Ham n'Eggs. And now I've got 'ndigestion.
   Alan Bennett, *Getting On*, 1971

2 WAITER (*to customer*): That fine line between gracious attendance and fawning obsequiousness – tell me, sir, how close did I come?
   William Hamilton, *William Hamilton's Anti-Social Register*, cartoon, 1974

3 He ordered as one to the menu born.
   O. Henry

4 ERIC: Just outside town there was this little place with a sign that said, 'Topless Bar'. So we went in there.
   ERNIE: You took your wife into a topless bar?
   ERIC: Yes . . . anyway, it turned out to be a bit of a disappointment.
   ERNIE: How come?
   ERIC: Turned out to be a cafe with no roof on. Still, we decided to eat there. But just as they brought the food, it started to rain.
   ERNIE: Oh, no!
   ERIC: Oh, yes – it took us an hour and a half to finish the soup!
   Eric Morecambe and Ernie Wise, *The Morecambe and Wise Joke Book*, 1979

5 ERIC: We went out for a special meal one night. It was a very posh restaurant. Just to impress the wife, I ordered the whole meal in French. Even the waiter was surprised.
   ERNIE: Really?
   ERIC: Yes – it was a Chinese restaurant.
   ERNIE: Was it good value?
   ERIC: Terrific value! For a pound each they serve you all the food you can eat.
   ERNIE: Fantastic!

ERIC: The trouble is, they only give you one chopstick.
Eric Morecambe and Ernie Wise, *The Morecambe and Wise Joke Book*, 1979

6 ERNIE: Waiter – there's a fly in my soup!
ERIC: They don't care what they eat, do they, sir?
ERNIE: But what's it doing there?
ERIC: It looks like the breaststroke to me, sir.
ERNIE: I can't believe it! A fly in my soup!
ERIC: Don't make a fuss, sir, they'll all want one.
ERNIE: But it looks like it's dead!
ERIC: Yes, it's the heat that kills them.
Eric Morecambe and Ernie Wise, *The Morecambe and Wise Joke Book*, 1979

7 Our order is taken ... by a waitress wearing a cowboy hat, a miniskirt, a fringed vest, boots and red garters. 'The key to a successful restaurant,' O'Donoghue says, 'is dressing girls in degrading clothes.'
Michael O'Donoghue, quoted by Paul Slansky in *Playboy*, 1983

8 *Chinese Food*: You do not sew with a fork, and I see no reason why you should eat with knitting needles.
Miss Piggy, *Miss Piggy's Guide to Life (As Told to Henry Beard)*, 1981

9 During dinner, it may be necessary to excuse yourself for a telephone call. However, it is far preferable to have a phone brought to the table ... as a general rule, white telephones go with fish and poultry, and black ones with anything else. If you are calling during dessert, a small after-dinner phone should be used ... if you are satisfied, say something like, 'Yes, it is a very nice, light telephone, with a good, clear tone and a smooth, almost velvety action.'
Miss Piggy, *Miss Piggy's Guide to Life (As Told to Henry Beard)*, 1981

10 Eating places with live plants in their windows are always good. Restaurants with peppermills the size of fire extinguishers and big red menus with the entrees spelled with *f*'s instead of *s*'s are always expensive. Italian restaurants with

more than 120 entrees are always disappointing. There are no good French restaurants in states which have a *K* in their names. (New Yorque is the exception that proves the rule, whatever that means.)
Miss Piggy, *Miss Piggy's Guide to Life (As Told to Henry Beard)*, 1981

See also Eating; Food; Hotels; Lunch; Tipping; Waiters; Wine.

RETIREMENT

1 Retirement means twice as much husband on half as much money.
Anon.

2 Retirement at sixty-five is ridiculous. When I was sixty-five, I still had pimples.
George Burns

3 ... one sure way of shortening life.
Frank Conklin

4 I married him for better or worse, but not for lunch.
Hazel Weiss, after her husband, George Weiss, retired as general manager of the New York Yankees, 1960

See also Old Age.

RETRACTIONS

1 *I* have reconsidered it; *you* have changed your mind; *he* has gone back on his word.
Competition, *New Statesman*

2 Man does not live by words alone, despite the fact that sometimes he has to eat them.
Adlai Stevenson

REVENGE

1 ... she got even in a way that was almost cruel. She forgave them.
Ralph McGill, on Eleanor Roosevelt

2 It's far easier to forgive an enemy after you've got even with him.
Olin Miller

REVOLUTION

1 Insurrection, *n.* an unsuccessful revolution.
Ambrose Bierce, *The Devil's Dictionary*, 1911

2 The successful revolutionary is a statesman, the unsuccessful one a criminal.
Erich Fromm, *Escape from Freedom*, 1941

3 Steal This Book.
Abbie Hoffman, title of revolutionary
manual, 1971

4 The first duty of a revolutionary is to get
away with it.
Abbie Hoffman, 1970

5 A revolution requires of its leaders a
record of unbroken fallibility. If they do
not possess it, they are expected to invent
it.
Murray Kempton, *Part of Our Time*, 1955

6 Women hate revolutions and revolutionists. They like men who are docile, and
well-regarded at the bank, and never late
at meals.
H. L. Mencken, *Prejudices*, Fourth Series,
1924

7 Revolutions have never lightened the
burden of tyranny: they have only shifted
it to another shoulder.
George Bernard Shaw, *Man and Superman*, 1903

See also Protest; Terrorism; War.

RICH AND POOR

1 The poor have more children, but the
rich have more relatives.
Anon.

2 Q: Why did Robin Hood only rob the
rich?
A: Because the poor had no money.
The Big Book of Jokes and Riddles, 1978

3 ROBIN HOOD: Here is the way it works:
we take from the rich and give to the poor
– keeping only enough for salaries, travel,
equipment, depreciation, and so on, and
so on.
Al Ross, cartoon in the *New Yorker*

4 I've been rich and I've been poor; rich is
better.
Sophie Tucker

See also Begging; Debt; Extravagance;
Money; Poverty; Wealth.

RIDDLES

1 Q: What happens when the human body
is completely submerged in water?
A: The telephone rings.
The Big Book of Jokes and Riddles, 1978

2 Q: What has four wheels and flies?
A: A garbage truck.
Anon.

3 Q: What has sixteen legs, fourteen tes-
ticles and two tiny breasts?
A: Snow White and the Seven Dwarfs.
Anon.

4 Q: What's green and pecks on trees?
A: Woody Wood Pickle.
The Big Book of Jokes and Riddles, 1978

5 Q: What's grey, has four legs and a trunk?
A: A mouse going on holiday.
Anon.

6 Q: What's worse than an octopus with
tennis-elbow?
A: A centipede with athlete's foot.
The Big Book of Jokes and Riddles, 1978

7 GEORGE: What is it that sings and has
four legs?
GRACIE: Two canaries.
George Burns and Gracie Allen, *The
Robert Burns Panatela Program*, CBS Radio,
1932

See also Comedy; Humour; Tom
Swifties; Wit.

RIGHTS

1 The right to be heard does not include
the right to be taken seriously.
Hubert Humphrey

2 What men value in this world is not rights
but privileges.
H. L. Mencken, *Minority Report*, 1956

ROCK 'N' ROLL

1 Dicky Hart and the Pacemakers.
Name of band, London, 1984

2 Rock 'n' roll is trying to convince girls to
pay money to be near you.
Richard Hell, rock musician

3 ... so I think now that Bangla Desh is really, y'know, the most important thing ... and y'know, it's really great the way George has fixed it up, y'know, so you can take care of it, y'know, just by sort of buying the album, y'know. 'Cos y'know, that's where the Seventies are at, I think, y'know ...
Tony Hendra and Michael O'Donoghue, National Lampoon*'s Radio Dinner*, 1972

4 The greatest line in rock 'n' roll is, 'Awopbopaloobop Alopbamboom'. Top that if you can!
Wilko Johnson, rock musician (Attrib.)

5 I tried to charm the pants off Bob Dylan but everyone will be disappointed to learn that I was unsuccessful. I got close ... a couple of fast feels in the front seat of his Cadillac.
Bette Midler, *Rolling Stone*, 1982

6 Good rock stars take drugs, put their penises in plaster of paris, collectivize their sex, molest policemen, promote self-curiosity, unlock myriad spirits, epitomize fun, freedom and bullshit. Can the busiest anarchist on your block match *that*?
Richard Neville, *Playpower*, 1970

7 I bit the head off a live bat the other night. It was like eating a Crunchie wrapped in chamois leather.
Ozzy Osborne, rock musician

8 I don't know anything about music. In my line you don't have to.
Elvis Presley (Attrib.)

9 ... after *Sticky Fingers* Mick [Jagger] became a debutant. Can't open a paper now without seeing a picture of him at some film opening cooing into Baryshnikov's ear ... The cat's gone high rent. I mean, the First Lady of Canada starts hanging out with him, and *she's* accused of social climbing ... Maybe he gets off on fashion shows or having Elaine personally come to his table to make sure all the shrimp on his plate are facing north.
Garry Trudeau, 'The Jimmy Thudpucker Interview', *Rolling Stone*, 1978

10 C'mon Jimmy, get a move on! It's studio time! ... As you may recall, Thudpucker, every nine months, you emerge from your hermitage to provide your legion of admirers with one crisply produced state-of-the-art rock 'n' roll masterpiece!
Garry Trudeau, 'The Jimmy Thudpucker Interview', *Rolling Stone*, 1978

11 For most rockers, the only thing standing between them and total illiteracy is the need to get through their Mercedes-Benz owner's manuals.
Garry Trudeau, 'The Jimmy Thudpucker Interview', *Rolling Stone*, 1978

12 ... in the music industry a legend is usually no more than someone with two consecutive hit singles.
Garry Trudeau, 'The Jimmy Thudpucker Interview', *Rolling Stone*, 1978

13 The Filthy Swine, with their folk hit 'My Girl's Head Comes to a Point' again head the Top Twenty this week. The Bedbugs' 'Chewing Old Socks With You' goes down to third place and Cliff Alopecea moves up with 'Individual Fruit Pie of Love'.
Wanda Drainstorm's 'My Old Plastic Granny' stays steady at number four and the Cockroaches have rocketed up from eleventh to fifth place with 'Love Crawled Under the Door'.
The Drips, whose 'Softening of the Brain' kept fifth place for three weeks running, suddenly collapsed and fell out of the charts altogether. Their manager has had them destroyed.
Peter Simple (Michael Wharton), ' "Pop Notes" by Jim Droolberg', *Daily Telegraph*

See also The Beatles; Jazz; Music and Musicians; Rock 'n' Roll – Critics; The Rolling Stones; Songs and Singers.

ROCK 'N' ROLL – CRITICS

1 If a horse could sing in a monotone, the horse would sound like Carly Simon, only a horse wouldn't rhyme 'yacht', 'apricot' and 'gavotte'.
Robert Christgau, reviewing Carly Simon's 'You're So Vain', 1972

2 Persistence beyond the call of talent.
   Robert Christgau, on singer Terry Reid

3 This may be catchy but I refuse to get
   caught; they may be good at what they do
   but what they do is so disgusting, that
   only makes it worse.
   Robert Christgau, reviewing Seals and
   Crofts' *Unborn Child*, 1974

See also Critics – The Artist's View; Rock
'n' Roll.

ROGUES

1 Time wounds all heels.
   Jane Ace

2 His lack of education is more than com-
   pensated for by his keenly developed
   moral bankruptcy.
   Woody Allen, *Esquire*, 1975

See also Morality; Standards.

THE ROLLING STONES

1 He moves like a parody between a
   majorette girl and Fred Astaire.
   Truman Capote, of Mick Jagger (Attrib.)

2 If the Stones' lyrics made sense, they
   wouldn't be any good.
   Truman Capote (Attrib.)

3 He's stoned on himself. He's always in
   complete control and the whole thing is
   manipulation. It really bothers me that a
   twerp like that can parade around and
   convince everybody that he's Satan.
   Ry Cooder, on Mick Jagger

4 Nine months of listening to the Rolling
   Stones is not my idea of heaven.
   Mick Jagger, after completing the record
   Love You Live, 1977

5 Jagger has got this marvelous sense of the
   day in which a family breaks up. The son
   throws acid in the mother's face, the
   mother stomps the son's nuts in and then
   the fat cousin comes and says, what is
   everybody fighting for, let's have dinner.
   And they sit down . . . British family life
   continues.
   Norman Mailer (Attrib.)

6 Mick Jagger has big lips. I saw him suck

an egg out of a chicken. He can play a
tuba from both ends. This man has got
child-bearing lips . . .
   Joan Rivers, *An Audience with Joan Rivers*,
   London Weekend Television, 1984

See also The Beatles; Music and Musicians; Rock 'n' Roll; The Sixties; Songs
and Singers.

ROMANCE

1 In a mountain greenery
   Where God paints the scenery
   With the world we haven't a quarrel.
   Here a girl can map her own
   Life without a chaperone.
   It's so good it must be immoral.
   It's not amiss
   To sit and kiss.
   For me and you
   There are no blue laws.
   Life is more delectable
   When it's disrespectable.
   Bless our mountain greenery home.
   Lorenz Hart, 'Mountain Greenery', song,
   1926

2 I found the ideal girl. Her father is a
   bookmaker and her brother owns a liquor
   store.
   Joe E. Lewis

3 ERIC: She's a lovely girl . . . I'd like to
   marry her, but her family objects.
   ERNIE: Her family?
   ERIC: Yes, her husband and four kids.
   Eric Morecambe and Ernie Wise, *The
   Morecambe and Wise Joke Book*, 1979

4 CELIA: Oh Charles – a woman needs
   certain things. She needs to be loved,
   wanted, cherished, sought after, wooed,
   flattered, cossetted, pampered. She
   needs sympathy, affection, devotion,
   understanding, tenderness, infatuation,
   adulation, idolatry – that isn't much to
   ask Charles.
   Barry Took and Marty Feldman, *Round
   the Horne*, BBC Radio, 1966

5 The very essence of romance is uncer-
   tainty. If ever I get married, I'll certainly
   try to forget the fact.
   Oscar Wilde, *The Importance of Being
   Earnest*, 1895

6 Where one goes wrong when looking for the ideal girl is in making one's selection before walking the full length of the counter.
P. G. Wodehouse, *Much Obliged, Jeeves*, 1971

See also Courting; Flirtation; Love; Proposals; Seduction; Sex.

FRANKLIN D. ROOSEVELT
President of the United States, 1933–1945

1 ... the man who started more creations than were ever begun since Genesis – and finished none.
Hugh Johnson, Director, National Recovery Administration, 1933–1934, 1937

2 If he became convinced tomorrow that coming out for cannibalism would get him the votes he so sorely needs, he would begin fattening a missionary in the White House backyard come Wednesday.
H. L. Mencken (Attrib.)

See also The Presidency; Washington.

THEODORE ROOSEVELT
President of the United States, 1901–1909

1 One always thinks of him as a glorified bouncer engaged eternally in cleaning out bar-rooms – and not too proud to gouge when the inspiration came to him, or to bite in the clinches.
H. L. Mencken, *Prejudices*, Second Series, 1920

2 The great virtue of my radicalism lies in the fact that I am perfectly ready, if necessary, to be radical on the conservative side.
Theodore Roosevelt, 1906

See also The Presidency; Washington.

ROYALTY

1 PETE: ... do you know, at this very moment, Her Majesty is probably exercising the royal prerogative.
DUD: What's that then, Pete?
PETE: Don't you know the royal preroga-

tive? It's a wonderful animal, Dud. It's a legendary beast, half bird, half fish, half unicorn, and it's being exercised at this very moment. Do you know that legend has it that e'er so long as the royal prerogative lives, happiness and laughter will reign throughout this green and pleasant land.
DUD: And the yeoman will stand tall upon this sceptred isle, Pete.
Peter Cook and Dudley Moore, *The Dagenham Dialogues*, 1971

2 Part of a royal education is
To be resigned
To your behind
Becoming numb.
The worst of every coronation is
We always wish we hadn't come.
Noël Coward, 'Coronation Chorale', song from *The Girl Who Came to Supper*, 1963

3 Everyone likes flattery; and when you come to Royalty you should lay it on with a trowel.
Benjamin Disraeli, to Matthew Arnold (Attrib.)

4 One day there will only be five kings left: hearts, spades, diamonds, clubs, and England.
King Farouk of Egypt, 1953

5 After you've met one hundred and fifty lord mayors, they all begin to look the same.
King George V (Attrib.)

6 I was taught a kind of theoretic republicanism which was prepared to tolerate a monarch so long as he recognized that he was an employee of the people and subject to dismissal if he proved unsatisfactory. My grandfather, who was no respecter of persons, used to explain this point of view to Queen Victoria, and she was not altogether sympathetic.
Bertrand Russell, *Portraits from Memory*, 1956

7 Prince Charles is planning to record his own version of Frank Sinatra's hit, 'My Way'. He's going to call it 'One Did It One's Way'.
Neil Shand

8 We're the envy of the world, we are, having a Royal Family. It's the one thing in the world no one else has got. An' don't talk to me about Norway, and Holland, and Sweden and all that rubbish. I'm talking about *Royalty*. Not bloody cloth-cap kings riding about on bikes. I mean, that's not Royalty. You'll never see our Queen on a bike. She wouldn't demean herself.

    Johnny Speight, *The Thoughts of Chairman Alf (Alf Garnett's Little Blue Book)*, 1973

9 Wednesday July 29th
ROYAL WEDDING DAY!!!!!
How proud I am to be English!
Foreigners must be sick as pigs!
We truly lead the world when it comes to pageantry!
. . . Prince Charles looked quite handsome in spite of his ears. His brother is dead good-looking; it's a shame they couldn't have swapped heads just for the day. Lady Diana melted my heartstrings in her dirty white dress. She even helped an old man up the aisle. I thought it was very kind of her considering it was her wedding day.

    Sue Townsend, *The Secret Diary of Adrian Mole Aged 13¾*, 1982

10 The kingly office is entitled to no respect. It was originally procured by highwayman's methods; it remains a perpetuated crime, can never be anything but the symbol of a crime. It is no more entitled to respect than is the flag of a pirate.

    Mark Twain, *Notebook*, 1935

11 Good kings are the only dangerous enemies that modern democracy has.

    Oscar Wilde, *Vera, or The Nihilists*, 1883

See also The Aristocracy; Class; The Ruling Class; Society; Queen Victoria.

RUGBY

1 His air was that of a man who has been passed through a wringer, and his eyes, what you could see of them, had a strange, smouldering gleam. He was so encrusted with alluvial deposits that one realized how little a mere bath would ever be able to effect. To fit him to take his place in polite society, he would certainly have to be sent to the cleaner's. Indeed, it was a moot point whether it wouldn't be simpler just to throw him away.

    P. G. Wodehouse, *Very Good, Jeeves*, 1930

2 Rugby football is a game I can't claim absolutely to understand in all its niceties, if you know what I mean. I can follow the broad, general principles, of course. I mean to say, I know that the main scheme is to work the ball down the field somehow and deposit it over the line at the other end, and that, in order to squelch this programme, each side is allowed to put in a certain amount of assault and battery and do things to its fellow-man which, if done elsewhere, would result in fourteen days without the option, coupled with some strong remarks from the Bench.

    P. G. Wodehouse, *Very Good, Jeeves*, 1930

See also Sport.

THE RULING CLASS

1 Political toleration is a by-product of the complacency of the ruling class. When that complacency is disturbed there never was a more bloody-minded set of thugs than the British ruling class.

    Michael Foot

2 There is no connection between the political ideas of our educated class and the deep places of the imagination.

    Lionel Trilling, *The Liberal Imagination*, 1950

See also The Aristocracy; Class; The Establishment; House of Lords; Royalty.

RUSSIA AND THE RUSSIANS

1 HILARY: One of the advantages of living in Russia is that it's one of the few places where smoking doesn't cause cancer. At least the authorities don't say it does, so one must presume it doesn't.

    Alan Bennett, *The Old Country*, 1978

2 I cannot forecast to you the action of Russia. It is a riddle wrapped in a mystery inside an enigma.
Winston Churchill, BBC Radio, 1939

3 In Russia they treated me like a Czar – and you know how they treated the Czar.
Bob Hope

4 I'm always thinking of Russia,
I can't keep her out of my head,
I don't give a damn for Uncle Sham,
I am a left-wing radical Red.
H. H. Lewis, *Thinking of Russia*, 1932

5 Ideas in modern Russia are machine-cut blocks coming in solid colors; the nuance is outlawed, the interval walled up, the curve grossly stepped.
Vladimir Nabokov, *Pale Fire*, 1962

6 *Racial characteristics*: brutish, dumpy, boorish lard-bags in cardboard double-breasted suits. Lickspittle slaveys to the maniacal schemes of their blood-lusting Red overlords. They make bicycles out of cement and can be sent to Siberia for listening to the wrong radio station.
P. J. O'Rourke, 'Foreigners Around the World', *National Lampoon*, 1976

7 The Soviet Union would remain a one-party nation even if an opposition party were permitted – because everyone would join that party.
Ronald Reagan, *Observer*, 1982

8 In the United States you have freedom of speech. You can go up to Ronald Reagan and say, 'I don't like Ronald Reagan.' In the Soviet Union you have the same thing. You can go up to Chernenko and say, 'I don't like Ronald Reagan.'
Yakov Smirnoff, Russian emigré comedian, quoted in *Newsweek*, 1984

9 There are no unemployed either in Russia or in Dartmoor jail, and for the same reason.
Philip Snowden, Labour politician, 1932

10 Q: What is a Russian string trio?
A: A Russian string quartet that has returned from the West.
David Steel, quoted in the *Observer*, 1984

See also Communism; Marxism; Socialism.

SAN FRANCISCO

1 When you get tired of walking around San Francisco, you can always lean against it.
'San Francisco', *Transworld Getaway Guide*, 1975–1976

2 San Francisco rock, San Francisco writing, it's always real lightweight, ephemeral stuff. Nothing *important* has ever come out of San Francisco, Rice-A-Roni aside.
Michael O'Donoghue, quoted in *Playboy*, 1983

3 My favorite city is San Francisco, because it's gay. They teach the kids in school: A C DC E F G . . .
Joan Rivers, *An Audience with Joan Rivers*, London Weekend Television, 1984

4 . . . the city that never was a town.
Will Rogers

5 The coldest winter I ever spent was a summer in San Francisco.
Mark Twain (Attrib.)

See also America and the Americans; California.

SATIRE

1 What arouses the indignation of the honest satirist is not, unless the man is a prig, the fact that people in positions of power or influence behave idiotically, or even that they behave wickedly. It is that they conspire successfully to impose upon the public a picture of themselves as so very sagacious, honest and well-intentioned. You cannot satirize a man who says, 'I'm in it for the money and that's all there is to it.'
Claud Cockburn, *Cockburn Sums Up*, 1981

2 FIRST SATIRIST: The kind of satire I prefer to do is the take-off on the little man . . . his troubles, his pet peeves . . . the little unnoticed bedevilments of life that may not give the audience a belly laugh, mind you, but will give them a smile of recognition. 'Yes – I'm like that,' they'll say. 'There I am. There you are. There we all are. Little Man. Peering off into the middle distance . . . there's my wife. There's my next door neighbor . . .'
SECOND SATIRIST: Together?
FIRST SATIRIST: Smut is *not* satire.
SECOND SATIRIST: Smut, dear sir, is our *only* satire.
Jules Feiffer, introduction, *Feiffer's Album*, 1963

See also Comedy; Humour; Laughter; The Sixties; Wit.

SAYINGS

1 If a thing's worth doing, it's worth doing badly.
G. K. Chesterton

2 A chrysanthemum by any other name would be easier to spell.
William J. Johnston, *Reader's Digest*

3 People who live in glass houses have to answer the bell.
Bruce Patterson

See also Epigrams; Maxims; Proverbs; Quotations.

SCANDALS

1 Scandal is merely the compassionate allowance which the gay make to the humdrum.
Saki (H. H. Munro), *Reginald at the Carlton*, 1904

2 One should never make one's *debut* with a scandal. One should reserve that to give an interest to one's old age.
Oscar Wilde, *The Picture of Dorian Gray*, 1891

See also Gossip; Sex.

SCHIZOPHRENIA

1 So I'm cured of schizophrenia – but where am I now that I need me?
   Graffito, New York, 1981

2 Two in every one people in this country are schizophrenic.
   Graffito, Exeter, 1985

3 You're never alone with schizophrenia.
   Badge, London, 1983

4 Roses are red,
   Violets are blue.
   I'm a schizophrenic
   And so am I.
   Billy Connolly

See also Insanity; Psychiatry; Psychoanalysis; Psychology.

SCHOOL

1 O vain futile frivolous boy. Smirking. I won't have it. I won't have it. I won't have it. Go find the headmaster and ask him to beat you within an inch of your life. And say please.
   Alan Bennett, *Forty Years On*, 1968

2 Headmasters have powers at their disposal with which Prime Ministers have never yet been invested.
   Winston Churchill, *My Early Life*, 1930

3 BOB: The first week I met you, five years of age, at Bygate Infants, you split my head open with a brick in the sandpit.
   TERRY: You stole my plasticine!
   BOB: No excuse for splitting one's head open with a brick!
   TERRY: See? You sulked about that all these years. Should have picked up the brick and hit me back. Instead of which you went home and told your mother.
   BOB: Of course I told me mother. What am I supposed to say when I go home after my first day at school with blood streaming down my new Aertex shirt – I cut myself shaving?
   Dick Clement and Ian La Frenais, 'Conduct Unbecoming', *The Likely Lads*, BBC TV

4 Stand firm in your refusal to remain conscious during algebra. In real life, I assure you, there is no such thing as algebra.
   Fran Lebowitz, *Social Studies*, 1981

5 School days, I believe, are the unhappiest in the whole span of human existence. They are full of dull, unintelligible tasks, new and unpleasant ordinances, brutal violations of common sense and common decency.
   H. L. Mencken, *The Baltimore Evening Sun*, 1928

6 ERNIE: They must have thought you were very clever at school.
   ERIC: They did. Every time the teacher asked a question, I was the first to put up my hand.
   ERNIE: That *was* clever.
   ERIC: You bet – by the time I got back, the question had been answered.
   Eric Morecambe and Ernie Wise, *The Morecambe and Wise Joke Book*, 1979

7 Show me the man who has enjoyed his schooldays and I will show you a bully and a bore.
   Robert Morley, *Robert Morley: Responsible Gentleman*, 1966

8 No one ever got a word of sense out of any schoolmaster. You may, at a pinch, take their word about equilateral hexagons but life, life's a closed book to them.
   John Mortimer, *A Voyage Round My Father*, screenplay, 1982

9 SKOOL FOOD
   Or the piece of cod which passeth understanding.
   Geoffrey Willans and Ronald Searle, 'Down With Skool!', *The Compleet Molesworth*, 1958

10 The job of masters is suposed to be to teach boys lessons e.g. geog lat fr. div hist bot. arith algy and geom.
   Actually most of them prefer BEER and PUBS. They are always late for brekfast not like keen alert boys who goble force poridge cereal with grate gusto and look scorn on masters pale yelow faces when they see a skool sossage. Then is the time to ask Would

you like some cream sir? or Gosh look at my egg sir its all runny. (Manners.)
Geoffrey Willans and Ronald Searle, 'Down With Skool!', *The Compleet Molesworth*, 1958

11 The Only good thing about skool are the BOYS wizz who are noble brave fearless etc. although you have various swots, bulies, cissies, milksops greedy guts and oiks with whom I am forced to mingle hem-hem. In fact any skool is a bit of a shambles.
Geoffrey Willans and Ronald Searle, 'Down With Skool!', *The Compleet Molesworth*, 1958

12 My school motto was '*Monsanto incorpori glorius maxima copia*' which in Latin means, 'When the going gets tough, the tough go shopping.'
Robin Williams, interview in *Playboy*, October 1982

13 ... the bearded bloke stepped to the footlights and started making a speech. From the fact that he spoke as if he had a hot potato in his mouth without getting a raspberry from the lads in the ringside seats, I deduced that he must be the headmaster.

With his arrival in the spotlight, a sort of perspiring resignation seemed to settle on the audience ... The speech was on the doings of the school during the past term, and this part of a prize-giving is always apt rather to fail to grip the visiting stranger.
P. G. Wodehouse, *Right Ho, Jeeves*, 1934

See also Childhood; Children; Examinations; Sex Education; Teachers.

SCIENCE AND SCIENTISTS

1 A drug is a substance that when injected into a guinea pig produces a scientific paper.
Anon.

2 Irreproducible research too often leads to great discoveries.
Journal of Irreproducible Results

3 Scientists discovered a link between silicon and melba toast. After fifteen years of exposure to air, silicon turns into melba toast, according to a group of University of California researchers. The findings caused panic among computer makers and other businesses that rely on the silicon chip. However, makers of processed-cheese spreads were elated at the news.
Off The Wall Street Journal, 1982

4 ... modern science was largely conceived of as an answer to the servant problem and ... is generally practiced by those who lack a flair for conversation.
Fran Lebowitz, *Metropolitan Life*, 1978

5 ... the further back one goes ... the science one does encounter is of a consistently higher quality. For example, in studying the science of yesteryear one comes upon such interesting notions as gravity, electricity, and the roundness of the earth – while an examination of more recent phenomena shows a strong trend toward spray cheese, stretch denim, and the Moog synthesizer.
Fran Lebowitz, *Metropolitan Life*, 1978

6 Scientists – a crowd that when it comes to style and dash makes the general public look like the Bloomsbury Set.
Fran Lebowitz, *Metropolitan Life*, 1978

7 Although this may seem a paradox, all exact science is dominated by the idea of approximation. When a man tells you that he knows the exact truth about anything, you are safe in inferring that he is an *inexact* man.
Bertrand Russell

See also Relativity; Vivisection.

SCOTLAND AND THE SCOTS

1 There are few more impressive sights in the world than a Scotsman on the make.
J. M. Barrie, *What Every Woman Knows*, 1908

2 One often yearns
For the land of Burns –
The only snag is
The haggis!
Lils Emslie, *Other People's Clerihews*, 1983

3 For the wife she used to ramble through
   me pooches
   When I was fast asleep aneath the quilt
   In the morning when I woke
   I was always stoney broke
   That's the reason noo I wear a kilt.
   Harry Lauder, 'That's the Reason Noo I
   Wear a Kilt', song, 1906

4 Is anything worn beneath the kilt?
   No, it's all in perfect working order!
   Spike Milligan, *The Great McGonagall
   Scrapbook*

5 SEAGOON: Who's this approaching
   wearing a transparent kilt?
   MACGOONIGAL: That is a special kilt
   designed for patriotic Scottish nudists.
   Spike Milligan, *The Goon Show*, BBC
   Radio, 1959

6 No McTavish
   Was ever lavish.
   Ogden Nash, 'Genealogical Reflection',
   Hard Lines, 1931

7 *Racial characteristics*: sour, stingy, depressing beggars who parade around in
   schoolgirls' skirts with nothing on underneath. Their fumbled attempt at speaking the English language has been a
   source of amusement for five centuries,
   and their idiot music has been dreaded
   by those not blessed with deafness for at
   least as long.
   P. J. O'Rourke, 'Foreigners Around the
   World', *National Lampoon*, 1976

8 It requires a surgical operation to get a
   joke well into a Scotch understanding.
   Sydney Smith, *Lady Holland's Memoir*,
   1855

9 It is never difficult to distinguish between
   a Scotsman with a grievance and a ray of
   sunshine.
   P. G. Wodehouse, *Blandings Castle and
   Elsewhere*, 1935

See also Britain and the British.

THE SEA

1 HILARY: Quite candidly, I've never seen
   the point of the sea. Except where it
   meets the land. The shore has point, the
   sea none.
   Alan Bennett, *The Old Country*, 1978

2 I'm Millie, a messy old mermaid,
   Out and about all the day,
   Combing my hair – what little is there –
   And just shouting my voice away.
   If I am a bit thin and p'raps minus a fin,
   It's a sin to suppose that I show it.
   What a failure I've been in the last forty
   years,
   Every sailor I've seen must have wool in
   his ears,
   If a whaler harpooned me I'd give him
   three cheers,
   I'm well on the rocks and I know it.
   Douglas Byng, 'Millie the Mermaid – A
   Lament', *Byng Ballads*

See also Fish and Fishing; Holidays; The
Navy; Ships; Swimming.

THE SEASONS

1 Winter is what people go south during.
   Anon.

2 First a howling blizzard woke us,
   Then the rain came down to soak us,
   And now before the eye can focus –
   Crocus.
   Lilja Rogers, *Reader's Digest*, 1964

3 Now is the winter of our discontent made
   glorious summer by central heating.
   Jack Sharkey, *Playboy*, 1965

4 The first day of spring was once the time
   for taking the young virgins into the
   fields, there in dalliance to set an example in fertility for Nature to follow. Now
   we just set the clock an hour ahead and
   change the oil in the crankcase.
   E. B. White, *One Man's Meat*, 1944

5 It's a sure sign of summer if the chair gets
   up when you do.
   Walter Winchell

SEDUCTION

1 Music helps set a romantic mood. Some
   men believe the only good music is live
   music. Imagine her surprise when you
   say, 'I don't need a stereo – I have an
   accordian!' Then imagine the sound of a
   door slamming.
   Martin Mull, *Playboy*, 1978

2 BUD: Cheers.
FRAN: Cheers.
BUD: You know what we're going to do after dinner?
FRAN: The dishes?
Billy Wilder and I. A. L. Diamond, *The Apartment*, screenplay, 1960

See also Courting; Flirtation; Petting; Romance; Sex; Sin.

SELF-DEFENCE

1 I can take care of myself. In case of danger I have this cutlass that I carry around with me . . . and in case of real emergency, I press the handle and it turns into a cane so I can get sympathy.
Woody Allen

2 I'm not a fighter, I have bad reflexes. I was once run over by a car being pushed by two guys.
Woody Allen

See also Fighting.

SELFISHNESS

1 'From now on I'm thinking only of me.'
Major Danby replied indulgently with a superior smile: 'But, Yossarian, suppose everyone felt that way.'
'Then,' said Yossarian, 'I'd certainly be a damn fool to feel any other way, wouldn't I?'
Joseph Heller, *Catch-22*, 1961

See also Opportunism.

SELLING

1 FIRST SALESMAN: I made some very valuable contacts today.
SECOND SALESMAN: I didn't get any orders either.
Anon.

2 *January cover*: If You Don't Buy This Magazine, We'll Kill This Dog.

February editorial page: Remember it? The dog that was going to be killed if you didn't buy the issue? You people are really incredible. You had us kill that sweet pooch. And don't for a minute go blaming us. We held the gun, but you sure as hell pulled the trigger . . . though there are those among you who did buy three or four issues to take up whatever slack existed. Those people are to be commended. But it wasn't enough. It was for everyone to pull his or her share. And you didn't.
National Lampoon, 1973

See also Consumers; Shopping.

THE SENATE

1 Draco wrote his laws in blood; the Senate writes its laws in wind.
Tom Connally

2 Office hours are from twelve to one with an hour off for lunch.
George S. Kaufman

See also Congress; Politics and Politicians; The Presidency; The Vice-Presidency; Washington.

SERVANTS

1 I know it's draggy having the au-pair feeding with us; but one has to be madly democratic if one wants to keep them.
Marc, *The Trendy Ape*, cartoon, 1968

2 Actually, I vote Labour – but my butler's a Tory.
Earl Mountbatten of Burma, to a Tory canvasser, 1945 (Attrib.)

3 Before the cleaning lady arrives, it is necessary to vacuum the entire house and straighten up all the rooms, because she works for friends of yours the other six days of the week and you don't want her to tell them how you really live . . .
. . . It is perfectly proper to ask your cleaning lady to iron, wash windows, polish silver, do the grocery shopping, and clean up after the dog. You can also ask her to jump through a flaming hoop with a cold leg of mutton in her mouth for all the good it will do you. She's going to dust a little, and that's it, no matter what.
P. J. O'Rourke, *Modern Manners*, 1983

4 The cook was a good cook, as cooks go; and as cooks go, she went.
Saki (H. H. Munro), *Reginald*, 1904

5 When domestic servants are treated as human beings, it is not worth while to keep them.
   George Bernard Shaw, *Maxims for Revolutionists*, 1903

6 CECILY: I am afraid that I disapprove of servants.
   CARR: You are quite right to do so. Most of them are without scruples.
   Tom Stoppard, *Travesties*, 1974

7 It has been my experience, sir, that no lady can ever forgive another lady for taking a really good cook away from her.
   P. G. Wodehouse, *Carry on, Jeeves*, 1925

8 My experience, sir, is that when the wife comes in at the front door the valet goes out at the back.
   P. G. Wodehouse, *Carry on, Jeeves*, 1925

See also Class.

THE SEVENTIES

1 Ten years ago wives were wives, rather than women, and 'affirmative action' was popping them right in the orthodontia when they stopped baking chocolate-chip cookies in their spare time and started screwing around.
   Now, however, it wasn't that simple. Wife-beating, in Marin in the seventies, was considered a crime against humanity second only to lighting a cigarette in a crowded elevator. Not only couldn't Harvey shake Kate until she lost her contact lenses; he couldn't even close her charge accounts.
   Cyra McFadden, *The Serial*, 1977

2 The seventies saw the spread of California culture (or 'life-style' as it came to be called), oozing from the canyons and condos of that state and slopping itself into the brainpans of previously rational and intelligent people.
   Many among us began applying the words 'therapy' and 'training' to every conceivable activity. And in fact much of the weirdness of the seventies was simply ordinary everyday activities raised to the level of great metaphysical significance.
   National Lampoon, 1980

See also The Fifties; The Sixties.

SEX

1 Sex is bad for one. But it's good for two.
   T-shirt, London, 1978

2 I believe that sex is a beautiful thing between two people. Between *five*, it's fantastic . . .
   Woody Allen, *The Nightclub Years, 1964–1968*, record, 1972

3 I finally had an orgasm . . . and my doctor told me it was the *wrong* kind.
   Woody Allen, *Manhattan*, screenplay, 1979

4 Is sex dirty? Only if it's done right.
   Woody Allen, *Everything You Always Wanted To Know About Sex*, screenplay, 1972

5 'Just put it this way, in my time I've been to bed with well over a hundred women.'
   Rosenberg had made some notes of the answers to all his questions until this last one, at which to Jake's distinct annoyance he merely nodded.
   Kingsley Amis, *Jake's Thing*, 1978

6 I've tried several varieties of sex. The conventional position makes me claustrophobic. And the others either give me a stiff neck or lockjaw.
   Tallulah Bankhead (Attrib.)

7 LADY RUMPERS: And then you took me.
   SIR PERCY: I took *you*? You took *me*. Your Land Army breeches came down with a fluency born of long practice.
   Alan Bennett, *Habeas Corpus*, 1973

8 WICKSTEED: What did he look like?
   LADY RUMPERS: As I say there was a black-out. I saw his face only in the fitful light of a post-coital Craven A.
   Alan Bennett, *Habeas Corpus*, 1973

9 There's a sexual revolution going on, and I think that with our current foreign policy, we'll probably be sending troops in there any minute to break it up.
   Mel Brooks (Attrib.)

10 We all know girls do it. But if you ask them to do it, they say no. Why? Because they want to be proper. Finally, after thirteen years of courtship and dates and

so on, one night they get drunk and they do it. And *after* they've done it, that's all they want to do. Now they're fallen, now they're disgraced, and all they want is to do it. You say, 'Let's have a cup of tea.' No, let's do it. 'Let's go to the cinema.' No, I'd rather do it.
Mel Brooks, quoted in *Time Out*, 1984

11 It doesn't matter what you do in the bedroom as long as you don't do it in the street and frighten the horses.
Mrs Patrick Campbell

12 The good thing about masturbation is that you don't have to dress up for it.
Truman Capote (Attrib.)

13 Sex is only the liquid centre of the great New Berry Fruit of friendship.
Jilly Cooper, *Super-Jilly*, 1977

14 What men desire is a virgin who is a whore.
Edward Dahlberg, *Reasons of the Heart*, 1965

15 At certain times I like sex – like after a cigarette.
Rodney Dangerfield

16 If it weren't for pickpockets, I'd have no sex life at all.
Rodney Dangerfield

17 He had ambitions, at one time, to become a sex maniac, but he failed his practical.
Les Dawson, *The Les Dawson Joke Book*, 1979

18 In the case of some women, orgasms take quite a bit of time. Before signing on with such a partner, make sure you are willing to lay aside, say, the month of June, with sandwiches having to be brought in.
Bruce Jay Friedman, 'Sex and the Lonely Guy', *Esquire*, 1977

19 One of the great breakthroughs in sex has been the discovery of all the new erogenous zones. Once it was thought there were only a handful. Now they are all over the place, with new ones being reported every day. Don't try to go at too many at once. If you do, they will cancel one another out, with some of the tra-

ditional old-line ones being neutralized. A sensitive partner can help by tapping you on the shoulder and saying, 'You are tackling too many erogenous zones.'
Bruce Jay Friedman, 'Sex and the Lonely Guy', *Esquire*, 1977

20 Seamed stockings aren't subtle but they certainly do the job. You shouldn't wear them when out with someone you're not prepared to sleep with, since their presence is tantamount to saying, 'Hi there, big fellow, please rip my clothes off at your earliest opportunity.' If you really want your escort paralytic with lust, stop frequently to adjust the seams.
Cynthia Heimel, *Sex Tips for Girls*, 1983

21 We, being modern and liberated and fully cognizant of women's sexual, intellectual, emotional and economic oppression, can never for a moment cease our vigilance against the imperialistic male supremacist. We must never relax our guard against his chauvinistic sexual fantasies.
So don't even for an instant consider keeping the following hidden in the back of your closet: a see-through nurse's uniform ... a cheerleader's costume ... a little black French maid's outfit ...
And if you do, don't tell anyone.
Cynthia Heimel, *Sex Tips for Girls*, 1983

22 Woody Allen was right when someone asked him if he thought sex was dirty and he said, 'If you do it right.' Sex is not some sort of pristine, reverent ritual. You want reverent and pristine, go to church.
Cynthia Heimel, *Sex Tips for Girls*, 1983

23 He moved his lips about her ears and neck as though in thirsting search of an erogenous zone. A waste of time, he knew from experience. Erogenous zones were either everywhere or nowhere.
Joseph Heller, *Good as Gold*, 1979

24 There was little she [Dori Duz] hadn't tried and less she wouldn't.
Joseph Heller, *Catch-22*, 1961

25 *Hospitals, to play*: to engage in congress, or to play cars and garages or hide the sausage.

Hots, to have the H's for: to be romantically attracted to.
Qantas hostie: a desirable sexual partner.
Barry Humphries, glossary from *Bazza Pulls It Off*

26 The zipless fuck is absolutely pure . . . and it is rarer than the unicorn.
Erica Jong, *Fear of Flying*, 1973

27 A woman occasionally is quite a serviceable substitute for masturbation. It takes an abundance of imagination, to be sure.
Karl Kraus

28 'Goodness, what beautiful diamonds.'
'Goodness had nothing to do with it, dearie.'
Vincent Laurence, *Night after Night*, screenplay (starring Mae West), 1932

29 'What, twins again, Mrs Lovejoy! Do you always have twins?'
'Oh no, Vicar! Lots of times we don't have anything at all!'
Donald McGill, seaside postcard, 1930s

30 My own belief is that there is hardly anyone whose sexual life, if it were broadcast, would not fill the world at large with surprise and horror.
W. Somerset Maugham

31 Sex is one of the nine reasons for re-incarnation . . . The other eight are unimportant.
Henry Miller, *Big Sur and the Oranges of Hieronymus Bosch*, 1957

32 I like the girls who do,
I like the girls who don't;
I hate the girl who says she will
And then she says she won't.
But the girl that I like best of all
And I think you'll say I'm right –
Is the one who says she never has
But looks as though she . . .
'Ere, listen . . .
Max Miller, *The Max Miller Blue Book*, 1975

33 . . . she said, 'Do you mind if I sit down, 'cos I'm pregnant?' I said, 'You don't look it. How long have you been pregnant?' She said, 'Only ten minutes – but doesn't it make you feel tired?'
Max Miller, *The Max Miller Blue Book*, 1975

34 There was a little girl
Who had a little curl
Right in the middle of her forehead.
When she was good, she was very, very good
And when she was bad, she was very, very popular.
Max Miller, *The Max Miller Blue Book*, 1975

35 The orgasm has replaced the Cross as the focus of longing and the image of fulfilment.
Malcolm Muggeridge, *The Most of Malcolm Muggeridge*

36 Sex – the poor man's polo.
Clifford Odets (Attrib.)

37 There are a number of mechanical devices which increase sexual arousal, particularly in women. Chief among these is the Mercedes-Benz 380SL convertible.
P. J. O'Rourke, *Modern Manners*, 1983

38 . . . there is no petting . . . Modern couples just strip their clothes off and go at it . . . blame must . . . be placed on ex-President Nixon's decision to let the US dollar float in relation to other Western currencies. More than a decade of monetary instability has conditioned people to utilize their assets immediately. If the sex urge is not spent forthwith, it might degenerate into something less valuable – affection, for instance.
P. J. O'Rourke, *Modern Manners*, 1983

39 If all the girls attending it were laid end to end, I wouldn't be at all surprised.
Dorothy Parker, of the Yale Prom

40 Familiarity breeds contempt – and children.
Mark Twain, *Notebook*, 1935

41 All this fuss about sleeping together. For physical pleasure I'd sooner go to my dentist any day.
Evelyn Waugh, *Vile Bodies*, 1930

42 To err is human – but it feels divine.
Mae West

43 'But what *is* the love-life of newts, if you boil it right down? Didn't you tell me

once that they just waggled their tails at each other in the mating-season?'

'Quite correct.'

'Well, all right if they like it. But it's not my idea of molten passion.'

P. G. Wodehouse, *The Code of the Woosters*, 1938

See also Birth Control; Bisexuality; Flirtation; Homosexuality; Kissing; Love; Orgies; Petting; Pregnancy; Promiscuity; Prostitution; Scandals; Seduction; Sex Education; Sexual Attraction; Sexual Perversions; Sin.

SEX EDUCATION

1 My father told me all about the birds and the bees. The liar – I went steady with a woodpecker till I was twenty-one.
   Bob Hope

2 All teaching in all subjects aims to stimulate interest. It would be odd if this were not true of sex lessons.
   Roger Probert, Birmingham headmaster, 1973

See also School; Sex.

SEXUAL ATTRACTION

1 Alcestis had exercised a mysterious attraction and then an unmysterious repulsion on two former husbands, the second of whom had to resort to fatal coronary disease to get away from her.
   Kingsley Amis, *Jake's Thing*, 1978

2 Such precepts are arguable, I know, but I've always gone along with the view that, first, the surest guarantee of sexual success is sexual success (you can't have one without the other and you can't have the other without the one), and, second, that the trappings of sexual success are only fleetingly distinguishable from sexual success itself.
   Martin Amis, *Success*, 1978

3 I am the world's sexiest man. Mr Burton and Mr Sinatra take second place to me in the sex-appeal stakes.

   Sex-appeal isn't just straight teeth, a square jaw and a solid torso. Look at me. I'm sixty-three and first thing in the morning I have a face like a woollen mat. And yet I am the most desirable man in the world. Indeed, if I put my mind to it I am sure I could pass the supreme test and lure Miss Taylor away from Mr Burton.
   Noël Coward (Attrib.)

4 I am going to hire a hit man and have that little wart rubbed out. I will not have him fouling this beautiful earth. Do you know what that little scum has done? He has wormed his way into my affections.
   Cynthia Heimel, 'LA Blues', *Playboy*, 1984

5 Those hot pants of hers were so damned tight, I could hardly breathe.
   Benny Hill, *The Benny Hill Show*, Thames TV, 1984

6 A girl whose cheeks are covered with paint
   Has an advantage with me over one
      whose ain't.
   Ogden Nash, 'Biological Reflection', *Hard Lines*, 1931

7 I have a big flaw in that I am attracted to thin, tall, good-looking men who have one common denominator. They must be lurking bastards.
   Edna O'Brien, 1979

8 . . . he's got – I don't mean to be – well, he looks like he's got a *cheese danish* stuffed in his *pants*!
   Tom Wolfe, *The Bonfire of the Vanities*, 1984

See also Flirtation; Infatuation; Kissing; Sex.

SEXUAL EQUALITY

1 A woman's place is in the House, and the Senate.
   Slogan on American T-shirt

2 LEE-ANN: No, you're wrong. You're emancipated. Not like me.
   FLORA: Oh yes. Twenty years of education, moral tuition, perseverance and honest toil, and we're all responsible women. Prepared to tackle the major problems of the age. Ready to meet our husbands right in the middle of the intellectual arena. So long as the Avon Lady

doesn't call, or we aren't too busy selling each other Tupperware for five per cent commission.
Malcolm Bradbury and Christopher Bigsby, *The After Dinner Game*, BBC TV, 1975

3 A country that can put men on the moon can put women in the Constitution.
Margaret Heckler

4 Women who insist on having the same options as men would do well to consider the option of being the strong, silent type.
Fran Lebowitz, *Metropolitan Life*, 1978

See also Equality; Feminism.

SEXUAL PERVERSIONS

1 An Argentine gaucho named Bruno
Once said, 'There is something I do know:
A woman is fine
And a sheep is divine,
But a llama is Numero Uno!'
Anon.

2 The Marquis de Sade and Genet
Are most highly thought of today,
But torture and treachery
Are not my sort of lechery,
So I've given my copies away.
W. H. Auden, *New York Review of Books*, 1966

3 I had to give up masochism – I was enjoying it too much . . .
Mel Calman, *Dr Calman's Dictionary of Psychoanalysis*, 1979

4 The uncertain and frenetic nature of modern life has led to the increasing popularity of mild bondage. When you're tied to the bed, at least you know where you're going to be for the next few minutes. And dominant partners enjoy the sense of having control over a situation, something they never get in real life. The dominant partner should show courtesy, however, and not abuse that position of control. It would be rude to get your sexual satisfaction by tying someone to bed and then leaving him or her there and going out with someone more attractive.
P. J. O'Rourke, *Modern Manners*, 1983

See also Sex.

WILLIAM SHAKESPEARE

1 I know not, sir, whether Bacon wrote the words of Shakespeare, but if he did not it seems to me he missed the opportunity of his life.
James Barrie, speech, 1925

2 The remarkable thing about Shakespeare is that he really is very good, in spite of all the people who say he is very good.
Robert Graves

3 Brush up your Shakespeare,
Start quoting him now,
Brush up your Shakespeare
And the women you will wow.
With the wife of the British embessida
Try a crack out of *Troilus and Cressida*,
If she says she won't buy it or tike it
Make her tike it, what's more, *As You Like It*.
If she says your behavior is heinous
Kick her right in the *Coriolanus*,
Brush up your Shakespeare
And they'll all kowtow.
Cole Porter, 'Brush Up Your Shakespeare', song, 1949

4 *Hamlet*
Prince Hamlet thought Uncle a traitor
For having it off with his Mater;
Revenge Dad or not?
That's the gist of the plot,
And he did – nine soliloquies later.
Stanley J. Sharpless, *New Statesman*

5 I don't know if you ever came across a play of Shakespeare's called *Macbeth*? If you did, you may remember this bird Macbeth bumps off another bird named Banquo and gives a big dinner to celebrate, and picture his embarrassment when about the first of the gay throng to turn up is Banquo's ghost, all merry and bright, covered in blood. It gave him a pretty nasty start, Shakespeare does not attempt to conceal.
P. G. Wodehouse, *Nothing Serious*, 1950

See also Acting; Actors and Actresses; Books; The English Language; Language; Literature; The Theatre; Writers; Writing.

SHIPS

1 The new nuclear submarine we have now is the best. It stays under water for two years and only comes up to the surface so the crew can re-enlist.
Dick Gregory, 1960

2 . . . a luxury liner is really just a bad play surrounded by water.
Clive James, *Unreliable Memoirs*, 1980

3 A ship is always referred to as 'she' because it costs so much to keep one in paint and powder.
Chester Nimitz, American admiral, speech, 1940

4 The Captain was on the bridge, pretty sure that he knew the way to New York but, just to be on the safe side, murmuring to himself, 'Turn right at Cherbourg, and then straight on.'
P. G. Wodehouse, *Plum Pie*, 1966

See also The Navy; The Sea; Travel.

SHOPPING

1 A safety check would reveal that there isn't a shopping cart that does not have all four wheels working. Unfortunately, all four are locked in stable directions. Three wheels want to shop and the fourth wants to go to the parking lot.
Erma Bombeck, *If Life is a Bowl of Cherries – What am I Doing in the Pits?*, 1978

See also Consumerism; Consumers; Selling.

SHOW BUSINESS

1 PERFORMING SEAL (*to another performing seal*): Of course, what I'd *really* like to do is direct.
Mort Gerberg, cartoon in the *New Yorker*

2 I do twenty minutes every time the refrigerator door opens and the light comes on.
Debbie Reynolds (Attrib.)

See also Acting; Actors and Actresses;

Ballet; Circus; Dance; Film; Music and Musicians; Songs and Singers; Television; The Theatre.

SILENCE

1 Drawing on my fine command of language, I said nothing.
Robert Benchley (Attrib.)

2 Silence is one of the hardest arguments to refute.
Josh Billings, *The Complete Works of Josh Billings*, 1919

3 Silence – that unbearable repartee.
G. K. Chesterton (Attrib.)

4 A man is known by the silence he keeps.
Oliver Herford

5 Never assume that habitual silence means ability in reserve.
Geoffrey Madan, *Twelve Reflections*, 1934

6 Silence – the most perfect expression of scorn.
George Bernard Shaw, *Back to Methuselah*, 1921

See also Ear; Noise.

SIN

1 Christ died for our sins. Dare we make his martyrdom meaningless by not committing them?
Jules Feiffer

2 Sin is a dangerous toy in the hands of the virtuous. It should be left to the congenitally sinful, who know when to play with it and when to let it alone.
H. L. Mencken, *The American Mercury*, 1929

3 Pleasure is something that you feel that you should really enjoy, which is really virtuous, but you don't; and sin's something that you're quite sure you shouldn't enjoy but do.
Ralph Wightman, *Any Questions*, BBC Radio, 1961

See also Evil; Religion; Sex; Temptation; Vice.

SINCERITY

1 It is dangerous to be sincere unless you are also stupid.
   George Bernard Shaw

2 A little sincerity is a dangerous thing, and a great deal of it is absolutely fatal.
   Oscar Wilde, 'The Critic as Artist', 1890

THE SIXTIES

1 The hippies have usurped the prerogatives of children – to dress up and be irresponsible.
   Anon., quoted in the *Atlantic Monthly*, 1967

2 Sexual intercourse began
   In nineteen sixty-three
   (Which was rather late for me) –
   Between the end of the *Chatterley* ban
   And the Beatles' first LP.
   Philip Larkin, 'Annus Mirabilis', *High Windows*, 1974

3 Fashions changed, changed again, changed faster and still faster: fashions in politics, in political style, in causes, in music, in popular culture, in myths, in education, in beauty, in heroes and idols, in attitudes, in responses, in work, in love and friendship, in food, in newspapers, in entertainment, in fashion. What had once lasted a generation now lasted a year, what had lasted a year lasted a month, a week, a day.
   Bernard Levin, *The Pendulum Years*, 1970

4 It was a credulous age, perhaps the most credulous ever, and the more rational, the less gullible, the decade claimed to be, the less rational, the more gullible, it showed itself. Never was it easier to gain a reputation as a seer, never was a following so rapidly and readily acquired. Teachers, prophets, sibyls, oracles, mystagogues, avatars, haruspices and mullahs roamed the land, gathering flocks about them as easily as holy men in nineteenth-century Russia, and any philosophy, from Zen Buddhism to macrobiotics and from violence as an end in itself to total inactivity as an end in *it*self, could be sure of a respectful hearing and a group of adherents, however temporary their adherence might prove.
   Bernard Levin, *The Pendulum Years*, 1970

5 We began to realize that behind every hip-head record company there lurks a giant oil concern. You can't avoid it. Every time you buy a record, you're offing a whale.
   Michael O'Donoghue, *Rolling Stone*, 1972

6 They'd go up to a table and tell people, 'Hello, I'm your waitress. How's your energy today? Our lunch special is the Gestalt Suchi – we give you a live fish, and you take the responsibility for killing it.'
   Robin Williams, interview in *Playboy*, 1982

See also The Beatles; The Fifties; The Rolling Stones; Satire.

SKIING

1 I went skiing last week and broke a leg. Fortunately, it wasn't mine.
   Anon.

2 There are two main forms of this sport: Alpine skiing and Nordic skiing. Alpine skiing involves a mountain and a $5,000 to $10,000 minimum investment, plus $300,000 for the condo in Aspen and however much you spend on drugs. It is a sport only a handful of people ever master, and those who do, do so at the expense of other skills like talking and writing their own name.
   National Lampoon, 1979

3 The sport of skiing consists of wearing three thousand dollars' worth of clothes and equipment and driving two hundred miles in the snow in order to stand around at a bar and get drunk.
   P. J. O'Rourke, *Modern Manners*, 1983

See also Sport; Travel.

SLEEP

1 Laugh and the world laughs with you, snore and you sleep alone.
   Anthony Burgess, *Inside Mr Enderby*, 1968

2 No civilized person goes to bed the same day he gets up.
   Richard Harding Davis

3 Late last night I slew my wife,
   Stretched her on the parquet flooring;
   I was loth to take her life,
   But I *had* to stop her snoring!
   Harry Graham, 'Necessity', *Ruthless Rhymes*, 1899

4 The amount of sleep required by the average person is about five minutes more.
   Max Kauffmann

5 You can't sleep until noon with the proper élan unless you have some legitimate reason for staying up until three (parties don't count).
   Jean Kerr, *Please Don't Eat the Daisies*, 1957

6 I love sleep because it is both pleasant and safe to use. Pleasant because one is in the best possible company and safe because sleep is the consummate protection against the unseemliness that is the invariable consequence of being awake. What you don't know won't hurt you. Sleep is death without the responsibility.
   Fran Lebowitz, *Metropolitan Life*, 1978

7 12.35 p.m. – The phone rings. I am not amused. This is not my favorite way to wake up. My favorite way to wake up is to have a certain French movie star whisper to me softly at two thirty in the afternoon that if I want to get to Sweden in time to pick up my Nobel Prize for Literature I had better ring for breakfast. This occurs rather less often than one might wish.
   Fran Lebowitz, *Metropolitan Life*, 1978

8 ERIC: You know, I heard something this morning that really opened my eyes.
   ERNIE: What was it?
   ERIC: An alarm clock!
   Eric Morecambe and Ernie Wise, *The Morecambe and Wise Joke Book*, 1979

9 I did not sleep. I never do when I am over-happy, over-unhappy, or in bed with a strange man.
   Edna O'Brien, *The Love Nest*, 1963

10 You can hit my father over the head with a chair and he won't wake up, but my mother, all you have to do to my mother is cough somewhere in Siberia and she'll hear you.
   J. D. Salinger, *The Catcher in the Rye*, 1951

11 Early to rise, early to bed, makes a man healthy, wealthy and dead.
   James Thurber, 'The Shrike and the Chipmunks', *Fables for Our Time*, 1951

12 There ain't no way to find out why a snorer can't hear himself snore.
   Mark Twain, *Tom Sawyer Abroad*, 1894

See also Bed; Dreams; Insomnia.

SMELLS

1 I did not realize what it had done to my breath – one doesn't with garlic – until this afternoon when I stood waiting for somebody to open a door for me and suddenly noticed that the varnish on the door was bubbling.
   Frank Muir, *You Can't Have Your Kayak and Heat It*, 1973

See also The Nose; Perfume.

SMILES

1 She gave me a smile I could feel in my hip pocket.
   Raymond Chandler, *Farewell, My Lovely*, 1940

2 'But I should like to come,' Miss Spence protested, throwing a rapid Gioconda at him.
   Aldous Huxley, *Mortal Coils*, 1922

3 He smiled, bunching his fat cheeks like twin rolls of smooth pink toilet paper.
   Nathaniel West, *Miss Lonelyhearts*, 1933

4 What magic there is in a girl's smile. It is the raisin which, dropped in the yeast of male complacency, induces fermentation.
   P. G. Wodehouse, *The Girl on the Boat*, 1922

See also Happiness; Laughter; Teeth.

SMOKING

1 As ye smoke, so shall ye reek.
   Anon., *Reader's Digest*, 1949

2 I read in the *Reader's Digest* that cigarettes are bad for you. So I had to give up reading the *Reader's Digest*.
   Anon.

3 They smoke cigarettes *professionally*. The smoke is inhaled very sharply and the teeth are bared. Then the head turns to give you a profile and the smoke is exhaled slowly and deliberately and the grey jet stream becomes a beautiful blue cloud of smoke. What are they trying to tell us?
   Jeffrey Bernard, *Spectator*, 1982

4 I never smoked a cigarette until I was nine.
   W. C. Fields (Attrib.)

5 Tobacco is a dirty weed. I like it,
   It satisfies no normal need. I like it,
   It makes you thin, it makes you lean,
   It takes the hair right off your bean
   It's the worst darn stuff I've ever seen.
   I like it.
   Graham Lee Hemminger, 'Tobacco', *Penn State Froth*, 1915

6 Smoking is, if not my life, then at least my hobby. I love to smoke. Smoking is fun. Smoking is cool. Smoking is, as far as I am concerned, the entire point of being an adult.
   Fran Lebowitz, *Social Studies*, 1981

7 Smoking is very bad for you and should only be done because it looks so good. People who don't smoke have a terrible time finding something polite to do with their lips.
   P. J. O'Rourke, *Modern Manners*, 1983

8 Usually we trust that nature has a master plan. But what was it she expected us to do with tobacco?
   Bill Vaughan

9 A cigarette is the perfect type of a perfect pleasure. It is exquisite and it leaves one unsatisfied.
   Oscar Wilde, *The Picture of Dorian Gray*, 1891

10 LADY BRACKNELL: . . . Do you smoke?
   JACK: Well, yes, I must admit I smoke.
   LADY BRACKNELL: I am glad to hear it.

A man should always have an occupation of some kind. There are far too many idle men in London as it is.
   Oscar Wilde, *The Importance of Being Earnest*, 1895

11 Mr Howard Saxby, literary agent, was knitting a sock. He knitted a good deal, he would tell you if you asked him, to keep himself from smoking, adding that he also smoked a good deal to keep himself from knitting.
   P. G. Wodehouse, *Cocktail Time*, 1958

See also Drugs.

SNEEZING

1 Florence felt the swift on-coming of a sneeze. She fumbled in her bag for a handkerchief, and rattled richly among the nine coppers. Several violent explosions followed, and when the spasm subsided, she found her father spraying the air round him with his flask of disinfectant.
   'Perhaps it would be wiser if you sat a little further off,' he said.
   E. F. Benson, *Paying Guests*, 1929

See also The Nose.

SNOBBERY

1 FIRST LADY: Breeding isn't everything, is it?
   SECOND LADY: No, but it's lots of fun.
   Joey Adams

2 Auntie Muriel is unambiguous about most things. Her few moments of hesitation have to do with the members of her own family. She isn't sure where they fit into the Great Chain of Being. She's quite certain of her own place, however. First comes God. Then comes Auntie Muriel and the Queen, with Auntie Muriel having a slight edge.
   Margaret Atwood, *Life Before Man*, 1979

3 She [his aunt] was a bit of a social climber – although very much on the lower slopes. I was once on a tram with her going past the gas works in Wellington Road and she said, 'Alan, this is the

biggest gas works in England. And *I* know the manager.'
Alan Bennett, *The South Bank Show*, London Weekend Television, 1984

4 And there is . . . that rich man in Chelsea who is so snobbish that he will not even drive in the same car as his chauffeur.
David Frost and Antony Jay, *To England with Love*, 1967

5 . . . the idiot who praises, with
   enthusiastic tone,
All centuries but this, and every country but his own.
W. S. Gilbert and Arthur Sullivan, *The Mikado*, 1885

6 A certain amount of judicious snobbery is quite a good thing, besides being amusing.
A. L. Rowse

7 He found it very difficult to admit that there were any Royalties whom he did not know personally. The nearest he ever came to it was in saying of the King of Saxony: 'I knew him very well – by sight.'
Bertrand Russell, *Portraits from Memory*, 1956

See also Haughtiness; Society.

SOCCER

1 . . . he became, if not a master, then an aspiring student of the synonym. On his great days he could avoid using the precise word throughout the duration of a report. He was a man of his time: he never in his life referred to a match as a 'clash'; and only rarely as a 'match'; it was a 'derby', 'duel', 'contest', 'tourney', 'battle', 'renewal of hostilities', 'struggle' ('epic', or, at best, 'titanic'). It was almost unknown for one of his players to shoot or head a goal. They 'drove home', 'converted', 'nodded', 'equalized', 'netted', 'notched', 'reduced the leeway', 'increased their advantage', 'applied the finishing touch' or 'left the custodian helpless'.
John Arlott, 'Football Phrases from Regnar's Thesaurus', *Guardian*, 1972

2 He had a special set of phrases for Christmas Day matches. 'The opposing leader set the sphere a-rolling (it was simply rolling in non-holiday matches) in a seasonable snowstorm.' Occasionally he would note that 'the holiday spirit was much in evidence', or in more extreme circumstances that 'a few spectators, alas, had celebrated not wisely, but too well'.
   If the referee seemed harsh on Rangers, 'the arbiter showed little seasonal good will towards the homesters': if he gave a penalty to the other side, 'the official proved a veritable Father Christmas to the visitors'. The scorer of a goal had 'earned his slice of chicken'.
John Arlott, 'Football Phrases from Regnar's Thesaurus', *Guardian*, 1972

3 The centre forward said, 'It was an open goal – but I put it straight over the crossbar! I could kick myself!' And the manager said, 'I wouldn't bother, you'd probably miss!'
David Frost, *TVam*, 1984

4 [Italian defender] Tardelli's been responsible for more scar tissue than the surgeons of Harefield hospital.
Jimmy Greaves, ITV World Cup Panel, 1982

5 Look, if you're in the penalty area and aren't quite sure what to do with the ball, just stick it in the net and we'll discuss all your options afterwards.
Bill Shankly, soccer manager, to player (Attrib.)

6 Some people think football is a matter of life and death . . . I can assure you it is much more serious than that.
Bill Shankly, 1973

7 Maybe Napoleon was wrong when he said we were a nation of shopkeepers . . . Today England looked like a nation of goalkeepers . . .
Tom Stoppard, *Professional Foul*, BBC TV, 1977

8 Football is all very well as a game for rough girls, but it is hardly suitable for delicate boys.
Oscar Wilde (Attrib.)

9 I said, 'What is the matter with you Tom, what's the trouble?' He said, 'I've got a bad back,' so I told him, I said, 'There's no need to worry about that – our team's got two.'
   Robb Wilton, *BBC Light Programme*, 1952

See also Sport.

SOCIALISM

1 'Rabbi, can one build socialism in one country?'
   'Yes, my son, but one must live in another.'
   Anon., quoted in the *Spectator*, 1984

2 HECKLER: What about the workers' wages?
   CANDIDATE: When my party comes to power, workers' wages will be doubled!
   HECKLER: And what about the whores and tarts who defile our streets?
   CANDIDATE: My friend, when my party comes to power they will be driven underground.
   HECKLER: There you go again. Favouring the bloody miners!
   Ian Aitken, *Guardian*

3 GEORGE: Fabled names in the annals of the New Left. All with monosyllabic names . . . Stan, Mike, Les, Norm. As if to have two syllables in one's name were an indication of social pretension.
   Alan Bennett, *Getting On*, 1971

4 The function of socialism is to raise suffering to a higher level.
   Norman Mailer

5 As far as Socialism means anything, it must be about the wider distribution of smoked salmon and caviar.
   Sir Richard Marsh, former Labour Cabinet Minister, quoted in the *Observer*, 1976

6 As with the Christian religion, the worst advertisement for Socialism is its adherents.
   George Orwell, *The Road to Wigan Pier*, 1937

7 The typical Socialist . . . a prim little man with a white-collar job, usually a secret teetotaller and often with vegetarian leanings.
   George Orwell, *The Road to Wigan Pier*, 1937

8 We should have had socialism already, but for the socialists.
   George Bernard Shaw (Attrib.)

9 Many people consider the things which government does for them as social progress, but they consider the things government does for others as socialism.
   Earl Warren

10 At one time Socialism might have been a good idea. Its inspiration, in those days, was generous and humane. Nowadays, it can appeal only to those whose social maladjustment might otherwise push them into the criminal classes, or whose intellectual inadequacies make them hungry for a dogmatic system in which they can hide their inability to think for themselves.
   Auberon Waugh, *Spectator*, 1984

11 We'll find it very difficult to explain to the voters that simply by taking over Marks & Spencer we can make it as efficient as the Co-op.
   Harold Wilson, 1973

See also Communism; Equality; The Labour Party; Marxism; Trades Unions.

SOCIETY

1 So You Want to Be a Social Climber?
   Of all the occupations dealt with here, this is undoubtedly the easiest to crack. It is also, alas, the hardest to stomach – a fact that seems to have had surprisingly little effect upon the hordes that crowd the field.
   Fran Lebowitz, *Metropolitan Life*, 1978

2 Dear Miss Manners,
   If you had a single piece of advice to offer a couple who want to break into society, what would it be?

   Gentle Reader,
   Don't bother.
   Judith Martin, *Miss Manners' Guide to Excruciatingly Correct Behaviour*, 1982

3 I love London Society! I think it has immensely improved. It is entirely composed now of beautiful idiots and brilliant lunatics. Just what Society should be.
   Oscar Wilde, *An Ideal Husband*, 1895

4 High society is for those who have stopped working and no longer have anything important to do.
   Woodrow Wilson

5 I sat next to the Duchess at tea;
   It was just as I feared it would be:
   Her rumblings abdominal
   Were truly phenomenal,
   And everyone thought it was me!
   Woodrow Wilson

See also The Aristocracy; Parties.

SOCIOLOGY

1 *The Good Samaritan for Sociologists*
   A man was attacked and left bleeding in a ditch. Two sociologists passed by and one said to the other, 'We must find the man who did this – he needs help.'
   Anon.

2 ... the science with the greatest number of methods and the least results.
   J. H. Poincaré, French scientist and mathematician

SONGS AND SINGERS

1 I studied all the rhymes that all the
      lovers sing;
   Then just for you I wrote this little
      thing.
   Blah, blah, blah, blah moon,
   Blah, blah, blah above;
   Blah, blah, blah, blah croon,
   Blah, blah, blah, blah love.
   Tra la la la, tra la la la la, merry month
      of May;
   Tra la la la, tra la la la la, 'neath the
      clouds of gray.
   Blah, blah, blah your hair,
   Blah, blah, blah your eyes;
   Blah, blah, blah, blah care,
   Blah, blah, blah, blah skies.
   Tra la la la, tra la la la la, cottage for two,

Blah, blah, blah, blah, blah, darling with
   you.
   Ira Gershwin, 'Blah, Blah, Blah', song from *Delicious*, 1931

2 I can hold a note as long as the Chase National Bank.
   Ethel Merman

3 Once in every lifetime a really beautiful song comes along ... Until it does, I'd like to do this one.
   Cliff Richard, stage act, 1983

See also Folk Songs; Jazz; Music and Musicians; Opera; Rock 'n' Roll; The Theatre.

SOUTH AFRICA

1 South Africa is developing a nubitron. The nuclear device, still in its earliest stages of development, would destroy non-whites, while leaving property and Caucasians unharmed. The nubitron would be used for peaceful purposes, diplomats said in Pretoria.
   Off The Wall Street Journal, 1982

SPACE

1 Space ... is big. Really big. You just won't believe how vastly hugely mind-bogglingly big it is. I mean, you may think it's a long way down the road to the chemist, but that's just peanuts to space.
   Douglas Adams, *The Hitch-hiker's Guide to the Galaxy*, 1979

2 Space isn't remote at all. It's only an hour's drive away if your car could go straight upwards.
   Sir Fred Hoyle, *Observer*, 1979

See also The Future; Travel.

SPAIN AND THE SPANIARDS

1 ERNIE: Didn't you know any Spanish?
   ERIC: I knew two words and they reckon that's all you need to know for honeymooning in Spain.
   ERNIE: And what are they?
   ERIC: 'Manana' – that means 'Tomor-

row'. And 'Pyjama' – that means 'Tonight'.

Eric Morecambe and Ernie Wise, *The Morecambe and Wise Joke Book,* 1979

SPEAKERS AND SPEECHES

1 An after-dinner speech should be like a lady's dress: long enough to cover the subject and short enough to be interesting.
Anon.

2 He's a man who is never lost for a few appropriated words.
Anon.

3 Speeches are like steer horns – a point here, a point there and a lot of bull in between.
Liberty

4 I stand up when he nudges me. I sit down when they pull my coat.
Ernest Bevin, Labour politician

5 I do not object to people looking at their watches when I am speaking – but I strongly object when they start shaking them to make certain they are still going.
Lord Birkett, MP and lawyer (Attrib.)

6 Some microphones work great as long as you blow into them. So you stand there like an idiot blowing and saying, 'Are we on? Can you hear me?' Everyone admits they can hear you blowing. It's only when you speak the microphone goes dead.
Erma Bombeck, *If Life is a Bowl of Cherries – What am I Doing in the Pits?,* 1978

7 A heavy and cautious responsibility of speech is the easiest thing in the world: anybody can do it. That is why so many tired, elderly and wealthy men go in for politics.
G. K. Chesterton (Attrib.)

8 Desperately accustomed as I am to public speaking.
Noël Coward, opening charity bazaar at Oxford (Attrib.)

9 Spontaneous speeches arc seldom worth the paper they are written on.
Leslie Henson, quoted in the *Observer,* 1943

10 The toastmaster introduced the speaker with great fervor, stressing her years of faithful service to the club and eulogizing her ability and charm. Somewhat overwhelmed, the speaker faced the audience. 'After such an introduction,' she said disarmingly, 'I can hardly wait to hear what I've got to say.'
Adnelle H. Heskett, *Reader's Digest*

11 I wasn't allowed to speak while my husband was alive, and since he's gone no one has been able to shut me up.
Hedda Hopper, *From under Your Hat,* 1952

12 Why don't th' feller who says, 'I'm not a speechmaker,' let it go at that instead o' givin' a demonstration.
Kin Hubbard

13 A toastmaster is a man who eats a meal he doesn't want so he can get up and tell a lot of stories he doesn't remember to people who've already heard them.
George Jessel

14 The human brain starts working the moment you are born and never stops until you stand up to speak in public.
Sir George Jessel, industrialist and Justice of the Peace

15 When audiences come to see us authors lecture, it is largely in the hope that we'll be funnier to look at than to read.
Sinclair Lewis

16 A speech is like a love affair. Any fool can start it, but to end it requires considerable skill.
Lord Mancroft

17 A speaker who does not strike oil in ten minutes should stop boring.
Louis Nizer

18 Speeches are like babies – easy to conceive but hard to deliver.
Pat O'Malley

19 He can take a batch of words and scramble them together and leaven them properly with a hunk of oratory and knock the White House doorknob right out of a candidate's hand.
Will Rogers, on William Jennings Bryan

20 I am the most spontaneous speaker in the world because every word, every gesture, and every retort has been carefully rehearsed.
  George Bernard Shaw

21 The last time I was in this hall was when my late beloved boss, Frank Knox, the Secretary of the Navy, spoke here, and it was a better speech he gave than the one I'll be giving tonight. I know. I wrote them both.
  Adlai Stevenson

22 It usually takes me more than three weeks to prepare a good impromptu speech.
  Mark Twain

23 I like the way you always manage to state the obvious with a sense of real discovery.
  Gore Vidal, *The Best Man*, 1960

24 I always said Little Truman [Capote] had a voice so high it could only be detected by a bat.
  Tennessee Williams (Attrib.)

25 It just shows, what any member of Parliament will tell you, that if you want real oratory, the preliminary noggin is essential. Unless pie-eyed, you cannot hope to grip.
  P. G. Wodehouse, *Right Ho, Jeeves*, 1934

See also Audiences; Hecklers; Pronunciation; Voices.

SPECTACLES

1 Men seldom make passes
  At girls who wear glasses.
  Dorothy Parker, 'News Item', 1927

See also Eyes.

SPOONERISMS

1 Kinquering Congs their titles take.

You have deliberately tasted two worms and you can leave Oxford by the town drain.

Yes, indeed; the Lord is a shoving leopard.

We all know what it is to have a half-warmed fish within us.
  Rev. W. A. Spooner, Warden of New College, Oxford (mostly apocryphal)

SPORT

1 When it comes to sports I am not particularly interested. Generally speaking, I look upon them as dangerous and tiring activities performed by people with whom I share nothing except the right to trial by jury.
  Fran Lebowitz, *Metropolitan Life*, 1978

2 I hate sports as rabidly as a person who likes sports hates common sense.
  H. L. Mencken

3 ERNIE: Excuse me, won't you – I'm a little stiff from badminton.
  ERIC: It doesn't matter where you're from.
  Eric Morecambe and Ernie Wise, *The Morecambe and Wise Joke Book*, 1979

4 Serious sport has nothing to do with fair play. It is bound up with hatred, jealousy, boastfulness, disregard of all rules and sadistic pleasure in witnessing violence: in other words it is war minus the shooting.
  George Orwell, 'The Sporting Spirit', 1945

5 They thought lacrosse was what you find in la church.
  Robin Williams, interview in *Playboy*, 1982

See also Cricket; Soccer; Tennis.

STANDARDS

1 FRANKLIN: Have you ever thought, Headmaster, that your standards might perhaps be a little out of date?
  HEADMASTER: Of course they're out of date. Standards always are out of date. That is what makes them standards.
  Alan Bennett, *Forty Years On*, 1968

See also Morality; Virtue.

STATUS

1 This is my executive suite and this is my executive vice-president, Ralph

Anderson, and my executive secretary, Adele Eades, and my executive desk and my executive carpet and my executive wastebasket and my executive ashtray and my executive pen set and my . . .
Henry Martin, cartoon in the *New Yorker*

See also Class.

STRENGTH

1 I can lick my weight in wildflowers.
W. C. Fields (Attrib.)

See also The Body; Exercise.

STUPIDITY

1 GEORGE: Gracie, let me ask you something. Did the nurse ever happen to drop you on your head when you were a baby?
GRACIE: Oh, no, we couldn't afford a nurse, my mother had to do it.
GEORGE: You had a smart mother.
GRACIE: Smartness runs in my family. When I went to school I was so smart my teacher was in my class for five years.
George Burns and Gracie Allen, stage routine, 1920s

2 GROUCHO MARX: . . . you've got the brain of a four-year-old boy, and I bet he was glad to get rid of it.
S. J. Perelman and others, *Horsefeathers*, screenplay, 1932

3 . . . she does not understand the concept of Roman numerals. She thought we just fought World War Eleven.
Joan Rivers, *An Audience with Joan Rivers*, London Weekend Television, 1984

4 James's uncle had just about enough brain to make a jay-bird fly crooked.
P. G. Wodehouse, 'The Man Upstairs', 1914

5 Veronica Wedge was a girl of a radiant blonde loveliness. Nature had not given her more than about as much brain as would fit comfortably into an aspirin bottle, feeling no doubt that it was better not to overdo the thing, but apart from that she had everything.
P. G. Wodehouse, *Galahad at Blandings*, 1965

See also Ignorance.

STYLE

1 Style is knowing who you are, what you want to say, and not giving a damn.
Gore Vidal, *Daily Express*, 1973

2 In matters of grave importance, style, not sincerity, is the vital thing.
Oscar Wilde, *The Importance of Being Earnest*, 1895

See also Clothes; Fashion; Looks; Taste.

THE SUBURBS

1 With four walk-in closets to walk in,
Three bushes, two shrubs, and one tree,
The suburbs are good for the children,
But no place for grown-ups to be.
Judith Viorst, *It's Hard to be Hip over Thirty . . .* , 1968

SUCCESS

1 Behind every successful man there stands an amazed woman.
Anon.

2 The penalty of success is to be bored by the people who used to snub you.
Nancy Astor

3 I don't think the state does enough for artists and writers generally in the way of subsidy and tax relief and so on. I mean, as an artist and a writer, I have to be surrounded by beautiful things and beautiful people. And beautiful people cost money.
Alan Bennett, 'The Lonely Pursuit', *On the Margin*, BBC TV, 1966

4 It is difficult to make a reputation, but it is even more difficult seriously to mar a reputation once properly made – so faithful is the public.
Arnold Bennett

5 If at first you don't succeed, try, try again. Then quit. No use being a damn fool about it.
W. C. Fields (Attrib.)

6 Gold no longer pretended to understand the nature of success. Instead, he pre-

tended not to. He knew the components that were necessary: none.

Or maybe one: dumb luck.
Joseph Heller, *Good as Gold*, 1979

7 There's no secret about success. Did you ever know a successful man that didn't tell you all about it.
Kin Hubbard, *Abe Martin's Primer*, 1914

8 Nothing succeeds like reputation.
John Huston

9 Success didn't spoil me; I've always been insufferable.
Fran Lebowitz

10 The worst part of having success is to try finding someone who is happy for you.
Bette Midler (Attrib.)

11 The secret of success is to offend the greatest number of people.
George Bernard Shaw (Attrib.)

12 It is fatal to be appreciated in one's own time.
Osbert Sitwell, quoted in the *Observer*, 1924

13 All you need in this life is ignorance and confidence, and then success is sure.
Mark Twain (Attrib.)

14 Failure is very difficult for a writer to bear, but very few can manage the shock of early success.
Maurice Valency

15 The usual drawback to success is that it annoys one's friends so.
P. G. Wodehouse, 'The Man Upstairs', 1914

See also Achievement; Failure; Winning.

SUICIDE

1 There are many who dare not kill themselves for fear of what the neighbours will say.
Cyril Connolly, *The Unquiet Grave*, 1944

2 Cliffy the Clown says: You can help solve the OVERPOPULATION PROBLEM this quick, easy way! THIS YEAR, WHY NOT COMMIT SUICIDE!? . . . Just leave a note telling your loved ones that you did it to help stave off worldwide famine and they will respect and admire you for your courage . . .
Robert Crumb, *Zap: The Original Zap Comix*, No. 6, 1973

3 Suicide is belated acquiescence in the opinion of one's wife's relatives.
H. L. Mencken, *A Mencken Chrestomathy*, 1949

4 I know a hundred ways to die.
I've often thought I'd try one:
Lie down beneath a motor truck
Some day when standing by one.
Or throw myself from off a bridge –
Except such things must be
So hard upon the scavengers
And men that clean the sea.
I know some poison I could drink,
I've often thought I'd taste it.
But mother bought it for the sink,
And drinking it would waste it.
Edna St Vincent Millay, *From a Very Little Sphinx*, 1929

5 The thought of suicide is a great consolation: by means of it one gets successfully through many a bad night.
Friedrich Wilhelm Nietzsche, *Beyond Good and Evil*, 1886

6 Guns are always the best method for a private suicide. They are more stylish looking than single-edged razor blades and natural gas has gotten so expensive. Drugs are too chancy. You might miscalculate the dosage and just have a good time.
P. J. O'Rourke, *Modern Manners*, 1983

7 Razors pain you;
Rivers are damp;
Acids stain you;
And drugs cause cramp.
Guns aren't lawful;
Nooses give;
Gas smells awful;
You might as well live.
Dorothy Parker, 'Résumé', *Enough Rope*, 1926

See also Death; Despair.

SUPERSTITION

1 DUD: It's very unlucky to put the sugar in before the milk, didn't you know that? . . . it has terrible effects on your life . . . My Aunt Dolly put the sugar in before the milk one day and over the next forty years she lost all her teeth.
Peter Cook and Dudley Moore, *The Dagenham Dialogues*, 1971

See also Astrology; The Occult.

SURPRISE

1 . . . Aunt Agatha, whose demeanour was now rather like that of one who, picking daisies on the railway, has just caught the down express in the small of the back.
P. G. Wodehouse, 'Aunt Agatha Takes the Count', *The Inimitable Jeeves*, 1923

2 I don't know if you have ever leaped between the sheets, all ready for a spot of sleep, and received an unforeseen lizard up the left pyjama leg? It's an experience which puts its stamp on a man.
P. G. Wodehouse, *Thank You, Jeeves*, 1934

SURVIVAL

1 He had decided to live forever or die in the attempt, and his only mission each time he went up was to come down alive.
Joseph Heller, *Catch-22*, 1961

SWEARING

1 *Madame Bovary* is the sexiest book imaginable. The woman's virtually a nymphomaniac but you won't find a vulgar word in the entire thing.
Noël Coward (Attrib.)

2 Swearing was invented as a compromise between running away and fighting.
Finley Peter Dunne

3 *Heck on Earth*. Heck is a place where God sends people when they say things like 'Aw, shoot' instead of 'shit'. Visionaries see it as a warm cloakroom, or perhaps a bus terminal at 3:00 a.m. in August.
Michael McCormick, P. J. O'Rourke and Michael Civitello, 'Sin Sundries', *National Lampoon*, 1981

See also The English Language; Language; Obscenity; Vulgarity.

SWEDEN AND THE SWEDES

1 *Racial characteristics*: tedious, clean-living boy scout types, strangers to graffiti and littering but who are possessed of an odd suicidal mania. Speculation is that they're slowly boring themselves to death. This is certainly the case if their cars and movies are any indication.
P. J. O'Rourke, 'Foreigners Around the World', *National Lampoon*, 1976

2 First impressions of Stockholm Paradise, second Limbo. Girls very pretty and not disfigured by paint and hairdressing. All look sexually and socially satisfied.
Evelyn Waugh, *Diary*, 1947

See also Europe and the EEC.

SWIMMING

1 GREENSLADE: Ten miles he swam – the last three were agony.
SEAGOON: They were over land. Finally I fell in a heap on the ground. I've no idea who left it there.
Spike Milligan, *The Goon Show*, 1954

See also The Sea; Sport.

SWITZERLAND AND THE SWISS

1 *Racial characteristics*: mountain Jews in whose icy clutches lay the fruits of grave misdeeds committed in every clime.
P. J. O'Rourke, 'Foreigners Around the World', *National Lampoon*, 1976

2 In Switzerland they had brotherly love, five hundred years of democracy and peace, and what did they produce? The cuckoo clock.
Graham Greene and Orson Welles, *The Third Man*, screenplay, 1949

3 The only nation I've ever been tempted to feel really racist about are the Swiss – a whole country of phobic handwashers living in a giant Barclays Bank.
Jonathan Raban, *Arabia through the Looking Glass*, 1979

4 . . . the train passed fruit farms and clean villages and Swiss cycling in kerchiefs, calendar scenes that you admire for a moment before feeling an urge to move on to a new month.
  Paul Theroux, *The Great Railway Bazaar*, 1975

5 Switzerland is simply a large, humpy, solid rock, with a thin skin of grass stretched over it.
  Mark Twain, 'A Tramp Abroad', 1880

See also Europe and the E.E.C.

SYMPATHY

1 To be sympathetic without discrimination is so very debilitating.
  Ronald Firbank, *Vainglory*, 1915

2 When you are in trouble, people who call to sympathize are really looking for the particulars.
  Edgar Watson Howe, *Country Town Sayings*, 1911

See also Adversity.

TALENT

1 I think this is the most extraordinary collection of talent, of human knowledge, that has ever been gathered together at the White House – with the possible exception of when Thomas Jefferson dined alone.
   John F. Kennedy, at White House dinner honouring Nobel Prize winners, 1962

See also Genius.

TASTE

1 Good taste is better than bad taste, but bad taste is better than no taste.
   Arnold Bennett, quoted in the *Observer*, 1930

2 Your right to wear a mint-green polyester leisure suit ends where it meets my eye.
   Fran Lebowitz, *Metropolitan Life*, 1978

3 MRS ALLONBY: The Ideal Man ... should never run down other pretty women. That would show he had no taste or make one suspect that he had too much.
   Oscar Wilde, *A Woman of No Importance*, 1893

See also Appearance; Fashion; Looks; Style.

TATTOOS

1 On the chest of a barmaid in Sale
   Were tattooed the prices of ale,
   And on her behind,
   For the sake of the blind,
   Was the same information in Braille.
   Anon.

2 I attribute my whole success in life to a rigid observance of the fundamental rule – never have yourself tattooed with any woman's name, not even her initials.
   P. G. Wodehouse, *French Leave*, 1956

See also The Body.

TAXATION

1 I believe we should all pay our tax bill with a smile. I tried – but they wanted cash.
   Anon.

2 TAXMAN: The position is that if I don't have one thousand pounds from you soon, you're going to jail.
   BUSINESSMAN: Now you're talking. Here's one thousand pounds in used notes.
   TAXMAN: Let me give you a receipt.
   BUSINESSMAN: What, a thousand nicker in cash and you're going to put it through the books?
   Guardian

3 Why does a slight tax increase cost you two hundred dollars and a substantial tax cut save you thirty cents?
   Peg Bracken

4 Any reasonable system of taxation should be based on the slogan of 'Soak the Rich'.
   Heywood Broun

5 I have always paid income tax. I object only when it reaches a stage when I am threatened with having nothing left for my old age – which is due to start next Tuesday or Wednesday.
   Noël Coward (Attrib.)

6 The income tax has made more liars out of the American people than golf has.
   Will Rogers (Attrib.)

7 Taxes, after all, are the dues that we pay for the privileges of membership in an organized society.
   Franklin D. Roosevelt, speech, Worcester, Mass., 1936

8 Income tax returns are the most imaginative fiction being written today.
   Herman Wouk

9 The income tax people are very nice.
They're letting me keep my own mother.
Henny Youngman

See also Government; Money.

TEACHING

1 For every person wishing to teach, there
are thirty not wanting to be taught.
Anon.

2 Teachers are overworked and under-
paid. True, it is an exacting and exhausting business, this damming up the flood
of human potentialities.
George B. Leonard, *Education and Ecstasy*

3 The decent docent doesn't doze:
He teaches standing on his toes.
His student dassn't doze – and does,
And that's what teaching is and was.
David McCord, 'History of Education'

4 The teacher should never lose his
temper in the presence of the class. If
a man, he may take refuge in profane
soliloquies; if a woman, she may follow
the example of one sweet-faced and
apparently tranquil girl – go out in the
yard and gnaw a post.
William Lyon Phelps, *Teaching in School
and College*

5 He who can, does. He who cannot,
teaches.
George Bernard Shaw, *Maxims for Revolutionists*, 1903

6 ... everybody who is incapable of learning has taken to teaching – that is really
what our enthusiasm for education has
come to.
Oscar Wilde, 'The Decay of Lying', 1889

See also Education; School; Sex Education; University.

TECHNOLOGY

1 Sattinger's Law: It works better if you
plug it in.
Arthur Bloch, *Murphy's Law and Other
Reasons Why Things Go Wrong*, 1977

2 Technology has brought meaning to the
lives of many technicians.
Ed Bluestone, 'Maxims', *The National
Lampoon Encyclopaedia of Humor*, 1973

3 Modern technology
owes ecology
an apology.
Alan M. Eddison, *Worse Verse*, 1969

4 Our toaster works on either AC or DC,
but not on bread. It has two settings – too
soon or too late.
Sam Levenson, *In One Era and Out the
Other*

See also Computers; Electricity; Inventions; Modern Life; Video Games.

TEENAGERS

1 Cute teenagers exist only on television, I
suspect. I know there are none in my
neighborhood.
Robert MacKenzie, *TV Guide*, 1979

2 The best way to keep children home is to
make the home atmosphere pleasant –
and let the air out of the tires.
Dorothy Parker

See also Adolescence; Childhood; Children; Parents; Youth.

TEETH

1 POLLY: Why is it only teeth that decay
... You don't always have to go to the
doctor's to have holes in your arms stopped up, do you? It's a flaw in the design.
Alan Bennett, *Getting On*, 1971

2 ... that dear little baby tooth, with a
small tag attached, reading: 'The first
bicuspid that little Willie lost. Extracted
from Daddy's wrist on April 5, 1887.'
W. C. Fields, *Let's Look at the Record*, 1939

3 I taste the flavor of your thumbs
While you massage my flabby gums.
Ernest A. Hooton, 'Ode to a Dental
Hygienist'

4 I've got a tooth that's driving me to
extraction.
Charlie McCarthy (Edgar Bergen), *The
Chase and Sanborn Hour*, NBC Radio, 1937

5 All joys I bless, but I confess
There is one greatest thrill:
What the dentist does when he stops the buzz
And puts away the drill.
Christopher Morley, 'Song in a Dentist's Chair'

See also Smiles.

TELEGRAMS

1 ... and then I want to end up NORWICH. Yes, well it's an epigrammatic way of saying KNICKERS OFF READY WHEN I COME HOME. It's the initial letters, you see, of each word. I know 'Knickers' is spelled with a 'K'. I did go to Oxford – that was one of the first things they taught us. Yes. And in a perfect world it would be KORWICH. But it doesn't have quite the same idiomatic force I think as NORWICH *does* it?
Alan Bennett, 'The Telegram', *On the Margin*, BBC TV, 1966

See also Communications; Telephones.

TELEPHONES

1 You have reached the — family. What you hear is the barking of our killer Doberman pinscher, Wolf. Please leave a message after the tone.
An answering machine message in California, quoted in *Life*, January 1984

2 I answer the phone 'Dickerson here' because I'm Dickerson and I'm here. Now what the hell do you want, Martha?
Charles Barsotti, *Kings Don't Carry Money*, cartoon, 1981

3 A man telephoned a friend at two o'clock in the morning. 'I do hope I haven't disturbed you,' he said cheerily.
'Oh, no,' the friend replied, 'that's quite all right. I had to get up to answer the telephone anyway.'
Carl Brandt

4 They [wives] are people who think when the telephone bell rings, it is against the law not to answer it.
Ring Lardner, *Say It with Oil*, 1923

5 ERIC: Hey, answer the phone! Answer the phone!
ERNIE: But it's not ringing!
ERIC: Why leave everything till the last minute?
Eric Morecambe and Ernie Wise, *The Morecambe and Wise Joke Book*, 1979

6 Public telephones in Europe are like our pinball machines. They are primarily a form of entertainment and a test of skill rather than a means of communication.
Miss Piggy, *Miss Piggy's Guide to Life (As Told to Henry Beard)*, 1981

7 Well, if I called the wrong number, why did you answer the phone?
James Thurber, cartoon in the *New Yorker*

See also Communications; Telegrams.

TELEVISION

1 Photography is going to marry Miss Wireless, and heaven help everybody when they get married. Life will be very complicated.
Marcus Adams, Society photographer, quoted in the *Observer*, 1925

2 Television is the first truly democratic culture – the first culture available to everybody and entirely governed by what the people want. The most terrifying thing is what the people do want.
Clive Barnes, *New York Times*, 1969

3 I've been in this business a long time. I was on television when it was radio. When I started people thought television was impossible, and a lot of them still do.
Milton Berle, *Variety*, 1978

4 Television is more interesting than people. If it were not, we should have people standing in the corners of our rooms.
Alan Coren, *The Times*

5 Time has convinced me of one thing. Television is for appearing on, not looking at.
Noël Coward (Attrib.)

6 It is a medium of entertainment which permits millions of people to listen to the

same joke at the same time, and yet remain lonesome.

T. S. Eliot, quoted in the *New York Post*, 1963

7 It's amazing how many people see you on TV. I did my first television show a month ago, and the next day five million television sets were sold. The people who couldn't sell theirs threw them away.
Bob Hope, 1950

8 All you have to do on television is be yourself, provided, that is, that you have a self to be.
Clive James, *Observer*, 1981

9 Disaster. The Festival committee say our Tariq Ali Protest Half-hour is ineligible as light entertainment – it's technically inadmissable because he doesn't sing a duet on a tall stool.
Marc, *The Trendy Ape*, cartoon, 1968

10 De Gaulle is one of the few politicians who has grasped the point that the balance of advantage is always with the man being interviewed if he cares to seize it. I saw him on French television being asked why he had delayed releasing the Ben Barka story till after the presidential election. Instead of getting hot under the collar, sending for the French equivalent of Sir Hugh Greene, transferring his favours to Radio Monte Carlo, or otherwise manifesting his displeasure, he just hung his old, battered head sheepishly, and muttered in a woeful, strangled voice: '*C'etait mon inexperience!*'
Malcolm Muggeridge, letter to *The Times*, 1966

11 I have had my television aerials removed. It's the moral equivalent of a prostate operation.
Malcolm Muggeridge

12 Television has lifted the manufacture of banality out of the sphere of handicraft and placed it in that of a major industry.
Nathalie Sarraute

13 Television is now so desperately hungry for material that they're scraping the top of the barrel.
Gore Vidal, 1955

14 I hate television, I hate it as much as peanuts. But I can't stop eating peanuts.
Orson Welles, quoted in the *New York Herald Tribune*, 1956

See also Show Business; Television – Commercials; Television – Game Shows; Television – Shows.

TELEVISION – COMMERCIALS

1 TV personality Speedy Alka-Seltzer came out of the medicine cabinet this week and admitted that he was a Bi-carbonate. Fearful over possible criticism, the beloved Speedy threw himself into a bathtub and effervesced to death.
'Weekend Update', *Saturday Night Live*

2 Dogs who earn their living by appearing in television commercials in which they constantly and aggressively demand meat should remember that in at least one Far Eastern country they *are* meat.
Fran Lebowitz, *Social Studies*, 1981

See also Advertising; Television.

TELEVISION – GAME SHOWS

1 And those quiz shows! A woman won a vacation and dropped dead from the shock, but the sponsors kept their word. They sent her body to Bermuda for two weeks.
Milton Berle, *Variety*

2 Hello, good evening and welcome to *Blackmail*. And to start tonight's programme, we go north to Preston in Lancashire and Mrs Betty Teal. Hello Mrs Teal! Now Mrs Teal, this is for fifteen pounds and it's to stop us revealing the name of your lover in Bolton. So, Mrs Teal, send us fifteen pounds by return of post please and your husband Trevor and your lovely children, Diane, Janice and Juliet, need never know the name of your lover in Bolton.
Graham Chapman, John Cleese, Eric Idle, Terry Jones and Michael Palin, *And Now for Something Completely Different*, screenplay, 1971

3 ANNOUNCER: It's time once again to play *Catch It and You Keep It* and here's your host, Bob Benson!
BOB BENSON: Hi, folks! For you new-comers to *Catch It and You Keep It*, here's how we play the game: I'm standing on a balcony on the tenth floor of the CBS Studios. The contestants are gathered below me in the parking lot. My assist-ants and I will throw prizes down to the crowd and if they catch them, they keep them!
Tony Hendra and Michael O'Donoghue, National Lampoon's *Radio Dinner*, record, 1972

4 *The Napalm Show*: Host Don Rickles welcomes a celebrity panel to view obscure talent. If, after thirty seconds, the contestant is deemed untalented by the panel, he is sprayed with a toxic defoliant. Tonight a man dry-cleans a goat.
Mario A. J. Mondelli, Jr, Competition, *New York Magazine*, 1976

5 *The $25,000 Sky Jump*: Dressed as fowls of their choice, contestants compete for cash prizes while free-falling from a 747.
Frank Russo, competition, *New York Magazine*, 1976

See also Competitions; Television; Tele-vision – Shows.

TELEVISION SHOWS

1 *The Young Podiatrists*: Hard-hitting drama about the new breed of foot doctors who try to live in and yet change a world not of their own making.
National Lampoon, 1978

2 *Closet Queen*: Victoria rearranges her wardrobe again and her clothes are not amused.
David J. Mackler, competition, *New York Magazine*, 1976

3 *Insect Theater*: Common garden spiders are featured this week in an uncommon production of *Death of a Salesman*.
Jeff Monasch, competition, *New York Magazine*, 1976

4 *Georgette*: Hilarious complications abound at Ted's funeral, with Phyllis arriving from San Francisco, Rhoda from New York, and Mary and Lou from Minneapolis, only to discover that Carlton has drunk all the embalming fluid.
Edward Pinsky, competition, *New York Magazine*, 1976

5 *Snoopy Visits the PLO*: Special. Snoopy and the entire gang put on a special show for PLO rebels, interview their leaders, join in Palestinian folk songs. Narrated by Vanessa Redgrave.
Gerald Sussman, *Not Quite TV Guide*, 1983

See also Television; Television – Game Shows.

TEMPER

1 MRS ALLONBY: Nothing is so aggravat-ing as calmness. There is something positively brutal about the good temper of most modern men. I wonder we women stand it as well as we do.
Oscar Wilde, *A Woman of No Importance*, 1893

TEMPERANCE

1 Sobriety's a real turn-on for me. You can see what you're doing.
Peter O'Toole, 1983

See also Abstinence; Drink; Prohibition.

TEMPTATION

1 I can resist everything except temptation.
Oscar Wilde, *Lady Windermere's Fan*, 1892

2 . . . there are terrible temptations that it requires strength, strength and courage to yield to.
Oscar Wilde, *An Ideal Husband*, 1895

See also Flirtation; Sin.

TENNIS

1 Another play is the rearrange the string number. Never take the rap for a bad return or no return. Whenever you hit a ball into the net, or miss it entirely, bring

the game to a grinding halt by checking the strings of your racket, spending sometimes as much as five minutes separating them and testing their strength. This absolves you of any of the responsibility for a bad shot.

Erma Bombeck, *If Life is a Bowl of Cherries – What am I Doing in the Pits?*, 1978

2 I have finally mastered what to do with the second tennis ball. Having small hands, I was becoming terribly self-conscious about keeping it in a can in the car while I served the first one. I noted some women tucked the second ball just inside the elastic leg of their tennis panties. I tried, but found the space already occupied by a leg. Now, I simply drop the second ball down my cleavage, giving me a chest that often stuns my opponent throughout an entire set.

Erma Bombeck, *If Life is a Bowl of Cherries – What am I Doing in the Pits?*, 1978

3 No doubt about it . . . every day in every way, my game grows stronger. I saw one enthusiast the other day playing with his racket out of the press. I'll have to try that.

Erma Bombeck, *If Life is a Bowl of Cherries – What am I Doing in the Pits?*, 1978

4 'If only I could have a transsexual operation,' I told my wife, 'I know I could improve my forehand.' She was very sympathetic: 'Do it if you think it will help your game.'

But if I had the operation and then women started beating me, instead of men, it would make me sick.'

'Women beat you now,' she said.

Art Buchwald

5 Nastase is a Hamlet who wants to play a clown, but he is no good at it: his gags are bad, his timing is terrible and he never knows how he's going over – which last drawback is the kiss of death for a comic.

Clive James, *Observer*, June 1975

6 Ladies, here's a hint; if you're playing against a friend who has big boobs, bring her to the net and make her hit backhand volleys. That's the hardest shot for the well-endowed. 'I've got to hit over them or under them, but I can't hit through,' Annie Jones used to always moan to me. Not having much in my bra, I found it hard to sympathize with her.

Billie Jean King, *Autobiography*, 1983

See also Sport.

TERRORISM

1 Perhaps one of the more noteworthy trends of our time is the occupation of buildings accompanied by the taking of hostages. The perpetrators of these deeds are generally motivated by political grievance, social injustice, and the deeply felt desire to see how they look on TV.

Fran Lebowitz, *Metropolitan Life*, 1978

See also Protest; Revolution; War.

MARGARET THATCHER

1 She sounded like the Book of Revelations read out over a railway station public address system by a headmistress of a certain age wearing calico knickers.

Clive James, of Margaret Thatcher on television, *Observer*, 1979

2 I am a great admirer of Mrs Thatcher. She's one of the most splendid headmistresses there has ever been.

Arthur Marshall, *Any Questions*, BBC Radio, 1982

3 . . . she is democratic enough to talk down to anyone.

Austin Mitchell, *Westminster Man*, 1982

4 Margaret Thatcher will never speak well on television. Her impulse to tell the microphone to pull itself together is too great.

Edward Pearce, *The Senate of Lilliput*, 1983

5 Mrs Thatcher took a chopper
Slashed Health Welfare good and proper,
Saying as she did so, 'Super!
After all – there's always BUPA.'

Stanley J. Sharpless, *New Statesman*, 1984

6 If I were married to her, I'd be sure to have dinner ready when she got home.
   George Shultz, American Secretary of State (Attrib.)

See also The Falklands; House of Commons; Parliament; Politics and Politicians.

THE THEATRE

1 He directed rehearsals with all the airy deftness of a rheumatic deacon producing *Macbeth* for a church social.
   Noël Coward, on producer J. R. Crawford (Attrib.)

2 I don't like propaganda in the theatre unless it is disguised so brilliantly that the audience mistakes it for entertainment.
   Noël Coward (Attrib.)

3 Since the war a terrible pall of significance has fallen over plays.
   Noël Coward (Attrib.)

4 It's a most unusual play,
   Feel like throwing my tickets away,
   'Cos the boy gets the boy
   And the girl gets the girl
   And it's way too far off Broadway.
   . . . There's no lighting
   There's no costumes
   Oh what art!
   If there only
   Were no houselights
   I would sneak up the aisle and depart!
   Allan Sherman, 'It's a Most Unusual Play', *My Name is Allan*, record, 1965

5 Show me a congenital eavesdropper with the instincts of a Peeping Tom and I will show you the makings of a dramatist.
   Kenneth Tynan, *Pausing on the Stairs*, 1957

See also Acting; Actors and Actresses; William Shakespeare; Theatre – Critics.

THEATRE – CRITICS

1 If the writing of *This was a Man* was slow, the production by Basil Dean was practically stationary. The second act dinner scene between Francine Larrimore and

Nigel Bruce made *Parsifal* in its entirety seem like a quick-fire vaudeville sketch.
   Noël Coward, of the Broadway production of his *This was a Man*, 1926

2 The day I shall begin to worry is when the critics declare: 'This is Noël Coward's greatest play'. But I know they bloody well won't.
   Noël Coward (Attrib.)

3 Richard Briers last night played Hamlet like a demented typewriter.
   W. A. Darlington, reviewing *Hamlet*, *Daily Telegraph*

4 All through the five acts . . . he played the King as though under momentary apprehension that someone else was about to play the Ace.
   Eugene Field, reviewing Creston Clarke's *King Lear*, *Denver Tribune, c.* 1880

5 I have knocked everything except the knees of the chorus girls, and God anticipated me there.
   Percy Hammond, *New York Herald Tribune*

6 *Celebration*: as in 'a joyous celebration', a phrase popularly employed by Australian drama critics to describe plays by heavily-subsidised left-wing authors which invariably unite the whimsical and the incomprehensible.
   Barry Humphries, glossary from *A Nice Night's Entertainment*, 1981

7 As swashbuckling Cyrano, Mr Woodward's performance buckles more often than it swashes.
   Kenneth Hurren, reviewing *Cyrano de Bergerac*, 1970

8 I think *The Amorous Prawn* is perhaps the most grisly, glassy-eyed thing I have encountered in the theatre for a very long time, and even outside the theatre its like is rarely met with except on a fishmonger's slab, and now I feel very ill indeed, and would like to lie down. Before doing so I should say that *The Amorous Prawn* is a farce made out of cobwebs and mothballs, my old socks, empty beer bottles, copies of the *Strand Magazine*, dust, holes, mildew, and Mr Ben Travers's discarded typewriter ribbons

... And now I really must go and lie down and hope I shall feel better in the morning.

Bernard Levin, reviewing *The Amorous Prawn*, 1959

9 Miss Moira Lister speaks all her lines as if they are written in very faint ink on a teleprompter slightly too far away to be read with comfort.

Bernard Levin, reviewing *The Gazebo*, 1960

10 I didn't like the play but then I saw it under adverse conditions – the curtain was up.

Groucho Marx (Attrib.)

11 Miss Stapleton played the part as though she had not yet signed the contract with the producer.

George Jean Nathan, reviewing *The Emperor's Clothes*, 1953

12 Go to the Martin Beck Theater and watch Katharine Hepburn run the gamut of emotions from A to B.

Dorothy Parker, reviewing *The Lake*, 1933

13 ... she had the temerity to wear as truly horrible a gown as I have ever seen on the American stage. There was a flowing skirt of pale chiffon – you men don't have to listen – a bodice of rose-colored taffeta, the sleeves of which ended shortly below her shoulders. Then there was an expanse of naked arms, and then, around the wrists, taffeta frills such as are fastened about the unfortunate necks of beaten white poodle-dogs in animal acts. Had she not luckily been strangled by a member of the cast while disporting this garment, I should have fought my way to the stage and done her in myself.

Dorothy Parker, reviewing *The Silent Witness, New Yorker*, 1931

14 ... now that you've got me right down to it, the only thing I didn't like about *The Barretts of Wimpole Street* was the play.

Dorothy Parker, *New Yorker*, 1931

15 It isn't what you might call sunny. I went into the Plymouth Theater a comparatively young woman, and I staggered out of it three hours later, twenty years older, haggard and broken with suffering.

Dorothy Parker, reviewing Tolstoy's *Redemption, Vanity Fair*, 1918

16 *The House Beautiful* is the play lousy.

Dorothy Parker, *Life*

17 Geraldine McEwan, powdered white like a clownish whey-faced doll, simpered, whined and groaned to such effect as the Queen, that Edward's homosexuality became both understandable and forgivable.

Milton Schulman, reviewing *Edward II*, 1968

18 CHAIRMAN: Is this piece the bold experiment some people hold it to be? Is it a shameless plagiarism from the pen of a true primitive of the theatre – as someone has said – or is it neither of these things? Denzil Pepper – what do you make of this?

PEPPER: This is a hotchpotch. I think that emerges quite clearly. The thing has been thrown together – a veritable ragbag of last year's damp fireworks, if a mixed metaphor is in order.

MISS SALT: Yes. I think it *is* what we must call a hotchpotch. I do think, though ... I do think, and this is the point I feel we ought to make, it is, surely, isn't it, an *inspired* hotchpotch?

N. F. Simpson, *A Resounding Tinkle*, 1958

19 MISS SALT: I know Mustard Short is more familiar than I am *about* the attitude to this kind of thing in James Joyce – isn't this ... haven't we got here an actual *repudiation* on the Joycean model *of* orderliness in a way the writers Spenser was attacking had not?

PEPPER: I'm not at all happy about letting him get away with it on his own terms like that. After all, what happens when a boxer gets knocked out in the ring? He's lost the fight. It's as simple as that. He's lost the fight and it makes no difference that his manager or someone announces through the loudspeaker afterwards that lying flat on his back was a deliberate repudiation of the vertical.

N. F. Simpson, *A Resounding Tinkle*, 1958

20 MUSTARD: Could he, I wonder, be satirizing satire?
CHAIRMAN: A skit on satire itself. How does that strike you, Miss Salt?
MISS SALT: Yes. Yes, I think it very likely. I'm wondering whether perhaps rather than 'skit' the word 'parody' would hit off better what it is he's trying for here. Could he be parodying the whole thing? The whole concept? A parody *of* a skit, if that's possible.
PEPPER: If this is a parody of a skit at all, it must be a parody of a skit *on* something.
MUSTARD: A parody of a skit on satire?
N. F. Simpson, *A Resounding Tinkle*, 1958

See also Critics – The Artist's View; The Theatre.

THIRST

1 I feel as if somebody stepped on my tongue with muddy feet.
W. C. Fields, *Never Give a Sucker an Even Break*, screenplay, 1941

See also Drink.

THE THIRTIES

1 No member of our generation who wasn't a Communist or a dropout in the thirties is worth a damn.
Lyndon Baines Johnson (Attrib.)

See also The Forties.

THREATS

1 Young man, if there is such a thing as a tartuffe, you are just that thing. One more peep out of you and I'll give you a sound trundling.
W. C. Fields, *You Can't Cheat an Honest Man*, screenplay, 1939

THRIFT

1 Just about the time you think you can make both ends meet, somebody moves the ends.
Pansy Penner, *Reader's Digest*

See also Budgets; Economy; Meanness.

TIPPING

1 DRIFTWOOD (GROUCHO MARX): Do they allow tipping on the boat?
STEWARD: Oh, yes, sir!
DRIFTWOOD: Have you got two fives?
STEWARD: Yes, sir!
DRIFTWOOD: Well then, you won't need the ten cents I was going to give you.
George S. Kaufman and Morrie Ryskind, *A Night at the Opera*, screenplay, 1935

2 ERNIE: Is this my bill?
ERIC: Yes, sir.
ERNIE: I'm terribly sorry – it looks as if I've got just enough money to pay for the dinner but I've got nothing to tip you with.
ERIC: Let me add that bill up again, sir.
Eric Morecambe and Ernie Wise, *The Morecambe and Wise Joke Book*, 1979

3 There are several ways of calculating the tip after a meal. I find that the best is to divide the bill by the height of the waiter. Thus, a bill of $12.00 brought by a six foot waiter calls for a $2.00 tip.
Miss Piggy, *Miss Piggy's Guide to Life (As Told to Henry Beard)*, 1981

4 'She once tipped me half a crown.'
'You will generally find that women loosen up less lavishly than men. It's something to do with the bone structure of the head.'
P. G. Wodehouse, *Uncle Dynamite*, 1948

See also Restaurants; Waiters.

TOLERANCE

1 I count myself very fortunate that as a person and as a writer I've known people of all sizes. I've known some very small people, very small people indeed. I've also known some very tall people. And, of course, I've known quite a few who came somewhere in between. But knowing in this way, people of literally all sizes, I think my attitude is perhaps more liberal and more tolerant than someone who, whether rightly or wrongly, has confined himself to people of his own size.
Alan Bennett, 'The Lonely Pursuit', *On the Margin*, BBC TV, 1966

2 Sometimes with secret pride I sigh
To think how tolerant am I;
Then wonder which is really mine;
Tolerance, or a rubber spine?
Ogden Nash, 'Yes and No', *I'm a Stranger Here Myself*, 1938

TOM SWIFTIES

1 'Doctor, I keep thinking I'm a gun,' the patient declared repeatedly.
Anon.

2 'I'm only a cartoon character and can always be erased,' said Mickey Mouse self-effacingly.
Anon.

3 'I'm simply not a nice girl,' she whispered tartly.
Anon.

4 'I've gained over fifty pounds,' he explained roundly.
Anon.

5 'Welcome to the annual teetotalers awards banquet,' the MC began drily.
Anon.

6 'Why, that chicken has no beak,' the man pronounced impeccably.
Anon.

See also Humour; Riddles.

TRADES UNIONS

1 SHOP STEWARD: From now on all wages are doubled, holidays are increased to twelve weeks and we shall only work Fridays.
VOICE FROM THE BACK: Not *every* bloody Friday?
Guardian

2 MRS WICKSTEED: I'm going to my cake-decorating class. I don't really want to, but we're electing a new secretary and it's like everything else: if the rank and file don't go, the militants take over.
Alan Bennett, *Habeas Corpus*, 1973

3 Unions run by workers are like alcoholic homes run by alcoholics, a sure recipe for tyranny.
Roy Kerridge, *The Lone Conformist*, 1984

4 Unionism seldom, if ever, uses such power as it has to insure better work; almost always it devotes a large part of that power to safeguarding bad work.
H. L. Mencken, *Prejudices*, Third Series, 1922

5 MINISTER OF LABOR: . . . the workers of Freedonia are demanding shorter hours.
FIREFLY (GROUCHO MARX): Very well, we'll give them shorter hours. We'll start by cutting their lunch hour to twenty minutes.
Arthur Sheekman and Nat Perrin, *Duck Soup*, screenplay, 1933

See also The Labour Party; Socialism; Work.

TRAMPS

1 Trailer for sale or rent,
Rooms to let fifty cents,
No phone, no pool, no pets
I ain't got no cigarettes.
Ah, but two hours of pushing broom buys a
Eight-by-twelve four-bit room
I'm a man of means by no means
King of the Road.
Roger Miller, 'King of the Road', song, 1964

2 To listen to tramps talking about 'the road' you would imagine they were perpetually on the move from Plymouth to Dover, Scapa Flow to Beachy Head. Actually, this fabled 'road' was usually the highway between the seafront and Manor House toilets, the convent and off-licence.
Roy Kerridge, *The Lone Conformist*, 1984

See also Begging; Poverty.

TRAVEL

1 *Unhelpful Advice For Foreign Tourists:*
When travelling by train, remember that it is considered impolite not to help anyone who is doing *The Times* crossword puzzle.

Comments from the public are always welcome in courts of law. When you start speaking, an usher will call 'Silence in

court' to ensure that you are heard without interruption.
Peter Alexander

London barbers are delighted to shave patrons' armpits.
V. F. Corleone

Most foreign tourists know that in London they are encouraged to take a piece of fruit, free of charge, from any open-air stall or display.
Michael Lipton

Competition, *New Statesman*, 1967

2 *Unhelpful Advice for Foreign Tourists:*
Women are not allowed upstairs on buses; if you see a woman there ask her politely to descend.
David Gordon

Try the famous echo in the British Museum Reading Room.
Gerard Hoffnung

On first entering an Underground train, it is customary to shake hands with every passenger.
R. J. Phillips

Competition, *New Statesman*, 1967

3 There are two classes of travel – first class, and with children.
Robert Benchley

4 It is easier to find a traveling companion than to get rid of one.
Art Buchwald, *Vogue*, 1954

5 The whole object of travel is not to set foot on foreign land. It is at last to set foot on one's own country as a foreign land.
G. K. Chesterton

6 The passenger's always right, my boys,
The passenger's always right.
Although he's a drip
He's paid for his trip,
So greet him with delight.
Agree to his suggestions,
However coarse or crude,
Reply to all his questions,
Ply him with drink – stuff him with food.
Noël Coward, 'The Passenger's Always Right', song from *Sail Away*, 1962

7 The Taj Mahal
And the Grand Canal
And the sunny French Riviera
Would be less oppressed
If the Middle West
Would settle for somewhere rather
  nearer.
Please do not think that I criticize or
  cavil
At a genuine urge to roam,
But why oh why do the wrong people
  travel
When the right people stay back home?
Noël Coward, 'Why Do the Wrong People Travel?' song from *Sail Away*, 1962

8 When one realizes that his life is worthless he either commits suicide or travels.
Edward Dahlberg, *Reasons of the Heart*, 1965

9 To give you an idea how fast we traveled: we left Spokane with two rabbits and when we got to Topeka, we still had only two.
Bob Hope

10 I suggested that she take a trip round the world.
'Oh, I know,' returned the lady, yawning with ennui, 'but there's so many other places I want to see first.'
S. J. Perelman, *Westward Ha!*, 1948

11 Continental breakfasts are very sparse, usually just a pot of coffee or tea and a teensy roll that looks like a suitcase handle. My advice is to go right to lunch without pausing.
Miss Piggy, *Miss Piggy's Guide to Life (As Told to Henry Beard)*, 1981

12 Like Webster's Dictionary,
We're Morocco bound.
Jimmy Van Heusen and Johnny Burke, title song, *Road to Morocco*, 1942

See also Flying; Holidays; Hotels; The Mediterranean; Railways; Ships; Xenophobia.

HARRY S. TRUMAN President of the United States, 1945–1953

1 To err is Truman.
Republican Party slogan, 1948

2 Truman . . . seemed to stand for nothing more spectacular than honesty in war contracting, which was like standing for virtue in Hollywood or adequate rainfall in the Middle West.
George E. Allen, *Presidents Who Have Known Me*

3 Mr Truman believes other people should be 'free to govern themselves as they see fit' – so long as they see fit to see as we see fit.
I. F. Stone

4 My choice early in life was either to be a piano-player in a whorehouse or a politician. And to tell the truth, there's hardly any difference.
Harry S. Truman, 1962

See also The Presidency; Washington.

TRUST

1 I never trust a man until I've got his pecker in my pocket.
Lyndon Baines Johnson (Attrib.)

See also Belief; Faith.

TRUTH

1 It has always been desirable to tell the truth, but seldom if ever necessary.
A. J. Balfour

2 I welcome the opportunity of pricking the bloated bladder of lies with the poniard of truth.
Aneurin Bevan, replying to a House of Commons speech by Winston Churchill

3 I should think it hardly possible to state the opposite of the truth with more precision.
Winston Churchill, replying to a House of Commons speech by Aneurin Bevan

4 Pressed for rules and verities,
All I recollect are these:
Feed a cold to starve a fever.
Argue with no true believer.
Think too-long is never-act.
Scratch a myth and find a fact.
Phyllis McGinley, *Times Three: 1932– 1960,* 1960

5 I never know how much of what I say is true.
Bette Midler, *A View from A Broad,* 1980

6 Truth is a rare and precious commodity. We must be sparing in its use.
C. P. Scott, *Spectator,* 1982

7 I never give them hell. I just tell the truth and they think it's hell.
Harry S. Truman, quoted in *Look,* 1956

8 If one tells the truth, one is sure, sooner or later, to be found out.
Oscar Wilde, 'Phrases and Philosophies for the Use of the Young', 1894

9 . . . the truth is a thing I get rid of as soon as possible! Bad habit, by the way. Makes one very unpopular at the club . . . with the older members. They call it being conceited.
Oscar Wilde, *An Ideal Husband,* 1895

10 The truth is rarely pure and never simple. Modern life would be very tedious if it were either, and modern literature a complete impossibility.
Oscar Wilde, *The Importance of Being Earnest,* 1895

See also Belief; Credulity; Fact.

UNEMPLOYMENT

1 He was fired with enthusiasm because he wasn't fired with enthusiasm.
Anon.

2 'I quit because the boss used repulsive language.'
'What did he say?'
'He said, "You're fired!"'
Anon.

3 Despite all the suggestions I've made over the years, Dobkins, I've never been able to fire you with enthusiasm. Until now.
David Frost, 'The Sack and How to Give It', *We British*, BBC TV, 1975

4 Dobkins, I just don't know *what* we'd do without you. But we're going to try.
David Frost, 'The Sack and How to Give It', *We British*, BBC TV, 1975

5 Tell me, Dobkins: how long have you been with us – not counting today?
David Frost, 'The Sack and How to Give It', *We British*, BBC TV, 1975

6 It's no use saying the Labour Government works if one and a half million do not.
Joe Haines, *Daily Mirror*, 1977

7 There comes a time in every man's life when he must make way for an older man.
Reginald Maudling, on being dropped from Mrs Thatcher's Shadow Cabinet, 1976

8 My brother-in-law . . . I wish he would learn a trade, so we'd know what kind of work he was out of.
Henny Youngman

See also Resignation; Work.

UNHAPPINESS

1 I have always disliked myself at any given moment; the total of such moments is my life.
Cyril Connolly, *Enemies of Promise*, 1938

2 Men who are unhappy, like men who sleep badly, are always proud of the fact.
Bertrand Russell

3 Noble deeds and hot baths are the best cures for depression.
Dodie Smith, *I Capture the Castle*, 1948

4 Those who are unhappy have no need for anything in this world but people capable of giving them their attention.
Simone Weil, *L'Attente de Dieu*, 1949

See also Despair; Happiness.

UNIVERSITY

1 I was a modest, good-humoured boy. It is Oxford that has made me insufferable.
Max Beerbohm, 'Going Back to School'

2 PATTERSON: Doesn't he have a gown?
FLORA: Battersea Tech. They just award them clean overalls on graduation.
Malcolm Bradbury and Christopher Bigsby, *The After Dinner Game*, BBC TV, 1975

3 Oxford was like a chat show but with more people.
Alan Coren, *The Late Clive James*, Channel Four, 1984

4 University politics are vicious precisely because the stakes are so small.
Henry Kissinger

5 Like so many ageing college people, Pnin had long ceased to notice the existence of students on the campus.
Vladimir Nabokov, *Pnin*, 1957

See also Education; Teachers.

VANITY

1 The last time I saw him he was walking down Lover's Lane holding his own hand.
Fred Allen

2 Colonel Chase openly used spectacles for reading when he was alone, and furtively in company, slipping them off if he thought they would be noticed, for they were a little out of keeping with that standard of perfect health and vigour of which he was so striking an example.
E. F. Benson, *Paying Guests*, 1929

3 There but for the grace of God, goes God.
Winston Churchill, on Stafford Cripps (Attrib.)

4 I am bursting with pride, which is why I have absolutely no vanity.
Noël Coward, quoted by Kenneth Tynan in *The Sound of Two Hands Clapping*, 1975

5 I think a lot of Bernstein – but not as much as he does.
Oscar Levant, of Leonard Bernstein

6 What the world needs is more geniuses with humility. There are so few of us left.
Oscar Levant

7 I have little patience with anyone who is not self-satisfied. I am always pleased to see my friends, happy to be with my wife and family, but the high spot of every day is when I first catch a glimpse of myself in the shaving mirror.
Robert Morley, *Playboy*, 1979

8 The affair between Margot Asquith and Margot Asquith will live as one of the prettiest love stories in all literature.
Dorothy Parker, *New Yorker* review of *Lay Sermons* by Margot Asquith, 1927

9 Never underestimate a man who over-estimates himself.
Franklin D. Roosevelt, on General Douglas MacArthur

10 You're so vain.
You probably think this song is about you.
Carly Simon, 'You're So Vain', song, 1972

11 There is no human problem which could not be solved if people would simply do as I advise.
Gore Vidal (Attrib.)

12 To love onself is the beginning of a life-long romance.
Oscar Wilde, 'Phrases and Philosophies for the Use of the Young', 1894

See also Actors and Actresses; Boasts; Egotism; Narcissism; Pride.

VEGETABLES

1 The local groceries are all out of broccoli,
Loccoli.
Roy Blount, Jr, 'Against Broccoli', *Atlantic Monthly*

2 Vegetables are interesting but lack a sense of purpose when unaccompanied by a good cut of meat.
Fran Lebowitz, *Metropolitan Life*, 1978

3 I have no religious or moral objection to vegetables but they are, as it were, dull. They are the also-rans of the plate. One takes an egg, or a piece of meat, or fish, with pleasure but then one has, as a kind of penance, to dilute one's pleasure with a damp lump of boskage.
Frank Muir, *You Can't Have Your Kayak and Heat It*, 1973

See also Eating; Food; Fruit, Vegetarianism.

VEGETARIANISM

1 Vegetarians have wicked, shifty eyes and laugh in a cold, calculating manner. They pinch little children, steal stamps, drink water, favour beards.
Beachcomber (J. B. Morton), 'By the Way', *Daily Express*

2 No more the milk of cows
  Shall pollute my private house
  Than the milk of the wild mares of the
    Barbarian;
  I will stick to port and sherry,
  For they are so very, very,
  So very, very, very Vegetarian.
    G. K. Chesterton, 'The Logical Vegeta-
    rian', 1914

3 Most vigitaryans I iver see looked
  enough like their food to be classed as
  cannybals.
    Finley Peter Dunne, *Mr Dooley's Philoso-
    phy*, 1900

4 Vegetarianism is harmless enough,
  though it is apt to fill a man with wind and
  self-righteousness.
    Sir Robert Hutchinson, President, Royal
    College of Physicians, 1938–1941

5 I'm very fond of pigs; but I don't find it
  difficult to eat them.
    Robert Runcie (Archbishop of Canter-
    bury), 1980

6 I did not become a vegetarian for my
  health. I did it for the health of the
  chickens.
    Isaac Bashevis Singer

7 The first time I tried organic wheat
  bread, I thought I was chewing on
  roofing material.
    Robin Williams, interview in *Playboy*,
    October 1982

See also Cults; Eating; Food; Fruit;
Vegetables.

VENICE

1 Streets flooded. Please advise.
    Robert Benchley, telegram to home on
    arriving in Venice (Attrib.)

2 Venice is like eating an entire box of
  chocolate liqueurs in one go.
    Truman Capote (Attrib.)

See also Italy and the Italians.

VETERINARIANS

1 The best doctor in the world is a
  veterinarian. He can't ask his patients
  what is the matter – he's got to just
  know.
    Will Rogers, *The Autobiography of Will
    Rogers*, 1949

See also Animals; Pets.

VICE

1 Vice is its own reward.
    Quentin Crisp, *The Naked Civil Servant*,
    1968

See also Evil; Prostitution; Sex; Sin;
Virtue.

THE VICE-PRESIDENCY

1 You really do get a chance to meet
  dead leaders ... it's known as quiet
  diplomacy.
    George Bush, on the number of state
    funerals he'd attended in four years as
    Vice-President. Speech in Washington,
    1985

2 Once there were two brothers; one ran
  away to sea, the other was elected Vice-
  President – and nothing was ever heard
  of them again.
    Thomas Marshall

3 The Vice-Presidency is sort of like the
  last cookie on the plate. Everybody insists
  he won't take it, but somebody always
  does.
    Bill Vaughan

QUEEN VICTORIA

1 LADY D: Is there anything in the newspaper this morning, Withers?
  WITHERS: They have named another
  battleship after Queen Victoria, ma'am.
  LADY D: Another? She must be beginning to think there is some resemblance.
    Alan Bennett, *Forty Years On*, 1968

VICTORY AND DEFEAT

1 In defeat unbeatable; in victory unbearable.
    Winston Churchill, of Field Marshall
    Montgomery of Alamein

See also Success; War; Winning.

VIDEO GAMES

1 It was a little all-too-devouring, just gobble, gobble, gobble. No social content.
Ralph Nader, on 'Pac-Man'

See also Computers; Technology.

THE VIETNAM WAR

1 Bombing can end the war – bomb the
Pentagon now!
Graffito, New York, 1970

2 DICK: We've come a long way since that
first Thanksgiving dinner in Plymouth,
when the Pilgrims sat down at the table
with the Indians to eat turkey.
TOM: Boy, I'll say we've come a long way.
Now we're in Paris, sitting down at a
table with the Viet Cong eating crow.
The Smothers Brothers Comedy Hour, CBS,
1968

3 Draft Beer, Not Students
Slogan on badge

4 End the Vietnam War and bring our kids
home. From Canada.
Graffito

5 Hey, all you kids of draft age – you can
count on Agnew to lay down your life for
his country.
Anon.

6 Napalm is a figment of the collective
imagination of the commie pinko hippie
yippie leftist queers – Agnew.
Graffito, Vietnam, 1971

7 The Cave at the End of the Tunnel.
Humiliating Defeat with Honor.
National Lampoon, 1975

8 Victory in Vietnam will not determine
who is right, only who is left.
Graffito

9 We are the unwilling, led by the unqualified, doing the unnecessary for the
ungrateful.
Graffito, American air base, Vietnam, 1970

10 We met the enemy and he was us.
General William C. Westmoreland
(Attrib.)

11 What do you get when you cross poly-
styrene with benzene and flammable
liquid hydrocarbons?
An armed guard for your campus re-
cruiters!
P. J. O'Rourke, 'Lab Riot', *The National
Lampoon Encyclopaedia of Humor*, 1973

12 The draft is white people sending black
people to fight yellow people to protect
the country they stole from red people.
Gerome Ragni and James Rado, *Hair*,
1967

See also Richard Nixon; Protest; The
Sixties; War.

VIOLINS

1 If it isn't a Stradivarius, I've been robbed
of 110 dollars.
Jack Benny (Attrib.)

See also Music and Musicians; Songs and
Singers.

VIRGINITY

1 There was a young lady called Wylde,
Who kept herself quite undefiled
By thinking of Jesus
Contagious diseases,
And the bother of having a child.
Anon., *Some Limericks* by Norman Douglas,
1917

2 Nature abhors a virgin – a frozen asset.
Clare Boothe Luce

3 I've been around so long, I knew Doris
Day before she was a virgin.
Groucho Marx (Attrib.)

See also Abstinence; Chastity.

VIRTUE

1 Righteous people terrify me . . . virtue is
its own punishment.
Aneurin Bevan (Attrib.)

2 What, after all, is a halo? It's only one
more thing to keep clean.
Christopher Fry, *The Lady's Not for Burning*, 1948

3 Vice
Is Nice
But a little virtue

Won't hurt you.
  Felicia Lamport, 'Axiom to Grind', *Scrap Irony*, 1961

4 He hasn't a single redeeming vice.
  Oscar Wilde (Attrib.)

See also Vice.

VIVISECTION

1 The mouse is an animal which, killed in sufficient numbers under carefully controlled conditions, will produce a Ph.D. thesis.
  The Journal of Irreproducible Results

See also Animals; Science and Scientists.

VOICES

1 My Aunt Dahlia has a carrying voice . . . If all other sources of income failed, she could make a good living calling the cattle home across the Sands of Dee.
  P. G. Wodehouse, 'Jeeves and the Song of Songs', *Very Good, Jeeves*, 1930

See also Speakers and Speeches.

VULGARITY

1 INTERVIEWER: You've been accused of vulgarity.
  BROOKS: Bullshit!
  Mel Brooks, interview in *Playboy*, 1975

See also Obscenity; Swearing.

WAITERS

1 DINER: I'd complain about the service if I could find a waiter to complain to.
Mel Calman, *How to Survive Abroad*, cartoon, 1971

2 By and by
God caught his eye.
David McCord, 'Epitaph on a Waiter', *Odds without Ends*, 1945

See also Food; Hotels; Restaurants; Tipping.

WALES AND THE WELSH

1 A Welshman is a man who prays on his knees on Sundays and preys on his neighbours all the rest of the week.
Anon.

2 When all else fails
try Wales.
Christopher Logue, 'To a Friend in Search of Rural Seclusion'

3 The land of my fathers? My fathers can have it.
Dylan Thomas (Attrib.)

4 There are still parts of Wales where the only concession to gaiety is a striped shroud.
Gwyn Thomas, *Punch*, 1958

5 We can trace nearly all the disasters of English history to the influence of Wales.
Evelyn Waugh, *Decline and Fall*, 1928

See also Britain and the British.

GEORGE WALLACE Governor of Alabama and Independent Presidential Candidate, 1968

1 I don't think you'll have to worry that this mental midget, this hillbilly Hitler from Alabama, is anywhere near becoming the nominee of the Democratic Party.
Julian Bond, Black activist

2 It's high time the rednecks came back to Washington. There are a hell of a lot more rednecks out there than people who eat crêpes suzette.
Mickey Griffin, campaign organizer for George Wallace

See also America – The South; Politics and Politicians.

WAR

1 A general and a bit of shooting makes you forget your troubles . . . it takes your mind off the cost of living.
Brendan Behan, *The Hostage*, 1958

2 I have never understood this liking for war. It panders to instincts already catered for within the scope of any respectable domestic establishment.
Alan Bennett, *Forty Years On*, 1968

3 WICKSTEED: Oh Mavis and Audrey and Lilian and Jean
Patricia and Pauline and NAAFI Christine
Maureen and Myrtle I had you and more
In God's gift to the lecher the Second World War.
Alan Bennett, *Habeas Corpus*, 1973

4 I'm sick of war for many reasons,
Three of them will do:
It's 1815,
I am French
And this is Waterloo.
Mel Brooks, 'To be or Not to be', song, 1984

5 There was very little actual shooting in Belgium, but there was plenty of mortar and artillery fire, and it was very noisy, and I thought I would not want to be in the war very long, because of the noise.
Mel Brooks, quoted by Kenneth Tynan in *Show People*, 1980

6 A prisoner of war is a man who tries to kill you and fails, and then asks you not to kill him.
  Winston Churchill, quoted in the *Observer*, 1952

7 Nothing in life is so exhilarating as to be shot at without result.
  Winston Churchill, *The Malakand Field Force*, 1898

8 Men love war because it allows them to look serious. Because it is the one thing that stops women laughing at them.
  John Fowles, *The Magus*, 1965

9 But that was war. Just about all he could find in its favor was that it paid well and liberated children from the pernicious influence of their parents.
  Joseph Heller, *Catch-22*, 1961

10 I hated the bangs in the war: I always felt a *silent* war would have been far more tolerable.
  Pamela Hansford Johnson, *Observer*, 1967

11 And while Hitler might chortle that his secret weapon was a mighty *Luftwaffe* designed to obliterate the Royal Air Force, England's leaders knew that their secret weapon was that they didn't *have* a Royal Air Force.
  Bruce McCall, 'That Fabulous Battle of Britain', *Zany Afternoons*, 1983

12 So it was that ordinary British housewives bent to the task of knitting sandbags, smiling cheerfully among the ungodly mess, while all British manhood flocked to join the army and don the uniform – for there was only one to go around, and they had to take turns.
  Bruce McCall, 'That Fabulous Battle of Britain', *Zany Afternoons*, 1983

13 Uncle Jason, an ace in the Royal Flying Corps
  grew up and old into a terrible borps.
  He'd take off from tables to play the Great Worps
  stretch out his arms and crash to the florps.
  His sister, an exSister (now rich) of the Porps,
  would rorps forps morps: 'Encorps! Encorps!'
  Roger McGough, 'Uncle Terry', *Sporting Relations*, 1974

14 Jaw-jaw is better than war-war.
  Harold Macmillan, speech, 1958

15 War may make a fool of man, but it by no means degrades him; on the contrary, it tends to exalt him, and its net effects are much like those of motherhood on women.
  H. L. Mencken, *Minority Report*, 1956

16 At Victoria Station the R.T.O. gave me a travel warrant, a white feather and a picture of Hitler marked 'This is your enemy.' I searched every compartment but he wasn't on the train.
  Spike Milligan, *Adolf Hitler: My Part in His Downfall*, 1971

17 ERNIE: Where did you spend your war years?
  ERIC: Everywhere. I fought with Mountbatten in Burma, with Alexander in Tunis, with Monty at Alamein ... I couldn't get on with anyone.
  Eric Morecambe and Ernie Wise, *The Morecambe and Wise Joke Book*, 1979

18 The quickest way of ending a war is to lose it.
  George Orwell, 'Shooting an Elephant', 1950

19 History is littered with wars which everybody knew would never happen.
  Enoch Powell, 1967

20 No battle is worth fighting except the last one.
  Enoch Powell (Attrib.)

21 You can't say civilization don't advance ... for every war they kill you a new way.
  Will Rogers

22 All wars are popular for the first thirty days.
  Arthur Schlesinger, Jr

23 Wars make for better reading than peace does.
  A. J. P. Taylor, *Observer*, 1981

24 'I gather it's between the Reds and the Blacks.'

'Yes, but it's not quite as easy as that. You see, they are all Negroes. And the Fascists won't be called black because of their racial pride so they are called White after the White Russians. And the Bolshevists *want* to be called black because of *their* racial pride. So when you *say* black you mean red, and when you *mean* red you say white and when the party who call themselves blacks say traitors they mean what *we* call blacks, but what *we* mean when *we* say traitors I really couldn't tell you... But, of course, it's really a war between Russia and Germany and Italy and Japan who are all against one another on the patriotic side. I hope I make myself plain?'
Evelyn Waugh, *Scoop*, 1938

25 As long as war is regarded as wicked, it will always have its fascination. When it is looked upon as vulgar it will cease to be popular.
Oscar Wilde, 'The Critic as Artist', 1890

See also The Army; Courage; Enemies; The Falklands; Fighting; Heroes; The Navy; Terrorism; Victory and Defeat; The Vietnam War.

WASHINGTON

1 Washington – Hubbub of the Universe.
Anon., *Reader's Digest*

2 There's nothing so permanent as a temporary job in Washington.
George Allen

3 When I first went to Washington, I thought, what is I'il ole me doing with these ninety-nine great people? Now I ask myself, what am I doing with these ninety-nine jerks?
S. I. Hayakawa, US Senator

4 I love to go to Washington – if only to be near my money.
Bob Hope

5 I find in Washington that when you ask what time it is you get different answers from Democrats and Republicans; 435 answers from the House of Representatives; a 500-page report from some consultants on how to tell time; no answer from your lawyer and a bill for $1,000.
R. Tim McNamar, Deputy Secretary of the Treasury under President Reagan

6 Washington is the only place where sound travels faster than light.
C. V. R. Thompson, *Reader's Digest*, 1949

7 The District of Columbia is a territory bounded on all sides by the United States of America.
Irving D. Tressler, *Reader's Digest*, 1949

See also Congress; Politics and Politicians; The Presidency; The Senate; The Vice-Presidency.

WATERGATE

1 Dick Nixon before he dicks you.
Car sticker, Washington, 1974

2 RICHARD NIXON: I admit my men made a sad mistake – they got caught.
Anon.

3 I suppose we should all sing 'Bail to the Chief'.
Howard Baker, Republican Senator, 1974

4 A group of politicians deciding to dump a President because his morals are bad is like the Mafia getting together to bump off the Godfather for not going to church on Sunday.
Russell Baker, *New York Times*, 1974

5 If [President Nixon's secretary] Rosemary Woods had been Moses' secretary, there would be only eight commandments.
Art Buchwald, 1974

6 I'm a fan of President Nixon. I worship the quicksand he walks on.
Art Buchwald, 1974

7 [Presidential Press Secretary] Ron Ziegler has done for Government credibility what the Boston Strangler did for door-to-door salesmen.
Art Buchwald, 1974

8 ... we've passed from the age of the common man to the common crook.
J. K. Galbraith, 1974

9 This we learn from Watergate,
That almost any creep'll
Be glad to help the Government
Overthrow the people.
   E. Y. Harburg, *At this Point in Rhyme*, 1976

See also Richard Nixon; Washington.

WEALTH

1 The Pluto-American Anti-Defamation
League said it will bring pressure to bear
on media to up-grade the image of incredibly rich people. The newly-formed
group, which hopes to combat negative
portrayals of incredibly rich people on
television and in print, cited the crucial
role that incredibly rich people have
played in American history, and hopes to
restore incredible richness as a 'positive
aspect of American life'.
   Off The Wall Street Journal, 1982

2 The rich man has his motorcar,
His country and his town estate.
He smokes a fifty-cent cigar
And jeers at Fate.
He frivols through the livelong day,
He knows not Poverty her pinch.
His lot seems light, his heart seems gay,
He has a cinch.
Yet though my lamp burns low and dim,
Though I must slave for livelihood –
Think you that I would change with
   him?
You bet I would!
   Franklin P. Adams, *By and Large*, 1914

3 Lord Finchley tried to mend the 'lectric
light himself; it struck him dead and
serve him right; it is the business of the
wealthy man to give employment to the
artisan.
   Hilaire Belloc

4 The Rich arrived in pairs
And also in Rolls Royces;
They talked of their affairs
In loud and strident voices.
(The Husbands and the Wives
Of this select society
Lead independent lives
Of infinite variety.)
   Hilaire Belloc, 'The Garden Party', *Ladies
   and Gentlemen*, 1932

5 The rich are the scum of the earth in
every country.
   G. K. Chesterton, *The Flying Inn*, 1912

6 Down with the idle rich!
The bloated upper classes.
They drive to Lord's
In expensive Fords
With their jewelled op'ra glasses.
   Noël Coward, 'Down with the Whole
   Damn Lot!', song from *Co-optimists*, 1928

7 Wealth is not without its advantages, and
the case to the contrary, although it has
often been made, has never proved
widely persuasive.
   J. K. Galbraith, *The Affluent Society*, 1958

8 Nouveau is Better than No Riche at All.
   Monsieur Marc, New York Society hairdresser. Title of his autobiography, 1983

9 God shows his contempt for wealth by
the kind of person he selects to receive it.
   Austin O'Malley

10 A fool and his money are soon married.
   Carolyn Wells

11 No woman can be too rich or too thin.
   Duchess of Windsor (Attrib.)

See also Extravagance; Money; Philanthropy; Rich and Poor.

WEATHER

1 And here is the weather forecast.
Tomorrow will be muggy. Followed by
Toogy, Weggy, Thurgy and Frigy.
   Anon.

2 It was so cold, the wolves were eating the
sheep just for the wool.
   Anon.

3 A: It's raining cats and dogs!
B: I know – I've just stepped into a
poodle.
   Anon.

4 Satellite photography in the 1970s gave
rise to the long-range weather forecast, a
month at a time. This in turn gave rise to
the observation that the long-range
weather forecast was wrong most of the
time. In turn, this gave rise to the dropping of the long-range weather forecast,

and to the admission that really accurate forecasting could only cover the next day or two, and not always then.

Miles Kington, *Nature Made Ridiculously Simple*, 1983

WEDDINGS

1 A delighted incredulous bride
Remarked to the groom at her side:
'I never could quite
Believe till tonight
Our anatomies *would* coincide'.
Anon.

2 If it were not for the presents, an elopement would be preferable.
George Ade, *Forty Modern Fables*, 1901

3 Dear Mrs A.
Hooray Hooray
At last you are deflowered.
On this as every other day
I love you. Noël Coward
Noël Coward, wedding telegram to Gertrude Lawrence, 1940

4 As soon as our engagement appeared in *The Times* wedding presents poured in . . . the majority were frightful, and they came in cohorts – fifteen lamps of the same design, forty trays, a hundred and more huge glass vases. They were assembled at Grosvenor Place . . . When the presents were all arranged Lady Evelyn looked at them reflectively.
'The glass will be the easiest,' she said. 'It only needs a good kick.' She said silver was more of a problem. 'Walter and I had such luck, *all* ours was stolen while we were on honeymoon.'
Diana Mosley, *A Life of Contrasts*, 1977

5 We're having a little disagreement. What *I* want is a big church wedding with bridesmaids and flowers and a no-expense-spared reception and what *he* wants is to break off our engagement.
Sally Poplin

6 When two people are under the influence of the most violent, most insane, most delusive, and most transient of passions, they are required to swear that they will remain in that excited, abnor-mal, and exhausting condition continuously until death do them part.
George Bernard Shaw, 'Preface', *Getting Married*, 1908

7 Nothing so surely introduces a sour note into a wedding ceremony as the abrupt disappearance of the groom in a cloud of dust.
P. G. Wodehouse, *A Pelican at Blandings*, 1969

See also Couples; Courting; Engagements; Flirtation; Honeymoons; Proposals; Romance; Seduction; Sex; Sexual Attraction.

HAROLD WILSON Prime Minister of Great Britain, 1964–1970, 1974–1976 (Labour Party)

1 The only reason Harold Wilson as a child had to go to school without boots on, was that his boots were probably too small for him.
Harold Macmillan (Attrib.)

See also House of Commons; The Labour Party; Parliament; Politics and Politicians; Socialism; Trades Unions.

WOODROW WILSON President of the United States, 1913–1921

1 Mr Wilson's name among the Allies is like that of the rich uncle, and they have accepted his manners out of respect for his means.
Morning Post, London, 1919

2 The spacious philanthropy which he exhaled upon Europe stopped quite sharply at the coasts of his own country.
Winston Churchill, *The World Crisis*, 1929

3 Mr Wilson's mind, as has been the custom, will be closed all day Sunday.
George S. Kaufman

4 I feel certain that he would not recognize a generous impulse if he met it on the street.
William Howard Taft (Attrib.)

See also The Presidency; Washington.

WINE

1 The point about white Burgundies is that I hate them myself. They so closely resemble a blend of cold chalk soup and alum cordial with an additive or two to bring it to the colour of children's pee.
Kingsley Amis, *The Green Man,* 1969

2 When it came to writing about wine, I did what almost everybody does – faked it.
Art Buchwald

3 FLETCHER: I'd like to warn you, gentlemen, that this should be sipped delicately like a fine liqueur. It shouldn't be gulped down by the mugful. If you do that you will lose the flavour and the bouquet. You will also lose your power of speech.
Dick Clement and Ian La Frenais, *Porridge,* BBC TV, 1976

4 A good general rule is to state that the bouquet is better than the taste, and vice versa.
Stephen Potter, *One-upmanship,* 1952

5 Its a Naïve Domestic Burgundy, Without Any Breeding, But I think you'll be Amused by its Presumption.
James Thurber, *Men, Women and Dogs,* cartoon, 1943

See also Champagne; Cheese; Drink; Food.

WINNING

1 Winning isn't everything – it's the only thing.
Vince Lombardi

See also Achievement; Competitions; Leadership; Records; Success; Television – Game Shows; Victory and Defeat.

WIT

1 Wit ought to be a glorious treat, like caviare; never spread it around like marmalade.
Noël Coward

2 Wits have one thing in common with bores: they recognize at sight and avoid one another, fearing competition.
Hesketh Pearson, *Lives of the Wits,* 1962

3 There are men who fear repartee in a wife more keenly than a sword.
P. G. Wodehouse, *Jill the Reckless,* 1921

See also Comedy; Humour; Laughter; Satire.

WOMEN

1 My vigor, vitality and cheek repel me. I am the kind of woman I would run away from.
Nancy Astor

2 Behind almost every woman you ever heard of stands a man who let her down.
Naomi Bliven

3 There are three things a woman ought to look – straight as a dart, supple as a snake, and proud as a tiger lily.
Elinor Glyn, *The Sayings of Grandmama and Others,* 1908

4 The word LADY: Most Often Used to Describe Someone You Wouldn't Want to Talk to for Even Five Minutes.
Fran Lebowitz, *Metropolitan Life,* 1978

5 There is only one political career for which women are perfectly suitable; diplomacy.
Clare Booth Luce, *Observer,* 1982

6 A woman will flirt with anyone in the world as long as other people are looking on.
Oscar Wilde, *The Picture of Dorian Gray,* 1891

7 Every woman is a rebel, and usually in wild revolt against herself.
Oscar Wilde, *A Woman of No Importance,* 1893

8 MRS ALLONBY: Man, poor, awkward, reliable, necessary man belongs to a sex that has been rational for millions and millions of years. He can't help himself. It is in his race. The History of Women is very different. We have always been picturesque protests against the mere existence of common sense. We saw its dangers from the first.
Oscar Wilde, *A Woman of No Importance,* 1893

See also Housewives; Mothers; Mothers-in-law; Women – The Male View.

WOMEN – THE MALE VIEW

1 A man without a woman is like a neck
without a pain.
Graffito, Los Angeles, 1984

2 You asked me if I knew women ... Well,
one of the things I do *not* know about
them is what they talk about while the
men are talking. I must find out some
time.
Edward Albee, *Who's Afraid of Virginia
Woolf?*, 1962

3 I remembered Cliff Wainwright saying
once that women were like the Russians
– if you did exactly what they wanted all
the time you were being realistic and
constructive and promoting the cause of
peace, and if you ever stood up to them
you were resorting to cold-war tactics
and pursuing imperialistic designs and
interfering in their internal affairs. And
by the way of course peace was more
peaceful, but if you went on promoting
its cause long enough you ended up
Finlandized at best.
Kingsley Amis, *Stanley and the Women*,
1984

4 ... this may sound ridiculous, but I've
never to this day really known what
most women think about anything. Completely closed book to me. I mean, God
bless them, what would we do without
them? But I've never understood them. I
mean, damn it all, one minute you're
having a perfectly good time and the next,
you suddenly see them there like – some
old sports jacket or something – literally
beginning to come apart at the seams.
Alan Ayckbourn, *Absurd Person Singular*,
1974

5 But no woman, so he often thought,
had any head for cards; the finesse and
subtlety of the game was beyond them,
and Miss Howard was wise in refusing to
play at all. He wished her refusal to play
had extended to the use of the piano.
E. F. Benson, *Paying Guests*, 1929

6 ... why haven't women got labels on
their foreheads saying, 'Danger: Government Health Warning: women can
seriously damage your brains, genitals,
current account, confidence, razor
blades and good standing among your
friends.'
Jeffrey Bernard, *Spectator*, 1984

7 Certain women should be struck regu-
larly, like gongs.
Noël Coward, *Private Lives*, 1930

8 Women are like elephants to me; they're
nice to look at but I wouldn't want to own
one.
W. C. Fields (Attrib.)

9 Women have more imagination than
men. They need it to tell us how wonderful we are.
Arnold H. Glasow

10 A: Do you believe in clubs for women?
B: Only if every other form of persuasion
fails.
Max Kauffmann

11 In point of morals, the average woman is,
even for business, too crooked.
Stephen Leacock, *The Woman Question*

12 Women are irrational, that's all there is
to that!
Their heads are full of cotton, hay and
rags!
They're nothing but exasperating,
irritating,
Vacillating, calculating, agitating,
Maddening and infuriating hags!
Alan Jay Lerner and Frederick Loewe, 'A
Hymn to Him,' song from *My Fair Lady*,
1956

13 On one issue at least, men and women
agree; they both distrust women.
H. L. Mencken

14 When women kiss, it always reminds one
of prize fighters shaking hands.
H. L. Mencken, *Sententiae*, 1920

15 After equality, wage parity, liberation of
body and soul, and the extension for the
ratification of the ERA, women still can't
do the following:
*Start barbecue fires. *Hook up a stereo.
*Shine shoes. *Anything on a roof.
*Decide where to hang a picture. *In-
vestigate mysterious house noises at

night. *Kill and dispose of large insects. *Walk past a mirror without stopping to look.

P. J. O'Rourke and John Hughes, 'Planet of the Living Women', *National Lampoon*, 1979

16 When a man takes an interest in a woman's body she accuses him of only taking an interest in her body, but when he doesn't take an interest in her body she accuses him of taking an interest in someone else's body.

P. J. O'Rourke and John Hughes, 'Planet of the Living Women', *National Lampoon*, 1979

17 *Women Jokes*. It is important to remember when making jokes about women, that they are *not* a minority, they *weren't* captured on another continent and brought here in leg-irons (funny shoes, yes, but not leg-irons) and Hitler *didn't* blame them for Germany's loss of World War I. Therefore you can make any kind of fun of them you want.

P. J. O'Rourke and John Hughes, 'Planet of the Living Women', *National Lampoon*, 1979

18 I used to be in favour of women priests but two years in the Cabinet cured me of them.

Norman St John-Stevas, ex-member of Mrs Thatcher's Government, 1981

19 Women and elephants never forget an injury.

Saki (H. H. Munro), *Reginald*, 1904

20 Changeable women are more endurable than monotonous ones. They are sometimes murdered but seldom deserted.

George Bernard Shaw

21 A woman's place is in the wrong.

James Thurber (Attrib.)

22 I hate women because they always know where things are.

James Thurber

23 I am afraid that women appreciate cruelty, downright cruelty, more than anything else. They have wonderfully primitive instincts. We have emancipated them, but they remain slaves looking for their masters all the same.

Oscar Wilde, *The Picture of Dorian Gray*, 1891

24 The history of women is the history of the worst form of tyranny the world has ever known. The tyranny of the weak over the strong. It is the only tyranny that lasts.

Oscar Wilde, *A Woman of No Importance*, 1893

25 The only way to behave to a woman is to make love to her, if she is pretty, and to someone else, if she is plain.

Oscar Wilde, *The Importance of Being Earnest*, 1895

26 Women, as some witty Frenchman once put it, inspire us with the desire to do masterpieces, and always prevent us from carrying them out.

Oscar Wilde, *The Picture of Dorian Gray*, 1891

27 Women have a wonderful instinct about things. They can discover everything except the obvious.

Oscar Wilde, *An Ideal Husband*, 1895

28 Hysteria is a natural phenomenon, the common denominator of the female nature. It's the big female weapon, and the test of a man is his ability to cope with it.

Tennessee Williams, *The Night of the Iguana*, 1961

29 I've said it before and I'll say it again – girls are rummy. Old Pop Kipling never said a truer word than when he made that crack about the f. of the s. being d. than the m.

P. G. Wodehouse, *Right Ho, Jeeves*, 1934

30 You know, the more I see of women, the more I think that there ought to be a law. Something has got to be done about this sex, or the whole fabric of Society will collapse, and then what silly asses we shall all look.

P. G. Wodehouse, *The Code of the Woosters*, 1938

See also Men – The Female View; Women.

WORDS

1 If there's one word that sums up everything that's gone wrong since the war, it's
'workshop'.
Kingsley Amis, *Jake's Thing*, 1979

2 I always wanted to write a book that
ended with the word 'mayonnaise'.
Richard Brautigan, *In Watermelon Sugar*,
1969

See also The English Language; Language; Names; Pronunciation.

WORK

1 Work was like cats were supposed to be;
if you disliked and feared it and tried to
keep out of its way, it knew at once and
sought you out . . .
Kingsley Amis, *Take a Girl Like You*,
1960

2 Anyone can do any amount of work,
provided it isn't the work he is supposed
to be doing at that moment.
Robert Benchley

3 Work is much more fun than fun.
Noël Coward

4 Work expands so as to fill the time available for its completion.
C. Northcote Parkinson, *Parkinson's Law*,
1957

5 For this real or imagined overwork there
are, broadly speaking, three possible
remedies. He (A) may resign; he may ask
to halve the work with a colleague called
B; he may demand the assistance of two
subordinates, to be called C and D. There
is probably no instance, however, in history of A choosing any but the third
alternative.
C. Northcote Parkinson, *Parkinson's Law*,
1957

6 One of the symptoms of approaching
nervous breakdown is the belief that
one's work is terribly important. If I were
a medical man, I should prescribe a holiday to any patient who considered his
work important.
Bertrand Russell, *The Autobiography of
Bertrand Russell*, Vol. 2, 1968

7 Work is the curse of the drinking classes.
Oscar Wilde (Attrib.)

See also The Boss; Collaboration; Lazi-
ness; The Office; Trades Unions;
Unemployment.

WRITERS

1 After being turned down by numerous
publishers, he decided to write for
posterity.
George Ade

2 T. S. Eliot is quite at a loss
When clubwomen bustle across
At literary teas
Crying: – 'What, if you please,
Did you mean by *The Mill on the Floss*'
W. H. Auden, 'T. S. Eliot', *Collected Poems*,
1977

3 Of all the honours that fell upon
Virginia's [Woolf] head, none, I think,
pleased her more than the *Evening
Standard* Award for the Tallest Woman
Writer of 1927, an award she took by a
neck from Elizabeth Bowen. And rightly,
I think, for she was in a very real sense the
tallest writer I have ever known. Which is
not to say that her stories were tall. They
were not. They were short. But she did
stand head and shoulders above her con-
temporaries, and sometimes of course,
much more so.
Alan Bennett, *Forty Years On*, 1968

4 We're all miners in our family. My father
was a miner. My mother *is* a miner.
These are miner's hands. We're all
artists I suppose, really, only I was the
first one who had this urge to express
myself on paper rather than at the coal
face. But under the skin I think I'm still a
miner. I suppose in a very real sense I'm a
miner writer.
Alan Bennett, 'The Lonely Pursuit', *On the
Margin*, BBC TV, 1966

5 H. L. Mencken suffers from the delusion that he is H. L. Mencken. There is
no cure for a disease of that magnitude.
Maxwell Bodenheim (Attrib.)

6 Of course, no writers ever forget their
first acceptance . . . One fine day when I

was seventeen I had my first, second and third, all in the same morning's mail. Oh, I'm here to tell you, dizzy with excitement is no mere phrase!
Truman Capote

7 That's not writing – that's typing.
Truman Capote, of Jack Kerouac (Attrib.)

8 Writing a book is an adventure: it begins as an amusement, then it becomes a mistress, then a master, and finally a tyrant.
Sir Winston Churchill

9 In America only the successful writer is important, in France all writers are important, in England no writer is important, in Australia you have to explain what a writer is.
Geoffrey Cotterell

10 Some day I hope to write a book where the royalties will pay for the copies I give away.
Clarence Darrow

11 My aged friend, Mrs Wilkinson,
Whose mother was a Lambe,
Saw Wordsworth once, and Coleridge, too,
One morning in her p'ram
Birdlike the bards stooped over her –
Like fledgling in a nest:
And Wordsworth said, 'Thou harmless babe!'
And Coleridge was impressed.
The pretty thing gazed up and smiled,
And softly murmured, 'Coo!'
William was then aged sixty-four
And Samuel sixty-two.
Walter de la Mare, 'The Bards'

12 Nat Hawthorne concealed his asperity
By a surface of delicate clarity;
He produced ambiguity
In rich superfluity,
And laudably free from vulgarity.
Hawthorne's writing achieved perspicuity
Continuity, beauty, acuity;
He won lasting glory
In romance and story –

Though some have complained of tenuity.
Richard Harter Fogle, 'Ambiguity, Perspicuity', *The Laurel Review*, 1910

13 Higgledy-piggledy
Thomas Stearns Eliot
Wrote dirty limericks
Under the rose,
Using synecdoches,
Paranomasias,
Zeugmas, and rhymes he de-
Plored in his prose.
Anthony Hecht, 'Vice', *Jiggery-Pokery: A Compendium of Double Dactyls*, 1966

14 No author is a man of genius to his publisher.
Heinrich Heine

15 They're fancy talkers about themselves, writers. If I had to give young writers advice, I would say don't listen to writers talk about writing or themselves.
Lillian Hellman

16 The most essential gift for a good writer is a built-in shock-proof shit-detector.
Ernest Hemingway

17 The novelist, afraid his ideas may be foolish, slyly puts them in the mouth of some other fool and reserves the right to disavow them.
Diane Johnson, *New York Times Book Review*, 1979

18 He writes the worst English that I have ever encountered. It reminds me of a string of wet sponges; it reminds me of tattered washing on the line; it reminds me of stale bean soup, of college yells, of dogs barking idiotically through endless nights. It is so bad that a sort of grandeur creeps into it. It drags itself out of the dark abysm of pish, and crawls insanely up to the topmost pinnacle of posh. It is rumble and bumble. It is flap and doodle. It is balder and dash.
H. L. Mencken, on Warren G. Harding, *Baltimore Evening Sun*, 1921

19 Almost anyone can be an author; the business is to collect money and fame from this state of being.
A. A. Milne

20 Oscar and George Bernard
    Cannot be reconciled.
    When I'm Wilde about Shaw
    I'm not Shaw about Wilde.
    Freddie Oliver, *Worse Verse*, 1969

21 When one says that a writer is fashionable one practically always means that he is admired by people under thirty.
    George Orwell

22 Writing is the only profession where no one considers you ridiculous if you earn no money.
    Jules Renard

23 It is part of prudence to thank an author for his book before reading it, so as to avoid the necessity of lying about it afterwards.
    George Santayana

24 The profession of book-writing makes horse racing seem like a solid, stable business.
    John Steinbeck

25 Some American writers who have known each other for years, have never met in the daytime or when both were sober.
    James Thurber

26 With a pig's eyes that never look up, with a pig's snout that loves muck, with a pig's brain that knows only the sty, and with a pig's squeal that cries only when he is hurt, he sometimes opens his pig's mouth, tusked and ugly, and let's out the voice of God, railing at the whitewash that covers the manure about his habitat.
    William Allen White, on H. L. Mencken, 1928

27 . . . the dullest speeches I ever heard. The Agee woman told us for three quarters of an hour how she came to write her beastly book, when a simple apology was all that was required . . .
    P. G. Wodehouse, *The Girl in Blue*, 1970

28 Success comes to a writer, as a rule, so gradually that it is always something of a shock to him to look back and realize the heights to which he has climbed.
    P. G. Wodehouse

See also Books; Creativity; Critics –
The Artist's View; Literature; Novels; Poets and Poetry; Publishers; Reading; William Shakespeare; Writing.

WRITING

1 I love being a writer. What I can't stand is the paperwork.
   Peter De Vries

2 I write when I'm inspired, and I see to it that I'm inspired at nine o'clock every morning.
   Peter De Vries

3 The tools I need for my work are paper, tobacco, food and a little whiskey.
   William Faulkner

4 The ideal view for daily writing, hour on hour, is the blank brick wall of a cold storage warehouse. Failing this, a stretch of sky will do, cloudless if possible.
   Edna Ferber

5 Cut out all those exclamation marks. An exclamation mark is like laughing at your own joke.
   F. Scott Fitzgerald, quoted in *Beloved Infidel*, 1959

6 Mostly, we authors must repeat ourselves – that's the truth. We have two or three great moving experiences in our lives – experiences so great and moving that it doesn't seem at the time that anyone else has been caught up and pounded and dazzled and astonished and beaten and broken and rescued and illuminated and rewarded and humbled in just that way ever before.
   F. Scott Fitzgerald

7 Writing is easy; all you do is sit staring at a blank sheet of paper until the drops of blood form on your forehead.
   Gene Fowler

8 Nothing you write, if you hope to be any good, will ever come out as you first hoped.
   Lillian Hellman

9 For forty-odd years in this noble profession
   I've harbored a guilt and my conscience is smitten.

So here is my slightly embarrassed
confession –
I don't like to write, but I love to have
written.
Michael Kanin, 'My Sin', *Dramatists Guild Quarterly*

10 So far as good writing goes, the use of the exclamation mark is a sign of failure. It is the literary equivalent of a man holding up a card reading LAUGHTER to a studio audience.
Miles Kington, *Punch*, 1976

11 A good many young writers make the mistake of enclosing a stamped, self-addressed envelope, big enough for the manuscript to come back in. This is too much of a temptation for the editor.
Ring Lardner, *How to Write Short Stories*

12 Contrary to what many of you might imagine, a career in letters is not without its drawbacks – chief among them the unpleasant fact that one is frequently called upon to sit down and write.
Fran Lebowitz, *Metropolitan Life*, 1978

13 Oh, shun, lad, the life of an author.
It's nothing but worry and waste.
Avoid that utensil,
The laboring pencil,
And pick up the scissors and paste.
Phyllis McGinley, 'A Ballad of Anthologies', 1941

14 There are three rules for writing the novel. Unfortunately, no one knows what they are.
W. Somerset Maugham (Attrib.)

15 Only ambitious nonentities and hearty mediocrities exhibit their rough drafts. It's like passing round samples of one's sputum.
Vladimir Nabokov

16 One thing that literature would be greatly the better for
Would be a more restricted employment by authors of simile and metaphor.
Authors of all races, be they Greeks,
    Romans, Teutons or Celts,
Can't seem just to say that anything is

the thing it is but have to go out of
their way to say that it is like
something else.
Ogden Nash, 'Very Like a Whale', *The Primrose Path*, 1935

17 The secret of popular writing is never to put more on a given page than the common reader can lap off it with no strain whatsoever on his habitually slack attention.
Ezra Pound

18 What no wife of a writer can ever understand is that a writer is working when he's staring out of the window.
Burton Rascoe

19 If you caricature friends in your first novel they will be upset, but if you don't, they will feel betrayed.
Mordecai Richler, *GQ*, 1984

20 Alexander Woollcott says good writers should never use the word 'very'. Nuts to Alexander Woollcott.
H. Allen Smith (Attrib.)

21 There's nothing to writing. All you do is sit down at a typewriter and open a vein.
Red Smith

22 Writing a play is like smashing that [glass] ashtray, filming it in slow motion, and then running the film in reverse, so that the fragments of rubble appear to fly together. You start – or at least I start – with the rubble.
Tom Stoppard, quoted in Kenneth Tynan's *Show People*, 1980

23 'He's supposed to have a particularly high-class style: "Feather-footed through the splashy fen passes the questing vole" . . . would that be it?'
'Yes,' said the Managing Editor. 'That must be good style. At least it doesn't sound like anything else to me.'
Evelyn Waugh, *Scoop*, 1938

24 Novel-writing is a highly skilled and laborious trade of which the raw material is every single thing one has ever seen or heard or felt, and one has to go over that vast, smouldering rubbish-heap of experience, half stifled by the fumes and

dust, scraping and delving until one finds a few discarded valuables.

Evelyn Waugh, *The Essays, Articles and Reviews of Evelyn Waugh*, 1984

25 No passion in the world is equal to the passion to alter someone else's draft.
H. G. Wells

26 I was working on the proof of one of my poems all the morning, and took out a comma. In the afternoon I put it back again.
Oscar Wilde (Attrib.)

27 Ambrose isn't a frightfully hot writer. I don't suppose he makes enough out of a novel to keep a midget in doughnuts for a week. Not a really healthy midget.
P. G. Wodehouse, *The Luck of the Bodkins*, 1935

See also Books; Creativity; Literature; Novels; Poets and Poetry; Publishers; Reading; Writers.

XENOPHOBIA

1 With its open door immigration policy, the United States is perhaps the only state not afflicted with xenophobia, but the very warp and weave of our national fiber is even now being eaten away by swarms of wops, dps, prs, coons and foreigners generally.
The National Lampoon Encyclopaedia of Humor, 1968

2 I don't hold with abroad and think that foreigners speak English when our backs are turned.
Quentin Crisp, *The Naked Civil Servant*, 1968

3 There have been many definitions of hell, but for the English the best definition is that it is a place where the Germans are the police, the Swedish are the comedians, the Italians are the defence force, Frenchmen dig the roads, the Belgians are the pop singers, the Spanish run the railways, the Turks cook the food, the Irish are the waiters, the Greeks run the government and the common language is Dutch.
David Frost and Antony Jay, *To England with Love*, 1967

4 The great and recurring question about abroad is, is it worth getting there?
Rose Macaulay (Attrib.)

5 Abroad is unutterably bloody and foreigners are fiends.
Nancy Mitford, *The Pursuit of Love*, 1945

6 Foreigners may pretend otherwise, but if English is spoken loudly enough, anyone can understand it, the British included.

Actually, there's no such thing as a foreign language. The world is just filled with people who grunt and squeak instead of speaking sensibly. French may be an exception. But since it's impossible to figure out what French people are saying, we'll never know for sure.
P. J. O'Rourke, *Modern Manners*, 1983

7 If the French were really intelligent, they'd speak English.
Wilfrid Sheed, 'Taking Pride in Prejudice', *GQ*, 1984

8 The points i wish to make about the world are contained in the molesworth newsletter.
(a) the rusians are roters.
(b) americans are swankpots.
(c) the french are slack.
(d) the germans are unspeakable.
(e) the rest are as bad if not worse than the above.
(f) the british are brave super and noble cheers cheers cheers.
Geoffrey Willans and Ronald Searle, 'Down With Skool!', *The Compleet Molesworth*, 1958

9 '*Faute de* what?'
'*Mieux*, m'lord. A French expression. We should say "For want of anything better."'
'What asses these Frenchmen are. Why can't they talk English?'
'They are possibly more to be pitied than censured, m'lord. Early upbringing no doubt has a lot to do with it.'
P. G. Wodehouse, *Ring for Jeeves*, 1953

See also Countries; Foreigners; Travel.

YOUTH

1 Youth would be an ideal state if it came a little later in life.
   Lord Asquith, 1923

2 The youth of the present day are quite monstrous. They have absolutely no respect for dyed hair.
   Oscar Wilde, *Lady Windermere's Fan*, 1892

3 To win back my youth ... there is nothing I wouldn't do – except take exercise, get up early, or be a useful member of the community.
   Oscar Wilde, *A Woman of No Importance*, 1893

See also Adolescence; Childhood; Teenagers.

YUGOSLAVIA

1 It's a very long flight to Yugoslavia and you land in a field of full-grown corn. They figure it cushions the landing ... Now, at night, you can't do anything, because all of Belgrade is lit by a ten-watt bulb, and you can't go anywhere, because Tito has the car. It was a beauty, a green '38 Dodge. And the food in Yugoslavia is either very good or very bad. One day, we arrived on location late and starving and they served us fried chains. When we got to our hotel rooms, mosquitoes as big as George Foreman were waiting for us. They were sitting in armchairs with their legs crossed.
   Mel Brooks, interview in *Playboy*, 1975

INDEX

References marked with an asterisk indicate collaboration with other writers or composers.